METAPHOR AND COMPOSITION
IN 1 PETER

SOCIETY
OF BIBLICAL
LITERATURE

DISSERTATION SERIES
David L. Petersen, Old Testament Editor
Pheme Perkins, New Testament Editor

Number 131

METAPHOR AND COMPOSITION
IN 1 PETER

by
Troy W. Martin

Troy W. Martin

METAPHOR AND COMPOSITION
IN 1 PETER

Scholars Press
Atlanta, Georgia

METAPHOR AND COMPOSITION
IN 1 PETER

Troy W. Martin

Ph.D., 1990
University of Chicago

Advisor:
Hans Dieter Betz

Library of Congress Cataloging in Publication Data

Martin, Troy W.
  Metaphor and composition in 1 Peter / Troy W. Martin.
  p. cm. — (Dissertation series / Society of Biblical
  Literature ; no. 131)
  Originally presented as the author's thesis (Ph.D.)—University
  of Chicago, 1990.
  Includes bibliographical references.
  ISBN 1-55540-664-5. — ISBN 1-55540-665-3 (pbk.)
  1. Bible. N.T. Peter, 1st—Language, style. I. Title.
II. Title: Metaphor and composition in 1st Peter. III. Title:
series (Society of Biblical Literature) ; no. 131.
BS2795.2.M37 1992
227'.92066—dc20
                                                91-41515
                                                CIP

Printed in the United States of America
on acid-free paper

I lovingly dedicate this book to my wife

SHERYL

with gratitude for her sacrifice, determination, and loyalty.

PREFACE

I would be remiss if I failed to mention the many people who participated in this dissertation process. I thank my advisor and *Doktorvater*, Hans Dieter Betz, who promptly read and returned the various drafts of my dissertation. His advice and breadth of knowledge led me to new insights and strengthened my dissertation immensely. I thank my readers, Arthur Droge and Arthur Adkins, for their investment of time and effort. I am grateful to all of the individuals who helped me acquire the languages necessary to complete this project. In particular, I thank the late Dr. David Wilmot, who deepened my understanding of Greek and with whom I first read 1 Peter in the original language. I thank April Wilson and Hans and Arlene Schmidt for facilitating my use of the German language. My special thanks are due to my proofreaders, Wells Hansen, Val Schuller, and especially Joseph Bennington. Although all of these proofreaders devoted significant effort to the project, Joseph Bennington committed many hours and days to the careful reading of the English text, and I owe a special debt of gratitude to him. I am especially grateful to my friends and supporters at Chicago First Church of the Nazarene and their pastor, Richard Young, for providing me with the means and the time to complete my research. I thank my colleagues at Olivet Nazarene University for their understanding and support during the writing of this project. I am grateful to David Whitelaw, my divisional chairman, who arranged my schedule so that I could finish the manuscript. I owe a debt of gratitude to Saint Xavier College for providing me with the time and resources for revising my dissertation for publication. During the years I have devoted to this project, I have gained a new appreciation for my family. My father and mother, Troy and Lavalta Martin, as well as my sisters, Pam Billings and Susan Etter, have supported me financially and emotionally throughout my academic preparation. My wife, Sheryl, and my daughters, Andrea and Amie, have extended encouragement and understanding that I desperately needed. Without their sacrifice, this project could not have succeeded. I thank them for their enormous contribution to this project. These individuals as well as many others participated in this dissertation, and I am grateful for them all. With their help I hope that my labors serve to elucidate 1 Peter for contemporary Christianity and the broader world of biblical research.

144 - 186

CONTENTS

INTRODUCTION

"An exegetical step-child" is certainly a strange phrase to describe a New Testament book, yet this is the description John Elliott gives to 1 Peter.[1] Throughout the long history of New Testament exegesis, 1 Peter has remained enigmatic. Scholars have searched for an appropriate exegetical perspective by which the book could be correctly understood. 1 Peter has been related to the letters of Paul, the Gospels, the Acts of the Apostles, Revelation, and the other Catholic Epistles. It has been compared with much less success to the other Petrine writings. It has been considered as a letter of instruction, admonition, or consolation; and it has even been explained in terms of a sermon or liturgy. In spite of all this effort, the problem of interpretation remains. How should I Peter be conceived? What type of letter does it purport to be? What theme or themes control the composition both in the selection and in the arrangement of topics? These questions are all subsumed under the broader question: How can 1 Peter be interpreted?

The problem of the literary character of 1 Peter lies underneath and complicates all of these exegetical problems. As Martin Dibelius astutely observed, "A clear concept of a document's literary character is necessary in order to understand it as a whole."[2] Both literary genre and compositional structure are fundamental issues that must be settled before interpretation can properly proceed. Yet, in the case of 1 Peter, these issues have never been resolved. In a recent collection of articles on 1 Peter, three different literary analyses were proposed, none of which

---

[1]John H. Elliott, "The Rehabilitation of an Exegetical Step-Child: 1 Peter in Recent Research," *Journal of Biblical Literature* 95(1976): 243-254.

[2]Martin Dibelius, *James: A Commentary on the Epistle of James*, trans. M. A. Williams, Hermeneia (Philadelphia: Fortress Press, 1976), 1.

agreed with the other.[3] With so little agreement on the literary character and compositional structure of 1 Peter, the final article in that collection was appropriately entitled, "Once Again: The Plan of 1 Peter."[4]

One of the contributors to that collection succinctly stated the literary problem of 1 Peter:

> First, while there is a general consensus that the evidence of 1 Peter indicates its coherence, there is no agreement on the literary structure of 1 Peter. Second, past proposals for the structure of 1 Peter and past accounts of its theology have been undecided as to the literary and theological relationship between various sections and divisions of the epistle: this includes the relationship between 1:3-12 and 1:13-5:11. Third, there is still no consensus on the major theme of 1 Peter or on how its different motifs relate to each other.[5]

With these important literary issues still unresolved, 1 Peter is indeed "an exegetical step-child."

In an effort to "rehabilitate" 1 Peter, this dissertation will resolve the problem of the literary character of the document.   In the course of this study, the literary genre will be identified, the compositional structure will be exposed, and the thematic motif will be explicated. These literary issues will be resolved by following an explicit agenda.   First, the compositional analyses of previous scholarship will be surveyed. Included in this survey will be an evaluation of the usefulness of each of the various types of analysis for resolving these literary issues.   Second, letter conventions will be examined to determine their relevance for resolving the literary character of 1 Peter.   Third, the genre of paraenesis will be studied to discover its significance for explaining the composition of 1 Peter.   Finally, the literary devices of metaphor and transition will be employed in order to resolve residual problems in the literary structure of the document.   Hopefully, this agenda and the resolution of these literary issues will contribute to the "rehabilitation" of 1 Peter.

---

[3]David W. Kendall, "The Literary and Theological Function of 1 Peter 1:3-12," 103-120; Earl Richard, "The Functional Christology of First Peter," 121-139; and Charles H. Talbert, "Once Again: The Plan of 1 Peter," 141-151, in *Perspectives on 1 Peter*, ed. Charles H. Talbert, National Association of Baptist Professors of Religion 9 (Macon, Georgia: Mercer University Press, 1986).

[4]Talbert, 141.

[5]Kendall, 103-104.

CHAPTER 1

HISTORY OF RESEARCH

Petrine research and interpretation has a long and rich tradition. Within this tradition, numerous attempts have been made to expose the compositional structure of 1 Peter. This chapter will survey the various compositional analyses that have been proposed. These analyses will be grouped into six analytical traditions, and the originator and some of the more important adherents of each of these traditions will be discussed. This chapter will discuss the older analyses first and then procede to more modern views.

Compositional Analyses Prior to
Urbanus Holzmeister

Before describing the older analyses of the compositional structure of 1 Peter, perhaps we should defend the selection of Holzmeister as the watershed between the older and more recent scholarship. First, his massive commentary appeared in 1937 just a few years after the last of the analytical types came to expression. Since that time, there have been no new approaches to the analysis of 1 Peter.[1] Second, Holzmeister is aware of analytical types and attempts to describe several of them.[2] Indeed, the

---

[1]One exception to this statement is Emilie T. Sander, "ΠΥΡΩΣΙΣ and the First Epistle of Peter 4:12" (Th.D. diss., Harvard, 1966). On page x she says, "There are a number of elements which contribute to seeing in 1 Peter at least some signs of a 'testament' form. . . ." This attempt to link 1 Peter to a "testament form" does suggest a new approach to the compositional analysis of 1 Peter, but her arguments and method are so weak that the suggestion cannot be seriously considered.

[2]Urbanus Holzmeister, *Commentarius in Epistulas SS. Petri et Iudae Apostolorum*, Cursus Scripturae Sacrae (Paris: P. Lethielleux, 1937), 165-172. His presentation of the compositional types is not as complete as the presentation in this dissertation, but it is

idea of presenting a history of scholarship for the various types of analyses arose from reading his commentary. Third, this commentary has not received the recognition it deserves. It is well researched and contains a rich treasure of material. It is my hope that designating this commentary as the watershed between older and more modern scholarship will draw attention to its importance.[3]

Type 1

Although he is not the first to comment on 1 Peter, Pseudo-Euthalius deserves first mention in the history of research on the composition of our letter.[4] Pseudo-Euthalius elaborated a compositional perspective that greatly influenced the views of succeeding Petrine scholars. He conceived of 1 Peter as an instructional letter [διδασκαλικὴ ἐπιστολή] written to Jewish Christians in order to establish them in their faith.[5] He then enumerated the instructional subjects as follows:

> Main ideas of 1 Peter:
> I. Concerning the new birth in Christ and endurance of temptations and the salvation faith announced beforehand by the prophets (1:3-12)
>
> II. Concerning hope and holiness and the obligatory steadfast conduct in sonship (1:13--2:10)
>
> III. Concerning living in Christ worthy of sonship for the glory of God in regard to those outside (2:11-12)

---

nevertheless useful. Particularly useful is the discussion of the compositional analyses in the margins of the Greek manuscripts of 1 Peter.

[3]Previous scholarship has not completely ignored the immense contribution of Holzmeister. Elliott, "Rehabilitation," 249, says, "A thoroughgoing investigation of the literary style, structure, and redactional techniques of 1 Peter has yet to be made. The ground work, however, has been laid." He mentions Holzmeister as the one who has laid this ground work. W. J. Dalton, *Christ's Proclamation to the Spirits*, Analecta Biblica 23 (Rome: Pontifical Biblical Institute, 1965), 73, says, "Holzmeister is an exception among the commentators in presenting and justifying a detailed plan of the epistle."

[4]For a discussion of the divisions of 1 Peter found in the manuscripts see Holzmeister, 165-167.

[5]Pseudo-Euthalius, "Elenchus Capitum septem Epistolarum Catholicarum," in *Patrologia Graeca*, ed. J. P. Migne, vol. 85, 680, says, "Peter himself writes this instructional letter to the Diaspora Jews who had become Christians. For since they had believed from the Jews, he establishes them."

IV. Concerning obedience toward rulers, brotherly love, and godliness (2:13-17) Wherein [ἐν ᾧ]

1. Concerning submission of slaves and patient enduring of evil on account of Christ (2:18-25)

2. Concerning obedience of wives and harmony toward their husbands and the salvation of Sarah as a model (3:1-6)

3. Concerning the association of husbands with their wives (3:7)

4. Concerning the gracious bearing of evil toward all of which the generousness of God to Noah is a type However, sympathy is upon us through the baptism of Christ. (3:8-22)

V. Concerning the putting away of evil deeds and taking up the fruits in the Spirit according to the distribution of gifts because it is necessary to conquer the physical passions by partnership with Christ and by hope in Him to bear the hurts from others (4:1-19)

VI. Exhortation to the elders concerning the oversight of the flock wherein there is the notion of the common humblemindedness of all toward each for victory against the devil (5:1-9)

VII. Entreaty on behalf of the perfection of those who believe (5:10-11)[6]

This enumeration of subjects leads to the conception that 1 Peter is desultory in composition with the subjects simply stated one after the other without any attempt to interrelate them.[7] Although Pseudo-Euthalius does not explicitly state the compositional principle that gives order to his analysis, it clearly resides in the subjective decision of the author. Attempting to instruct his readers, the author chooses which subjects he will treat and discusses them one after the other. Pseudo-Euthalius does not attempt to uncover the principles that influenced the author's selection and arrangement of topics. Thus, Pseudo-Euthalius does not provide a satisfactory explanation of how the subjects were selected or why they are arranged in their present form. He is content to leave his analysis at the level of a description of the contents. This conception of 1 Peter's composition holds throughout ancient exegesis and continues to influence some modern analyses of 1 Peter.[8]

---

[6]Ibid., 680-681.

[7]This concurs with paraenetic documents in general. See Chapter 3 below.

[8]A. Jülicher, *Einleitung in das Neue Testament*, 6th ed.(Tübingen: J. C. B. Mohr, 1906), 176, succinctly stated this position: "An outline determined previously by the author can not be found because it never existed." Walter Bauer, *Die Katholischen Briefe*

Type 2

Pseudo-Oecumenius closely follows Pseudo-Euthalius' compositional analysis. His method is simple description of the contents, and there is no attempt to uncover the underlying rationale for the selection and arrangement of topics.[9] In spite of imitating his predecessor, however, he does make an important contribution to the compositional analysis of the letter. He comments on 3:8, "After ceasing from his instruction pertaining to men and women, he makes a common exhortation to all."[10] This recognition of the distinction between exhortation to specific groups and to the group at large later becomes an important analytical criterion for describing the composition of 1 Peter. Pseudo-Oecumenius, however, does not utilize this distinction in his analysis of the letter as a whole.

Although Pseudo-Hilarius Arelatensis does not develop a comprehensive analysis of 1 Peter, he does point out several compositional breaks in the text utilizing the criteria of subject matter and instruction pertaining to all or to specific groups. He comments on 2:13, "Now Peter, the head of the Church, imposes a common rule of daily conduct and joins all members of the church in concord."[11] His comment on 2:17 indicates that he conceived of this passage as rules for the entire community. He says, "These restraining obligations are for all."[12] After noting that the next verse, 2:18, is directed to servants, he says, "This is the beginning of a discourse. . . ."[13] He is using the criterion of a change in audience as a basis for the compositional break. He also utilizes the criterion of a change in subject matter as his comments in 3:1 and 4:12 indicate.[14] Thus, this

---

des Neuen Testaments, Religionsgeschichtliche Volksbücher für die deutsche christliche Gegenwart 1.20 (Tübingen: J. C. B. Mohr, 1910), 22, agrees with the position of Jülicher: "It is wasted effort to attempt to ferret out an arrangement in 1 Peter that the author had laid out at the beginning of the work and then followed."

[9]Pseudo-Oecumenius, "Commentarii in epistolas catholicas," in *Patrologia Graeca*, ed. J. P. Migne, vol. 119, 509.

[10]Ibid., 549B.

[11]Pseudo-Hilarius Arelatensis, "Expositio in epistolas catholicas," in *Patrologia Latina*, ed. J. P. Migne, Supplement III, 91.

[12]Ibid., 92.

[13]Ibid.

[14]Ibid., 93 and 102.

commentator relies on the criteria of subject matter and audience to perceive the compositional breaks in the text.

In contrast to his predecessors, the Venerable Bede uses the criteria of general and specific exhortation to develop a comprehensive compositional analysis of 1 Peter. He comments on 2:11:

> Up to this point blessed Peter has been instructing the church in general, enlarging on either the benefits by which the divine condescension deigned to call us to salvation or on the gifts which he deigned once to honor the Jews but now us. From this point on he skillfully urges the various classes of the faithful not to show themselves unworthy of so great a grace of the spirit by living according to their bodily desires. . . . Therefore, he particularly addresses first those who are free and slaves, then women and men, and then after a passage of general exhortation he points out to the old and young also how they ought to conduct themselves.[15]

Bede proposes an analysis that consists of four parts of alternating general and specific exhortation with the former in 1:1--2:10 and 3:8--4:19 and the latter in 2:11--3:7 and 5:1-5.

Bede easily established his comprehensive compositional analysis since it was based upon an objective criterion of exhortation to the whole group or to subgroups. The issue posed by this type of analysis is whether or not this criterion is valid for understanding the compositional structure of the letter. Did the author select and arrange his material with this criterion in mind? I would answer this question both positively and negatively. In 2:11--3:12, there is alternation from general to specific exhortation. As I shall demonstrate later, this entire passage is a major compositional unit; and within this unit, the author has chosen to address the whole group, then subgroups, and afterwards the whole group again. This criterion is valid for identifying smaller subsections of the epistle, but it is not adequate for delineating the major sections of the epistle as Bede desires to do. This type of analysis is used repeatedly by later scholars; however, it is not a satisfactory explanation for the composition of 1 Peter.

Martinus Legionensis followed Bede's compositional analysis but stated more clearly that 5:5b-11 contains general admonitions. He comments on this verse, ". . . following on generally, he subjoined

---

[15]Bede the Venerable, *The Commentary on the Seven Catholic Epistles*, trans. David Hurst (Kalamazoo, Michigan: Cistercian Publications, 1985), 89.

admonition."[16] Thus, he arrives at a compositional analysis that has two sections of specific admonitions (2:11--3:7; 5:1-5a) separating three sections of general admonitions (1:1--2:10; 3:8--4:19; 5:5b-11). Although Bede implied that the last section was composed of general admonitions, Martinus Legionensis made this point explicit.[17]

As this analytical tradition progresses, some scholars begin to understand general and specific admonitions in terms of abstract or concrete admonitions rather than in terms of a general or specific audience. By general and specific admonitions, they mean admonitions that do not pertain to a particular situation in life and those that do. On the basis of this understanding, they divide the letter into general admonitions (1:13--2:10) and special admonitions (2:11--5:9). Ernst Theodor Mayerhoff is the earliest representative of this shift in understanding. He outlines the letter as follows:

> After the compressed, thoughtful salvation wish for the readers (1:1-2), the passage that establishes the paraenetical section follows as the first part of the epistle (1:3-12): The praise of God for the living hope of salvation co-divided to those who are born again.
>
> Second part of the letter: Admonitions
>
> A. General 1:13--2:10
>
> I. In view of the inner man alone 1:13-21
>
> II. In view of him as a member of a larger whole 1:22--2:10
>
> B. Special Admonitions
>
> I. In relation to the interactions of Christians with the unbelieving 2:11--4:19
>
> II. In relation to the interaction of Christians with one another 4:7-11; 5:5
>
> III. In relation to God 5:5-7
>
> IV. In relation to the devil 5:8-9[18]

Clearly, Mayerhoff's understanding of general and specific admonitions differs from that of Bede and leads to a different analysis of the letter.

---

[16]Martinus Legionensis, "Expositio in epistolam I B. Petri apostoli," in *Patrologia Latina*, ed. J. P. Migne, vol. 209, 247-248.

[17]Among modern critical exegetes, E. T. Mayerhoff, *Historische-critische Einleitung in die petrinischen Schriften* (Hamburg: Friedrich Perthes, 1835) is an advocate of this position.

[18]Ibid., 97-98.

Karl Reinhold Jachmann accepts Mayerhoff's analysis and explains more explicitly his understanding of general and specific admonitions. He describes the contents of Chapter 1 as follows, "The content of Chapter 1 falls into two passages of which the first contains a reminder of the Christian calling and the certainty of salvation (1:1-13) and the second contains general exhortations toward a conduct of life conformed to the rules (1:14--2:10)."[19] He proceeds to describe the contents of Chapter 2, "The first 10 verses belong to the preceding, which contains general exhortations.   In the following, specific exhortations on particular relationships of civic and domestic life are employed."[20] For Jachmann, special admonitions are those that pertain to particular relationships in life, whereas general admonitions refer to conduct of life in general.

Mayerhoff and Jachmann's view of general and specific admonitions becomes very persuasive for commentators like W. M. L. de Wette[21] and Hermann Couard[22] but suffers from subjectivity. Whereas Bede's analysis was based upon the objective criteria of general and specific audience, their analysis is based upon a vague understanding of general and specific admonitions. Contrary to the view of these scholars, the command to love one another in 1:22 does not differ from the same command in 4:8. This modification of Bede's analytical criteria is not a valid method of analysis.

Type 3

Like his predecessors, Martin Luther utilized the criteria of changes in subject and audience in his compositional analysis.[23] Unlike his

---

[19]Karl Reinhold Jachmann, *Commentar über die katholischen Briefe mit genauer Berücksichtigung der neuesten Auslegungen* (Leipzig: Johann Ambrosius Barth, 1838), 120.

[20]Ibid., 136.

[21]W. M. L. de Wette, *Die katholischen Briefe, griechisch, mit kurzem Commentar* (Halle: Eduard Anton, 1847), 585, 591.

[22]Hermann Couard, *Die Briefe des Petrus, Judas und Johannes* (Potsdam: August Stein, 1895), 22, 31, 50.

[23]Martin Luther, "Sermons on the First Epistle of St. Peter," in *Luther's Works*, ed. Jaroslav Pelikan, vol. 30: *The Catholic Epistles*, trans. Martin H. Bertram (Saint Louis: Concordia Publishing House, 1967), 81-82, says commenting on 2:18, "So far St. Peter has taught us that we must be submissive to secular authority and show it honor. . . . This is stated about government in general and is teaching for everyone. But now the

predecessors, however, Luther only used these criteria to distinguish the epistle's smaller sections. In identifying the main sections of the epistle, he appealed to the epistle's theme, which he identified as proclamation of the gospel. In an important passage, he identifies this theme:

> Accordingly, this epistle of St. Peter is also one of the noblest books in the New Testament; it is the genuine and pure gospel. For St. Peter does the same thing that St. Paul and all the evangelists do; he teaches the true faith and tells us that Christ was given to us to take away our sin and to save us. . . .[24]

He goes on to describe the first two chapters:

> This is the first chapter of this epistle. In it you see how masterfully St. Peter preaches faith and treats of it. Hence one sees clearly that this epistle is the true Gospel. Now the second chapter follows. It will teach us how we should conduct ourselves toward our neighbor so far as deeds are concerned.[25]

Luther's analysis is succinctly expressed in his comment on 2:1, "Here the apostle begins to teach what the works and fruits of a Christian life should be. For we have said often enough that a Christian life is composed of two parts: faith in God and love toward one's neighbor."[26] Thus, Luther divides the epistle into two main sections. The first section is contained in Chapter 1 and treats of faith in God. The second section extends from 2:1 to 5:11 and deals with Christian conduct. This distinction will be explained later as the interplay between the indicative, which states the fact of salvation, and the imperative, which states the duties of the saved. The difficulty with this position is that the imperatives begin in 1:13, not in 2:1. If the indicative section is limited to 1:3-12 as later exegetes will do, then this analysis does little more than emphasize the introductory nature of 1:3-12 and the paraenetic nature of 1:13--5:11. This division is supported by the conventions of ancient letter writing, but the problem of how to analyze the body of the letter, 1:13--5:11, remains. In spite of these

---

apostle continues and speaks of the kind of power that does not extend to a community but pertains only to particular persons."

[24]Ibid., 4.

[25]Ibid., 46.

[26]Ibid., 47.

difficulties, however, Luther's criterion of statement contrasted with command will be used extensively by later scholars.[27]

Benedictus Aretius is strongly influenced by the tradition that identifies 1 Peter as a teaching letter, but his analysis of the overall plan of the letter most resembles Luther. A statement of his analysis follows:

> The apostle Peter teaches what great benefices God confers on the elect by knowledge of the Gospel and moreover that this understanding is in sole conformity with the teachings of the prophets and therefore these ancient and certain benefices must be preserved. Then he proceeds to rules and he summons all to virtues of the newborn man. Not only in general, but he proceeds to special rules: namely, what the subjects owe to a magistrate; what the servants owe to masters; what the wife owes to the husband; what the husband owes to the wife; what the teacher owes to the flock; what the flock owes to the teachers; and many similar things that represent the true Christian philosophical ethic.[28]

His analysis differs from Luther's in that he limits the first section to 1:3-12, whereas Luther includes all of chapter 1 in the first section. Aretius' analysis thus states that 1:3-12 teaches the readers that God has conferred great benefices upon them and that as a consequence 1:13--5:11 exhorts them to live virtuously as newborn men and women. Like others, he uses the analytical principle of general and specific exhortation to analyze this second section. Aretius' modification of Luther's position is an improvement since the analysis based on the statement of regeneration and its subsequent duties now corresponds to the formal criteria of indicative (1:3-12) and imperative (1:13--5:11).[29]

Although Johann Gerhard follows the same analysis as Aretius, he raises an important question regarding the composition of 1 Peter. Gerhard comments on an unnamed commentator's analysis:

---

[27]John Calvin follows Luther's analysis stating, "After having taught the faithful that they had been regenerated by the word of God [chapter 1], he now exhorts them to lead a life corresponding with their birth." John Calvin, *Commentaries on the Catholic Epistles*, trans. John Owen (Edinburgh: T. Constable, 1855), 61.

[28]Benedictus Aretius, *Commentarii in Domini nostri Jesu Christi Novum Testamentum* (Geneva: Petrum & Iacobum Chouet, 1607), 845. See also the discussion of the propositio on page 846.

[29]Nicolus Serarius, *Prolegomena Bibliaca et Commentaria in omnes Epistolas Canonicas* (Paris: Balthasar Lippius, 1612), 26-27, resembles Aretius' analysis except that he divides 1:3-12 into two parts: a blessing (1:3-5) and a consolation (1:6-12).

Although this partition can be treated usefully in certain instances, nevertheless in it two things are chiefly lacking. 1) In this case, what single thing establishes the essential goal of the Epistle, namely the exhortation toward the sacred conduct of life and character, since the Epistle confirms what the Apostle wants to teach most of all: that the teaching of the Gospel, which they had embraced by faith, is infallibly true and for the sake of this to exhort them to steadfastness in faith.[30]

What is the theme that unifies the teaching and the exhortations? Gerhard has correctly observed that simply stating that the exhortations are based on the teaching in 1:3-12 does not supply an ordering rationale for them. Although, he has raised an important question, he continues to use the analytical principle of general and specific exhortation and thus does not resolve the question.[31]

Type 4

A fourth approach to the compositional analysis of 1 Peter divides the letter into a few major sections based upon thematic and literary considerations. J. A. Bengel is an early representative of this type of analysis. He identifies three sections of the epistle from the various descriptions of the readers. First, they are described as those born again of God, and this description forms the basis for 1:3--2:10 where the author mentions the benefits of God toward believers and the duties of believers toward God. Three motives for conduct further divide this section into three subsections: (a) God has regenerated believers to a lively hope, and, therefore, they are to hope to the end (1:3-13); (b) As obedient sons they are to bring forth to their heavenly Father the fruit of faith (1:14-21); and (c) Being purified by the Spirit, they are to love with a pure heart (1:22--2:10). Second, the readers are described as strangers in the world, a theme that governs the material from 2:11--4:11. This description of the readers enables the author to call upon them to abstain from fleshly lusts (2:11) and to maintain good conduct (2:12--3:14) and a good profession (3:15--4:11). Bengel further divides the exhortations on good conduct into specific (2:13--3:7) and general (3:8-15) admonitions. Third, the author describes the readers as fellow partakers of future glory calling upon them to sustain

---

[30]Johann Gerhard, *Commentarius super Priorem D. Petri Epistolam* (Hamburg: Zacharia Hertelius, 1709), 13-14.

[31]Ibid., 14.

adversity, and this theme controls the material in 4:12--5:11. The author applies this theme to everyone in general (4:12-19) and to each one in his own particular condition (5:1-11).[32] In order to further support this tripartite thematic analysis, Bengel appeals to a literary consideration saying, "The title *ἀγαπητοί, beloved*, twice made use of, separates the second part from the first, ii.11, and the third part from the second, iv.12."[33] Thus, by thematic and literary considerations, Bengel analyzes the epistle into three major sections and then subdivides these sections into smaller units.[34]

This type of analysis makes enormous progress in understanding the composition of 1 Peter. The theme of the description of the readers lends compositional unity to the writing mitigating against the desultory composition of those who view 1 Peter as a series of disjointed teachings and admonitions. In this analysis, the analytical device of general and specific admonitions is not utilized to identify the major sections of the letter but only subsections. Thus, this approach avoids the problems of those who use this device as their primary method of analysis. Bengel's analysis does not attempt to artificially divide the letter into indicative and imperative but allows the natural divisions of the text to surface. The value of this type of analysis is demonstrated by the wide acceptance it gains among subsequent exegetes.

J. C. W. Augusti follows in this analytical tradition generally adhering to the major sections delineated by Bengel but demonstrating some obvious problems in Bengel's analysis. He separates 1:3-12 from Bengel's first section identifying it as a section in its own right.[35] Many commentators will follow Augusti in this modification of Bengel's view.

---

[32]John Albert Bengel, *Gnomon of the New Testament*, vol. 5, trans. Andrew Fausset (Edinburgh: T.& T. Clark, 1860), 43-44.

[33]Ibid., p. 44.

[34]Johannes Tobias Beck, *Erklärung der Briefe Petri* (Gütersloh: C. Bertelsmann, 1896), 29-30, 151-152, and 180-181, identifies the descriptive terms in the superscription as the controlling ideas of each of these three sections. Thus, ἐκλεκτοί, παρεπίδημοι, and διασπορά are predicated of the readers in 1:1 and these determine the content of the three sections identified by Bengel.

[35]J. C. W. Augusti, *Die Katholischen Briefe* (Lemgo: Meyersche Buchhandlung, 1801), 212-213, says, "With this verse, 1:13, begins the section that runs until Chapter 2:10. In the preceding section it was proven that the religion of Jesus is the most excellent and the blessedness of Christians is great. Now follows the exhortations to make yourself worthy of this great blessedness and to cease from the sins by which it is disturbed."

Augusti also shifts the beginning of the third section from 4:12 to 4:8.[36]
This shift represents a pervasive problem concerning the exact limits of the
second and third sections of Bengel's analysis. Subsequent exegetes are
unable to consistently establish the limits of these sections. This problem
indicates that Bengel's thematic analysis is inadequate to fully account for
the material in each of the sections. Although his thematic analysis
illustrates the correct method to use in a compositional analysis of 1 Peter,
he has not sufficiently demonstrated the controlling themes nor the limits
and boundaries of each major section.

Although he ignores Bengel's suggestion that the description of the
readers provides the basis for the compositional analysis of 1 Peter, J. E.
Huther maintains the tripartite division of the letter by arguing that the
admonitions in 1 Peter fall into three classes.[37] The first class (1:13--2:10)
is linked to the thought of the glory promised to the Christians while the
second class (2:11--4:6) is connected with the position of Christians in the
world and the third class (4:7--5:9) with their position in the church.[38]
Huther attempts to demonstrate the coherence of each section by
articulating a broad, vague description of the section's contents. His
analytical argument is circular. For example, the first class of admonitions
is controlled by the thought of the glory promised to Christians, but it is
these admonitions themselves that provide the substance for this theme.
Huther does not demonstrate that other documents advocating this theme
also include these admonitions. Thus, the composition of 1 Peter itself
forms the basis for Huther's compositional analysis and this argument is
clearly circular. Although he maintains Bengel's tripartite division of the
letter, Huther's analysis is inferior to Bengel's because the former has
ignored the latter's important insight that the description of the readers
provides the appropriate basis for the compositional analysis of 1 Peter.

---

[36]Ibid., 245-246. He says when commenting on the content of Chapter 4, "The
new passage should begin only at verse 8 and the first 7 verses should be connected with
the preceding. The example of Jesus should obligate us to a virtue-filled life (verses 1-7).
Exhortation on brotherly love and kindness (verses 8-11). Sufferings are to be endured
with steadfastness and trust in God (verses 12-19)."

[37]J. E. Huther, *Kritisch-exegetisches Handbuch über den 1. Brief des Petrus, den
Brief des Judas und den 2. Brief des Petrus*, Kritisch-exegetischer Kommentar über das
Neue Testament 12 (Göttingen: Vandenhoeck und Ruprecht, 1851), 9-10.

[38]Ibid., 9-11.

Siegfried Goebel likewise follows in this analytical tradition, but he argues in contrast to Bengel and Huther that the composition is not based on a description of the readers nor on various kinds or classes of admonitions but upon the reasons or arguments that substantiate the admonitions.[39] Although the encomium on the Christian hope in 1:3-12 is the general basis for all the admonitions in the letter, a specific basis is provided for each individual series of exhortations.[40] In 1:13--2:3 the nature of God and His word substantiate the exhortation[41] while in 2:4-32, the admonitions are based on the notion of the readers as the true people of God.[42] The consummation of all things and the last judgment provide the impetus for the exhortations in 4:1-19, and the last section of exhortation arises from the perilous times in which Christians live.[43] Goebel's analysis suffers from insensitivity to literary and thematic considerations. He identifies a major break between verses three and four of Chapter 2, but verse four begins with a prepositional phrase with a relative pronoun that clearly takes κύριος in verse three as its antecedent. Thus, on literary

---

[39]Goebel is not the first to utilize this type of analysis, but he is the first to use it in a comprehensive analysis of the letter. Johann Martin Usteri, *Wissenschaftlicher und Praktischer Commentar über den ersten Petrusbrief* (Zürich: S. Hohr, 1887), viii and Ernst Kühl, *Die Briefe Petri und Judae*, Kritisch-exegetischer Kommentar über das Neue Testament 12 (Göttingen: Vandenhoeck & Ruprecht, 1887), 261, have already noted that the admonitions following 4:7 are based upon the consideration of the approaching consummation of all things.

[40]Siegfried Goebel, *Die Briefe des Petrus, griechisch, mit kurzer Erklärung* (Gotha: Friedrich Andreas Perthes, 1893), 9, comments on 1:3-9 saying, "The exhortation to the readers is grounded on this encomium on the Christian hope. . . ." Goebel is reiterating a position that was first worked out in detail by Georg Seyler, "Über die Gedankenordnung in den Reden und Briefen des Apostels Petrus," *Theologische Studien und Kritiken* 5 (1832): 44-70. Seyler rejects previous scholarship that viewed 1 Peter as a series of disjointed thoughts or exhortations. He argues for unity of thought in 1 Peter but only discusses 1:3-12 and claims that everything else in the letter is based upon this passage. According to him, 1:3-12 is a description of the Christian hope in regard to its source (1:3), its object (1:4), the condition of its fulfillment (1:5), its efficacy (1:6-7), and the testimony for its certainty (inward testimony 1:8-9; outward testimony 1:10-12). Everything else in the letter is an expansion of these themes or an admonition based upon these themes. Since Seyler does not analyze the rest of the letter, we are left to wonder what outline he would have devised. His identification of hope as the unifying theme of the letter is taken up later by B. Weiss, who does provide an analysis of 1 Peter.

[41]Goebel, 9.

[42]Ibid., 10.

[43]Ibid., 30.

grounds, there should not be a major break between these verses. Goebel states that the third section of the letter begins in 4:1 although the theme of suffering that is discussed at the end of Chapter 3 continues in Chapter 4. In addition to these major difficulties, Goebel does not sufficiently demonstrate that the arguments he adduces are sufficient to explain the material in each of the respective sections.

Julius Kögel is also a representative of this analytical tradition. He attempts to demonstrate that 1 Peter is not a series of disjointed admonitions but a letter the parts of which are connected by the practical issues addressed by the author.[44] On this basis he divides the body of the letter into four parts. The first part deals with the issue of the actuality of the present possession of salvation (1:3--2:10) while the second part treats the issue of the readers' place in the world (2:11--4:6). Part three discusses the issue of the approaching end (4:7-19), and the fourth part contains concluding admonitions to submit to God and resist evil (5:1-11).[45] Kögel argues that the composition of 1 Peter and the unity of its thought are based upon the issues addressed by the author.[46] He attempts to resolve the problem of his analysis by saying, "Unity is not uniformity, and a writing that is so exclusively practical as this one brings with it a looser and freer combination and connection of thoughts. . . ."[47] In spite of this statement, Kögel cannot escape the fact that his analysis is grounded in the subjectivity of the author of 1 Peter. Kögel does not demonstrate the logical connection between the sections but relies on the author's selection of material as the unifying factor. Since he does not confirm his thematic analysis with a literary analysis, his outline of 1 Peter has little, if any, objectivity and, therefore, is not a satisfactory analysis of the letter.

From the preceding discussion, it is evident that several problems arise in this analytical tradition initiated by Bengel. The most serious problem concerns the identification of the controlling themes for each section of the letter. Bengel identified the descriptions of the readers as the controlling themes for the various sections while Huther proposed different classes of admonitions and Goebel various types of ethical arguments as the

---

[44]Julius Kögel, *Die Gedankeneinheit des Ersten Briefes Petri*, Beiträge zur Förderung christlicher Theologie 6 (Gütersloh: C. Bertelsmann, 1902), 8-9.

[45]Ibid., 176-177.

[46]Ibid., 26.

[47]Ibid., 8.

controlling themes. In contrast to all of these approaches, Kögel argued that the practical concerns of the author are sufficient to differentiate among the various sections of the letter. In this analytical tradition, there is no consensus regarding the controlling themes nor concerning the identification of these themes. This is a serious problem in Petrine studies that still awaits resolution. In addition to this major problem, there are minor problems in this analytical tradition, such as the relationship of 1:3-12 to the rest of the letter, the number of major sections, and the exact limits of each of these sections. In order for this analytical tradition to provide a viable analysis of 1 Peter, these problems must be resolved.

Types 5 and 6

Adolf von Harnack proposed a novel solution to the long debate concerning the recipients of the letter. He agreed with those who advocated Jewish recipients because of the salutation in 1:1, but he also agreed with those who advocated Gentile recipients because of the material in the body of the letter. He concluded that the salutation (1:1-3), as well as the conclusion (5:12-14), was not part of the original document but was a later addition. He went on to describe the document not as a letter but as a sermon.[48] Harnack thus became the earliest representative of two types of analysis that often occur together. His comments provided the agenda for those who doubted the integrity of the letter and sought to partition it [Type 5] as well as for those who doubted that it was a real letter at all and sought to explain its composition on liturgical grounds [Type 6]. Since the history of these two types of analysis is intertwined, the representatives of both types will be discussed together.

J. H. A. Hart is an important representative of the partitionist position. He observed that the epistle contained two conclusions (4:11; 5:10), which he maintained argued against the letter's unity.[49] Since the

---

[48]Adolf von Harnack, *Geschichte der altchristlichen Litteratur bis Eusebius*, vol. 1: *Die Chronologie der altchristlichen Litteratur bis Eusebius* (Leipzig: J. C. Hinrich, 1897), 451, says, "If 1:1-2 and 5:12-14 are ignored, then the writing represents, similar to Ephesians, not a letter but rather a homiletic treatise. . . ."

[49]J. H. A. Hart, *The First Epistle General of Peter*, The Expositor's Greek Testament 5 (Grand Rapids: Eerdmans, 1897), 3, says, ". . . it contains two formal and solemn conclusions (4:11; 5:10) . . . in this the document bears witness to its own disunity."

address indicated that the letter was circular or encyclical, he suggested that a letter addressed to different communities "should contain alternative or additional letters, if the writer was aware that the conditions or circumstances were not identical in every case."[50] He argued that the first letter was read if the community were not actually enduring persecution while the second letter was addressed to the communities experiencing persecution. Hart's partition of the letter between verses 11 and 12 of Chapter 4 has a profound effect upon several Petrine exegetes, particularly those who advocate a liturgical analysis. However, his unprecedented explanation of two alternative letters gained very little recognition.[51]

Just as Hart developed Harnack's notion of partition, Hermann Gunkel developed his suggestion that the document is actually a sermon. He writes in his commentary:

> If we disregard the few things that have the form of the letter, i.e., for the most the superscription and conclusion, then we will have to accept for the main part that it imitates the preaching in the community. Accordingly, the thanksgiving is at the beginning (1:3f.) and the benediction at the conclusion (5:10f.); therefore, the praises at the end of passages are met with the "Amen" of the community (4:11; 5:11); and there are the statements to various groups (2:18ff.). Above all there is the unique manner of thought flow. The author does not feel the need as we would today of an arrangement that organizes the whole into a unity. Rather, he permits himself to be led here and there by the inspiration of the moment according to the manner of an extemporaneous speech. Repetitions are very frequent. Passages into which the whole is divided and which are seldom longer than ten verses customarily stand fairly loosely side by side. These passages are seldom collected under a basic thought (2:11--3:6). They also frequently have in themselves a very loose arrangement that is clearly prominent in 3:17-22.[52]

Gunkel's development of Harnack's suggestion serves as an agenda for later liturgical analyses. His allusion that the author does not speak every word but others speak within the letter, such as the community expressing the "Amen" in 4:11 and 5:11, later becomes an important explanation for many features of the text. His explanation that the flow of thought is determined

---

[50]Ibid., 4.

[51]C. F. D. Moule, "The Nature and Purpose of 1 Peter," *New Testament Studies* 3 (1956-1957): 1-11, advocates this position but with no reference to Hart. J. W. C. Wand, *The General Epistles of St. Peter and St. Jude*, Westminster Commentaries (London: Methuen & Co., 1934), 1-2, states that Hart's suggestion is probable.

[52]Hermann Gunkel, *Der erste Brief des Petrus*, Die Schriften des Neuen Testaments 2 (Göttingen: Vandenhoeck & Ruprecht, 1906), 530.

by the conventions of a sermon becomes the basic feature of this type of analysis. Gunkel does not collect ancient Christian sermons in order to determine the sermonic conventions, but he simply relies on his own subjective understanding of these conventions. This serious methodological flaw pervades this type of analysis down to the present.[53] Gunkel, building upon Harnack, expresses a view of 1 Peter that becomes dominant in the twentieth century.

Combining the partition and homiletic theories into one hypothesis, Richard Perdelwitz developed a literary analysis that partitioned the letter into two parts: a baptismal sermon and a letter for persecuted Christians. In his literary analysis, he observed that the treatment of suffering in 4:12 is different from the preceding treatment of that subject.[54] He noticed many repetitions such as 4:14-15 compared with 3:14 and 4:13 compared with 1:7.[55] These observations along with his observation of a benediction in 4:11 led him to theorize that 1 Peter consists of two documents.[56] The first document is a baptismal homily addressed to recent converts and includes 1:3--4:11. Perdelwitz explained the frequent occurrence of νῦν (1:12; 2:10, 25; 3:21) and ἄρτι (1:6,8; 2:2) as a result of the actual rite in progress. It is just at this moment, at baptism, that the illumination of those addressed has come about. Thus, Perdelwitz disagrees with the previous explanation that these temporal adverbs derived from the

---

[53]This flaw is evident in the work of William L. Schutter, *Hermeneutic and Composition in 1 Peter*, Wissenschaftliche Untersuchungen zum Neuen Testament 2.30 (Tübingen: J. C. B. Mohr (Paul Siebeck), 1989), passim. He identifies 1 Peter as a midrashic homily but then does not provide an analysis of the literary composition of such homilies.

[54]Richard Perdelwitz, *Die Mysterienreligion und das Problem des I. Petrusbriefes* (Giessen: Alfred Töpelmann, 1911), 12, says, "There is an important observation made only by very few exegetes that the treatment of suffering in our letter shows two very different points of view. In Chapter 4:12 the sufferings are present. . . . The situation in 1:6; 3:13,14,17 is entirely different because here all is hypothetical." Perhaps one of the exegetes mentioned by Perdelwitz was Ernst Kühl who was the first to offer a suggestion as to why persecution is perceived differently before and after 4:12. He explains in *Die Briefe Petri und Judae*, 30-31, that the hypothetical references to suffering refer to persecution by the heathen of which the author has no information while the actual references to suffering pertain to the innercommunity persecution of unbelieving Jews of which the author is acutely aware. Kühl's explanation has not been accepted by anyone.

[55]Perdelwitz, 13.

[56]Ibid., 14-15.

eschatological outlook of the author.[57] In the History of Religions segment of his study, he attempts to demonstrate that the purpose of this homily is to demonstrate the superiority of Christian baptism to the initiation rites of the Mystery Cults. The second document was a letter intended for persecuted Christians who lived in areas where these cults flourished and consists of 1:1-2; 4:12--5:13. He conjectured that both these documents were kept in the archive of the community and later redacted together to produce the document known as 1 Peter.[58] Perdelwitz is credited as being the first to suggest that 1 Peter was a baptismal homily although, as we have seen, he was not.[59] Nevertheless, his analysis provides the basis for the analyses of Windisch, Streeter, Beare, Preisker, and Cross.[60]

Wilhelm Bornemann agreed that 1 Peter was a baptismal homily, but he disagreed that the letter should be partitioned. He states his historical reconstruction, "After they had sung and prayed, leaders of the community first speak some words of greeting. Then Silvanus is invited to speak. He first reads Psalm 34 and then attaches to it the speech that is contained for us in 1 Peter 1:3--5:11."[61] Thus, he conceives of 1 Peter as a baptismal homily delivered by Silvanus based on Psalm 34. He specifies that this occurred about 90 CE in a city of Asia Minor. Reasoning from this fanciful historical reconstruction, he offers an analysis of 1 Peter. He says that Silvanus admonishes the community as children of God in their individual ranks to serve God (1:13--3:14). He reminds them that they must represent the primary concerns of the Gospel in word and holy conduct (3:15--4:11) and that they must suffer according to God's will

---

[57]Ibid., 18.

[58]Ibid., 26.

[59]F.L. Cross, *1 Peter: A Paschal Liturgy* (London: A.R. Mowbray, 1954), 28, says, "We have added reason for considering sympathetically the views of those scholars who have held that a large part, or even the whole, of I Peter is a Baptismal Homily. To the best of my knowledge the suggestion was first made by R. Perdelwitz. . . ."

[60]Hans Windisch, *Die Katholischen Briefe*, 2d ed., Handbuch zum Neuen Testament 4.2 (Tübingen: J. C. B. Mohr (Paul Siebeck), 1930); Burnett Hillman Streeter, *The Primitive Church* (New York: The Macmillan Company, 1929); F. W. Beare, *The First Epistle of Peter* (Oxford: Basil Blackwell, 1958); Herbert Preisker, "Anhang zum ersten Petrusbrief," in Hans Windisch, *Die katholischen Briefe*, 3d ed., Handbuch zum Neuen Testament 4.2 (Tübingen: J. C. B. Mohr (Paul Siebeck), 1951), 152-162; Cross, *1 Peter*.

[61]Wilhelm Bornemann, "Der erste Petrusbrief: Eine Taufrede des Silvanus?" *Zeitschrift für die neutestamentliche Wissenschaft* 19 (1920): 161.

(4:12-19). The speaker finally urges the leaders and members to be conscious of their respective duties (5:1-11).[62] Bornemann's analysis demonstrates the inability of the baptismal sermon hypothesis to furnish an adequate compositional analysis of 1 Peter. By advocating a major break between 3:14 and 3:15, he ignores the literary evidence that indicates there is no break at this point. Since he does not collect and analyze Christian baptismal sermons, he has nothing with which to compare his analysis of 1 Peter. His hypothesis that 1 Peter is composed as a baptismal homily remains unfounded, and no one accepts his historical reconstruction.[63]

Hans Windisch's commentary illustrates the enormous impact that Perdelwitz's theory had on Petrine scholarship. In the first edition of his commentary appearing in 1911, he divides the letter into several small segments and does not always explain their interrelationships.[64] He identifies the purpose of the letter as an attempt to establish Gentile Christians in their faith.[65] Nowhere does Windisch mention the baptismal sermon theory. In his second edition in 1930, however, he heartily espouses Perdelwitz's theory accepting it as an adequate explanation of the composition of 1 Peter.[66]

This analytical tradition based upon a liturgical analysis of 1 Peter follows Perdelwitz and not Bornemann. Consequently, the liturgical-analytical tradition is usually combined with some type of partition theory. This homiletical-liturgical analysis of 1 Peter, as well as the partition theories, has had a profound impact upon Petrine studies in this century. It is surprising that the suggestions of Harnack, who is the originator of liturgical and partition theories, have influenced the analysis of 1 Peter so greatly. In the next section, where the scholarship of the past fifty years will be examined, the influence of this homiletical-liturgical analysis will be very evident.

---

[62]Ibid., 161-162.

[63]Streeter, 128-130, 136-139, may be an exception. He takes a position very similar to Bornemann when he conjectures that Ariston of Smyrna is the bishop responsible for the baptismal sermon and subsequent letter. He dates 1 Peter between 90 and 95 CE However, he appears to be working independently of Bornemann's article.

[64]Windisch, 46-47.

[65]Ibid., 47.

[66]Ibid., 1930[2], passim.

Compositional Analyses Since
Urbanus Holzmeister

Type 1

The old analysis that views 1 Peter as an instructional letter with a series of exhortations and teachings listed one after the other has become the preferred type of analysis for those scholars who cannot discern a coherent plan in 1 Peter. Hanns Lilje does not discern a coherent plan, which is evident in the following, "Some have correctly observed that 1 Peter in spite of the almost classical Greek in which it is written appears to lack a strict arrangement. However, how rich and full flows the stream of powerful early Christian thoughts, promises, and commands."[67] He further comments on 1:13-21, "One cannot deny that this second passage (1:13-21) confirms what we said about the lack of an essential order because one can scarcely discover an actual progression of thought."[68] After expressing these doubts concerning a compositional plan in 1 Peter, Lilje enumerates twelve instructional subjects in the letter that are very similar to those identified by Pseudo-Euthalius.[69]

Emphasizing the hortatory nature of 1 Peter, Ambroggi and Cranfield echo the same skepticism concerning ordered composition. Ambroggi states succinctly, "St. Peter did not intend to write an ordered tract of systematic doctrine but he wants especially to exhort and testify [παρακαλῶν καὶ ἐπιμαρτυρῶν 5:12]"[70] Cranfield concurs with Ambroggi:

> Exhortation and testimony–that well describes the letter. The two things are intertwined with each other. Whereas others might – more logically and more neatly maybe – put first testimony and then as a separate division the exhortation that follows from it, Peter's way is to weave the two strands together. . . .[71]

---

[67]Hanns Lilje, *Die Petrusbriefe und der Judasbrief*, Bibelhilfe für die Gemeinde, Neutestamentliche Reihe 14 (Kassel: J. G. Oncken, 1938), 17.

[68]Ibid., 20.

[69]Ibid., 10.

[70]Pietro De Ambroggi, *Le Epistole Cattoliche Di Giacomo, Pietro, Giovanni e Giuda*, La Sacra Biblia 14.1 (Torino: Marietti, 1947) 93.

[71]C. E. B. Cranfield, *The First Epistle of Peter* (London: S.C.M. Press, 1950), 122.

Both commentators then proceed to list the instructional subjects, which is typical for this type of analysis.[72]

The boldest expression of a lack of plan in 1 Peter is expressed by J. P. Love:

> Indeed, to attempt an outline of the letter is to invite failure, not because its method is nondescript, but because its themes are skillfully interwoven even as in the scheme of life itself. One may mark out great "doctrinal" passages such as 1:3-12, 2:6-10, 3:18-22, 4:12-19, and he may note that they alternate with such great exhortations to Christian living as are to be found in 1:13-22, 2:1-5, 2:11--3:12, 4:1-11, 5:1-11. But all such divisions into the doctrinal and hortatory give a pedantic formula that would be far from the author's intent. One may painstakingly outline the letter, showing how each verse fits into some such threefold scheme as "The Privileges of the Christian Life" (1:1--2:10); "The Duties of the Christian Life" (2:11--4:11); "The Trials of the Christian Life" (4:12--5:14). But he will come back to a rereading with a realization that privileges and duties and trials all appear, not neatly compartmentalized, but treated in all parts of the letter even as they enter into every phase of life itself. . . . The best method of study is not by an outline of contents but by the topics that keep coming up in cycles of thought.[73]

Clearly, Love does not think there is a coherent flow of thought in 1 Peter. Thus, he advocates that proper analysis will only attempt to identify the small teaching and paraenetic statements as they arise.

Like Love, many scholars adopt this type of analysis because of their dissatisfaction with other types of analyses. Jean-Claude Margot and Alan Stibbs strongly criticize the liturgical approach before adopting the type of analysis represented by Pseudo-Euthalius.[74] In similar fashion, W. C. van Unnik says, "It is impossible to distinguish as clearly as one can in many of Paul's letters between doctrinal and ethical sections. Therefore it will be better simply to summarize the contents as the letter proceeds."[75] Van Unnik then proceeds to simply list the instructional subjects. Clearly, these scholars are adopting this type of analysis because of the inadequacy of other explanations of the compositional structure of 1 Peter. They cannot

---

[72]Ambroggi, 98; Cranfield, 5.

[73]Julian Prince Love, "The First Epistle of Peter," *Interpretation* 8 (1954): 63-64.

[74]Jean-Claude Margot, *Les Epîtres de Pierre* (Genève: Labor et Fides, 1960), 11-13. Alan M. Stibbs, *The First Epistle General of Peter*, The Tyndale New Testament Commentaries (Grand Rapids: Eerdmans Publishing Co., 1959), 58-63.

[75]W. C. van Unnik, "Peter, First Letter of," *The Interpreters Dictionary of the Bible*, vol. 3: *K-O* (New York: Abingdon Press, 1962), 759.

discern a coherent plan in 1 Peter and are content to leave their analysis at the level of simple description.[76]

Most recently, Wolfgang Schrage has argued for the lack of compositional plan in 1 Peter. He states that although central themes can be identified, the individual exhortations are loosely arranged without strict order or system and that this desultory compositional scheme is characteristic of the paraenetic tradition. Although he identifies section headings, he cautions saying that the headings are only an attempt to give an overview of the section. Since the document is paraenetical, it has no explainable compositional structure.[77]

These modern representatives of this type of analysis have not removed the problems nor addressed the criticisms of Pseudo-Euthalius' approach. They neither can escape that their method leads to the conclusion 1 Peter is a desultory composition, nor can they explain the selection and arrangement of topics. Since the relationship between the various instructional materials are not explained, the context for each individual unit is vague and the proper perspective for interpretation is lost. Since this position is attained by default, an adequate explanation of 1 Peter's composition will render this type of analysis invalid. Obviously,

---

[76]This type of analysis is popular with devotional commentaries like Roland De Pury, *Pierres Vivantes* (Paris: Delachaux & Niestlé, 1944) and Eduard Schweizer, *Der erste Petrusbrief*, Prophezei (Zürich: Zwingli-Verlag, 1942).

[77]Horst Balz and Wolfgang Schrage, *Die "katholischen" Briefe*, Das Neue Testament Deutsch 10 (Göttingen: Vandenhoeck & Ruprecht, 1973), 64-65, says, "Although particular focal points can be recognized like the exhortation to fearlessness (3:6, 14) and brotherly love (1:22; 3:8), that does not dictate a strict arrangement. The headings in the exegesis are only an attempt to render a certain overview. Repetitions are frequent and passages belonging together like 4:10f. and 5:1f. always stand next to one another. The freer stringing together of individual exhortations without strict order and arrangement is a typical characteristic of the paraenetic tradition. . . . Nevertheless this does not deny that there are rudiments of an arrangement scheme as in James whose parallel passages in general have the same sequence as in 1 Peter. So it is scarcely accidental that the expressions of baptism are found especially in Chapter 1 (compare 1:2, 3), while the eschatological expressions as well as the questions of church order attach to the end of the letter (4:7, 13, 17 and 5:1 respectively). The clear order of the "haustafel" in Chapters 2 and 3 that exhorts the Christian to good works within the structures of society was bequeathed to the author already. In spite of the loose connections, the letter achieves with unusual forcefulness its chief concerns of witnessing and exhorting the Christian to obedience in life and suffering." Norbert Brox, *Der erste Petrusbrief*, Evangelisch-katholischer Kommentar zum Neuen Testament 21 (Zürich: Benziger Verlag, 1979), 35-38, takes a similar position in regard to the composition of 1 Peter.

the modern adherents of the Pseudo-Euthalian tradition have only restated his position without improving upon it.

Type 2

The analysis of the Venerable Bede that uses the criteria of audience for analyzing 1 Peter has been used extensively by more recent commentators. However, in contrast to Bede, no one uses the criteria of general or specific audience to delineate the major sections of the letter. Rather, they use his analytical criteria to differentiate the subsections of the letter while employing some other method of analysis to identify the letter's major sections. Holzmeister provides a paradigmatic example of how modern scholars use Bede's analytical method. He says in his commentary:

> The order of the epistle and the progress of the Apostle's argument seem to consist in this, that three themes are derived from holy writ, which commend a good and patient life: (1) God's great benefits that are brought together for us, (2) edification and discussion of the outward hostility facing Christians, (3) the divine judgment soon coming upon all. Nevertheless in applying these themes that are prominent in the individual parts of the epistle, the sacred writer naturally moves from general precepts to special and particular precepts, but does this in such a way that as the occasion necessitates, he may return to general precepts.[78]

Holzmeister uses major themes to demarcate three major sections in 1 Peter and then utilizes admonitions to everyone or to specific groups to identify the subsections. His use of general and specific audience to identify subsections of the letter rather than major sections is characteristic of the contemporary use of Bede's method.

This method of analysis is difficult to ignore because of the objective features of the text of 1 Peter. In 2:18 the author addresses slaves as a particular subgroup, then wives in 3:1, and finally husbands in 3:7. The "all" of 3:8 clearly indicates that the author has returned to addressing the entire group. In 5:1 the author again addresses a subgroup, "elders," and then another subgroup, "young men," in 5:5a. In 5:5b he again speaks to "all." Thus, almost all commentators are forced to recognize the distinction between general and specific admonitions as a valid criterion for a compositional analysis of 1 Peter. The problem with this analytical

---

[78]Holzmeister, 170.

criterion is to determine whether it delineates major sections or only subsections of the epistle. Recent scholarship has corrected Bede's error of applying this criterion to major sections of the epistle, demonstrating that this is only a valid criterion for determining the subsections.

Mayerhoff's variant form of Bede's analysis, which understands particular admonitions to refer to specific situations in life and general admonitions to refer to life in general, still finds adherents among more recent commentators. After identifying the major theme of the epistle as hope, Georg Staffelbach discusses the general and specific admonitions as follows, "On the basis of this hope we live consoled through this earthly life and we order our lives. In general we are appointed for eternal life (1:13--2:12), and in particular we live in the power of hope through the various relationships of life (2:13--5:11)."[79] Since Staffelbach does not improve upon the method of Mayerhoff, all the criticisms that were leveled against Mayerhoff apply to him as well.[80]

Type 3

The type of analysis that began with Martin Luther and attempted to identify doctrinal sections that support ethical sections has not been popular among Petrine scholars. Although this type of analysis has been used extensively in analyzing Paul's letters, it does not work very well in 1 Peter.[81] E. G. Selwyn has been the chief exponent of this method. He identifies three doctrinal sections: 1:3-12; 2:1-10; and 3:13--4:19, which provide the basis for three ethical sections: 1:13-25; 2:11--3:12; and 5: 1-11.[82] The problem with his analysis is the ethical material that occurs in the doctrinal sections and the doctrinal material that occurs in the ethical sections. For example, the doctrinal statements about Christ's sufferings in 2:21-24 occur in an ethical section, and the admonition in 2:2 appears in a doctrinal section. Selwyn cannot escape the conclusion that his analysis does not correspond to the formal features of the text.

---

[79]Georg Staffelbach, *Die Briefe der Apostel Jakobus und Judas, Petrus und Johannes* (Luzern: Räter & Cie, 1941), 41.

[80]See the criticisms of Mayerhoff above.

[81]Rudolf Bultmann, "Das Problem der Ethik bei Paulus," *Zeitschrift für die neutestamentliche Wissenschaft* 23 (1924): 123-140.

[82]Edward Gordon Selwyn, *The First Epistle of St. Peter* (London: Macmillan & Co., 1946), 4-6.

Indeed, in total disregard for the formal textual features, Max-Alain Chevallier, who also adopts this method, divides 1:3--2:10 into four sections of alternating doctrine and exhortation. The first (1:3-12) and third (2:1-5) parts concern doctrinal affirmation that is developed in the first part by indicative verbs but by imperatives in the third. The second (1:13-25) and fourth (2:6-10) parts give exhortations expressed in the second part by the imperative but in the fourth part by the indicative.[83] His identification of doctrinal sections developed by imperatival verbs and hortatory sections developed by indicative verbs is strange and cannot be substantiated. As these examples demonstrate, the frequent pervasive appearance of imperatival verbs from 1:13--5:12 renders this approach to an analysis of 1 Peter impossible, and very few scholars have utilized it.[84]

In spite of its difficulties, this method is not totally without merit. It does emphasize the foundational nature of 1:3-12. Johann Michl uses this method to arrive at the following analysis, "First Part. The bliss of Christians called to salvation, 1:3-12. Second Part. Implications for life, 1:13--5:11."[85] Michl's observation that 1:3-12 provides the basis for the exhortation in 1:13--5:12 is significant and can be substantiated by the fact that no imperatives occur in the former passage while in the latter passage imperatives form the structure of the text.[86] Thus, as it was for Luther, this method is also inadequate for more recent exegetes to explain the structure of the material in 1:13--5:12. It is, however, useful to demonstrate the unique status of 1:3-12 in relation to the rest of the epistle.

---

[83]Max-Alain Chevallier, "I Pierre 1/1 à 2/10: Structure Littéraire et Conséquences Exégètiques," *Revue d'Histoire et de Philosophie Religieuses* 51 (1971): 129-142.

[84]Except for Albert R. Jonsen, "The Moral Theology of the First Epistle of St. Peter," *Sciences Ecclésiastiques* 16 (1964): 93-105, I am unaware of anyone who adopts the conclusions of Selwyn's analysis.

[85]Johann Michl, *Die Katholischen Briefe*, Das Neue Testament 8.2 (Regensburg: Friedrich Pustet, 1953), 8. See also 193.

[86] Ἀγαλλιᾶσθε in 1:6 has frequently been taken as an imperative. It is however a futuristic present according to Leonhard Goppelt, *Der erste Petrusbrief*, Kritisch-exegetischer Kommentar über das Neue Testament 12.1, 8th ed. (Göttingen: Vandenhoeck & Ruprecht, 1978), 98-99. He says, "It promises future joy at the consummation like a futuristic present."

Type 4

Bengel's thematic analysis is the most popular method for explaining the composition of 1 Peter. In addition to Holzmeister, at least 29 scholars before him and 21 after him have utilized this method. In spite of its popularity, this method continues to encounter the same problems as it did before Holzmeister. The exact identification of the controlling theme of each section as well as the limits and extent of each section continues to pose problems. There is also no agreement upon the number of sections in 1 Peter. In addition, the relationship of 1:3-12 to the rest of the letter has never been established in this analytical tradition. These problems become apparent when the various adherents of this tradition are compared.

Regarding the relationship of 1:3-12 to the rest of the letter, many commentators follow Bengel by incorporating it into the first section of the letter, 1:3--2:10, implying that it forms the basis or rationale for the admonitions in this section but not for the whole letter. P. N. Trempelas' treatment of 1:3-12 is paradigmatic for these commentators. He outlines the passage as follows:

> The Privileges of a Christian and the Consequent Demand of Purity from him (1:3--2:10).
> a) Thanksgiving to God because of the bequest of salvation that has been provided to the Christians (1:3-12).
> b) Exhortations to a life worthy of the bequest of God (1:13--2:10).[87]

He identifies 1:3-12 as a thanksgiving for the bequest of God's salvation that provides the basis for the exhortations that follow in this section. The basis for the second section, 2:11--4:6, and the third, 4:7--5:11, is not provided by 1:3-12 but by duties that arise from Christian existence in the world and in the community respectively.[88] Holzmeister, Ketter, Lohse, Hunter, Schelkle, Dalton, Schiwy, Goppelt, Elliott, and Balch, all subscribe to this view of 1:3-12 held by Trempelas.[89]

---

[87]Π. N. Τρεμπελα, Ὑπόμνημα εἰς τὴν πρὸς Ἑβραίους καὶ τὰς ἑπτὰ Καθολικὰς ('Αθῆναι· 'Αδελφότης Θεολόγων ἡ Ζωή, 1941), 248, 253.

[88]Ibid., 266, 288.

[89]Holzmeister, 170; Peter Ketter, *Hebräerbrief, Jakobusbrief, Petrusbriefe, Judasbrief*, Die Heilige Schrift für das Leben erklärt 16.1 (Freiburg: Herder, 1950), 207; Eduard Lohse, "Paränese und Kerygma im 1. Petrusbrief," *Zeitschrift für die neutestamentliche Wissenschaft* 45 (1954): 47f.; A. M. Hunter and E. G. Homrighausen,

Other commentators differ with Bengel detaching 1:3-12 from the other sections of the letter arguing that this passage provides the rationale for the entire letter and not just the first section. R. C. H. Lenski provides a good example of the views of these commentators. He calls 1:3-12 "The Great Doxology."[90] For him, the remainder of the letter consists of exhortations based upon this doxology. He comments on 1:13, "With διό Peter bases his hortations on the entire preceding doxology in which he expects his readers to join. Realizing all that this doxology says of them in their blessed relation to God, the readers will be ready to respond to the admonitions that are then justified."[91] Clearly, this view of 1:3-12 differs from Bengel and the commentators who view this passage as a rationale only for the first section of the letter. Lenski is supported by Boismard, Schneider, Spicq, Kelly, Best, Michl, Kendall, and Kistemaker.[92]

As this discussion demonstrates, the relationship of 1:3-12 to the rest of 1 Peter has not been established by the analytical tradition initiated by Bengel. In addition to this problem, this tradition has not been able to

---

The Epistle of James, The First and Second Epistles of Peter, The First, Second, and Third Epistles of John, The Epistle of Jude, The Revelation of St. John the Divine, The Interpreter's Bible 12 (Nashville: Abingdon, 1957), 85; Karl Hermann Schelkle, *Die Petrusbriefe. Der Judasbrief*, Herders Theologischer Kommentar zum Neuen Testament 13.2 (Freiburg: Herder, 1961),vii; Dalton, *Proclamation*, 81; Günther Schiwy, *Weg ins Neue Testament*, Kommentar und Material, vol. 4, *Nachpaulinen* (Würzburg: Echter-Verlag, 1970), 189; Goppelt, *Petrusbrief*, 8; John H. Elliott, *A Home for the Homeless: A Sociological Exegesis of 1 Peter, Its Situation and Strategy* (Philadelphia: Fortress Press, 1981), 284; David L. Balch, *Let Wives Be Submissive: The Domestic Code in 1 Peter*, Society of Biblical Literature Monograph Series 26 (Chico, California: Scholars Press, 1981), 124.

[90]R. C. H. Lenski, *The Interpretation of the Epistles of St. Peter, St. John and St. Jude* (Columbus, Ohio: Lutheran Book Concern, 1938), 28.

[91]Ibid., 52.

[92]M. E. Boismard, "Pierre (Première Epître de)," *Dictionnaire de la Bible*, Supplément 7: *Pastorales-Pirot* (1966):1415; Johannes Schneider, *Die Briefe des Jakobus, Petrus, Judas, und Johannes*, Das Neue Testament Deutsch 10 (Göttingen: Vandenhoeck & Ruprecht, 1961), 44; Ceslas Spicq, *Les Épitres de Saint Pierre*, Sources Bibliques (Paris: Librairie Lecoffre, 1966), 37; J. N. D. Kelly, *A Commentary on the Epistles of Peter and Jude*, Black's New Testament Commentaries (London: A. & C. Black, 1969), 21-22; Ernest Best, *1 Peter*, The New Century Bible Commentary (Grand Rapids: Wm. B. Eerdmans Publishing Co., 1971), 73; Michl, *Briefe*, 455; Kendall, 104; Simon J. Kistemaker, *Exposition of the Epistles of Peter and of the Epistle of Jude*, New Testament Commentary (Grand Rapids: Baker Book House, 1987), 24.

establish the themes of each section. Few have followed Bengel's lead in identifying the themes of the sections by reference to the descriptions of the readers.[93] Almost all of the commentators since Holzmeister prefer to adhere to Huther's method of dividing the sections according to the various classes of admonitions or to Kögel's method of identifying the sections by the issues raised by the author.

Adherents of the former method are Lenski, Trempelas, Ketter, Lohse, Schneider, Schiwy, and Michl.[94] Lohse furnishes a good example of this method. He divides 1 Peter into three sections that are all characterized by paraenesis. In the first section, 1:3--2:10, the admonitions pertain to the holy people of God while in the second section, 2:11--3:12, the admonitions are structured around the notion of submission, and in the third section, 3:13--5:11, they are intended to comfort suffering Christians.[95]

Adherents of the latter method are Holzmeister, Boismard, Hunter, Schelkle, Dalton, Spicq, Best, Combrink, Calloud, Kendall, and Kistemaker.[96] Ceslas Spicq's treatment of 1 Peter supplies a paradigmatic example of this method.[97] He identifies 1 Peter as a "Pastoral Letter" in

---

[93]Kelly, 22, identifies the theme of the first section as "God's chosen people are called to holiness." However, he does not use the description of the readers to identify the themes in the remaining sections. Goppelt, *Petrusbrief*, 155-156, understands the description of the readers as strangers and aliens to form the basis of the entire letter but he is not as astute as Bengel in noticing the shift in the description of the readers among the various sections of the letter. The same comments apply to Elliott, *Home*, passim.

[94]Lenski, 52, 106; Τρεμπελα, 248, 266, 288; Ketter, 215f.; Michl, *Briefe*, 8; Lohse, "Paränese," 68-89; Schneider, 64f.; Schiwy, 189.

[95]Lohse, "Paränese," 73, 78, 80.

[96]Holzmeister, 170, Boismard, "Première Épître, de," 1415; Hunter, 85; Schelkle, *Petrusbrief*, vii; Dalton, *Proclamation*, 76-79; Spicq, *Épîtres*, 37-38; Best, *I Peter*, 84f.; H. J. B. Combrink, "The Structure of 1 Peter," *Neotestamentica* 9 (1975): 34-63; Jean Calloud and Francois Genuyt, *La Première Épître de Pierre*, Lectio Divina 109 (Paris: Cerf, 1982), 8-9; Kendall, 104-106; Kistemaker, 24.

[97]The works of Combrink and Calloud provide a dimension that Spicq's treatment lacks because they utilize modern linguistic theory in their analysis of 1 Peter. Combrink uses Discourse Analysis to divide the letter into cola. On page 35 he describes his method, "To determine the coherence of these cola, attention should be given to words or concepts which can be used for the same meaning and are therefore related to one another, as well as to the whole train of thought of a specific utterance." His synopsis of the letter on page 53f. indicates that he is identifying the sections of the letter by the issues raised by the author. His Discourse-Analysis method enables him to perceive the sentence structures but does not enable him to identify the larger sections and subsection. Hence, he resorts to the

which the author addresses issues that he considers important. The issue of the holiness of the Christian life is discussed in the first section, 1:3--2:10. In the second, 2:11--3:12, and the third, 3:13--4:19, sections, Christian living in various circumstances and in a hostile world are taken up respectively. In the last section, 5:1-11, the author discusses general pastoral concerns.[98]

As these examples demonstrate, there is no consensus concerning the proper method to employ in determining the various themes of each section. This is a pernicious problem for Bengel's analytical tradition.

Additional problems plague this analytical tradition. In this tradition, there is no consensus regarding the number or extent of each of the sections. The majority of commentators designate three sections, but Ketter, Spicq, Michl, and Elliott have four sections while Best and Kistemaker have five sections.[99] Since the first section, 1:13--2:10, is recognized by all, the division debate focuses on 2:11--5:11. How many sections are there and what are the limits of each section? Adherents of this analytical tradition have neither been able to answer these questions nor resolve the problems.

This popular analytical tradition initiated by Bengel is valuable in explaining the compositional structure of 1 Peter. However, in order to satisfactorily analyze 1 Peter, four problems in this tradition must be

---

thematic method to establish these larger sections. It should be noted that Combrink is building on the initial work of A. B. du Toit, "The Significance of Discourse Analysis for New Testament Interpretation and Translation: Introductory Remarks with Special Reference to 1 Peter 1:3-13," *Neotestamentica* 8 (1974): 54-79. In contrast to Combrink, Calloud's method, which he calls *analyse semiotique*, attempts to ascertain the larger sections of the letter. In addition to the linguistic markers that he identifies in the text, he gives ample attention to a discussion of themes, and his identification of each of the major sections still rests largely on thematic principles. For example, in the summary of his analysis on page 8, the theme of sanctification controls the material in 1:13-25 while the theme of edification determines the section in 2:1-10. Calloud's semiotic method does make an advance over previous thematic studies because of his sensitivity to linguistic markers that function as transitions within the text. As Chapter 4 of this dissertation will demonstrate, sensitivity to transitional markers is an important key for determining the compositional structure of 1 Peter.

[98]Spicq, *Les Épîtres*, 11, 37, 38.

[99]Ketter, 207, 233, 252, 261; Spicq, 37-38; Michl, *Briefe*, 8; John H. Elliott, *I-II Peter/Jude*, Augsburg Commentary on the New Testament (Minneapolis: Augsburg Publishing House, 1982), 67-68, 70; Best, *1 Peter*, 73f.; Kistemaker, 24.

addressed: What is the relationship of 1:3-12 to the rest of the letter?
What method should be used to identify the controlling theme in each
section? How many sections are there? What is the extent and limit of
each section? The resolution of these problems will form the agenda for
this dissertation.

Types 5 and 6

Since Holzmeister, the analytical traditions begun by Harnack have
produced at least six different conclusions regarding the composition of
1 Peter.[100]   Some argue that 1 Peter is composed of two letters while
others assert that it is a baptismal sermon in its entirety. Others allege that
it is a letter into which a baptismal sermon has been redacted while others
propose that the document is a baptismal sermon with a letter appended.
One scholar states that it is a letter containing two baptismal homilies. Still
others argue that the document is an account of a liturgical service. These
diverse conclusions demonstrate the lack of adequate method in this
analytical tradition. Inadequate method leads to some perplexing problems.
What method conclusively determines the partition of 1 Peter?   What
method determines whether 1 Peter is a letter or a baptismal homily?
Adherents of these analytical traditions have been unable to give
satisfactory answers to these questions as an examination of their positions
will indicate.

Following Hart, J. W. C. Wand and C. F. D. Moule maintain that
1 Peter is composed of two different letters. Both affirm the unity of
1 Peter by asserting that both letters were written by the same author at
the same time and were intended to circulate together. After criticizing
Streeter's partition theory as going much too far, Wand states his position:

> A more probable suggestion is that made by J. H. A. Hart in the *Expositor's
> Greek Testament.* He accepts the essential unity of the document but emphasizes
> the fact that it is addressed to a number of different churches. Not the whole of it
> need necessarily have been intended for every church. . . . This being so, it is

---

[100]Schutter, *Hermeneutic,* could be included in this discussion of analytical
traditions begun by Harnack since he claims that 1 Peter is a homilitic midrash. However,
his work will be discussed in detail in Chapter 4 with that of William Dalton because
Schutter bases his compositional analysis upon the methods first utilized by Dalton instead
of the compositional devices of a homilitic midrash.

possible that we have here two separate addenda meant to suit the circumstances of two different churches.[101]

Moule reiterates this position:

> In brief my suggestion is as follows: 1 Peter is genuinely epistolary and was written specifically for the communities indicated in the greeting; but since some of these communities were actually suffering persecution, while for others it was no more than a possibility, the writer sent two forms of epistle, one for those not yet under actual duress (1:1-4:11 and 5:12-14), and the other—terser and swifter—for those who were in the refining fire (1:1-2:10; 4:12-5:14). The messengers were bidden to read the appropriate part to each community according to the situation.[102]

Wand is led to his position because there are two doxologies in 1 Peter. He says, "The fact that there are two doxologies (iv.11; v.11), each of which might have served as a good finale, makes it difficult to believe that the work as it stands is an original and organic unit."[103] This line of reasoning is not persuasive because other Christian documents contain doxologies that do not provide sufficient grounds for partition.[104] Likewise, Moule's argument that differing attitudes toward persecution demand some form of partition theory is not conclusive. Perhaps there are other, more adequate solutions that explain the different perspectives toward suffering in the letter.

Like Perdelwitz and others, Wand and Moule have constructed a hypothetical historical situation in order to explain the composition of 1 Peter. Indeed, constructing fanciful historical scenarios is a favorite method of these analytical traditions, but this method is unsatisfactory because of the illusive subjective nature of the scenario. It is best to deal seriously with the text and avoid these fanciful reconstructions.

In contrast to Wand and Moule, Bo Reicke; Oscar Brooks; and, with reservations, G. R. Beasley-Murray affirm the unity of 1 Peter as a baptismal sermon. Reicke states in his commentary:

> The form in which the author has chosen to present his message is outwardly that of an epistle. It is introduced and closed by the forms of greeting common to

---

[101]Wand, 2-3.
[102]Moule, "Purpose," 11.
[103]Wand, 1.
[104]See Romans 11:36; *1 Clement* 32:4; 38:4 for examples.

epistles, i 1f., v 12ff. On closer examination it is evident, however, that First Peter is really a baptismal sermon in the form of an epistle, first directed to newly baptized people, i 1-iv 6, and after that to the congregation as a whole, iv 7-v 14. Baptism is alluded to in i 2 as shown by the reference to election "in the blood of Christ." This alludes to the communication of holy spirit at baptism, the promise of obedience given by the baptismal candidates, and their participation in Christ's atoning death through the waters of baptism. From that point on the awareness of the recent conversion of the hearers is maintained through the entire text until iv 6; it is only after this verse that the speaker addresses himself to Christians generally. In the earlier section, which constitutes the main portion of the epistle, the baptismal procedure is expressly affirmed in iii 21, where baptism is said to save the believers "now."[105]

In spite of his assertion, many have examined the epistle quite closely and found no evidence that it is really a baptismal sermon. Two major problems plague Reicke's method. First, the genre of a first-century baptismal homily has never been described. To explain the composition of 1 Peter as a baptismal homily is to explain one unknown by another. A label is not an explanation. Second, allusions to baptism do not make a baptismal sermon as Moule notes in the following:

> For my own part, I whole-heartedly agree that 1 Peter is concerned with baptism—who, indeed, could deny it? But this much is true, of course, of many other parts of the N.T. [Rom 4, Col 2, Heb 6, to go no further], and, in itself, it proves no more than that early church writers continually had the 'pattern' of baptism in mind. . . .[106]

These same problems plague Brooks' article,[107] and Beasley-Murray subscribes to the baptismal homily theory with great reservations, saying:

> It would be absurd to put forward the thesis that these Letters [Romans, Colossians, Hebrews] were written as baptismal treatises, but it is not absurd to suggest the same of I Pt. 1.3-4.11, even though it be a mistaken thesis. Whatever be the truth of its origin, I Pt. 1.3-4.11 is unique among New Testament writings in its fullness of baptismal allusions, as a glance through its contents serves to show. Accordingly, in the present stage of investigation, it would seem justifiable to put forward a modest claim. While proof is not forthcoming, the evidence suggests that I Pt 1.3-4.11 reflects the pattern of

[105]Bo Reicke, *The Epistles of James, Peter, and Jude*, The Anchor Bible 37 (Garden City, New York: Doubleday & Co., 1964), 74.

[106]Moule, "Purpose," 4.

[107]Oscar S. Brooks, "I Peter 3:21–The Clue to the Literary Structure of the Epistle," *Novum Testamentum* 16 (1974): 290-305.

baptismal instruction followed by the writer of the Letter, and may reproduce an address given by him to newly baptized converts. . . .[108]

His comments clearly indicate that the baptismal homily scenario is at best tenuous and, at worst, totally unfounded. It is not useful in explaining the composition of 1 Peter.

More in agreement with Perdelwitz is the position of F. W. Beare and A. R. C. Leaney who view 1 Peter as a baptismal homily with an appended letter. Beare states in his interpretation:

> This later part of the book is truly epistolary in form and in content, and to this the address (1:1-2) and the closing greetings (5:12-14) properly belong. Into this framework, the baptismal discourse has been intruded, possibly by a later editor, but more probably by the writer himself. For in recognizing the composite structure of the book, there is no need to postulate two different authors; on the contrary, there is every indication that the writer of the letter to the persecuted also composed the discourse to the newly baptized. . . . The Epistle will then have been sent forth by the writer in the form in which we now have it before us, even though the major portion was composed for a different purpose, and in more tranquil times; and the whole work receives a secondary unity from the circumstances of its publication.[109]

Leaney articulates the same position:

> We shall see that perhaps not all of it is–or was originally–a letter. The first clue is that the work makes a stop at 4:11 with a doxology, an ascription to God of glory and power, like the formal end of a sermon in church. . . . After this point, on the other hand, the work becomes very like a letter, since it refers clearly to an event now in progress, 'the fiery ordeal that is upon you' (4:12). . . . It seems therefore that some person or persons may have sent a discourse–perhaps a favorite sermon–to their Christian brethren on hearing that they were in danger of persecution.[110]

---

[108]G. R. Beasley-Murray, *Baptism in the New Testament* (London: Macmillan & Co., 1962), 255-256.

[109]Beare, *1 Peter*, 8.

[110]A. R. C. Leaney, *The Letters of Peter and Jude*, The Cambridge Bible Commentary (Cambridge: Cambridge University Press, 1967), 8. C E. B. Cranfield, *I & II Peter and Jude*, Torch Bible Commentaries (London: S. C. M. Press, 1960), 13, articulates this position with hesitation. He says, "Perhaps the most likely hypothesis is that in the composition of a letter to the churches indicated in 1.1 the substance of a sermon which was already in existence [in view of the allusions to baptism it may well have been a baptismal sermon] was incorporated (1.3-4.11) along with fresh material written with the

Again, there are major problems with method. Leaney argues that since
the first section ends with a doxology in 4:11, it is a sermon.
Inconsistently, he does not argue that the second section is a sermon
although it also concludes with a doxology in 5:11. None of these scholars
have established the genre of baptismal homily, nor have they convincingly
argued their claim that the tone of 1:3--4:11 differs from the tone of 4:12--
5:12. Indeed, Beare's contention that "there are no carefully constructed
periods or nicely balanced rhythms and antitheses" after 4:12 is simply
incorrect.[111] In 4:16, in connection with two disjunctive elements, there is
a nicely balanced antithesis that is exactly paralleled in 1:8, 12; 2:10; and
3:9. These scholars in the grand tradition of Harnack are attempting to
construct an historical scenario in order to explain the composition of
1 Peter. In the process they overlook the text itself, and thus their analyses
of the composition of 1 Peter are based largely on fantasy.

Even more speculative is the position of R. P. Martin, who asserts
that 1 Peter is a letter containing two baptismal homilies. One was
delivered before and the other after the rite of baptism.[112] Unfortunately,
he only states this position and does not discuss details nor offer support.

Sheer fantasy is the position of Herbert Preisker and F. L. Cross,
who argue that 1 Peter is an account of a baptismal liturgy in progress.
Preisker argues in a ten page addition to the third edition of Windisch's
commentary that 1 Peter is not only a baptismal sermon but the transcript
of a Roman baptismal liturgy.[113] He identifies eight segments in this
liturgy. The liturgy opens with a "prayer-psalm" in 1:3-12 followed by a
"teaching-discourse" in 1:13-21. The third segment is the baptismal act
itself that takes place immediately after the statements in 1:21. Like
Perdelwitz, he argues that this act is not described because of its mysterious
nature. Following the act of baptism, the officiant delivers a short
"baptismal dedication" in 1:22-25, and an inspired member of the

---

present situation of the particular churches in mind (1.1-2; 4.12-5.14)." This position
represents a shift from his position in his 1950 commentary on 1 Peter.

[111]Beare, *1 Peter*, 7.

[112]R. P. Martin, "The Composition of 1 Peter in Recent Study," in *Vox
Evangelica: Biblical and Historical Essays*, ed. idem (London: Epworth Press, 1962), 40.

[113]Windisch, 3d ed., 152-162.

congregation leads a "festal song" that is recorded in the first ten verses of Chapter 2. Segment six is an exhortation by a new officiant who speaks from 2:11--3:12. He is interrupted by the congregation bursting into a hymn about Christ (2:21-24). His exhortation ends when he is again interrupted by a "charismatic prophet" who delivers a "revelation" in 3:13--4:7a. The last segment contains the closing prayer in 4:7b-11. The remaining part of 1 Peter is a transcript of the worship of the whole church that followed the baptismal service. Cross follows Preisker but asserts more specifically that the liturgy in 1 Peter is a paschal liturgy.[114] Goppelt's comment on Preisker's work is very appropriate. He calls it a *"phantasievolle Hypothese."*[115] This liturgical hypothesis has never been established, and it has been frequently criticized by many scholars.[116]

In spite of inadequate method, the analytical traditions initiated by Harnack have had an enormous impact upon Petrine studies. Although they have not established their grand speculative conclusions regarding 1 Peter, these analytical traditions have made a form critical impact upon the view of Petrine compositional materials. M. É. Boismard rejects the homiletical theory of Perdelwitz and the liturgical theories of Preisker and Cross, but he maintains that 1 Peter contains a number of fragments from a primitive baptismal liturgy. In two articles entitled "Une Liturgie baptismale dans la Prima Petri," he argues that 1 Peter is neither itself a baptismal homily nor a liturgy but draws material from a baptismal liturgy.[117] His arguments are based upon a detailed comparison of parallel passages in Titus, 1 John, Colossians, and James. He further develops his theories in a monograph entitled, *Quatres hymnes baptismales dans la première épître de Pierre.*[118] The first hymn is found in 1 Peter 1:3-5; the second is reconstructed from scattered elements in 1:20; 3:18, 22; 4:6; the third is contained in 2:22-25; and the fourth is reconstructed by comparing 1 Peter

---

[114]Cross, passim.

[115]Goppelt, *Petrusbrief*, 39.

[116]T. G. C. Thornton, "I Peter, A Paschal Liturgy?" *Journal of Theological Studies* N.S. 12 (1961): 14, says, "The aim of this paper is to show that there is nothing distinctively Paschal about I Peter and that it can be called a liturgy if the word 'liturgy' is used in such a vague way as to make it almost meaningless." See also Kelly, 16-20.

[117]M. É. Boismard, "La typologie baptismale dans la première épître de saint Pierre," *La Vie Spirituelle* 94 (1956): 339-352.

[118]M. É. Boismard, *Quartes hymnes baptismales dans la première épître de Pierre,* Lectio Divina 30 (Paris: Cerf, 1961).

5:5-9 with James 4:6-10. His most mature thought is presented in his article on 1 Peter in the *Dictionnaire de la Bible*:

> It is, however, difficult to discern a logical division of the sections of the letter because the sections are following one another without apparent connection. The proposed divisions vary significantly from one to the other. It seems, therefore, that it should be legitimate to distinguish three grand parts corresponding to an exposition of the Christian life descending from the more general to the more particular.[119]

Boismard labels the first section (1:3-12) as a Christianized Jewish benediction formula. The second section (1:13--2:10) treats the theme of regeneration by God while the third section (2:11--5:11) expounds the moral requirements incumbent upon the new life of the Christian. Boismard does not analyze 1 Peter as a baptismal homily although he does recognize that baptismal and liturgical elements provide some of the material in 1 Peter. Few contemporary scholars would deny there are some baptismal and liturgical elements in 1 Peter although they do not totally agree with Boismard's identification of these materials.[120] Although it is useful for isolating smaller sections, this form-critical approach is not able to provide an adequate method for a comprehensive compositional analysis of 1 Peter.

Indeed, all of these diverse conclusions regarding the composition of 1 Peter that arise from the analytical traditions begun by Harnack are inadequate to provide a comprehensive compositional analysis. This analytical tradition has not been able to establish an acceptable method for determining whether the document is a letter or a homily. Neither has it been able to articulate a viable method for partitioning the document. Many fanciful scenarios and hypotheses have been proposed but without adequate substantiation. The composition of 1 Peter remains an unsolved riddle.

---

[119]Boismard, "Pierre (Première épître de)," 1415.

[120]Rudolf Bultmann, "Bekenntnis- und Liedfragmente im ersten Petrusbrief," *Coniectanea Neotestamentica* 11 (1947): 1-14; reprint, *Exegetica*, ed. Erich Dinkler (Tübingen: J. C. B. Mohr (Paul Siebeck), 1967), 285-297. Bultmann accepts Windisch's designation of 1:18-21; 2:21-25; and 3:18-22 as hymn fragments. These passages differ from the ones Boismard isolated.

Conclusion

This survey of Petrine scholarship demonstrates the need for an adequate method of analysis for explaining the composition of 1 Peter. Although many approaches have been proposed, none can claim to have resolved the enigma of 1 Peter's composition. An adequate method is needed that will not import an external construct in order to explain the compositional structure but will devise a construct that arises from the text itself. This method must identify the relationship of 1:3-12 to the rest of the letter. It must identify how many sections there are as well as the extent and limit of each section. In addition, this method of analysis must identify the controlling theme or themes in each section. This dissertation will develop and utilize such a method that can explain the composition of 1 Peter.

CHAPTER 2

LETTER FORMULAS IN 1 PETER

One of the most obvious features of 1 Peter is its epistolary form.[1] Even those who argue that it is really a homily in letter form tacitly admit the epistolary nature of the document. Indeed, 1 Peter corresponds to the definition of a letter developed by W. G. Doty, who states the following:

> A letter is a literary product, intended for a private or public reader/s, originally or only formally in letter form. Letter form is distinguished by (1) being sent or intended for sending, (2) from a writer or from writers, (3) to an addressee or to addressees, (4) with greetings, conclusion, or other formally stylized components, and usually (5) with reference to or clear intent to be a letter.[2]

Doty's description of letter form certainly fits 1 Peter in every detail. 1 Peter is a document composed in epistolary form.

1 Peter not only corresponds to the epistolary form, but it also answers to the epistolary situation. This situation involves the separation of at least two persons, one of whom wishes to communicate with the other. A letter may thus be described as "half of a dialogue."[3] Heikki

---

[1]Chevallier, 138, says, ". . . 1 Peter is homogenous. In particular, the address and the salutation are inserted at the appropriate position. It is impossible to deny that our text has a deliberate epistolary character, whether the letter is real or ficticious."

[2]W. G. Doty, "The Classification of Epistolary Literature," *The Catholic Biblical Quarterly* 31 (1969): 193.

[3]Demetrius, *De Elocutione*, 223, says, "We will next treat of the epistolary style, since it too should be plain. Artemon, the editor of Aristotle's *Letters*, says that a letter ought to be written in the same manner as a dialogue, a letter being regarded by him as one of the two sides of a dialogue." Text and translation by W. Rhys Roberts, *Aristotle: Poetics; Demetrius on Style*, Loeb Classical Library (Cambridge: Harvard University Press, 1932), 438-439. For other texts reflecting this same idea, see Abraham J.

Koskenniemi asserts that the basic form of the letter corresponds to a personal speech encounter. He proposes the following:

> The basic scheme of the Greek letter: prescript, letter-body proper, and concluding formulas, which remain unchanged until the fourth century CE, can be compared in its parts with a personal encounter. The prescript corresponds to the greeting; the concluding formulas to the leave-taking. These parts frame the epistolary encounter, and the epistolary situation puts its stamp on them to a greater degree than in the rest of the letter.[4]

1 Peter corresponds to the epistolary situation indicating a separation between the sender who is in *Babylon* (5:13) and the addressees who are in Asia Minor (1:1).[5] In this communicative situation, a prescript and concluding formulas are appropriate and are exhibited in the letter.

Since 1 Peter corresponds to the epistolary form and answers to the epistolary situation, the first step in a compositional analysis is to identify the letter formulas in the document.

The Prescript

The prescript in ancient Greek letters was very stylized. Francis Exler describes the basic formula saying, "The basic type of the opening phrase in the Greek letter is expressed by the formula: A- to B- χαίρειν. 'A' stands for the writer or addressant, 'B' for the addressee."[6] Given this description of the prescript, 1 Peter 1:1-2 is certainly composed as an epistolary prescript.

The writer is identified as Peter, an apostle of Jesus Christ. Compared to some other ancient letters, the identification of the writer has been expanded. Exler cites examples of this accepted convention saying,

---

Malherbe, "Ancient Epistolary Theorists," *Ohio Journal of Religious Studies* 5.2 (1977): 15; reprint, Atlanta, Georgia: Scholars Press, 1988.

[4]Heikki Koskenniemi, *Studien zur Idee und Phraseologie des griechischen Briefes bis 400 n. Chr.* (Helsinki: Suomalaien Tiedeakatemia, 1956), 155.

[5]Many scholars think that *Babylon* is a code name for Rome. See Claus-Hunno Hunzinger, "Babylon als Deckname für Rom und die Datierung des 1. Petrusbriefes," in *Gottes Wort und Gottes Land*, Festschrift für Hans-Wilhelm Hertzberg, ed. Henning Graf Reventlow (Göttingen: Vandenhoeck & Ruprecht, 1965), 67-77.

[6]Francis Exler, "The Form of the Ancient Greek Letter: A Study in Greek Epistolography" (Ph.D. diss., Catholic University of America, 1923), 23.

"In familiar letters there was a tendency of giving expression to the friendship existing between the writer and his correspondents by the addition of appropriate words to the salutation."[7] The identification of the writer as an apostle definitely establishes a particular relationship between him and the reader of the letter. Whether or not the writer is indeed an apostle or even truly Peter, the letter makes this claim and establishes this relationship.[8]

This expanded identification of the writer is paralleled in the Pauline corpus. John White argues that Saint Paul was the creator of the apostolic letter tradition.[9] He asserts, "The apostle Paul was the primary influence in the formation of the Christian letter tradition or, at least, the apostolic letter tradition which we find in the NT."[10] He goes on to say:

---

[7]Ibid., 62.

[8]It is beyond the scope of this dissertation to prove or disprove Petrine authorship. The discussions are voluminous and, as far as I can tell, incapable of definitive solution since we do not possess one clearly genuine Petrine writing with which to compare 1 Peter. The primary argument against Petrine authorship is the quality of Greek in which the letter is written. Selwyn, *1 Peter*, 9-17, mitigates this objection by suggesting that Silvanus was Peter's amanuensis. This objection to Petrine authorship is further undermined by the report of the grandsons of Jude, the brother of Jesus, who were poor Galilean farmers forced to make their defense before the Emperor Domitian. Their speech reported in Eusebius is fairly good Greek. Given the fact that Eusebius may be creating speeches for them as historians were apt to do, he nevertheless was constrained to fit the style and language of the speech into an expression appropriate for their status and situation in life. This report at least provides for the possibility that Galilean peasants could speak Greek with modest proficiency. See Eusebius, *Ecclesiastical History* III.20.1-7. In spite of the lack of a definitive solution, however, more recent scholarship generally accepts the letter as pseudonymous. For example, Norbert Brox, "Zur pseudepigraphischen Rahmung des ersten Petrusbriefes" *Biblische Zeitschrift* N.F. 19 (1975): 78-96, argues for pseudonymity on the basis that no one would ascribe this letter to Peter if his name did not stand in 1:1.

[9]Helmut Koester, "I Thess–Experiment in Christian Writing," in *Continuity and Discontinuity in Church History*, Essays Presented to George Hunston Williams, ed. F. Forrester Church and Timothy George, Studies in the History of Christian Thought 19 (Leiden: E. J. Brill, 1979), 33-44. Koester convincingly argues that Paul was the creator not only of the apostolic letter but also of the Christian letter in general. On page 33, he states, "I Thessalonians testifies to the creative moment, it is 'the Christian letter in the making.'"

[10]John L. White, "New Testament Epistolary Literature in the Framework of Ancient Epistolography," in *Aufstieg und Niedergang der römischen Welt* II.25.2, ed. Hildegard Temporini und Wolfgang Haase (Berlin: Walter de Gruyter, 1984), 1739.

The Pauline pattern of evoking apostolicity immediately in the opening address
(e.g., the use of the title, "apostle") is imitated in all of the pseudo-Pauline letters
and in 1,2 Pet., Jas., and Jude, though the latter epistles appeal, of course, to the
apostles under whose name they are written.[11]

The identification of the writer in 1 Peter follows the standard formula for
the prescript of a Christian letter and more specifically a Christian
apostolic letter.

The description of the addressees has likewise been greatly expanded
when compared to documentary letters. The addressees are identified as
the elect strangers of the Dispersion from five provinces of Asia Minor.
This expansion has been noted and studied for the Pauline letters. White
states in his study:

The recipients' own divinely determined status is identified through various
designations ("saints," "called," "sanctified," "beloved"). But Paul gives not
only a general Christian cast to the items of address. He particularizes the
qualification, on each occasion, so that the message of the individual letter
is anticipated.[12]

Leonhard Goppelt perceives 1 Peter to be following the same agenda. He
states, "The designation of the readers as παρεπίδημοι programmatically
introduces here the first part (1:3--2:10) and then in 2:11 fills out through
πάροικοι the program of the second part (2:11--4:11)."[13] Goppelt attempts
to make this designation of the readers the compositional theme of the
entire letter. The problem with his approach is that the first and third
sections of the letter do not contain this term, nor do they treat topics
usually associated with these themes. For example, Goppelt does not say
why this term does not also encompass the third part (4:12--5:11), but it is
clear that he understands this expansion of the description of the readers to
be programmatic for the letter that follows.

The description of the readers as παρεπίδημοι is more
programmatic for the letter than Goppelt realizes. Not only does this term
strike a major theme in the letter, but it also signals an agenda for the
letter. This agenda utilizes metaphor as a compositional device. A debate
rages among ancient commentators whether the phrase παρεπίδημοι

[11]Ibid., 1752.
[12]Ibid., 1740.
[13]Goppelt, *Petrusbrief*, 79.

διασπορᾶς exclusively limits the letter to Jewish readers or permits some
Gentile readers. The debate is explained quite fully by Wilhelm Steiger:

> The immediate design of the writer of the Epistle is limited to a particular sort of
> Christian, by all those, who believe it to have been exclusively intended, either
> for Jewish or Gentile churches. In reference to the former, which Eusebius (h.e.
> iii 4), Jerome (Catal.), Didymus, Epiphanius (Haer. xxvii. 6), Oecumenius, and
> Theophylact, the Scoliast in Matthai, Erasmus, Calvin, Beza, W. Est, Baronius
> (Ann. 1.1), Salmasius, Grotius, Ik. Capellus, Hammond, Bengel, Hensler,
> Bertholdt, Hug, De Wette, think they find in the expression παρεπίδημοι
> διασπορᾶς, the Epistle itself speaks nothing, but much against it. . . . There is a
> positive ground why we should necessarily conclude, that the Epistle was written
> to the Gentile Christians as Augustine (c. Faust. xxii. 89), Procopius (in Isa.
> xv.20), Cassiodor (de Inst. div. litt., T.II.516), Osiander, Wetstein, Hallet,
> Brehme (comm. in Ep. ad Hebr. p. 46, sp.; comp. also Didymus on ch. ii.10),
> apprehend, or at least to churches, which not only were composed of heathen and
> Jewish Christians, as Flacius, Calov, Wolf, Carpzov, Pott, Haenlein, Eichhorn,
> Schott, believe, but as Guerike rightly judges, consisted in most part of
> Gentile Christians.[14]

Steiger concluded that the phrase referred primarily to Gentile Christians
because of statements in the body of the letter like 4:3.[15] Having concluded
that the readers were Gentile or at least predominantly Gentile, he faced
the problem of how this phrase could be applied to them. He concluded
that the use of these terms is metaphorical and cites many examples of this
usage in early Christianity.[16] He recognizes that the older commentators,
Oecumenius, Theophylact, and Didymus recognized the metaphorical use
of these terms. However, they still asserted that the addressees were Jewish
because of Paul's statement in Galatians that Peter was the apostle to the
Jews. By Steiger's time, this argument had lost its force and continued to
decline as Petrine authorship became more and more questionable. Thus,
Steiger's revival of the notion that these terms are metaphorical and do not
necessarily imply that the readers were Jewish Christians proved to be a
powerful argument, regarding the conception of the addressees of the
letter. This understanding of the phrase as a metaphor has important

---

[14]Wilhelm Steiger, *Exposition of the First Epistle of Peter*, trans. Patrick Fairbairn
(Edinburgh: Thomas Clark, 1836), 19-20. The original German edition was published
in 1832.

[15]Ibid., 20-21, says, ". . . at least one passage in the Epistle clearly designates the
reader as having once been a heathen. . . . The principal passage is found in Chap. iv.3."

[16]Ibid., 22-24.

implications for an analysis of the composition of 1 Peter because it signals the use of metaphor in the letter.

Just as the Petrine conventions relating to the writer and the addressee have been expanded in a Christian direction, so also has the greeting, χαίρειν. Again, much of the pioneering work in this area has involved the Pauline letters. White says, "Paul departs from the customary form of the inside address, 'A- to B- χαίρειν,' by substituting for χαίρειν a separate and fuller salutation, 'Grace to you and peace.'"[17] Ernst Lohmeyer has demonstrated that this practice corresponds to the oriental practice of separating address and greeting.[18] 1 Peter follows this convention and corresponds even more fully to the oriental custom as noted by White:

> All the pseudo-Pauline letters imitate Paul's opening greetings. Four (1,2 Pet., Jude, 2 Jn.) of the remaining epistles separate the greetings from the address and express the greeting as a prayer, in the Pauline manner, though the statement of the prayer as a wish in the form, εἰρήνη πληθυνθείη (1,2 Pet., Jude) indicates greater dependence upon the Greek OT.[19]

White notes that this greeting is paralleled in the letters of Nebuchadnezzer and Darius in the LXX of Daniel 3:98 and 4:34 as well as in the letters of *1 Clement*, Polycarp to the *Philippians*, and the *Martyrdom of Polycarp*. I would add that this greeting, εἰρήνη πληθυνθείη, is found in the letters of Gamaliel, which provide a more exact parallel than those mentioned by White.[20]

---

[17]White, "Epistolary Literature," 1740.

[18]Ernst Lohmeyer, "Probleme paulinischer Theologie I: Die brieflichen Grussüberschriften," *Zeitschrift für die neutestamentliche Wissenschaft* 26 (1927): 158-173.

[19]White, "Epistolary Literature," 1752.

[20]David E. Aune, *The New Testament in Its Literary Environment*, Library of Early Christianity (Philadelphia: The Westminster Press, 1987), 185, cites the parallels to this salutation. He says, "The presence of an optative verb in the salutation in 1-2 Peter, Jude, *1 Clement*, Polycarp's *Philippians*, and the *Martyrdom of Polycarp* reflects another distinctive pattern: 'May grace and peace be multiplied to you' (1 Peter 1:2; cf. *1 Clement*, preface). . . . A similar salutation occurs in three letters attributed to a Rabbi Gamaliel (I or II?), written in Aramaic, possibly the preferred language of written communication in the eastern Diaspora: 'May your well-being [selam] increase!' (J. *Sanh.* 18d; B. *Sanh.* 18d; *Tos. Sanh.* 2.6). Two letters from the Aramaic section of Daniel have the same salutation (Dan. 3:31; 6:26). The Theodotianic Greek text of Daniel 4:1 and 6:26 ['may peace be multiplied to you'] is verbally identical with 1 Peter 1:2 [though the Christian term 'grace'

Not only does 1 Peter 1:1-2 correspond in form to an epistolary prescript, but it also corresponds in function. Koskenniemi states the function of the prescript, "Originally, the prescript had a very practical purpose: It should give information about the sender and the addressee."[21] He proceeds to argue that as the prescript develops, it functions in the letter as a greeting functions in a personal encounter.[22] Since a letter is "half a dialogue," the prescript functions as the greeting to this "dialogue." The first two verses of 1 Peter perform this function. Information about the sender and addressees is given, and a phrase of greeting is "pronounced" by the sender.

This discussion of the material in 1 Peter 1:1-2 indicates composition according to the convention of an epistolary prescript. The formulas have been Christianized, but they nevertheless correspond both in form and function to the prescripts of other ancient letters. Thus, we may conclude that 1 Peter 1:1-2 is the epistolary prescript for this document.[23]

The Thanksgiving-Healthgiving
Clause

According to Exler, a healthgiving clause follows the prescript:

> In the first part we take up the "initial" phrases which occur at the beginning of the letter proper, and follow immediately upon the opening formula. They are subdivided into three sections: the ἐρρῶσθαι wish, the ὑγιαίνειν wish without and with the proscynesis, and the ἀσπάσασθαι wish.[24]

In contrast to Exler, White separates this clause from the body of the letter saying:

> Since they, like the formulas which introduce and conclude the letter, serve the same broad purpose of enhancing the correspondents' relationship, it is more

---

is missing]. Further, the three letters of Gamaliel were encyclicals directed to three regional groups of Diaspora Jews, the brothers of Upper and Lower Galilee, of the Upper and Lower South, and of Babylonia. James, 1-2 Peter, and Jude have some of the characteristics of these and other Jewish encyclical letters."

[21]Koskenniemi, 156.

[22]Ibid., 156-158.

[23]This position is in agreement with Schutter, *Hermeneutic*, 24.

[24]Exler, 101.

accurate to regard them as opening and closing conventions than as phrases in the body.[25]

The health wish thus forms the second part of an ancient letter. It occurs after the prescript and before the body of the letter.

White notes that this healthgiving clause was often replaced by a thanksgiving clause. He says, "Both the thanksgiving and the notice of arrival may occur in addition to, and may function as a surrogate form of, the more common assurance of health."[26] It is the thanksgiving, not the healthgiving clause, which predominates in the New Testament letters.

When we examine 1 Peter, there is no section of either healthgiving or thanksgiving but rather a blessing section.[27] This section comprises verses 3-12 as Goppelt notes in the following, "The entire passage, 1:3-12, grammatically forms a single sentence, which is formed in modest style through a series of relative clauses."[28] While the substitution of a blessing section for the thanksgiving section is unusual, it is by no means without precedent. White states, "1 Pet., like the Pauline tradition, employs an opening prayer of benediction which closes with an eschatological reference (1:1-9)."[29] This same substitution is made in 2 Corinthians 1:3 and Ephesians 1:3. White is probably correct when he asserts that this substitution reflects the liturgical setting of the letters.[30] The *Hodayot Psalms* from Qumran, as well as the *Odes of Solomon*, reflect this usage of εὐλογητός.[31]

At this point, a methodological decision must be made. One must decide whether liturgical materials influence epistolary formulas or

---

[25]John L. White, *Light from Ancient Letters* (Philadelphia: Fortress Press, 1986), 198.

[26]Ibid., "Epistolary Literature," 1735.

[27]Nils A. Dahl, "Adresse und Proömium des Epheserbriefs," *Theologische Zeitschrift* 7 (1951): 241-264, especially 250, calls this type of blessing section a *"Briefeingangs-Eulogie"* and cites 1 Peter 1:3f. as an example. He says on pages 251-252, "The function of the *Briefeingangs-Eulogie* is the same as the thanksgiving section. It is not a hymn placed at the beginning of the letter, but rather an epistolary introduction particularized by the epistolary situation."

[28]Goppelt, *Petrusbrief*, 91.

[29]White, "Epistolary Literature," 1753. Schutter, *Hermeneutic*, 24, agrees with White's position.

[30]White, "Epistolary Literature," 1739, says, "The liturgical setting of the letters is well illustrated by the opening prayers of thanksgiving or benediction."

[31]This term is a translation of the Hebrew term, בָּרוּךְ.

completely preempt the formulas. One must also determine whether liturgical materials perform epistolary functions or continue to perform their own functions. Those scholars who advocate a liturgical analysis of 1 Peter conclude that the liturgical materials maintain their own form, perform their own functions, and preempt the epistolary formulas.   I would argue, however, that although the epistolary formulas may be influenced somewhat by the liturgical materials, they nevertheless maintain their epistolary form and function. Although 1 Peter was used in a liturgical setting and was read in public worship services, it was read, heard, and used as a letter.

John White advocates a similar assessment of the Pauline letters:

> With the possible exception of Philemon, Paul's letters are much longer than the common familial letter. This characteristic is of a piece with a difference in style; Paul's letters being considerably more literary. These factors relate, in turn, to the unusual nature of the epistolary setting and the corresponding difference in function that the letter must serve. Apart from Philemon, and it is not entirely an exception, all of Paul's letters are addressed to Christian congregations with an eye to their corporate setting in worship. It is in his capacity as apostle, and customarily as founding Father, that Paul addresses Christian communities. It is this unusual epistolary dynamic that accounts for the peculiar combination of "private" sentiment and "official" authority, as well as the generally passionate/religious mood of Paul's letters.[32]

White does not think that liturgical materials are preempting the epistolary situation. Paul's letters are not sermons or liturgies in epistolary dress; rather they are letters that draw upon sermonic and liturgical materials.

White's perspective on Paul's letters is correct not only for them, but also for 1 Peter. Those who advocate that 1 Peter is a sermon or liturgy in letter form have not correctly understood the epistolary setting of 1 Peter. Therefore, I contend that the blessing section, corresponding to the thanksgiving and healthgiving clauses of other letters, is epistolary in both form and function. Although the blessing section utilizes liturgical elements, the epistolary situation determines its form.

In his important study of God and Christ hymns in early Christendom, Reinhard Deichgräber recognized the hymnic nature of this passage but argued that the entire passage is not hymnic in form since there is a shift from the "we-style" to the "you-style." He observes, "At the

---

[32]White, "Epistolary Literature," 1739.

end of verse 4, however, the 'we-style' shifts to the 'you-style' and the eulogy per se should not be extended past verse 5."[33]   He criticizes Windisch saying:

> Windisch correctly entitles the passage 1:3-12, "Eulogy of God for the salvation extended to Christians." The designation of the entire passage as a hymn is however unfortunate since only verses 3-4 and perhaps 5 comprise the essential eulogy.[34]

Deichgräber goes on to criticize Preisker, who identifies the entire passage as a "Gebetspsalm," saying that this is a remarkable prayer-psalm in which the listeners are addressed more than God.[35]   Clearly Deichgräber limits the "hymn" in this passage to verses 3-5 because of the "you-style" that pervades verses 5-12. Reflecting the epistolary situation, this "you-style" indicates that liturgical elements cannot completely account for the form of this passage.[36]   The epistolary situation drawing on liturgical elements determined the form. Thus, although this letter convention has undergone the same Christianizing process as the prescript, it assumes the form dictated by its epistolary context.

This blessing section not only exhibits epistolary form, but it also maintains the epistolary function that its position in the letter dictates. The blessing section follows immediately upon the prescript, precedes the body of the letter, and functions as a surrogate healthgiving clause. It is imperative for a correct compositional analysis of 1 Peter that the blessing

---

[33]Reinhard Deichgräber, *Gotteshymnus und Christushymnus in der frühen Christenheit: Untersuchungen zu Form, Sprache und Stil der frühchristlichen Hymnen* (Göttingen: Vandenhoeck & Ruprecht, 1967), 77.

[34]Ibid., note 1.

[35]Ibid., says, "In the exposition of H. Preisker (third edition of Windisch's Commentary) 1:3-12 forms a prayer-psalm with which the baptismal service is introduced. A remarkable prayer-psalm in which the listeners are addressed more than God."

[36]Paul Schubert, *The Form and Function of the Pauline Thanksgiving*, Beihefte zur Zeitschrift für die neutestamentliche Wissenschaft 20 (Berlin: Alfred Töpelmann, 1939), 37, says, ". . . the Pauline thanksgivings are not "addressed" to God, as we would expect in liturgical sentence structure. In a liturgical thanksgiving of the εὐχαριστῶ pattern we might expect, e.g., εὐχαριστῶ σοι, ὦ θεέ κτλ., or some other liturgical structural pattern . . . In other words, the thanksgiving structure is characterized by a basic bipolarity, a double focus around which all thoughts center: The addressant and the addressee." Schubert's analysis is true not only for Paul but also for Peter. His analysis indicates that the εὐλογητος section has not been lifted out of a liturgical setting wholesale but has been epistolized with the major focus being not on God but on the addressant and addressee.

section be understood in its epistolary context. It does not form part of the body of the letter but is a distinct segment of the letter with its own unique function.[37]

What is the function of the healthgiving, thanksgiving, or blessing clause?   Again, the most extensive work on these clauses has been performed within the Pauline corpus. Paul Schubert has established that the thanksgiving section of Paul's letters concluded the opening, suggested the purpose of the letter, and sometimes outlined its key topics.[38] Schubert's position can be illustrated by other letters from antiquity. In the letter of Epimacus to his Father, he says, "I thank my Lord Serapis that while I was in danger at sea, he saved me speedily."[39] This letter was written upon the safe arrival of Epimacus at Misene after sailing from Alexandria. This thanksgiving indicates the context within which this letter is to be read.[40] Further research has confirmed Schubert's position.[41]

Since it corresponds to the healthgiving clause, the blessing section of 1 Peter provides an important function in the letter.[42] It gives the context in which the letter is to be understood.[43] Given this necessary function,

---

[37]Both Dalton and Balch, who follows him, are incorrect in extending the blessing section through verse 25. They have not seriously considered either the epistolary form or function of this section. See Dalton, *Proclamation*, 79, and Balch, *Wives*, 124.

[38]Schubert, passim.

[39]Text and translation in Adolf Deissmann, *Light from the Ancient East*, trans. Lionel R. M. Strachan (Grand Rapids: Baker Book House, 1978), 179-180.

[40]Schubert, 180, says, "The function of the epistolary thanksgiving in the papyrus letters is to focus the epistolary situation, i.e., to introduce the vital theme of the letter."

[41]Stanley K. Stowers, *Letter Writing in Greco-Roman Antiquity*, Library of Early Christianity 5 (Philadelphia: The Westminster Press, 1986), 22, says, "Later study has confirmed and refined Schubert's results."

[42]Ludwig Joseph Hundhausen, *Die beiden Pontificalschreiben des Apostelfürsten Petrus*, vol. 1: *Das erste Pontificalschreiben des Apostelfürsten Petrus*, Festschrift für Pius IX (Mainz: Franz Kirchheim, 1873), 76, says, "On the basis of the truths and themes in the introduction, the Apostle exhorts the readers to place themselves in the correct spiritual conception and to direct their hope completely upon the future salvation."

[43]Relying on Dalton, Balch, *Wives*, 124, says, "Dalton (pp. 76-79) also makes the fundamental observation that, as in Romans and Hebrews, the opening address (1 Pet 1:1-2) is expanded to announce some of the chief themes to be treated in the first chapter. God the 'Father' is mentioned again only in the first chapter (1:17). The Spirit is mentioned only four times in the work (1:2, 11, 12; 4:14; but cp. 2:5, 3:18, 4:6), with three of these in the opening section. 'Jesus' occurs eight times in the whole letter (never after 4:11); half of these occurrences are in the first thirteen verses. Sanctification, obedience, and the sprinkling of blood, aspects of salvation mentioned in the opening address, all appear in the

this blessing section must be carefully interpreted in order to understand the context in which the body of 1 Peter should be read.

The syntax of 1 Peter 1:3-12 is difficult. It is one long, nominal sentence, taking ὁ θεὸς καὶ πατήρ [Father God] as its subject and the verbal adjective εὐλογητός [blessed be] as its predicate. The subject is more clearly defined by a dependent genitive phrase, "our Lord Jesus Christ" and by an attributive participle, ἀναγεννήσας [who has begotten (rebirthed) us]. The difficulty begins with the prepositional phrase εἰς ἐλπίδα ζῶσαν [for a living hope]. This phrase expresses the purpose of the verb ἀναγεννάω [I beget again] as in John 18:37, which reads, "ἐγὼ εἰς τοῦτο γεγέννημαι [I was begotten for this purpose.]"[44] The issue is whether this phrase is used alone or in connection with other phrases to express the object and purpose of the new birth.

Deichgräber connects εἰς ἐλπίδα [for hope] in verse 3 with εἰς κληρονομίαν [for an inheritance] in verse 4 and εἰς σωτηρίαν [for salvation] in verse 5. He thinks all of these parallel εἰς phrases express the purpose of ἀναγεννάω.[45] In support of his opinion, he cites the εἰς phrases in Ephesians 1:10 and 14. His example serves to disprove his position because the first εἰς phrase in verse 10 is not parallel to the two

---

second part of the chapter (1:13-25). There is an exhortation to holy living 'as children of obedience' (1:14; cp. 1:2, 22), which is followed and supported by a citation of Lev 19:2, 'You shall be holy, for I am holy' (1:16; cp. 1:2, 22). If they call God 'Father,' they will conduct themselves with fear during their time of exile (1:17; cp. 1:1 and 2:11), not according to the local traditions of their former 'Fathers,' but as persons ransomed by the 'blood' (1:19; cp. 1:2) of Christ. So the address is an announcement of the chief themes of the first chapter. . . ." While Dalton and Balch correctly point to the development in the blessing section of themes alluded to in the address, it is the blessing section that develops these themes and sets the context for the letter.

[44]Joseph Dey, Παλιγγενεσία. Ein Beitrag zur Klärung der religionsgeschichtlichen Deutung von Tit 3.5, Neutestamentliche Abhandlungen 17.5 (Münster: Verlag der Aschendorffschen Verlagsbuchhandlung, 1937), 151-153, also connects hope to the new birth. He says that 1 Peter emphasizes hope in his notion of the new birth more than Titus 3:5 does because Peter is dealing with Christians undergoing persecution.

[45]Deichgräber, 77, says, "It is important to observe . . . the threefold assertion of salvation's purpose through the εἰς phrases similar to Ephesians 1:10, 14." Gerhard Delling, "Der Bezug der christlichen Existenz auf das Heilshandeln Gottes nach dem ersten Petrusbrief," in Neues Testament und christliche Existenz, Festschrift für Herbert Braun, ed. Hans Dieter Betz and Luise Schottroff (Tübingen: J. C. B. Mohr, 1973), 97, takes a similar position.

εἰς phrases in verse 14. Furthermore, although the two εἰς phrases in verse 14 are parallel, they are juxtaposed without any intervening constructions, whereas the three εἰς phrases in 1 Peter are not juxtaposed since other prepositional phrases and grammatical constructions separate them. Deichgräber has not substantiated his position. There is a better explanation of these phrases.

Leonhard Goppelt agrees with Deichgräber that all three εἰς phrases are linked, but he does not think they are parallel. He distinguishes hope from the other two in the following manner:

> The new birth effects a transfer into a new life situation; namely, an inauguration of a living hope, an undeceptive genuine living hope. Ἐλπίς here is not an attitude but rather the thing anticipated, the secure safe future. "Inheritance" and "salvation" in verses 4 and 5 parallel hope and state its content. Born again are all to whom hope, namely, the inheritance, the salvation, and an assured safe future, is given.[46]

In his opinion, then, the second and third εἰς phrases state the content of the hope expressed in the first εἰς phrase. Ἐλπίς does not refer to an attitude but to the content of the thing hoped. He collapses the notion of hope into the notions of inheritance and salvation.[47]

Aside from this strange definition of hope, Goppelt's connection of all three of these phrases is improbable on grammatical grounds. Greek prepositions do not inflect; therefore, position and semantics determine syntax. Εἰς ἐλπίδα is near the verb ἀναγεννάω, which takes the preposition εἰς, implying the object or purpose of the new birth. The second phrase εἰς κληρονομίαν is near the noun ἐλπίς, which also takes the preposition εἰς, stating the object of the hope. Charles Bigg correctly perceives this relationship stating, "The pilgrim's hope is further defined by its object, the inheritance."[48] The third εἰς phrase is near the noun πίστις, which admits this construction as a statement of the object of faith. Therefore, these three εἰς phrases are neither parallel as Deichgräber

---

[46]Goppelt, *Petrusbrief*, 94.

[47]J. Ramsey Michaels, *1 Peter*, Word Biblical Commentary (Waco: Word Books, 1988), 19, adopts Goppelt's explanation completely.

[48]Charles Bigg, *The Epistles of St. Peter and St. Jude*, International Critical Commentary (Edinburgh: T.& T. Clark, 1901), 100.

suggests, nor are the latter two subsumed to the first as Goppelt surmised. They each relate in different ways syntacticly.

The following translation of 1 Peter 1:3-5 reflects the syntactic relationships of these various phrases:

> Blessed be the Father-God of our Lord Jesus Christ who according to His great mercy through the resurrection of Jesus Christ from the dead has begotten us into a living hope, a hope for an indestructible, incorruptible, and unfading inheritance that has been preserved in the heavens for you who by the power of God are guarded through faith in a salvation prepared to be revealed at the end time.

As in the prescript, metaphor plays an important role in the author's thought. Just as an earthly father begets a child who hopes to attain the inheritance from his Father, so also God, their heavenly Father, had begotten them and now they have expectation of receiving an inheritance. The author describes their hope as "living hope." Numerous commentators explain this concept in various ways, but according to the metaphor, it simply refers to a hope that is still capable of realization. A child may be born to a wealthy Father and have hope of attaining an inheritance, but if the father squanders his wealth, or if the child dies before the Father, the child's hope of an inheritance dies. Our author states two reasons why his readers' hope of an inheritance is still very much alive and capable of realization. First, their death cannot dash their hope because God has raised Jesus Christ from the dead ones. Our author assumes that his readers knew that just as Jesus had been raised, so also they would be raised. Second, their inheritance cannot be squandered because it is guarded or preserved [$\tau\epsilon\tau\eta\rho\eta\mu\acute{\epsilon}\nu\eta$] by God himself.[49] Indeed, it is God's guardianship that makes their inheritance incapable of embezzlement [$\check{\alpha}\phi\theta\alpha\rho\tau o\varsigma$], fraud [$\dot{\alpha}\mu\acute{\iota}\alpha\nu\tau o\varsigma$], or depreciation [$\dot{\alpha}\mu\acute{\alpha}\rho\alpha\nu\tau o\varsigma$]. Furthermore, God is guarding their inheritance in the heavens where it is safe from the vicissitudes of this world. For these two reasons, their hope is alive and capable of realization.

In this metaphor our author intercalates statements about the past, present, and future. His readers have been begotten in the past; on this

---

[49]The passive verb without a stated agent in Biblical Greek implies that God is the agent. See F. Blass and A. Debrunner, *A Greek Grammar of the New Testament and Other Early Christian Literature* (Chicago: The University of Chicago Press, 1961), 72.

basis, they hope in the present for a future inheritance. In verse 5 he further describes their present condition. They are guarded [φρουρέω] by God's power through faith in a future salvation. Paul uses this verb in Galatians 3:23-24 to refer to the Law's role as a παιδαγωγός [schoolmaster], who takes care of the child until he grows up and receives his inheritance. The point of Paul's metaphor in Galatians 3:23--4:7 is that the Law was the guardian until faith came, and now all those who believe in Jesus Christ are enjoying and using their inheritance–the possession of the spirit (Galatians 3:14; 4:6). In contrast to Paul, our author applies this metaphor of guardianship to the present state of his readers who are presently under a guardian who is none other than God Himself. Their faith in a future salvation is the intermediate agent through which God's power is made effective in guarding them. Our author implies that the maintenance of this faith is the only avenue through which God will continue to function as their guardian. If they cease believing, they would lose God's protection and perhaps never receive their inheritance. Although they have been begotten by God, their inheritance is still future and therefore tenuous. In the present they are under God's guardianship through the agency of their faith in a future salvation.

Many commentators conceive of the inheritance as synonymous with the salvation. However, our author does not equate these two terms. Salvation is merely one aspect of the total inheritance of Christians. It refers to their preservation and resurrection per se, whereas inheritance refers not only to the resurrection but also to their resurrected life and the glory associated with that life. He makes this two-fold distinction in 1:21 where he describes God as the One who raised Jesus from the dead ones and gave glory [δόξα] to Him. Their salvation is equated with Jesus' resurrection, but their inheritance is the glory [δόξα] God will give to them.[50] The relationship between these notions is not one of equality because inheritance includes not only salvation but much more. Our author does not speak in detail of other aspects of their inheritance. He rather focuses on salvation since the preservation of one's life makes possible the reception of the total inheritance. Indeed, our author speaks of the inheritance of his readers as the glorious things subsequent to the present

---

[50]In 5:10 he speaks of God calling them into His eternal glory [δόξα] but states that the blessings of their inheritance will only be realized after a short period of suffering.

sufferings of the Christians in 1:11. The only specific detail of that inheritance, however, is the reception of salvation in 1:9.

Our author does not conceive of salvation in Pauline notions of justification. For him, salvation rather refers to his readers' resurrection and the preservation of their lives.[51] In 1:5 he states that their salvation is not present but prepared to be revealed at the last time. In 1:9 he says that his readers will receive the end of their faith, and this end will be the preservation of their lives.[52] In 2:2 he speaks of desiring the "pure milk of the word" by which they may grow up into salvation.[53] The use of this milk metaphor in 1 Corinthians 3:2 and Hebrews 5:12-13 indicates that it refers to elementary Christian teaching. Its non-pejorative use here refers to Christian teaching both elementary and advanced.[54] In this passage, salvation is something to be attained in the future. In 3:20 he mentions the preservation of the lives of Noah and his family stating, that baptism correspondingly preserves his readers now. Some commentators use this verse to prove that our author conceived of salvation in present terms. However, when he explains in verse 21 how baptism saves now, he states that the cleansing does not save, but salvation is effected by the confession of a good conscience through the resurrection of Jesus Christ. Thus, the present preservation of the believers is only realized through their ultimate preservation in the resurrection. Baptism is conceived as an antitypal participation of the believer in the resurrection of Jesus.[55]

---

[51]Donald G. Miller, "Deliverance and Destiny," *Interpretation* 9 (1955): 421, says, "Although Peter insists that we have already been 'born anew' and are already growing unto salvation, he nevertheless keeps his doctrine of salvation oriented toward the end."

[52]Gerhard P. Dautzenberg, "Σωτηρία ψυχῶν (1 Petr 1:9)" *Biblische Zeitschrift* 8 (1964): 262-276, correctly concludes that this phrase means and should be translated "the rescuing of your lives." His arguments are drawn from Semitic influence on the Greek, but many of his assertions about this influence are incorrect.

[53]This is F. J. A. Hort's translation of this phrase. Although criticized by Michaels, *1 Peter*, 87, it is a more accurate translation than "pure spiritual milk," which Michaels prefers.

[54]Michaels, *1 Peter*, 88, says, "What then is the 'pure spiritual milk'? The uses of the metaphor in 1 Corinthians 3:2 and Hebrews 5:12-13, where 'milk' is elementary Christian teaching, could suggest that here too it refers to the instruction needed [both elementary and advanced] for the believer to 'grow up to salvation.'" Milk is a religious symbol found in many ancient cults and religions. Michaels has compiled many such parallels.

[55]For a discussion of the literature and difficulties of this passage, see Michaels, *1 Peter*, 194-222. On page 218, he comments on the phrase, "through the raising of Jesus

Although salvation is not used synonymously with inheritance, grace [χάρις] is. The author conceives of this inheritance as a grace [χάρις] or boon conferred by God upon his readers. In 1:13 he exhorts his readers to hope in the boon that will be brought to them at the ἀποκάλυψις of Jesus Christ.[56] In 5:12 he certifies that "this boon of God is genuine whereunto they should stand." This translation assumes definite resolutions to several grammatical difficulties in this verse, which reads in Greek, ταύτην εἶναι ἀληθῆ χάριν τοῦ θεοῦ εἰς ἣν στῆτε.

One problem involves the antecedent to ταύτην. Because of the absence of the article before ἀληθῆ χάριν, Usteri assumes the antecedent of both the demonstrative pronoun ταύτην and the relative pronoun ἣν to be persecution and translates, "This persecution is a real grace of God. Stand fast to meet it."[57] Bigg identifies the antecedent as ἐπιστολή stating, "'This' refers to the whole of the contents of the Epistle, whether doctrine or exhortation."[58] Both of these antecedents overlook the most probable grammatical antecedent, which is χάρις. Χάρις is nearer the two pronouns in question than the other suggested antecedents for these pronouns. Michaels argues against χάρις as the antecedent since the statement would be little more than a tautology: "the grace God holds in store for us is *true* grace from God."[59] His translation indicates that the statement is not a tautology because the adjective ἀληθῆ [true, genuine] occurs in the predicate but not in the subject. Ταύτην with its understood antecedent χάριν τοῦ θεοῦ [this grace of God] is the subject of the sentence. 'Αληθῆ functions as

---

Christ," saying, ". . . this phrase depends on σῴζει in v 21a: the water of baptism 'saves you through the raising of Jesus from the dead'—just as God brings about the new birth 'through the raising of Jesus Christ from the dead'—in 1:3. In both instances, God, who raised Jesus from the dead, is the implied subject (cf. 1:21), just as God was the implied subject in the deliverance of Noah from the disastrous flood [διεσώθησαν, v 20]. The resurrection of Jesus Christ is what makes an appeal or pledge to God 'out of a good conscience' efficacious, and guarantees eternal life to the one baptized. Unlike Paul, who characterizes baptism as a 'death' with Christ (Rom 6:3-4a) to be followed by a 'resurrection' identified as new life in the Spirit (Rom 6:4b-5; 8-11), Peter links baptism itself with Jesus' resurrection."

[56]Henry George Liddell, Robert Scott, and Henry Stuart Jones, *A Greek-English Lexicon* (Oxford: Clarendon Press, 1968), 1979, say, ". . . a favor done or returned, boon, χάριν φέρειν τινί confer a favour on one, do a thing to oblige him."

[57]Usteri, 227-229.

[58]Bigg, 196.

[59]Michaels, *1 Peter*, 308-309.

the predicate adjective and the phrase χάριν τοῦ θεοῦ is placed beside it for emphasis. Thus, the author testifies, "This grace from God is *genuine* grace from God."[60] Thus Michaels' criticism of a tautology is unfounded, and it is best to take χάρις as the antecedent of ταύτην. This sentence says something very important for the author of 1 Peter. 1 Peter 1:13 clearly states that this grace, referring to the inheritance, is future and still to be realized. The author wants to assure his readers who are enduring trials and persecutions that it is genuine.

Another problem with this verse involves the use of εἰς with a verb of rest where one would expect the preposition ἐν. Commentators are too hasty to dismiss this as one more example of the confusion of εἰς for ἐν in Koine Greek. Although there is confusion of these prepositions, the local use of these prepositions is consistent in the epistolary literature of the New Testament. Bauer states, "The Epistles and, still more surprisingly, Rev. exhibit a correct differentiation between εἰς and ἐν in the local sense except 1P 5:12."[61] Given the good quality of Greek in 1 Peter, it is even more surprising that he alone of all the New Testament writers did not differentiate between εἰς and ἐν. Grammarians refer to the construction involving a verb of rest and a preposition with the accusative as *Constructio Praegnans*. Smyth says that this construction "denotes motion previous to or following upon the action of the verb."[62] This construction allows our author to express exactly what he means. He is exhorting his readers in the present to stand or endure for a future boon or grace that will be bestowed upon them. Hermann von Soden articulates this understanding. He rejects the confusion of εἰς for ἐν. He thinks that here, as in 1:13, χάρις is regarded as future, and he translates this clause, ". . . this is the true grace of God whereunto stand fast."[63] This consistent use of

---

    [60]Goppelt, *Petrusbrief*, 350, note 26 says, "Ἀληθής in 1 Peter only here, of persons: 'truthful,' of things: 'true,' here: 'real,' 'genuine.'" Talbert, "Plan of 1 Peter," 144, correctly translates this verse. He says, "What is attested in 1 Peter 5:12 is stated in the following accusative with infinitive . . . 'this to be the true grace of God' . . . 'this is the true grace of God.'"

    [61]Blass, 110-111.

    [62]Herbert Wier Smyth, *Greek Grammar* (Cambridge: Harvard University Press, 1980), 368.

    [63]Hermann von Soden, *Hebräerbrief, Briefe des Petrus, Jakobus, Judas*, Hand-Commentar zum Neuen Testament 3.2 (Leipzig: J. C. B. Mohr, 1899), 166-167. On

χάρις in 1:13 and 5:12 forms an inclusio or ring structure that implies the compositional unity of this letter.

The relationship of inheritance to χάρις is analogous to the relationship of salvation to inheritance. Just as inheritance is inclusive of salvation plus much more, so also the term *grace* refers to the inheritance but also to other aspects of God's benevolence. In 2:19-20 present actions can accrue grace with God. The notion of grace in this passage approximates the notion of reward or blessing [64] In 3:7 our author refers to husbands and wives as "co-heirs of the grace of life." Here the meaning approximates the notion of gift.[65] In 4:10-11 he refers to those who have gifts of ministry as stewards of the manifold grace of God. In 5:5 he makes the same statement as Psalm 3:34 about God's giving grace to the humble. In 5:10 he speaks of the God of all grace. These conceptions of grace are, however, secondary to the primary use of grace as the synonym for the future inheritance of Christians.[66]

The metaphor of inheritance, as well as the interplay of past, present, and future, is continued in verses 6-9 of Chapter 1. Grammatical and syntactical problems continue to plague the interpretation of these verses of the blessing section. Since the blessing section in 1:3-12 is one long nominal sentence and since the independent clause occurs in verse 3, a long string of dependent clauses confronts the exegete in these verses. Sorting out these dependent clauses and following the flow of thought is a major task.

Verse 6 begins with a dependent clause, which reads ἐν ᾧ ἀγαλλιᾶσθε. The primary exegetical issue in this clause is the function of ἐν ᾧ. Is it used in an absolute sense meaning *since* or *while,* or does it have an antecedent? The resolution of this question affects the

---

page 167, he says, "The *grace* to which the author refers here is the *grace* of 1:13. Because it is being brought to them, he says, 'εἰς ἣν στῆτε.'"

[64]Walter Bauer, *A Greek-English Lexicon of the New Testament and Other Early Christian Literature*, trans. W. F. Arndt and F. W. Gingrich (Chicago: The University of Chicago Press, 1957), 885, says, "In these passages the meaning comes close to *reward* . . . also by metonymy *that which brings someone God's favor 1 Peter 2:19,20.*"

[65]Ibid., 886, translates this phrase, "fellow-heirs of the gracious gift that is life."

[66]In 1 Peter, grace is not viewed in Pauline terms as the antithesis of law as in Romans 6:14-16. Those who insist on reading 1 Peter through Pauline eyes overlook the use of the term *grace* to refer to the future inheritance of Christians.

understanding of the tense and mood of $d\gamma a\lambda\lambda\iota\tilde{a}\sigma\theta\epsilon$. Ancient commentators took the last three words of verse 5 $\dot{\epsilon}\nu$ $\kappa\alpha\iota\rho\tilde{\omega}$ $\dot{\epsilon}\sigma\chi\dot{a}\tau\omega$ as the antecedent to $\dot{\epsilon}\nu$ $\tilde{\omega}$, and they understood $d\gamma a\lambda\lambda\iota\tilde{a}\sigma\theta\epsilon$ as a future indicative verb. Didymus Alexandrinus translates this clause "in which you will rejoice [*exultabitis*]."[67] The Venerable Bede translates and comments as follows, "In which you will exult [*exultabitis*], etc. When he says, 'in which,' he refers to that time when a prepared salvation will be revealed and will be given to those who are worthy."[68] Theophylact has an interesting comment:

> Although you are grieved now, if it is necessary, that is if this is necessary, for not all the saints are afflicted. "In the last time, you shall rejoice [$d\gamma a\lambda\lambda\iota\dot{a}\sigma\epsilon\sigma\theta\epsilon$]," the $A\gamma a\lambda\lambda\iota\tilde{a}\sigma\theta\epsilon$ has been received for a future circumstance rather than a present circumstance as is declared below.[69]

He goes on to discuss the promises of the Lord in John 17:11 and 16:33 where affliction is promised in this world, but affliction will be turned into rejoicing in the future. Although these references could be multiplied, they are sufficient to demonstrate that the ancient tradition understood "at the last time" to be the antecedent of $\dot{\epsilon}\nu$ $\tilde{\omega}$ and then thought that the present $d\gamma a\lambda\lambda\iota\tilde{a}\sigma\theta\epsilon$ referred to the future.[70]

This ancient interpretation of the first clause of 1:6 held sway until challenged by Conrad Horneius, whose argument follows:

> In which circumstances you rejoice, now even for a while if it is allowed although you are grieved by sadness among the many temptations. . . . The ancient translator *has the future tense*, "in which you will rejoice". . . . But they translated it in that way primarily because they referred the phrase $\dot{\epsilon}\nu$ $\tilde{\omega}$, in which, taken independantly, to the final day and secondarily because this phrase seemed to have some appearance of incompatability; *you are rejoicing although*

---

[67]Didymus Alexandrinus, *Enarratio in Epistolas Catholicas*, in *Patrologia Graeca*, ed. J. P. Migne, vol. 39, 1756. This same translation is given by Eusebius Hieronymus, *Divina Bibliotheca*, in *Patrologia Latina*, ed. J. P. Migne, vol. 29, 877; Pseudo-Hilarius, 85; Martinus, 209:219.

[68]Beda Venerabilis, *Super Epistolas Catholicas Expositio*, in *Patrologia Latina*, ed. J. P. Migne, vol. 93, 43.

[69]Theophylact, *Expositio in Epistolam Primam S. Petri, in Patrologia Graeca*, ed. J. P. Migne, vol. 125, 1196.

[70]Walter Thiele, *Die Lateinischen Texte des 1. Petrusbriefes*, Vetus Latina: Aus der Geschichte der Lateinischen Bibel 5 (Freiburg: Verlag Herder, 1965), 84, says, "The future in 1:6 is easily understood after 1:5."

you are grieved by sadness . . . . But it is more correct that the present tense be retained, which has been received in the manuscripts, for the ἐν ᾧ refers to everything that precedes, certainly to the fact that God has regenerated them to a living hope or an eternal inheritance and that they are kept by faith for it just as Beza renders, *"Qua in re exultatis."* Neither is it incompatable for the same men to feel simultaneously both happy and sad since this happens for different reasons: for believers are grieved on account of present afflictions; but they rejoice on account of an eternal hope of retribution. . . . And Paul says in 2 Corinthians 6:10, "Being afflicted but always rejoicing. . . ."[71]

In contrast to the ancient interpretation, he understands ἐν ᾧ to refer to everything the author has said before verse 6.[72] Consequently, he concludes that ἀγαλλιᾶσθε is present in meaning as well as in form.

About 150 years after Horneius, S. F. N. Morus presented yet another resolution to the problems in this clause. He explains below:

"Therefore rejoice, even if for a little while in the present you are grieved by various miseries." Ἐν ᾧ is translated wherever it occurs in this Epistle by the Hebrew word, בַּאֲשֶׁר, which itself means, "therefore." Ἀγαλλιᾶσθε will be taken to be an imperative for the style is engaged in exhortation. Therefore the translation: "Therefore rejoice."[73]

He takes ἐν ᾧ in an absolute sense to mean "therefore." For him, the relative pronoun ᾧ has no antecedent. Furthermore, he takes ἀγαλλιᾶσθε as an imperative.[74]

We must choose among these three alternative understandings of the clause ἐν ᾧ ἀγαλλιᾶσθε. Although Morus' explanation is widely accepted by modern commentators, it should be rejected. The Greek language does allow for an absolute use of ἐν ᾧ to mean "while" or "therefore."[75]

---

[71]Conrad Horneius, *In Epistolam Catholicam Sancti Apostoli Petri Priorem Expositio Litteralis* (Braunschweig: Andrea Duncker, 1654), 16.

[72]His interpretation assumes that the relative pronoun ᾧ is neuter.

[73]S. F. N. Morus, *Praelectiones in Jacobi et Petri Epistolas*, ed. C. A. Donat (Leipzig: Sumtibus Sommeri, 1794), 105.

[74]This interpretation was first made by Augustine according to Τρεμπελα, 250.

[75]Smyth, 377, but especially 565, where he says, "The antecedent of a neuter relative is often omitted, leaving the relative with the force of a conjunction." He cites ἐν ᾧ as an example. The author of 1 Peter knows of this absolute use of ἐν ᾧ and uses it in 2:12; 3:16; and 4:4. In each of these occurrences of the phrase, there is no antecedent to the relative pronoun. In 3:19 ἐν ᾧ occurs with the antecedent πνεύματι and Bo Reicke, *The Disobedient Spirits and Christian Baptism*, Acta Seminarii Neotestamentici Upsaliensis 13 (Kopenhagen: Einar Munksgaard, 1946), 103, notes, "The ordinary opinion is that ἐν

However, this usage is very unlikely when there is a clear antecedent for the relative such as ἐν καιρῷ ἐσχάτῳ at the end of verse 5. Furthermore, his assertion that the verb ἀγαλλιᾶσθε is an imperative rather than an indicative fails to consider the form and function of the blessing section. In this section, the author is stating the context in which the letter should be read. The indicative, not the imperative, is the appropriate mood for his declarations. The imperatives do not begin until the body of the letter in 1:13. For these reasons, his explanation should be rejected.

Similarly Horneius' interpretation is not convincing. The antecedent of ᾧ is not everything that precedes, but rather ἐν καιρῷ ἐσχάτῳ at the end of verse 5. A similar construction occurs in 3:18-19. In these verses the antecedent of ᾧ is clearly the dative πνεύματι, which precedes and not everything that has been said before. Just as his understanding of the antecedent of ᾧ overlooks the most obvious solution, so also his understanding of ἀγαλλιᾶσθε as present tense ignores several important features of the text. The circumstantial participle λυπηθέντες depends upon the finite verb ἀγαλλιᾶσθε. It is aorist tense and signifies action prior to the action of the finite verb ἀγαλλιᾶσθε. If ἀγαλλιᾶσθε is present as Horneius argues, then the readers' grieving has taken place in the past. However, this aorist participle is modified by the adverb ἄρτι meaning "now" or "just now." The text clearly states that the grieving is taking place now.[76] The only way this present grieving can take place

_____

ᾧ in 1 Pet. III 19 refers to the πνεύματι in verse 18 immediately preceding it." In footnote 4 he states that this opinion is accepted with almost 100% unity and certainty. He spends the next 10 pages unsuccessfully attempting to refute this opinion. More reasonable is W. J. Dalton's position. In his article, "Interpretation and Tradition: An Example from 1 Peter," *Gregorianum* 49 (1968): 25, he says, "In this case ἐν ᾧ could be translated, 'in this process,' 'in these circumstances.' This interpretation cannot be ruled out. In the text of 1 Peter we have a number of cases where this usage appears (2:12; 3:16; 4:4, and possibly 1:6). Yet it should be noted that in the three clear cases above it is impossible to relate the relative pronoun with any preceding noun, while in 3:19 it is not merely possible but almost inevitable. When we have the relative actually following the noun, and when the phrase ἐν πνεύματι is one of the commonest in the New Testament . . . , then the reader is almost forced to take ἐν ᾧ as the equivalent of καὶ ἐν πνεύματι or καὶ ἐν τούτῳ τῷ πνεύματι. Hence this view is not merely supported by the majority of scholars, but can be seen to be more intrinsically probable."

[76]Herbert Braun, *Das Leiden Christi. Eine Bibelarbeit über den I. Petrusbrief*, Theologische Existenz heute 69 (München: Kaiser Verlag, 1940), 37-38, correctly recognizes the pervasive theme of suffering in 1 Peter. He says, "The suffering of

before the rejoicing of the finite verb is if that rejoicing is understood as future. Therefore, although *ἀγαλλιᾶσθε* is present in form, it must be future in meaning. Another feature of the text that he ignores is the antithesis set up by *ἀγαλλιᾶσθε* and *ἄρτι*. This antithesis functions only if *ἀγαλλιᾶσθε* has a future reference. These textual features undermine Horneius' interpretation.

Avoiding the criticisms leveled against Morus and Horneius, the ancient interpretation of this clause *ἐν ᾧ ἀγαλλιᾶσθε* best explains both the textual and contextual features of this passage. It appropriately recognizes the juxtaposition of this clause with *ἐν καιρῷ ἐσχάτῳ* at the end of verse 5 and maintains the anthesis between present and future, which is a basic feature of this blessing section. It also accounts best for the selection of the aorist tense of the participle *λυπηθέντε*s. The major problem with the ancient interpretation as Morus and Horneius recognized is that the verb *ἀγαλλιᾶσθε* is present in form, not future. Can the present tense form be used to refer to future action? Both Smyth and Bauer answer in the affirmative. Smyth says, "The present is used instead of the future in statements of what is immediate, likely, certain, or threatening."[77] Bauer reiterates, "In confident assertions regarding the future, a vivid, realistic present may be used for the future. . . . Ordinarily a temporal indication of the future is included."[78] This clause in 1 Peter 1:6 is a textbook example of the statements made by Smyth and Bauer complete with a temporal indication of the future, *ἐν ᾧ* meaning "at which last time." The closest parallel is found in Romans 2:16 where Paul says, "*ἐν ᾗ ἡμέρα κρίνει ὁ θεὸς τὰ κρυπτὰ τῶν ἀνθρώπων* [on which day God will judge the secrets of men]." The notion is clearly future, but the present tense *κρίνει* stands in the Nestle Edition, not the future tense *κρινεῖ*.[79] Clearly the present

---

Christians is a theme that not only resounds in 1 Peter but also is treated broadly and extensively. The selection of terms makes this clear to us. In this brief letter, there is mention eight times of the suffering of Christians, twice of their practice in patience, once of their affliction, and once of their many temptations." On pages 38-39, he goes on to argue that this suffering is directed to the individual Christian and not to the community as a whole.

[77]Smyth, 421.

[78]Blass, 168.

[79]It is unfortunate that this is a liquid verb, which differentiates between the two tenses in question only by the accent. The editors of the text have decided that the present

tense can be used for the future in certain circumstances. Thus, the present form of the verb ἀγαλλιᾶσθε does not disprove the ancient interpretation, and this interpretation remains superior to all others. This clause at the beginning of verse 6 should be translated "at which end time you will rejoice."

The remainder of verse 6 consists of a circumstantial participial clause that contrasts the present grief from manifold temptations with the future rejoicing mentioned at the beginning of the verse. The entire verse translates as follows: ". . . at which end time you will rejoice although for a little while now by necessity you are grieved by manifold trials."[80]

The nominal sentence of the blessing section continues after verse 6 with a ἵνα clause in verse 7, which gives the reason or purpose for the readers' being grieved by manifold temptations. The verse reads, ἵνα τὸ δοκίμιον ὑμῶν τῆς πίστεως πολυτιμότερον χρυσίου τοῦ ἀπολλυμένου, διὰ πυρὸς δὲ δοκιμαζομένου, εὑρεθῇ εἰς ἔπαινον καὶ δόξαν καὶ τιμὴν ἐν ἀποκαλύψει Ἰησοῦ Χριστοῦ. The passive verb εὑρεθῇ functions as a copulative verb taking τὸ δοκίμιον as its subject and πολυτιμότερον as its predicate adjective.

In spite of the grammar, most commentators understand *faith* [πίστις], not *test* [δοκίμιον] nor the variant *testing* [δόκιμον], as the subject of this clause. Bigg argues in his commentary:

> "Test" is here a quite impossible rendering; the means by which faith is tested is suffering, and suffering cannot be called more precious than gold, nor is it "found" in the Last Day. "The testing of your faith," for the same reasons, is hardly, if at all, less impossible. We are driven, therefore, to take δοκίμιον here as adjectival, and to translate "the tested residue of your faith," that faith which remains when all impure alloy has been burnt away.[81]

---

tense is the form that Paul used. Another example of a present used as a future occurs in Jesus' prophecy of his death and resurrection in Mark 9:31 where the present verb παραδίδοται is used. This use of the present is even more striking because when this prophecy is repeated in 10:33, the future tense παραδοθήσεται is used.

[80]Michaels, *1 Peter*, 28, says, "Εἰ δέον, whether ἐστίν is expressed or understood, should be read as a first-class conditional clause, referring in this instance to what is actually the case: i.e., not "if need be" but "since it is necessary" or "by necessity."

[81]Bigg, 104.

Deissmann contributed to this shift of the subject of this verb by pointing out that δοκίμιον and δόκιμον are interchangeably used in the Papyri of the first three centuries. They occur as adjectives almost equivalent in meaning to γνήσιον meaning genuine.[82] Blass-Debrunner took his contribution a step further and argued that a neuter singular adjective with a dependent genitive could be used as a substitution for the abstract noun.[83] Thus δοκίμιον is understood to mean "genuineness." Goppelt comments, "The affliction in the sense of a test should throw into bold relief τὸ δοκίμιον τῆς πίστεως, 'the genuineness of faith.'"[84] Michaels states more confidently, "But τὸ δοκίμιον in 1 Peter is virtually equivalent to the faith itself ['the genuineness of your faith' or 'your faith insofar as it is genuine. . . .']"[85]

Perhaps these commentators have been too hasty in their attempt to rearrange the grammar of this verse. Although they cannot conceive how the test or testing of faith can be considered to be more precious than gold, the author of 1 Peter can and does. He considers the difficulties and sufferings that are testing his readers' faith to be part of the sufferings of the Messiah. He speaks of the prophets' foretelling the sufferings of the Messiah (1:11) and of his readers' being partners in the sufferings of the Messiah (4:13). They share these sufferings with the broader Messianic community (5:9). As Messianic sufferings, their sufferings are according to the will of God (4:19) and, if handled properly, will lead to the Gentiles' glorifying God in the Day of Visitation (2:12). Indeed, their sufferings can only be correctly understood and will only be correctly understood at the Second Coming of Jesus Christ. The test or testing of their faith will be found to be more precious than gold, not in the present, but in the future (1:7).[86]

---

[82]Gustav Adolf Deissmann, *Bible Studies*, trans. Alexander Grieve (Edinburgh: T. & T. Clark, 1903), 259 ff.

[83]Blass, 138.

[84]Goppelt, *Petrusbrief*, 100.

[85]Michaels, *1 Peter*, 30.

[86]David Wenham, "Being 'Found' on the Last Day: New Light on 2 Peter 3.10 and 2 Corinthians 5.3," *New Testament Studies* 33 (1987): 477-479. He says on page 477, "Jesus' eschatological parables refer on several occasions to the returning lord 'finding' his servants (Mt 24:46/Lk 12:43, Mk 13:36, Lk 12:37, 38)." E. E. Ellis, "II Corinthians V.1-10 in Pauline Eschatology," *New Testament Studies* 6 (1959): 211-

1 Peter shares this positive notion of suffering with other New Testament writings. In 2 Corinthians 1:5-7 Paul states that the sufferings of the Messiah are abounding in him and his readers. In verse 7 he even speaks of his readers as partners of the sufferings. In 4:17 he refers to these sufferings as momentary and light and leading to an eternal weight of glory. Again in Philippians 3:10, he testifies that he has given up all things in order that he might know Christ, the power of his resurrection, and the partnership of his sufferings. Colossians 1:24 refers to the sufferings lacking in the tribulations of the Messiah. The writer conceives of his sufferings as filling up or completing the Messianic sufferings. The New Testament frequently mentions the Messianic tribulations (Matthew 24:21,29; Mark 13:19,24) and these become a major focus of the book of Revelation, where they are graphically detailed.

The New Testament in turn shares this notion with the broader world of Judaism. In her study of πύρωσις, Emilie T. Sander attempts to understand this term in its First Century Jewish and Christian contexts. She states, "The image of testing in 1P 1:6-7 . . . simply explicates in terms of purification by smelting the description in 1P 4:12, where this situation is described as πύρωσις."[87] She continues discussing the metaphor:

> As will be seen in the thesis proper, πύρωσις is an eschatological term denoting the end-time trial or ordeal which is expected before the final consummation and revelation of glory. This πύρωσις is for the testing of the church and the vindication of the elect. Thus the situation of πύρωσις has a πειρασμός character.[88]

Although she cites many parallels from Hellenistic Judaism, she devotes her attention to the Qumran literature, noting:

> The word translated πύρωσις in the LXX is the M.T. מצרף. . . . At Qumran מצרף occurs more frequently and it is a sectarian *terminus technicus* for the time or situation which the community sees as its own: the end-time with the ultimate

---

224, notes that εὑρίσκεσθαι is almost a technical term for being 'discovered' at the parousia, and he cites 1 Peter 1:7 as an example.

[87]Sander, 50.

[88]Ibid., xxvi.

ordeal before the consummation of the age to come. In this time the elect [= the members of the sect] will be vindicated and saved and the wicked annihilated.[89]

In this ancient context, the test or trial of faith had immense value for the eschatological community. Sufferings and tribulations were not viewed negatively but positively. In the end, those who suffer on account of their faith will be vindicated, and their suffering will be seen to have great value.

1 Peter 1:7 should be understood in this eschatological context. The test or testing of the readers' faith will be found to be more precious than gold at the revelation of Jesus Christ. Indeed, at that time, their testing will result in praise, glory, and honor.

Following verse 7, the nominal sentence continues with two relative clauses in verse 8 that have Ἰησοῦ Χριστοῦ as their antecedent. These relative clauses continue alternating among past, present, and future that is characteristic of this passage. Verse 8 begins ὃν οὐκ ἰδόντες ἀγαπᾶτε [whom although not having seen you love]. The aorist participle with the negative οὐ instead of the expected μή indicates that they have in fact not seen him in the past, but they still love him in the present.[90] The verse continues εἰς ὃν ἄρτι μὴ ὁρῶντες πιστεύοντες δὲ ἀγαλλιᾶσθε χαρᾷ ἀνεκλαλήτῳ καὶ δεδοξασμένῃ [in whom although not now seeing but now believing you will rejoice with a joy unspeakable and glorious].[91] The antithesis of the present between not seeing but believing is framed within a larger antithesis between present and future. This larger antithesis is staged by the adverb ἄρτι [now] and the present tense of ἀγαλλιᾶσθε used with a future meaning as in verse 6.[92] Ἀγαλλιᾶσθε is future in meaning because in verse 9 the present participle that indicates simultaneous action with the main verb refers to a future event; namely, receiving the end of their faith

---

[89]Ibid., 103.

[90]The contrast of οὐκ ἰδόντες with μὴ ὁρῶντες indicates that the author can factually state that they have not seen him, but he cannot be so sure about the present. Jesus Christ could be revealed at any moment, and then they would see him in the present.

[91]The compact construction of disjunction and antithesis found in the phrase μὴ ὁρῶντες πιστεύοντες δέ is a stylistic feature of this author. He uses the same construction in 1:12; 2:10; 3:9; and 4:16. This last occurrence completely refutes Beare's assertion that there are no carefully balanced antitheses after 4:11. He makes this assertion as a defense of his partition theory. See Beare, *1 Peter*, 7.

[92]The discussion of the tense of ἀγαλλιᾶσθε here parallels the discussion in verse 6. For the literature on this problem, see the discussion on verse 6 above.

to be the salvation of their lives.[93] It is at that time the readers will rejoice. This future time of rejoicing in Christ is contrasted with the present where faith in Christ, a faith not based on sight, describes the readers.

Verses 10-12 conclude the nominal sentence that began in verse 3. These verses propose that neither the prophets in the past nor the angels in the present really know what is foreordained until it is revealed to the elect people of the end time. Sander points out that this motif is similar to Qumran (1 Qp Hab vii. 4f.).[94]

Having carefully interpreted this blessing section, we can now understand the context in which 1 Peter should be read. The writer expresses a thoroughly eschatological concern. In the past, his readers have been begotten by God. This new status gives them hope for a future inheritance, an inheritance that includes but is not limited to the salvation of their lives. At the revelation of Jesus Christ, the readers will be vindicated and will rejoice to such a degree that it cannot even be expressed. Between past and future lies the present. This present is where the readers currently find themselves. In contrast to past and future, the present is characterized by manifold temptations and trials that bring grief and sorrow to the readers. These trials are viewed as part of the Messianic tribulations that must occur before the final consummation of all things. Although these tribulations will be brief, the readers still need to be guarded by the power of God. God's guarding power is made available to them through their faith in a future salvation. In these present circumstances, the author describes the readers as those who have hope for a future inheritance, faith in a future salvation, and love for a soon-returning Lord. It is in this eschatological context that this author addresses his readers. In the remainder of this letter, he will focus on the present but always with reference to these past events and to these future expectations.

---

[93]The adjective $\dot{\alpha}\nu\epsilon\kappa\lambda\alpha\lambda\dot{\eta}\tau\omega$ and the adjectival participle $\delta\epsilon\delta o\xi\alpha\sigma\mu\acute{e}\nu\eta$ also indicate a future joy. Gerhard Kittel, "$\delta o\kappa\acute{e}\omega$," in *Theological Dictionary of the New Testament*, ed. idem, vol. 2: Δ–H (Grand Rapids: Wm. B. Eerdmans Publishing Co., 1964), 250, says, "This means that when the NT refers to the eschatological participation of believers in $\delta\acute{o}\xi a$ this is simply part of the general statement of salvation history concerning the connexion and parallelism between the resurrection of Christ and the resurrection and new aeon of believers. Participation in $\delta\acute{o}\xi a$, whether here in hope or one day in consummation, is participation in Christ."

[94]Sander, xvii.

The Letter-Body

Although research on the letter-body progressed more slowly than studies on the other epistolary formulas, significant advances have been made in recent times. Doty remarked a decade and a half ago:

> Within the bodies of the Pauline letters, consistent use of formulae seems less likely—or at any rate no such consistent use has been identified. My own feeling is that in the body sections of the longer letters, at least, Paul had more inclination to strike out on his own and to be least bound by epistolary structures.[95]

He blamed this lack of progress on the diversity of the letter-body, which until then defied formal analysis.[96] This lacuna in epistolary studies was filled by the efforts of John White. In his Vanderbilt dissertation, White studied the form and function of the body of the Greek letter.[97] In his analysis he identified three parts of the letter-body: the body-opening, the body-closing, and the body-middle.[98] He explained both the formulaic features and the functions of each of these parts of the letter-body. As in other epistolary studies, he focused primarily on the Pauline letters. His analysis is not only useful to these letters, but it also explicates the letter-body of 1 Peter as I will demonstrate.

White's analysis proceeds by giving attention to the transitional devices in the letter-body. He distinguishes between general transitional devices that may be employed in all parts of the body, and specific transitional devices that gravitate to either the opening, closing, or middle of the body.[99] He also differentiates between transitional devices, indicating major or minor transitions. He identifies the transitions from opening to middle to closing as major transitions. In addition, major shifts

---

[95]William G. Doty, *Letters in Primitive Christianity*, Guides to Biblical Scholarship: New Testament Series (Philadelphia: Fortress Press, 1973), 35.

[96]Ibid., *Letters*, 34.

[97]John L. White, "The Form and Function of the Body of the Greek Letter: A Study of the Letter-Body in the Non-literary Papyri and in Paul the Apostle," *Society of Biblical Literature Dissertation Series* 2 (Missoula, Montana: University of Montana, 1972), passim.

[98]Ibid., "Form," 9, says, "The body, like the letter in general, may be divided into three discrete sections: body-opening; body-closing; and section between opening and closing ['body-middle']."

[99]Ibid., "Form," 11ff.

in subject matter within the body-middle are major transitions. Minor transitions allow for shifts to subtopics within the broader subject areas.

The Body-Opening

The specific transitional devices that he cites for the body-opening do not apply to 1 Peter 1:13.[100] He does not however claim to be exhaustive in his treatment. In a later publication, he broadens his understanding of requests to include the imperative of instruction or exhortation. He says in this publication:

> The fourth and final category is concerned with how requests or instructions introduce the body directly. The first of the two conventions listed under this fourth heading is the formulaic phrase, καλῶς ποιήσεις. . . . The second convention, non-formulaic instructions, employs the imperative of the verb at the beginning of the body to instruct or order the recipient to do something. Like the polite form of the request, an explanation usually accompanies the command.[101]

This imperatival convention of request signals the body-opening of 1 Peter. The imperative ἐλπίσατε states the request that the author is making upon the recipients. The independent clause signaled by this imperative only extends through verse 13. Thus, we may conclude that 1:13 forms the body-opening of 1 Peter.

Another epistolary formula that indicates 1:13 forms the body-opening is the inferential conjunction διό. White lists it only as a general transitional device stating, "For example, the conjunctions, οὖν, διό, and ὅθεν, are standard means of indicating the transition from the background to a statement of request."[102] Nevertheless, Sanders cites its use with the participle νήφοντες as a surrogate disclosure formula similar to the ones that introduce the Pauline body-opening. He comments on 1:13, "Vs. 13,

---

    [100]Ibid., "Form," 34-41, cites requests, joy expressions, and statements signaling previous communication as the formulas that connect the body-opening with the healthgiving or thanksgiving clause.
    [101]Ibid., *Light*, 211. He gives several references to letters utilizing this convention in footnote 102. Also see his article, "Introductory Formulae in the Body of the Pauline Letter," *Journal of Biblical Literature* 90 (1971): 91-97, where he lists six introductory formulae: (1) The Disclosure Formula, (2) The Request Formula, (3) Joy Expressions, (4) Expressions of Astonishment, (5) Statement of Compliance, and (6) Formulaic Use of the Verb of Hearing or Learning.
    [102]Ibid., *Light*, 211.

opening with διό, is slightly reminiscent of the Pauline introductory formula, as it is addressed to the νήφοντες."[103] Along with the imperative of request, this epistolary formula identifies 1:13 as the body-opening of 1 Peter and functions as the transition from the blessing section to the body of the letter.

White makes several observations about the body-opening that are important for understanding the function of 1:13 in 1 Peter. He notes in the following:

> The body-opening is the point at which the principal occasion for the letter is usually indicated. In addition, the body-opening must proceed, like spoken conversation, from a basis common to both parties. This is provided either by allusion to subject matter shared by both parties or by the addresser's disclosure of new information. The body-opening lays the foundation, in either case, from which the superstructure may grow.[104]

Functioning as the body-opening, the request made by the imperative ἐλπίσατε indicates the principal occasion of this letter. The author requests his readers to hope in the grace that will be brought to them at the revelation of Jesus Christ. This request alludes to subject matter already disclosed in the blessing section. There he has explained that they have been begotten for a living hope for a future inheritance. He now exhorts them to exercise that hope and intensifies his request by the addition of the adverb τελείως.[105] They should hope completely until their inheritance is realized. The remainder of the letter-body is simply a more complete explanation of what this request entails.[106] There are certain attitudes and actions that those who hope for an inheritance must exhibit, and these are explicitly stated. These conclusions, based upon an analysis of epistolary

---

[103]Jack T. Sanders, "The Transition from Opening Epistolary Thanksgiving to Body in the Letters of the Pauline Corpus," *Journal of Biblical Literature* 81 (1962): 357.

[104]White, "Form," 33.

[105]Henry A. Steen, "Les clichés épistolaires dans les lettres sur papyrus greques," *Classica et Mediaevalia* 1 (1938): 119-176, discusses the intensification of an imperative by the addition of an adverbial expression. He does not, however, cite this passage nor refer to this specific adverb.

[106]White, *Light*, 211, says, "There are a few examples in the present collection, however, of this polite request phrase introducing the body immediately, without the benefit of prior 'background' information. In these cases, an explanation for the request is usually provided subsequently within the letter. . . . Like the polite form of the request, an explanation usually accompanies the command."

formulas, indicate that Georg Seyler and Bernard Weiss were essentially correct in advocating hope as the central theme of this letter.[107]

The Body-Closing

Although the specific transitional devices mentioned in White's dissertation did not apply to the body-opening of 1 Peter, they do apply to the body-closing. Although he cites four specific transitional formulas occurring in the body-closing, only two, the disclosure formula and statements of responsibility, are relevant to 1 Peter.[108]

In regard to the disclosure formula he states, "The body-closing commonly employs only one disclosure formula . . . and it is the motivation for writing formula."[109] In the examples he gives, this formula takes either the aorist or perfect form of γράφω. The function of this disclosure formula is to call attention to the preceding information. White comments, regarding this function:

> The disclosure formula is roughly comparable to that of the fuller form in the body-opening; instead of calling attention to some information following, however, the addresser calls attention to the preceding information, or some aspect of the preceding information in the body.[110]

1 Peter 5:12 contains this disclosure formula. The aorist form of γράφω occurs with two participles, παρακαλῶν καὶ ἐπιμαρτυρῶν, which state the author's motivation for writing. This entire statement calls attention to the

---

[107]Seyler, 66, says, "Thus these verses (3-12) contain a description of the Christian hope according to its sources (v. 3), its object (v. 4), the condition of its fulfillment (v. 5), its efficacy (v. 6-7), and the testimony for its certainty (inward testimony (v. 8-9); outward testimony (v. 10-12). In general the position of these verses to the entire letter is noteworthy. Everything following is an exposition of this beginning and the tendencies developed through it. Nothing can be taken away without making the following admonitions groundless and invalid. Therefore, he proceeds to verse 13 not simply with διό, but he designates this life toward which he exhorts as a τελείως ἐλπίζειν." Bernhard Weiss, *Der petrinische Lehrbegriff* (Berlin: Wilhelm Schultze, 1885), 48-49, says, "This overview leads to the conclusion that hope not only forms the background of the entire letter and its dominant controlling viewpoint, but also in the few passages where it is specificly mentioned, its meaning for the instructional view of the Apostle is so central that it is not incorrect to call the author the Apostle of Hope."

[108]White, "Form," 45-49.

[109]Ibid., 45.

[110]Ibid.

previous information that he has shared with the recipients. Thus, this verse in both form and function represents a disclosure formula found in body-closings.[111]

In addition to this disclosure formula, there is a statement of responsibility that is characteristic of body-closings. White describes this statement as follows:

> The summons to responsibility, it was noted, may appear elsewhere in the body but neither as often nor with such variety of expression as in the body-closing. These phrases, like the motivation for writing formula, call attention to previous material in the body. Their function is to urge the addressee to be responsive regarding an earlier request.[112]

The last three words of 5:12 εἰς ἣν στῆτε correspond in function to this statement of responsibility. These words reiterate the basic request made in 1:13. The writer is exhorting his readers to stand fast for the grace they are to receive at the revelation of Jesus Christ. These last three words of verse 12 represent a statement of responsibility that is characteristic of body-closings.

This disclosure formula and statement of responsibility indicate that 1 Peter 5:12 forms the body-closing of the letter. White describes the overall function of the body-closing as follows:

> The transition from the middle of the body to the body-closing, like the transition from letter-opening to body-opening, is a major transition. But the phraseology and the idea [function] of the body-closing are even more stereotyped, perhaps, than the body-opening. The body-closing functions in two discrete, though not necessarily separate, ways: (1) as a means of finalizing the principal motivation for writing [by accentuating or reiterating what was stated earlier in the body]; (2) as a means of forming a bridge to further communication.[113]

---

[111]Robert W. Funk, "The Apostolic *Parousia*: Form and Significance," in *Christian History and Intrepretation*, Studies Presented to John Knox, ed. W. R. Farmer, C. F. D. Moule, and R. R. Niebuhr (Cambridge: University Press, 1967), 249-268, establishes the discussion of the apostolic presence as a formal structure of the Pauline letter. The presence is realized by either a letter, an emissary, or a personal visit. In 1 Peter there is no mention of a personal visit, but the letter itself and the mention of Sylvanus serve to make the presence of the apostle available to the readers.

[112]Ibid., 46.

[113]Ibid., 42.

The body-closing in 1 Peter 5:12 performs the first function. It finalizes the author's principal motivation for writing. It reiterates his testimony that he has disclosed the genuine grace of God to them and restates his basic request that they stand fast for that grace that will be brought to them at the revelation of Jesus Christ.

The Body-Middle

In 1 Peter there is clear evidence of the epistolary conventions of body-opening (1:13) and body-closing (5:12). Between these two conventions stands the body-middle (1:14--5:11). White notes the difficulties with this part of the letter-body saying:

> The body-opening and the body-closing are analyzed prior to the body-middle because the last is more difficult to delineate. The prior description of the body-opening and the body-closing is one way of circumscribing the boundaries of the section between, i.e., the body-middle. The body-middle, and its points of transition, is more difficult to define for the following reasons. (1) The common Greek letter of the Ptolemaic and Roman periods is generally short, and frequently the body-opening dovetails immediately into the body-closing or the letter-closing, i.e., there is no occasion for positing a body-middle. (2) The body of the letter is so fluid, on other occasions, that it is difficult to separate the body-middle from either the body-opening or the body-closing. (3) The transitions to the body-opening and the body-closing tend uniformly to be major, whereas transitions in the body-middle may mark either a major movement to a new subject or a more minor development of the present subject. The unequal weight of body-middle transitions prohibits a simple definition of the body-middle.[114]

---

[114]Ibid., 10, note 6. These difficulties in ascertaining the body-middle have led Schutter, *Hermeneutic*, 25-27, to incorrectly include parts of the body-middle in the body-opening and closing. He identifies the body-opening as 1:13--2:10 and the body-closing as 4:12-19 with 5:1-11 forming a concluding paraenesis. On page 26 he correctly observes, "Also, two formula do not appear until 5:12, the letter's close, whereas they would usually appear in the body-closing of Paul's letters, the motivation-for-writing formula and the responsibility formula." Schutter offers no rationale for his decision not to designate 1 Peter 5:12 as the body-closing. By his own admission, this verse has all the characteristics of a body-closing. Futhermore, he has incorrectly extended the body-opening to 2:10 because he has not recognized the use of metaphor as a major compositional device in the body-middle of 1 Peter. See Chapter 4 for a correct analysis of the body-middle based upon the compositional device of metaphor.

The use of letter formulas to analyze the composition of 1 Peter thus reaches its limit when the body-middle is encountered. Although the letter formulas indicate the extent of the body-middle (1:14--5:11), other analytical methods must be utilized if the composition of the body-middle is to be explained.[115] Since other methods are involved, an analysis of the composition of the body-middle will not be taken up here. The next two chapters of this dissertation will undertake this task.

The Greeting Section

Koskenniemi describes the greeting section of letters as follows:

> A frequently occurring and popular element in the phraseology of the letter is the greeting in its various forms. . . . The greeting could be of various types: either the writer greets the addressee, or he could greet another through the addressee, or unfamiliar persons introduce into the letter their greeting to the addressees. . . . In most cases these greetings are only stereotyped expressions. In the construction of the letter, their usual position is in a distinct passage at the close of the letter.[116]

He cites the verb ἀσπάζομαι as a typical formula for the greeting section.[117] In his analogy of the epistolary situation as a speech encounter, the greeting section of a letter corresponds to the leave-taking just as the prescript corresponds to the meeting.[118]

1 Peter 5:13-14a answers to Koskenniemi's description of the greeting.[119] The verb ἀσπάζομαι occurs twice, once in the indicative and once in the imperative. The indicative serves to allow unfamiliar people to greet the addressees. Although these people are unfamiliar, they are not

---

[115]Johannes Sykutris, "Epistolographie," in *Paulys Real-Encyclopädie der classischen Altertumswissenschaft*, vol. 4: *Supplement*, ed. Wilhelm Kroll (Stuttgart: J. B. Metzler, 1924), 199, says, "There is not much to say about the content of letters because it was very diverse depending upon the situation to which it pertained." Hendrikus Boers, "The Form Critical Study of Paul's Letters. I Thessalonians as a Case Study," *New Testament Studies* 22 (1974): 145, says, "The *formal* characteristics of the central section of the Pauline letter remain unclear."

[116]Koskenniemi, 148.

[117]Ibid., 149.

[118]Ibid., 155, says, "The prescript corresponds to the greeting; the concluding formulas to the leave-taking. These parts frame the epistolary encounter and the epistolary situation puts its stamp on them to a greater degree than in the rest of the letter."

[119]Schutter, *Hermeneutic*, 27, also identifies this material as formulaic greetings.

strangers. The philophronetic epistolary topos is established by the prepositional prefix σύν.[120] "The co-elect [συνεκλεκτή] in Babylon greet you."[121] With whom is the church or congregation in Babylon co-elect? In 1:1 the addressees are called the ἐκλεκτοί. The author is affirming common ground between the church in Babylon and the addressees.[122] The author's son Mark also sends greetings. It is not clear whether Mark is known or unknown to the addressees or whether this is a pseudepigraphic device.[123] In either case these statements are appropriate to the greeting section of a letter.

The imperative of ἀσπάζομαι summons the readers to greet one another with a kiss [φίλημα] of love. This statement is an interesting variation of a common greeting formula described by Koskenniemi. He states, "A definite group among the circle of those whom one could greet are the friends. They were frequently directed, "Greet all those who love you." This formula introduced in the first century CE continued throughout the centuries."[124] This variation in 1 Peter is a Christianization of the formula. It occurs frequently at the end of the Pauline letters as a "holy kiss" (Rom. 16:16; 1 Cor. 16:20; 2 Cor. 13:12; 1 Thess 5:26).[125] Goppelt asserts that this "kiss of love" underscores not only thoughts of

---

[120]Koskenniemi, 35-38, discusses this important epistolary topos.

[121]Hunzinger, 67-77, argues that "Babylon" as a nickname for "Rome" was only used after the destruction of the temple in 70 CE. He bases his argument on the fact that all the Jewish texts that speak of Rome as Babylon are post 70 CE. Since this nickname is used in 1 Peter 5:13, he concludes that it must be post 70 CE. It would be decisive for Petrine authorship if Hunzinger could prove his thesis. Unfortunately, his method only allows him to prove that "Babylon" as a nickname for Rome was used after 70 in connection with the destruction of the temple. By his method, however, he cannot prove that this nickname was not used earlier because of other connections of Rome with Babylon. The revolt of Judas the Galilean in 6 CE is sufficient to demonstrate that the Jewish state felt their subjugation to Rome.

[122]Michaels, *1 Peter*, 310, says, "Peter is affirming common ground between the συνεκλεκτή and his readers, not himself."

[123]Lewis R. Donelson, *Pseudepigraphy and Ethical Argument in the Pastoral Epistles* (Tübingen: J. C. B. Mohr (Paul Siebeck), 1986), 24, states in regard to the Pastoral Epistles, "Of course, it is my contention that the author did just that; in the interest of deception he fabricated all the personal notes, all the fine moments of deep piety, and all the careless but effective commonplaces in the letters."

[124]Koskenniemi, 150.

[125]White, "Epistolary Literature," 1740, arguing that Paul created the apostolic letter tradition, says, "The greetings depart from the common pattern, too, in the admonition, 'Greet one another with a holy kiss.'"

friendship but also brotherly relations.[126]   Again, philophronetic concerns are expressed in this greeting.

1 Peter 5:13-14a functions in its epistolary situation as leave-taking. It establishes a friendly if not familial relationship between the author, as well as those who are with him, and the recipients.   It alludes to the salutation in the prescript [συνεκλεκτή] as well as to other concerns expressed in the letter [i.e. ἀγάπη].   It is a fitting epistolary conclusion to this document.

The Farewell

Many letters in antiquity ended with some form of farewell.   Exler describes farewell formulas as follows:

> In the epistolary papyri of the Ptolemaic and the Roman periods, we find that certain letters regularly have for their closing formula the expression: ἔρρωσο [ἔρρωσθε], or its modifications; others end with the verb: εὐτύχει, later changed into διευτύχει; while a third group of letters has no special formula at all, but simply omits the final salutation.[127]

This word of farewell functions as the "good-by" of the speech encounter.

None of these terms occur in 1 Peter, but a Christianized variant does occur in the phrase εἰρήνη ὑμῖν πᾶσιν τοῖς ἐν Χριστῷ.[128]   White discusses a similar variant in the Pauline letters saying:

> Familial letters often close with greetings, health wish/or a word of farewell. Paul also closes his letters with greetings . . . , but he replaces the word of farewell with an expression of blessing, "The grace of our Lord Jesus Christ be with your spirit." Needless to say, this benediction reflects a Christian adaptation of the existing practice.[129]

He argues Paul created this apostolic epistolary practice that influenced other Christian letters including 1 Peter.   The phrase is slightly different in 1 Peter since "peace" is used instead of "grace."   The preference for this term may reflect the conflict situation that pervades the letter and probably

---

[126]Goppelt, *Petrusbrief*, 354, says, "The greeting is not just an expression of friendly thoughts but of brotherly relations."

[127]Exler, 69.

[128]Schutter, *Hermeneutic*, 27, identifies this material as the final benediction.

[129]White, "Epistolary Literature," 1740.

alludes to the same wish for peace in the prescript in 1:2.[130] This phrase
functions as an appropriate epistolary farewell to this letter.

Conclusion

This analysis of the letter formulas in 1 Peter establishes that the document
is composed as a letter. Although it draws on liturgical, paraenetic, and
other materials, all of these materials have been modified to fit the
epistolary situation. This analysis reveals the essential error of Harnack
who said, "If one ignores 1:1-2 and 5:12-14, then the document portrays
itself not as a genuine letter but as a sermonic treatise. . . ."[131] Even if the
prescript and the concluding formulas are removed, evidences of epistolary
form remain. The blessing section, while using liturgical materials, has
altered them to fit the epistolary situation. This alteration is evident in the
shift from "God" to "us" to "you." Not only has this blessing section been
formally altered to answer to the epistolary situation, but its function is
essentially epistolary. It provides the eschatological context within which
the letter is to be understood. In addition to the blessing section, the letter-
body gives evidence of epistolary form and function. The body-opening in
1:13 corresponds in both form and function to the body-opening of other
letters as also does the body-closing in 5:12. It begins with the conjunction
διό and contains an imperative that makes the essential request or command
of the letter. Correspondingly, the body-closing contains a disclosure
formula using the verb γράφω that states the reason for writing. It also
reiterates the basic request of the letter. For these reasons, I conclude that
this document has been composed as a letter.

Having been composed as a letter, the first level of the compositional
analysis of this document should identify the letter formulas as we have
done. This epistolary analysis provides the following outline of 1 Peter:

    1 The Prescript 1:1-2
    2 The Blessing Section 1:3-12

---

[130]Goppelt, *Petrusbrief*, 355, says, "The concluding blessing wish speaks not of
grace to the readers as in Paul, but--emphasizing the horizontal dimension--of peace, which
is the salvation relationship to God and to men (compare 1:2) and which overcomes the
conflict situation in hope, faith, and love (1:3-7)."

[131]Harnack, 451.

This analysis of epistolary formulas is effective for analyzing all parts of this document except the body-middle.[132] Since analysis of letter formulas is only able to delineate the extent of the body-middle, new analytical methods must be applied to this segment of the document in order to explain its internal composition. In the next chapter, form critical methods will be applied, and in the succeeding chapter, a literary and style analysis will be performed on the body-middle.

---

[132]Franz Schnider and Werner Stenger, *Studien zum neutestamentlichen Briefformular*, New Testament Tools and Studies 11 (Leiden: E. J. Brill, 1987) do not even treat the body-middle in their study of epistolary formulas. Although my analysis of the letter formulas is more specific in regard to function, it generally agrees with their analysis with two important exceptions. First, on pages 84-86 they identify 5:1-11 as the concluding paraenesis for the entire letter. I argue that 5:1-5 and 5:6-11 are two subsections of a larger section that includes 4:12--5:11. Thus 5:1-11 does not function as the concluding paraenesis of the entire epistle. See my analysis below on pages 240-264. Second, they identify a transition between the thanksgiving-healthgiving-blessing clause and the letter-body that leads into the major theme announced in the body-opening. They call this transition a "*briefliche Selbstempfehlung* [epistolary self-commendation]." They assume that the epistolary prescript and thanksgiving are equivalent to a rhetorical exordium. The exordium of a speech consists of two parts: the address and the *captatio benevolentiae*. They equate the address with the epistolary prescript and the *captatio benevolentiae* with the thanksgiving clause. Since the thanksgiving clause focuses on the addressees, the epistolary situation requires an additional passage that returns to the author and establishes his ethos. Schnider and Stenger, 64, designate 1 Peter 1:10-12 as a "*briefliche Selbstempfehlung*." Unfortunately for their argument, 1 Peter 1:10-12 does not return to a discussion of the author's ethos. Furthermore, the link they make between this passage and the author on pages 64-65 is so general that it does not serve the ethos function. Hence, the term "*briefliche Selbstempfehlung*" is inappropriate.

CHAPTER 3

FORM-CRITICAL ANALYSIS

Klaus Berger has remarked that letters form a major genre pressing other genres into its service. He says in his comprehensive treatment of genres:

> Letters are handed down from the antique world in nearly every possible prose genre [in Horace even in poetic form]. "Letter" is thus only a framing genre for an abundance of other genres pressed into its service. Nevertheless, the letter is not only an external transmission form of written communication, but it is also essentially a major genre with constitutive characteristics.[1]

He goes on to say that the great number of different literary forms and genres corresponds to the great variety of situations and groups.[2] His remarks emphasize the need to determine the genre of 1 Peter that occurs within its epistolary frame.[3] This task leads directly into the discipline of Form Criticism.

Form-critical methods are not new to the study of 1 Peter. Harnack, Perdelwitz, Bornemann, Preisker, and Cross have all applied these methods and concluded that 1 Peter is a baptismal sermon or baptismal liturgy.[4] Windisch, Bultmann, and Boismard have also used these methods to argue

---

[1]Klaus Berger, "Hellenistische Gattungen im Neuen Testament," *Aufstieg und Niedergang der Römischen Welt* 25.2 (1984): 1338.

[2]Berger, 1339.

[3]Dibelius, 1, says, "For the question of literary genre is not resolved by the recogniition of epistolary form. . . . Only the document itself can provide the necessary information as to its genre."

[4]Harnack, *Chronologie*, 451-465; Perdelwitz, passim; Bornemann, passim; Preisker, "Petrusbrief," 152-162; Cross, passim.

that several hymnic fragments have been incorporated into 1 Peter.[5] These form-critical studies of 1 Peter, however, have suffered from a lack of methodological control.[6] Those who argue for sermonic form have yet to produce another first-century baptismal sermon with which to compare 1 Peter.[7] The liturgies to which 1 Peter have been compared are all much later and thus of questionable usefulness for explicating the composition of 1 Peter. Responding primarily to Cross, T. G. C. Thornton criticizes this approach, saying:

> The aim of this paper is to show that there is nothing distinctively Paschal about 1 Peter and that it can only be called a liturgy if the word *liturgy* is used in such a vague way as to make it almost meaningless. . . . It is relevant to note that neither

---

[5]Windisch, passim; Bultmann, "Liedfragmente," 1-14; Boismard, "La Typologie," 339-352; idem, *Quatres Hymnes*; and idem, "Une Liturgie baptismale dans la Prima Petri," *Revue Biblique* 63 (1956): 182-208 and 64 (1957): 161-183.

[6]Aune, 197, says, "Modern scholars have labeled many early Christian compositions as 'sermons' or 'homilies.' Yet these interchangeable terms are not really labels for a literary genre, since New Testament scholarship has not yet been able to define what a sermon is." Even Schutter, *Hermeneutic*, 93, who identifies 1:14--2:9 as a homiletic midrash fails to explicate the compositional structure of a midrash. In appendix two on page 183, he says, "It is desirable for comparative purposes to analyze briefly several examples of homiletic midrash." In order for Schutter to substantiate his claim that 1 Peter is composed according to a homiletic midrash, it is not only desirable but absolutely necessary that a thorough analysis of homiletic midrashim be undertaken. On page 92-93, he admits that the essential features of 1 Peter that convince him that it belongs to the genre of homiletic midrash is the central place given the Old Testament in its organization. This feature is too vague to establish a genre.

[7]*Didache* 1-6 is an early Christian baptismal catechesis according to Chapter 7 verse 1. However, the value of this document for Petrine studies has not been recognized. A comparison of these two documents needs to be made. On the surface it appears that the documents are very different. The prominent emphasis on suffering is lacking in *Didache* 1--6. The prescriptions in *Didache* are much more diverse than in 1 Peter. Whereas 1 Peter uses aorist imperatives in the second person plural, *Didache* uses present imperatives, aorist imperatives, and future indicatives in both the singular and plural. Furthermore, the composition of *Didache* 1--6 is structured by the two ways scheme, which is almost entirely lacking in 1 Peter. Thus, 1 Peter is very different from the one baptismal catechesis that survives from the first or early second century. After examining the baptismal hypothesis, David Hill, "On Suffering and Baptism in 1 Peter," *Novum Testamentum* 18 (1976): 189, concludes, "To say that the letter, or most of it, is a baptismal homily or liturgy is to treat as explicit, direct, and prominent what is only implicit, presupposed, and subsidery. 1 Peter is paraenetical, not catechetical: and its main theme is the conduct of Christians in a situation of testing and adversity."

Melito's homily nor the oration attributed by some to Hippolytus is anything like
1 Peter either in form or in content.[8]

Thornton's criticism reveals a lack of methodological control among those
who argue on form-critical grounds that 1 Peter is a liturgy. Even those
who argue for hymnic fragments in 1 Peter suffer from this same lack of
control. David Henry Schmidt points out, "In summary, there is no clear
evidence that the writer of 1 Peter has used hymns. His good literary
style, particularly as it resembles artistic Periods in 1:3-12, has given rise
to speculations which do not have sufficient characteristics of hymns to be
called such."[9] These form-critical studies of 1 Peter have been less than
persuasive because of a lack of methodological control.

Indeed, form criticism itself has been criticized in contemporary
scholarship. In a recent article, Martin Buss argues that because of a lack
of methodological control, among other reasons, the term *form criticism*
should be dropped. He writes the following:

The term *form criticism* is difficult to use for several reasons. One lies in the fact
that it has developed three rather distinct meanings: a systematic or historical
study of genres [*Gattungsforschung* or *Gattungsgeschichte*]; a reconstruction of
oral tradition with attention to genres [for some, *Formgeschichte*]; and the
examination of a text as it stands [*Formkritik*, according to Wolfgang Richter].
Furthermore, the term is not one used in ordinary conversation or in writing
outside of biblical studies, so that it does not have the benefit of protection and
clarification by frequent usage. Most seriously, endeavors designated by that
phrase have often been based on the view that there is a firm conjunction between
linguistic form, content, and recurring circumstances in oral expression; closely
connected with this outlook is a belief that genres recognized in a given society
are clearly separated from one another.[10]

Clearly a definition of terms and a precise statement of method is in order
before one engages in a form-critical study of 1 Peter.

---

[8]Thornton, 14-15.

[9]David Henry Schmidt, "The Peter Writings: Their Redactors and Their
Relationships," (Ph.D. diss., Northwestern University, 1972), 56.

[10]Martin J. Buss, "Principles for Morphological Criticism: With Special Reference
to Letter Form," in *Orientation by Disorientation: Studies in Literary Criticism and Biblical
Literary Criticism*, Festschrift for William A. Beardslee, ed. Richard A. Spencer
(Pittsburgh: The Pickwick Press, 1980), 71.

In the present study, the term *form criticism* or its adjective *form-critical* will be used as a simple and neutral designation for the study of literary forms.[11] The philosophical and historical assumptions that have traditionally adhered in this term are not implied here. In this study, this term will be used to refer to a method of analysis that will attempt to explain the composition of the letter-body of 1 Peter by relating it to other compositions in the ancient world. This method will attempt to determine the genre of 1 Peter.

In his monumental study of Hellenistic genres, Klaus Berger makes several observations regarding the identification of genres. He identifies two basic methods for determining genre: the literary form and the social context. He says in his study, "The elements constitutive of a genre are determined in two possible ways. They are either immanent in the text, or they are sociological, that is oriented toward the communication situation and to their reception."[12] He explains in more detail what he means by these two methods:

> For the genre of Apology, a series of frequently occuring individual elements can be established like assertion of innocence, biographical material, and *captatio benevolentiae*. However, a particular literary form in the sense of a composition schema cannot be established. According to Veltman, the genre can only be defined on the basis of the arrangement of the individual parts and on the basis of the composition of the entire document. Even here various possibilities must be reckoned with. However, there are other genres that are identified through their compositional structure like the Gospels.[13]

According to Berger, literary form or social context are the two methods for determining genre. Both of these methods will now be used to determine the genre of 1 Peter.

---

[11]Ibid., 73, Buss says, "If the usage of the term 'form criticism' can be purged of certain philosophical and historical assumptions, that phrase may continue to be a convenient one in biblical studies. If not, one may need to adopt another, such as 'morphology.' Perhaps the expression 'the study of forms' can serve as a simple and neutral designation."

[12]Berger, "Gattungen," 1038.

[13]Ibid., 1038-1039.

*The Literary Form of 1 Peter
and of Paraenesis*

Perhaps the most prominent feature of the form of the material in 1 Peter is the presence of so many imperatives. Beginning in 1:13 and extending to 5:12, imperatives are strategically placed throughout the letter. James Moulton has noted that there are 28 imperatives within this section of 1 Peter.[14] Indeed, it is the imperatives with their supporting participles that form the framework of the body of 1 Peter and move the thought forward. Thus, the imperatives with their supporting participles determine the form of most of the material in the letter.

Turning to ancient literature, we find this same use of the imperative in speeches and writings that the ancients referred to as paraenesis. Pseudo-Isocrates' *Address to Demonicus* uses imperatives to form the framework of the address and to carry the thought forward.[15] He begins, following a lengthy introduction:

> First of all, then, show devotion to the gods, not merely by doing sacrifice, but also by keeping your vows; for the former is but evidence of a material prosperity, whereas the latter is proof of a noble character. Do honor to the divine power at all times, but especially on occasions of public worship; for thus you will have the reputation both of sacrificing to the gods and of abiding by the laws. Conduct yourself toward your parents as you would have your children conduct themselves toward you. Train your body, not by the exercises which conduce to strength, but by those which conduce to health. In this you will succeed if you cease your exertions while you still have energy to exert yourself. Be not fond of violent mirth, nor harbor presumption of speech; for the one is folly, the other madness. Whatever is shameful to do you must not consider it honorable even to mention. Accustom yourself to be, not of a stern, but of a thoughtful, mien; for through the former you will be thought self-willed, through the latter, intelligent. Consider that no adornment so becomes you as modesty, justice, and self-control; for these are the virtues by which, as all men are agreed, the character of the young is held in restraint. Never hope to conceal any shameful thing which you have done; for even if you conceal it from others, your

---

[14]James H. Moulton, *A Grammar of New Testament Greek* (Edinburgh: T. & T. Clark, 1906), 174.

[15]Isocrates may appear not to be a good parallel since he predates 1 Peter by several centuries, but Berger, "Gattungen," 1076, notes, "Since Isocrates, prose paraeneses have been handed down. In addition to the oldest prose paraeneses, 'To Nikocles' and 'Nikocles,' there is also the speech 'To Demonicus,' which represent the average prototype for the later genre."

own heart will know. Fear the gods, honor your parents, respect your friends, obey the laws.[16]

Pseudo-Isocrates clearly identifies this type of address as a paraenesis:

> Therefore, I have not invented a hortatory exercise, but have written a moral treatise; and I am going to counsel you on the objects to which young men should aspire and from what actions they should abstain, and with what sort of men they should associate and how they should regulate their own lives.[17]

Pseudo-Isocrates' *Address to Demonicus* is very similar in form to 1 Peter and is clearly labeled a paraenesis.[18]

Isocrates' *Address to Nicocles* is another example of a discourse that uses imperatives to form the framework of the discourse and to carry the thought forward. A typical section follows:

> Reflect on the fortunes and accidents which befall both common men and kings, for if you are mindful of the past you will plan better for the future. Consider that where there are common men who are ready to lay down their lives that they may be praised after they are dead, it is shameful for kings not to have the courage to pursue a course of conduct from which they will gain renown during their lives. Prefer to leave behind you as a memorial images of your character rather than of your body. Put forth every effort to preserve your own and your state's security, but if you are compelled to risk your life, choose to die with honor rather than to live in shame. In all your actions remember that you are a king, and take care never to do anything which is beneath the dignity of your station.[19]

Although this discourse is the first of a number of discourses in antiquity that came to be called περὶ βασιλείας,[20] Isocrates places it in the category

---

[16]Pseudo-Isocrates, *To Demonicus* 4-5. George Norlin, trans., *Isocrates*, vol. 1, The Loeb Classical Library (Cambridge: Harvard University Press, 1980), 10-13.

[17]Ibid., 3. Translation by Norlin, 7.

[18]Pseudo-Isocrates' distinction between a paraenesis and a protrepticus has led to a longstanding scholarly debate. Can such a distinction be made? Very often these terms appear to be used synonymously. Paulus Hartlich, Theodore Burgess, and Stanley Stowers have all contributed to this debate.

[19]Isocrates, *To Nicocles* 22. Translation by Norlin, 61.

[20]In *To Nicocles* 16, Isocrates says, "And yet the mere attempt is well worth while--to seek a field that has been neglected by others and lay down principles [νομοθετεῖν] for monarchies." Theodore C. Burgess, "Epideictic Literature" *Studies in Classical Philology* 3 (1902): 136, describes this speech as follows: "A large class of Greek orations under the title περὶ βασιλείας has this as the avowed purpose–to picture the ideal prince, to lay down the principles upon which he must base his rule, to present a code

of paraenesis when he says at the end, "Now I, for my part, have offered you all the good counsels [παρῄνεκα] which I know."[21] This discourse is thus another example of a discourse similar to 1 Peter, which uses imperatives to form the framework of the discourse and to carry the thought forward.

Yet another discourse similar to 1 Peter in its use of the imperatives is Isocrates' *Nicocles*. This document is unlike 1 Peter in its lengthy defense of rhetoric and monarchy. Isocrates explains the treatment of these subjects in a paraenesis saying, "But the reason why I have spoken at some length both about myself and the other subjects which I have discussed is that I might leave you no excuse for not doing willingly and zealously whatever I counsel and command."[22] After this explanation, he proceeds to the typical paraenesis:

> I declare it to be the duty of each one of you to perform whatever tasks you are assigned with diligence and justice; for if you fall short in either of these qualities, your conduct must needs suffer by that defect. Do not belittle nor despise a single one of your appointed tasks, thinking that nothing depends upon it; but, knowing that the whole depends for its success or failure on each of the parts, be careful in everything. Display no less concern in my interests than in your own, and do not think that the honors enjoyed by those who successfully administer my affairs are a small reward. Keep your hands off the possessions of others in order that you may be more secure in the possession of your own estates. You should be such in your dealings with others as you expect me to be in my dealings with you.[23]

The fact that Isocrates regards this discourse as a paraenesis is evident when he discusses types of discourses:

> I, myself, welcome all forms of discourse which are capable of benefiting us even in a small degree; however, I regard those as the best and most worthy of a king, and most appropriate to me, which give directions on good morals and good government; and especially those which teach how men in power should deal with the people, and how the rank and file should be disposed to their rulers. For

---

of morals and offer precepts appropriate for his guidance under any circumstances likely to arise under his administration of the sovereignty."

[21] Isocrates, *To Nicocles* 25. Translation by Norlin, 69.
[22] Ibid., 36. Translation by Norlin, 105.
[23] Ibid., 36-37. Translation by Norlin, 105.

I observe that it is through such discourses that states attain the highest prosperity
and greatness.[24]

This discourse is yet another example of the paraenetical use of imperatives
to structure the speech and to carry the thought forward.

Other discourses in antiquity that demonstrate this paraenetic form
are the speeches of generals to their troops.[25] In Plato's *Ion*, there is an
illuminating statement made by Socrates. He is dialoguing with the
rhapsodist Ion, who claims to know more about Homer than anyone else.
After Socrates has convinced Ion that a shepherd or a maid knows better
than the rhapsodist the sections of Homer dealing with their respective
duties, he asks, "Well, the rhapsodist will know 'the kind of speech that
suits a man'--a general exhorting [παραινοῦντι] his soldiers?"[26] Ion
answers, "Yes, that is the sort of thing the rhapsode will know."[27] This
statement indicates that paraenesis is the proper speech for a general to use
when addressing his troops.

Many examples of generals' speeches could be cited from the
historians, but the speech of Phormio in Thucydides provides a
paradigmatic example. After giving a long speech of encouragement, he
exhorts his troops:

As for you, keep good order [εὔτακτοι], stay near your ships [μένοντες], give
heed sharply to the word of command [δέχεσθε], especially since the two fleets
are at watch so near one another; and when it comes to action, regard discipline
and silence, which are generally advantageous in warfare, but especially so at sea,
as all important, and ward off [ἀμύνεσθε] the enemy yonder in a manner worthy
of your past exploits. The contest is a momentous one for you--whether you are
to shatter the hopes which the Peloponnesians have in their fleet, or to bring
closer home to the Athenians their fear about the sea. Once more I remind you
that you have beaten most of them already; and when men have once suffered

---

[24]Ibid., 28. Translation by Norlin, 81, 83.

[25]Burgess, 210-214, gives examples of these generals' speeches and lists their
most common topoi.

[26]Plato, *Ion* 540D. Lane Cooper, trans., "Ion," in *The Collected Dialogues of
Plato* , ed. Edith Hamilton and Huntington Cairns, Bollingen Series 71 (Princeton, New
Jersey: Princeton University Press, 1985), 226.

[27]Ibid.

defeat, their spirit is never the same as before if they are called upon to face the same dangers.[28]

In this speech Phormio wants to both encourage his troops and to make a paraenesis to them. The paraenesis is short but is structured by imperatives and their supporting participles; however, it is the imperatives that express the thought of the passage.

More contemporary with 1 Peter than the previous examples, Seneca discusses paraenesis in *Epistles* 94 and 95. These epistles are not constructed in the form of a paraenesis but present a conscious reflection upon the genre. Seneca is writing in Latin, but at the beginning of *Epistle* 95 he makes this helpful statement:

> You keep asking me to explain without postponement a topic which I once remarked should be put off until the proper time, and to inform you by letter whether this department of philosophy which the Greeks call *paraenetic*, and we Romans call the "preceptorial," is enough to give us perfect wisdom.[29]

Seneca equates "precept-giving" with "paraenesis." He illustrates what he means by precept-giving when he says, "For he who utters precepts says, 'If you would have self-control, you shall act [*facies*] thus and so.'"[30] Clearly, Seneca understands precept-giving to be the primary characteristic of paraenesis when he equates the two.

In her study of Seneca's moral epistles, Hildegard Cancik concludes that prescriptive speech is the essential characteristic of paraenesis. She says in her findings:

> From the duality of emotive and rational means that Seneca's method employs, a separation of two areas of argumentation forms arises. We call the one theoretical-doxographical and the other paraenetical. We want to describe both these areas in the following study beginning with the form of their smallest identifiable element, the sentence. The indicative sentence is treated in the former while the imperative sentence is treated in the latter. Under this aspect, the

---

[28]Thucydides, *History of the Peloponnesian War* II.89.9-11. Charles Smith, trans., *Thucydides*, The Loeb Classical Library (Cambridge: Harvard University Press, 1951), 431.

[29]Seneca, *Epistulae Morales* 95.1. R. M. Gummere, trans, *Seneca*, vol. 6, The Loeb Classical Library (Cambridge: Harvard University Press, 1971), 59.

[30]Seneca, 95.66.

theoretical can be characterized as descriptive speech and the paraenetical as prescriptive speech.[31]

Her study indicates that prescriptive speech, which utilizes the imperative, dominates paraenesis.

For her, prescriptive speech includes not only statements with imperatives but also statements that have surrogate imperatives. She illustrates in the following:

> We also designate as imperatival statements those sentences that from a morphological standpoint do not contain an imperative but that function imperatively or have a type of imperatival meaning so that they could be formulated with an imperative without loosing their function. This includes statements of duties, expressed especially by the gerund as well as by the future indicative, and formulas of moral sanction that imply the impossibility of an alternative decision.[32]

Thus, although the imperative is the primary vehicle for prescriptive speech, other devices are available.

Although I agree with Cancik's imperatival surrogates, Berger's expansion of the list to include the participle, infinitive, and adjective is problematic and leads to a misunderstanding of paraenetic texts.[33] Of course, the infinitive can function as an imperative[34] but what about the participle and the adjective?[35] J. H. Moulton argued that the use of the participle for the imperative is a Hellenistic development in the Greek language.[36] His argument was successfully refuted by David Daube, who

---

[31]Hildegard Cancik, *Untersuchungen zu Senecas Epistulae Morales*, Spudasmata 18 (Hildesheim: Georg Olms, 1967), 16.

[32]Ibid., 23, note 42.

[33]Berger, "Gattungen," 1076, says, "In the New Testament examples, the ethical exhortation is not exclusively based. Instead of an imperative, participles could also be used (i.e. Romans 12:9) as well as the infinitive (i.e. Romans 12:15) or the adjective of hortatory character (i.e. Romans 12:9)."

[34]It is able to function as an imperative because of its use in indirect discourse in Greek. In indirect discourse the tense of the verb in the direct discourse is maintained but the mood is changed. Thus the infinitive even in situations where the verb of saying has been ellipsed can serve as an imperative.

[35]In the discussion that follows, the comments and conclusions reached in regard to the participle, which is a verbal-adjective, will also apply to the adjective.

[36]Moulton, 180f., 232f.

developed an alternative explanation.[37] He suggested that the imperatival use of the participle was due to Semitic influence.[38] His notion of an imperatival participle is completely mistaken. The essential syntactical notion of the participle is subordination. To regard the participle as a verb that can occur in an independent clause completely disregards this essential notion. Many examples could be cited, but two will suffice. First, in his *Address to Demonicus*, Pseudo-Isocrates says, "First of all, then, show devotion [εὐσέβει] to the gods, not merely by doing sacrifice [θύων], but also by keeping [ἐμμένων] your vows."[39] Clearly the participles here are not surrogates for the imperative since Cancik says that surrogate imperatives can be expressed by the imperative without a shift in meaning. These participles are subordinated to the imperative εὐσέβει and express an adverbial notion that further explains or compliments the imperative. Another example can be taken from the speech of Phormio where he says, "As for you, keep good order [εὔτακτοι], stay near your ships [μένοντες], give heed [δέχεσθε] sharply to the word of command."[40] The English translator understands the adjective εὔτακτοι and the participle μένοντες to be imperatival equivalents. However, his translation has obscured the fact that both of these grammatical forms are subordinate to the imperative δέχεσθε. They give the attendant circumstances or the context within which the command in the imperative is to be carried out. "Keeping good order as you remain by the ships" is the context within which they are to "snap to" the commands. If the adjective and the participle had been expressed by the imperative, we should assume that the commander is facing a mutiny with disorderly soldiers attempting to desert. This obviously is not the case here. Phormio wants to remind them to give quick heed to their orders, and he assumes they will maintain order and stay at their post. Thus, the imperative or an acceptable equivalent, such as the future indicative, the infinitive, or the subjunctive, becomes the vehicle for the argument in a prescriptive statement while adjectives and participles give the attendant

---

[37]David Daube, "Participle and Imperative in 1 Peter," in E. G. Selwyn, *The First Epistle of Saint Peter*, Thornapple Commentaries (Grand Rapids: Baker Book House, 1981), 467-471.

[38]Ibid., 471, says, "It is suggested that the participles in question may be due to Hebrew or [though less probably] Aramaic influence."

[39]Pseudo-Isocrates, *To Demonicus* 4.

[40]Thucydides, *History* II.89.9. Translation by Smith, 431.

circumstances or context for the fulfillment of the imperatival command. The only exception to this rule is the adjective ending in -τεος. It can function as an imperative because of this suffix that denotes necessity. The use of an adjective ending in -τεος is still not an exact equivalent for the imperative because it does not specify the person as the imperative does. This feature makes it the preferred imperatival vehicle in "how-to manuals."[41] These manuals are not commands to specific persons but instructions for anyone. Thus, neither the participle nor the adjective functions as a surrogate for the imperative. This observation is very important for the analysis of paraenetic texts.[42]

We conclude that imperatives with their supporting participles and imperatival equivalents are the essential feature of prescriptive speech, which in turn is the essential mark of the paraenetic genre. The imperatives and supporting participles of 1 Peter clearly place this document within the context of prescriptive speech, and the prescriptive speech of 1 Peter formally classifies it within the paraenetic genre. There are other features of prescriptive speech exhibited by 1 Peter that confirm this conclusion.

Cancik describes these other features of prescriptive speech while discussing paraenetic arguments, saying:

> We observe first the elements of paraenetic arguments: The most important structural element, the imperative, has already been mentioned above [p. 16]. The most ordinary situation of its use are lists of commands, prohibitions, admonitions, warnings, etc. The combination of imperatival statements with declarations and consequences is more interesting. Further elements of prescriptive speech are exempla, examples, and comparisons that correspond to

---

[41]For example see Xenophon's *How to Hunt* or *How to be a Cavalry Commander*.

[42]The lack of methodological control relating to imperatival participles is evident in Michaels, *1 Peter*, 82-83. He comments on 2:1-3, "In this section Peter continues the practice of juxtaposing participles with aorist imperatives. In 1:13-14 the imperative was preceded by an aorist and a present participle and followed by another present participle [with all the participles consequently functioning as imperatives]; in 1:22-23 the imperative was both preceded and followed by perfect participles [signaling Peter's avoidance in that instance of the imperatival meaning]. Now he returns to the aorist participle, as in 1:13, and to the use of the participle as an imperative." Michaels speaks as if it is an established fact that aorist and present participles can function as imperatives while perfect participles cannot. To my knowledge, this fact has not been established, and I would argue that the perfect participles in 1 Peter indicate that the participles are circumstantial or adjectival, but not imperatival.

the theorems in the doxographical descriptive parts of Seneca's epistles. For example, *Epistle* 95.72 says, "It will be helpful not only to state what is the usual quality of good men, and to outline their figures and features, but also to relate and set forth what men there have been of this kind." Exempla, examples, and comparisons comply with this need since they arise from life itself and thus are suitable to again exert influence upon life. They are thus in place whenever things not words are concerned.[43]

According to Cancik then, the indicative can function in prescriptive speech when it describes a model to be emulated or avoided or when it gives the motivation for conduct. She bases her study on the linguistic theory of R. M. Hare, who classifies prescriptive language into the broad categories of imperatival statements and value-judgments.[44] He includes under value-judgments models, examples, and choices that are either commended or scorned.[45] He also includes in this category the supporting reasons for these choices.[46] So prescriptive speech also makes use of the indicative to describe exemplary models and to state reasons or motivations for the recommended conduct.

Seneca comments on the use of motivations for conduct in paraenesis. In *Epistle* 94, he sets out to refute the argument of Aristo the Stoic, who advocated that paraenesis is superfluous. In diatribe style he quotes Aristo's objection, "'But if,' comes the answer, 'your precepts are not obvious, you will be bound to add proofs; hence the proofs, and not the precepts, will be helpful.'"[47] Seneca goes on to say that bare precepts [*nuda praecepta*] are useful, but more persuasive are those that add a reason or motive for action. He says in *Epistulae Morales*:

---

[43]Cancik, 23.

[44]R. M. Hare, *The Language of Morals* (Oxford: Clarendon Press, 1952), 3. See also Cancik, 30-31.

[45]Hare, 129, says, "It should be pointed out that even judgements about past choices do not refer merely to the past. As we shall see, all value-judgements are covertly universal in character, which is the same as to say that they refer to, and express acceptance of, a standard which has an application to other similar instances. . . . To commend, as we have seen, is to guide choices."

[46]Ibid., 176, he says, ". . . if we make a particular moral judgement, we can always be asked to support it by reasons; the reasons consist in the general principles under which the moral judgement is to be subsumed."

[47]Seneca, *Epistle* 94.27. Translation by Gummere, 29.

Also, if rebuke gives one a sense of shame, why has not counsel the same power, even though it does use bare precepts? The counsel that assists suggestion by reason--which adds the motive for doing a given thing and the reward that awaits one who carries out and obeys such precepts--is more effective and settles deeper into the heart.[48]

From these comments of Seneca, it is evident that reason or motive for action is compatible with the literary form of paraenesis and was often added to bare "precepts."

This fact can also be demonstrated from the paraenetical discourses that have already been mentioned. For example, Pseudo-Isocrates' *Address to Demonicus* adds reasons for showing devotion to the gods and honoring the divine power. He reasons, "Do honor to the divine power at all times, but especially on occasions of public worship; for thus you will have the reputation both of sacrificing to the gods and of abiding by the laws."[49] Thus, it can be demonstrated that reasons and motivations for conduct, although not essential, are a feature of prescriptive speech and consequently of paraenesis.

Lorenz Nieder has conducted the most thorough examination of motivational statements in Christian paraenesis.[50] Focusing on the Pauline letters, he identifies 10 general sanctions in Pauline paraenesis.[51] The first sanction involves a consideration of God, specifically His will, judgment, and salvation. Considering the nature of God particularly in these three areas, Paul argues that his readers ought to behave morally. The second sanction centers on Christology. Motivations for ethical conduct associated with this sanction include the conception of the Lord, His example, sacrificial death, and redemption. "Christ Mysticism" comprises the third sanction discussed by Nieder. The conception of the Christian as a member of Christ or of His body induces him to moral conduct. The fourth, fifth and sixth sanctions, which are respectively the church, baptism, and reception of the Spirit, are closely associated with this conception. Because the church represents the true people of God, its members ought to act

---

[48]Ibid., 94.44. Translation by Gummere, 39, 41.

[49]Pseudo-Isocrates, *To Demonicus* 13. Translation by Norlin, 11.

[50]Lorenz Nieder, *Die Motive der religiös-sittlichen Paränese in den Paulinischen Gemeindebriefen*, Münchener Theologische Studien 12 (München: Karl Zink, 1956), passim, but especially 104-145.

[51]Ibid., 3, note 7, cites several monographs that treat ethical motivation in Paul.

accordingly. The symbolism of baptism as a washing and putting off of the old life and putting on of the new likewise prompts the adoption of a moral life. Reception of the indwelling Spirit also provides Paul with a basis for encouraging Christian conduct. The seventh, eighth, and ninth sanctions function by allusions to rewards and punishments. The new life of the Christian brings benefits that are in danger of being lost if moral conduct is not practiced. In view of the soon-approaching end and the dangers associated with it, Paul argues that Christians ought to live morally. The tenth and last Pauline sanction identified by Nieder comprises motivations that are drawn from Stoic and popular philosophy. These motivations include conduct based upon a consideration of "those outside," being independent, attaining reputation, and doing the appropriate or pleasing action. Nieder concludes his study stating that the overarching sanction of Pauline paraenesis is the love of God received through Christ.

This feature of prescriptive speech is a pervasive element in 1 Peter that utilizes many of the sanctions identified by Nieder as well as some others. After exhorting his readers to be holy, the author in 1:16 cites a scriptural passage that provides motivation for this action: "Be holy because I am holy." He provides similar motivation for his exhortation to build themselves into a spiritual temple by citing several biblical passages in 2:6-8 that refer to Christ as the keystone. Again in 5:5 he appears to quote scripture as a basis for his admonition to humble themselves. In 1:18, 23; 2:13, 21; 3:18; and 4:1 the admonitions are supported by Christological statements. In 1:18 and 23 the admonitions are supported by reference to the price or source of their redemption--namely the sacrificial death of Christ. In 2:13 they should submit to every human institution "on account of the Lord." Christ's example provides the motivation for the author's exhortations in 2:21f; 3:18f; and 4:1f. In numerous passages eschatological references provide motivation for conduct.[52] In 2:2 the

---

[52]Anton Grabner-Haider, *Paraklese und Eschatologie bei Paulus*, Neutestamentliche Abhandlungen N.F. 4 (Münster: Verlag Aschendorff, 1968), 108, identifies eschatology as the primary basis of Pauline paraenesis. He says, "The most comprehensive basis for paraenesis in Paul is the reference to the time. This time has become the last time and the endtime. . . ." Grabner-Haider, 71-94, demonstrates with examples how eschatology formed the basis for exhortation in Jewish apocalyptic and in Paul. A similar conclusion was reached by Herbert Preisker, *Das Ethos des Urchristentums* (Gütersloh: C. Bertelsmann, 1949), 247, where he says, "The Ethic is composed from rational [Stoic], moralizing [Judaism], and cultic [Mysteries] affiliations in

readers are exhorted to desire the sincere milk of the word so that they might have a share in the eschatological salvation. The eschatological blessing in 3:9, joy in 4:13, judgment in 4:17, and crown of glory in 5:4 all lend support for following the commands prescribed by the author. In 5:6 eschatological exaltation provides motivation for humbling themselves. A categorical statement that the end of all has arrived furnishes a reason for being wise and sober for prayers. Other less prominent motives for conduct are given in the letter. In 2:15 the recommended conduct arises from the will of God while in 3:4 it will lead to the praise of God. In 3:1 the recommended action impacts unbelieving husbands, and in 2:2 the unbelieving Gentiles are affected. Successful prayers are mentioned in 3:7 as a motivation for husbands to live with their wives κατά γνῶσιν. Ferdinand Hahn correctly states that no paraenesis in early Christianity was ever given without a Christological basis, but as the great variety of motivational statements here indicate, this Christological basis was not exclusive of other motivational statements.[53] Since these motivational statements are features of prescriptive speech and since prescriptive speech

---

the transcending sphere of the Kingdom-of-God-faith. This early Christian faith serves an ethic of eschatological certainty as an eschatological warrant." Hans Dieter Betz, "Das Problem der Grundlagen der paulinischen Ethik," *Zeitschrift für Theologie und Kirche* 85 (1988): 199-218, cautions against concluding that Paul simply took his ethic from Greek or Jewish moral systems. On page 201 he says, "The often expressed opinion nowadays that early Christianity simply adapted itself to the common moral conceptions stands in contradiction to what the sources report. Just as incorrect would be the assumption that early Christianity developed a completely new morality that had nothing to do with the common morality of antiquity or was simply opposed to it. Rather, it procedes also here according to the rule that Paul advances in 1 Thessalonians 5:21-22: 'Prove all things and hold to the good! Flee from evil in every form!' If it should procede according to this rule, then criteria must be put forward by which adequate supports can be distinguished from inadequate ones. This, in turn, presupposes ethical reflection that has to work with theological foundations." Betz further states that it is a mistake to isolate individual theological elements such as eschatology, baptism, the Spirit, or the Kerygma as the foundation for the Pauline ethic. He says on page 218, "Finally, the foundation of the ethic is nothing other than the entire theology, namely the righteousness of God from which everything is constructed."

[53]Ferdinand Hahn, "Die christologische Begründung urchristlicher Paränese" *Zeitschrift für die neutestamentliche Wissenschaft* 72 (1981): 99, says, "A paraenesis never existed in early Christianity without connection with the message of the Gospel and hence without a Christological basis."

is the basic indicator of a paraenesis, they confirm that in its literary form 1 Peter belongs to the paraenetic genre.

The other type of indicative statement utilized by prescriptive speech that Cancik and Hare identify are moral examples. Both Seneca and Pseudo-Isocrates concur with the appropriateness of moral example in prescriptive speech. Seneca quotes Posidonius:

> He remarks that it will also be useful to illustrate each particular virtue; this science Posidonius calls ethology, while others call it characterization. It gives the signs and marks that belong to each virtue and vice, so that by them distinction may be drawn between like things. Its function is the same as that of precept. For he who utters precepts says: "If you would have self-control, act thus and so!" He who illustrates, says: "The man who acts thus and so, and refrains from certain other things, possesses self-control." If you ask what the difference here is, I say that the one gives the precepts of virtue, the other its embodiment.[54]

Isocrates as well as Seneca supports the usefulness of moral examples for prescriptive speech and thus paraenesis. He cites the example of Demonicus' father as a moral example before he proceeds to imperatival statements. He says in his example:

> Nay, if you will but recall also your father's principles, you will have from your own house a noble illustration of what I am telling you. For he did not belittle virtue nor pass his life in indolence; on the contrary, he trained his body by toil, and by his spirit he withstood dangers. Nor did he love wealth inordinately; but, although he enjoyed the good things at his hand as became a mortal, yet he cared for his possessions as if he had been immortal. Neither did he order his existence sordidly, but was a lover of beauty, munificent in his manner of life, and generous to his friends; and he prized more those who were devoted to him than those who were his kin by blood; for he considered that in the matter of companionship nature is a much better guide than convention, character than kinship, and freedom of choice than compulsion. But all time would fail us if we should try to recount all his activities. On another occasion I shall set them forth in detail; for the present, however, I have produced a sample of the nature of Hipponicus, after whom you should pattern your life as after an ensample, regarding his conduct as your law, and striving to imitate and emulate your father's virtue; for it were a shame, when painters represent the beautiful among animals, for children not to imitate the noble among their ancestors. Nay, you must consider that no athlete is so in duty bound to train against his competitors as are you to take thought how you may vie with your father in his ways of life.

---

[54]Seneca, *Epistle* 95.65-66. Translation by Gummere, 99.

But it is not possible for the mind to be so disposed unless one is fraught with many noble maxims; for, as it is the nature of the body to be developed by appropriate exercises, it is the nature of the soul to be developed by moral precepts. Wherefore I shall endeavor to set before you concisely by what practices I think you can make the most progress toward virtue and win the highest repute in the eyes of all other men.[55]

Both Seneca and Pseudo-Isocrates establish the use of moral examples in the prescriptive speech of a paraenesis.[56]

Stanley Stowers stresses the importance of moral examples for prescriptive speech. He distinguishes between a simple and a complex hortatory letter saying:

A useful distinction that I shall employ is between simple and complex hortatory letters. Words of exhortation were common to everyday language and can occur here and there in all types of letters [simple hortatory letter]. . . . What all complex letters of moral exhortation have in common is an explicit or implicit model of what it means to be a good person in general or a good person in a certain role.[57]

For Stowers, the paraenetic letter in its entirety becomes a model for conduct. Everything in the letter serves this purpose, even the imperatival statements. He articulates his position as follows:

The model can be presented to the reader in various ways. A seemingly random series of precepts or virtues may actually provide an implicit pattern of character. Very frequently authors refer to historical and legendary examples. Sometimes letter writers also appeal to living examples, including examples of the author's own behavior that may be set forth for imitation.[58]

Thus, he subsumes every element of the complex prescriptive letter to the category of moral example.

---

[55]Pseudo-Isocrates, *To Demonicus* 9-12. Translation by Norlin, 9, 11.

[56]For further discussion of the paraenetic use of example see Abraham J. Malherbe, *Moral Exhortation, a Greco-Roman Sourcebook*, Library of Early Christianity 4 (Philadelphia: Westminster Press, 1986), 135-138. Also see his article, "Exhortation in First Thessalonians," *Novum Testamentum* 25 (1983): 246-249. For a reflection on Malherbe's position, see Leo G. Purdue, "Paraenesis and the Epistle of James," *Zeitschrift für die neutestamentliche Wissenschaft* 72 (1981): 245-246.

[57]Stowers, *Letter Writing*, 93-94.

[58]Ibid., 95.

1 Peter certainly exhibits this feature of paraenetic prescriptive speech, and Stowers identifies it as a complex hortatory letter.[59] It does indeed attempt to establish by precepts and examples the model of the good person. The good person who is described by 1 Peter is a person in a certain life role. He/she is a Christian, and 1 Peter exhorts him/her to play this role well. The letter describes the noble origin of Christians and the glorious goal awaiting Christians as well as the present conduct expected of them. Specific examples such as Christ (2:18f.; 3:18f.; and 4:1f.), Sarah (3:6), and the author himself (5:1f.) provide models for imitation. This description of the Christian life is not theoretical but prescriptive. The readers are being exhorted to emulate the model of the Christian life that the letter describes. We can conclude that not only in its use of imperatival statements and motivations for conduct but also in its use of moral example, 1 Peter reflects the literary form of the paraenetic genre.[60]

Another literary feature of paraenesis that is closely associated with moral examples is the use of antithesis. Malherbe states, "Antithesis is a common feature in the use of examples. An example could, for instance, be described antithetically, or a positive example could be balanced by or juxtaposed to a negative one."[61] Describing Pliny's *Letter to Avitus*, Stowers also cites antithesis as a feature of paraenesis:

> Pliny also uses himself as an example for imitation in his *Letter to Avitus* (2.6). He begins by recounting an incident where a dinner host displayed miserliness combined with self-indulgence. He then relates a conversation at the dinner where he took a stand against these vices by putting forth his own behavior as a contrast. Pliny thus employs the paraenetic device of antithetical models of behavior and then explicitly draws out principles of behavior.[62]

Instances of this paraenetic feature could be multiplied. Paraenesis frequently contrasts positive and negative models of behavior through the literary device of antithesis.

---

[59]Ibid., 97, says, "First Peter is a complex hortatory letter. . . ."

[60]Benjamin Fiore, *The Function of Personal Example in the Socratic and Pastoral Epistles*, Analecta Biblica 105 (Rome: Biblical Institute Press, 1986), has an extensive discussion of personal example in Christian paraenesis. For a critique of his contribution, see the review of this work by Hans Dieter Betz in *Journal of Biblical Literature* 107 (1988): 335-337.

[61]Malherbe, *Moral Exhortation*, 136.

[62]Stowers, *Letter Writing*, 101.

1 Peter also exhibits this feature of paraenesis. In 1:14-15 and 2:1-2 the author contrasts his readers' former way of life with their present way of life. In 1:18-19 he reminds them that they were not redeemed with corruptible things but with the precious blood of Christ, and in verse twenty three he states that their new birth is a result not of corruptible seed but of incorruptible. The readers are contrasted with unbelievers in 2:7-9 and 4:4-5. The author calls his readers to exercise their freedom not as a pretext for evil but as servants of God in 2:16, and in verse twenty he contrasts the misconduct of servants with the preferred good conduct. Chapter 3:3-4 compares the outward image of women with the inward character. In 3:9 the readers are urged not to revile but to bless. In 4:15-16 he urges them not to suffer as a malefactor but as a Christian. Finally, several negative administrative tendances are contrasted with their positive counterparts in 5:1-3. As these examples demonstrate, 1 Peter frequently uses antithesis that also indicates it is a paraenesis.

Before leaving this discussion of the literary form of paraenesis, some of the paraenetical terms in 1 Peter should be mentioned. In his argument that 1 Thessalonians is a paraenetic letter, Malherbe lists several hortatory terms that occur in the letter. He says in his article:

> To these features others can be added which are characteristic of hortatory speech. It is noteworthy, for example, that a wide range of hortatory terms occur in this short letter, and that they are scattered throughout the letter: παράκλησις (2:3), παρακαλέω (2:12; 3:2, 7; 4:1, 10, 18; 5:11, 14), παραμυθέομαι (2:12; 5:14), (δια)μαρτύρομαι (2:12; 4:6), στηρίζω (3:2), παραγγελία (4:2), παραγγέλλω (4:11), ἐρωτάομαι (5:12), νουθετέω (5:12, 14), ἀντέχομαι (5:14), and μακροθυμέομαι (5:14). Most of these terms appear as descriptions of different types of exhortation in the Greek and Roman sources, and their use in I Thessalonians shows that Paul is concerned with a wide variety of types of exhortation.[63]

Although all of these terms do not occur in 1 Peter, some of them do. Παρακαλέω stands in 2:11 and 5:1, 12. Ἐπιμαρτυρέω, an intensive form of μαρτυρέω, occurs in 5:12 and στηρίζω is used in 5:10.[64] Although all of these terms indicate that 1 Peter is a paraenetical document, the most important term is παρακαλέω.

63Malherbe, "First Thessalonians," 241.
64Grabner-Haider, 10-11, says that the term μαρτυρέω belongs to paraenesis.

The precise significance of παρακαλέω has been recently debated by scholars. V. P. Furnish, following H. Schlier[65] and W. Schrage,[66] argues that the term "itself embraces the twin aspects of Paul's preaching: the gift of God's love in Christ and the consequent demand of God upon men."[67] C. J. Bjerkelund demonstrated that the term could not support such a broad theological meaning since the function of the term was only to establish a fraternal atmosphere in which to make a formal request of the recipients. Thus, the function of the term is diplomatic rather than theological.[68] D. C. Verner agrees with Bjerkelund in his description of the essential function of the term, but he does not think the view of Furnish has been ruled out since context must also be taken into account.[69] Berger also agrees with Bjerkelund, stating, "When Paul begins his exhortation with παρακαλῶ, he subscribes to the language of a letter of request and implies a particular type of intimacy."[70] Pliny's *Letter to Maximus* illustrates a fusion of command and request. Pliny says in this letter:

---

[65]H. Schlier, "Vom Wesen der apostolischen Ermahnung nach Röm. 12:1-2," *Die Zeit der Kirche* (Freiburg: Herder, 1956), 74f.

[66]Wolfgang Schrage, *Die konkreten Einzelgebote in der paulinischen Paränese* (Gütersloh: Gütersloher Verlagshaus, 1961). His most significant contribution lies in his attempt to demonstrate the individual commands or precepts are not necessarily directed to actual circumstances although they can be. His work represents an attempt to correct the misconception of Dibelius that paraenesis is not directed to a specific situation. See 37f. and especially 46.

[67]V. P. Furnish, *Theology and Ethics in Paul* (Nashville: Abingdon, 1968), 109.

[68]C. J. Bjerkelund, *Parakalo: Form, Funktion und Sinn der parakalo–Sätze in den paulinischen Briefen* (Oslo: Universitetsforlaget, 1967), 156f. He concludes that παρακαλῶ is not a technical term for paraenesis and that it is rarely used in paraenetic letters. It most frequently occurs in private letters expressing a summons or request, that does not imply command. See pages 58, 87, and 110. Bjerkelund's study is marred by his failure to perceive the personal, intimate nature of paraenesis in Paul's culture. Since his definition of paraenesis was too narrow, he mistakenly excluded παρακαλῶ from paraenetic terms.

[69]D. C. Verner, *The Household of God: The Social World of the Pastoral Epistles*, Society of Biblical Literature Dissertation Series 71 (Chico, California: Scholars Press, 1983), 117, says, "Nevertheless, while Bjerkelund's case for the diplomatic function of parakalo-Sätze such as the one in Rom. 12:1-2 is convincing, there is no compelling reason why this passage cannot have more than one function. Thus, it does not appear that Bjerkelund's study refutes Furnish's basic perspective on the passage."

[70]Berger, "Gattungen," 1329.

Please believe, as I said at the start, that this letter was intended not to tell, but to remind you of your duties–though I know I am really telling you as well, as I am not afraid of letting my affection carry me too far; there is no danger of excess where there ought to be no limits.[71]

Pliny's statement confirms Bjerkelund's conclusion that in a paraenetical letter the term παρακαλῶ indicates a fusion of command and request, placing the exhortation within a familial or fraternal context.[72]

This term, which occurs three times in 1 Peter (2:11; 5:1, 12), is an important indicator of the paraenetical genre of the document. Berger says that the author's own description of his work is an important genre determiner. He comments about the use of this description in letters, "We call it a commentary when the author himself puts his own opinion about the interpretation of the document in the text itself. The means are of many types. In letters it is frequently, 'I am writing this so that. . . .'"[73] In 1 Peter 5:12 the author gives his commentary of the letter saying, "I have written to you exhorting [παρακαλῶν] and witnessing [ἐπιμαρτυρῶν] that this grace of God is genuine; for which grace, stand." Both of these terms are paraenetic terms and conclusively indicate that the author intended to write a hortatory or paraenetic letter. As Berger notes, the concluding imperative στῆτε confirms the paraenetic genre of 1 Peter. He explains, "The summary of the most important thing at the letter's end is the epideictic counterpart of the concluding paraenesis described under 'a' above. It is found in the New Testament in . . . 1 Peter 5:12b."[74] The author's own commentary in 5:12 that uses the term παρακαλῶ indicates 1 Peter belongs to the paraenetic genre.

Having examined the literary form of 1 Peter, two conclusions are in order before the social context of the paraenetic genre is examined. First, several literary features of 1 Peter place it within the genre of paraenesis. The prescriptive language in 1 Peter is an essential feature of paraenesis. The imperatives with their supporting participles, motivations

---

[71]Pliny, *Letter to Maximus* 8.24. B. Radice, trans., *Pliny: Letters and Panegyricus*, The Loeb Classical Library (Cambridge: Harvard University Press, 1969), 77.

[72]Grabner-Haider, 4, prefers the term "paraklesis" to "paraenesis" since the former term occurs in the New Testament itself.

[73]Berger, "Gattungen," 1048.

[74]Ibid., 1349.

for conduct, and moral examples, which often employ antithesis, are all marks of prescriptive speech. In addition, paraenetical terms, especially παρακαλῶ, indicate the paraenetical nature of 1 Peter. Second, although there are literary elements that frequently occur in this genre, the paraenetical genre is not determined by its compositional structure. Prescriptive speech uses many different devices and varies them in an infinite number of compositional schemes. Imperatives or imperatival equivalents, motivations for conduct, and moral examples have no fixed structure or order in this genre. According to Berger, if a genre is not constituted by a fixed literary form, it is determined by the social context in which it functions. We turn now to an examination of the social context of paraenesis.

The Social Context of 1 Peter
and of Paraenesis

Leo G. Perdue has made a significant contribution to the study of the social context of paraenesis. He differentiates between two aspects of the social context, which are the social setting and the social function.[75] These two aspects of the social context of 1 Peter will now be examined.

The Social Setting

Perdue discusses the difficulty of identifying the social setting of paraenesis because of the traditional nature of many admonitions that are applicable to many life situations. This problem is further complicated by the fact that many paraenetic texts do not speak either directly or indirectly about their social setting. In spite of this problem, he thinks it is possible to establish some general factors concerning the social setting of paraenesis.[76]

The first factor he discusses is the gift of paraenesis by an aged teacher or mentor who is facing death. He alludes to *Tobit* and *The Testaments of the Twelve Patriarchs* as examples of this social setting.[77] In *Epistle* 94 Seneca begins a long discussion concerning the question: "Is it not clear that we need someone whom we may call upon as our preceptor

---

[75]Perdue, 242.
[76]Ibid., 246-247.
[77]Ibid., 247.

in opposition to the precepts of men in general?"[78] He answers this
question by replying:

> We should, therefore, have a guardian, as it were, to pluck us continually by the
> ear and dispel rumors and protest against popular enthusiasms. For you are
> mistaken if you suppose that our faults are inborn in us; they have come from
> without, have been heaped upon us. Hence, by receiving frequent admonitions,
> we can reject the opinions which din about our ears.[79]

He emphasizes the necessity of a "preceptor" when he says, "It is therefore
indispensable that we be admonished, that we have some advocate with
upright mind, and, amid all the uproar and jangle of falsehood, hear one
voice only."[80] Seneca is arguing that everyone needs a "preceptor" who
gives precepts or paraenesis. This "preceptor," whether he be a teacher,
mentor, or some other authoritative figure, is an important element in the
social setting of paraenesis.

Stowers comments on this factor in the social setting when he
discusses the paraenetic, model letter of Libanius, saying:

> Libanius' model letter also illustrates the typical friendly context of paraenetic
> correspondence. Paraenesis required some type of positive relationship, e.g.,
> that of parent and child, or friendship. It was customary for the adviser to liken
> himself to a father exhorting his child. Friends were supposed to care for each
> other's character development. The author's self-presentation as a friend is often
> the relational framework for providing exhortation and specific advice.[81]

Thus the "preceptor" should have a friendly, positive relationship with
those he is exhorting.

This friendly setting is intensified in Christian paraenesis by the
adoption of family ethics. The giver of a Christian paraenesis is not only
an authoritative, aged, experienced figure such as a father or teacher, but
he is also a Christian brother. H. D. Betz describes this development in
Christian ethics, saying:

> This fact, however, implies that the terms [$\phi\iota\lambda\alpha\delta\epsilon\lambda\phi\iota\alpha$ and $\phi\iota\lambda\acute{\alpha}\delta\epsilon\lambda\phi$os] have
> already been transformed and no longer refer to family relationships, but to

---

[78]Seneca, *Epistle* 94.52. Translation by Gummere, 45.
[79]Ibid., 94.55-56. Translation by Gummere, 47.
[80]Ibid., 94.59. Translation by Gummere, 49.
[81]Stowers, *Letter Writing*, 95.

Christian "brotherhood." Apart from a few instances, ECL is not interested in the family relationship of "brotherhood," but instead "brotherhood" almost throughout ECL means "spiritual brotherhood." Along with this transformation, older *topoi* of family ethics now appear simply as Christian church ethics, the congregation becoming the household of God.[82]

The Christian "brotherhood" provided an ideal situation for the rise of "preceptors" and gave increased authority to their exhortations.[83] As a result, in Christian paraenesis as compared to that of the philosophers, there is less argument and more paternal exhortation.[84]

1 Peter certainly reflects this element of the paraenetic social setting. In 1:1 the author identifies himself as Peter the apostle of Jesus Christ. Although he is an authoritative figure, he does not exert his prerogative to command the recipients. Instead, he relates to them by using fraternal language. This language includes terms such as παρακαλῶ (2:11; 5:1, 12), ἀγαπητοί (2:11; 4:12), and ἀδελφότηs (5:9). He is experienced and qualified to give this paraenesis because he is a "co-elder" and "witness" of the sufferings of Christ as well as a "partner" of the glory about to be revealed (5:1). His most important qualification for giving this paraenesis is his being a "spiritual brother" to the recipients. In 1:3 he includes himself and his readers in the same spiritual family because they have all been "reborn." Peter as the "preceptor" enables this letter to exhibit the first element in the social setting identified by Perdue.

The second factor in the social setting discussed by Perdue is the separation of the teacher and his student.[85] Of course, this applies primarily to paraenetic letters and arises from the epistolary social setting rather than the paraenetic. In paraenetic letters, however, this separation of sender and addressee produces a potentially threatening situation of moral independence for the addressee. In the absence of his "preceptor," the addressee may suffer a moral lapse or at least moral discouragement. In this situation, the "preceptor" sends his paraenesis by a letter in order to

---

[82]Hans Dieter Betz, "De Fraterno Amore (Moralia 478A-492D)," in *Plutarch's Ethical Writings and Early Christian Literature*, ed. idem, Studia ad Corpus Hellenisticum Novi Testamenti 4 (Leiden: E.J. Brill, 1978), 232-233.

[83]Malherbe, "First Thessalonians," 252-253, discusses the use of "brotherhood" in Pauline paraenesis instead of "friendship."

[84]Albert Wifstrand, "Stylistic Problems in the Epistles of James and Peter," *Studia Theologica* 1 (1948): 172.

[85]Perdue, 248.

comfort and to encourage the recipient to maintain his/her morality. This factor is amply illustrated in 1 Peter. Throughout the letter, reference is made to the trials, persecutions, and sufferings of the recipients in the absence of the author, and yet he exhorts them to maintain their Christian conduct. He does not mention an intended visit to them as Paul frequently does, but he alludes to their meeting in the eschaton when the glory of Christ is revealed.[86] In 1:11 he mentions the glories in Christ that occur subsequent to the sufferings in Christ. In 1:7 he states that they will receive glory at the coming of Jesus Christ. Since he is also a partner in this glory (5:1), the coming of Jesus Christ will resolve the epistolary situation and unite the author with the recipients. At that time the threatening situation will be removed, but until then this paraenetic letter serves as a surrogate "Peter" for the recipients.

The third social-setting factor discussed by Perdue pertains to the recipient of the instruction.[87] He says in regard to this factor:

> Generally speaking, the recipient is young, inexperienced, and about to embark or recently has embarked on a new course of life, involving either entrance into a social group or elevation to a social position with new responsibilities. . . . In other words, some paraenetic texts are an important rite of passage often involving inexperienced novices who are going through either status elevation or initiation into a social group.[88]

If 1 Peter is considered to be a baptismal homily, then this social setting would apply. However, the exhortation to the elders in 5:1f. certainly does not correspond to this scenario. The references to suffering and grief that have already been endured by the recipients (1:6; 2:12; 4:12f.; 5:9) do not indicate they are inexperienced novices, experiencing a rite of passage or induction into the group. The author indicates they have already been inducted into the group when he mentions their election (1:1), new birth (1:3), and redemption (1:18). For these reasons, this social setting that Perdue discusses does not pertain to 1 Peter.

The fourth and final social setting discussed by Perdue does pertain to 1 Peter. In this setting, exhortations are given "at a time after incorporation and tend to call the recipients to a serious reflection upon

---

[86]Funk, "*Parousia*," 249-268.
[87]Perdue., 248.
[88]Ibid., 248.

their initial entrance into their present group or position."[89] Perdue asserts this is the social setting of the book of James:

> The audience addressed consists of Jewish Christians who have already entered the community, but at least some of the more affluent are experiencing major problems that tempt them to leave and return to the world. The paraenesis of James exhorts the audience to reflect upon their initial entrance into the community, to continue to dissociate themselves from the world, and to engage in more committed efforts towards a higher level of virtue and perfection. In fact, Chapter 4 recalls the language that was a part of the initial rite of passage into the community: "submission," "cleansing of hands," "purifying of the heart," "mourning," and "humiliation."[90]

Except for some minor variations, this description of the social setting of James also describes the social setting of 1 Peter. The community or communities have experienced manifold temptations and persecutions, and the author is encouraging them by reflection upon their entrance into the group, as well as their future hope, to stand firm. This situation provides the social setting for 1 Peter.

The correspondence of 1 Peter's social setting and the paraenetic social setting discussed by Perdue demonstrates that it belongs to the paraenetic genre. It completely reflects the social setting of paraenesis. A "preceptor," Peter, who is separated from these communities, writes to community members who have already been incorporated but who are experiencing adversity exhorting them to stand firm by reflecting upon their initiation into the group and the glorious future awaiting them. It is this social setting that conclusively identifies 1 Peter as a paraenesis.

The Social Function

In addition to the social setting of paraenesis, Perdue also discusses its social function:

> The primary function of paraenesis is socialization, defined by Berger and Luckmann as "the comprehensive and consistent induction of an individual into the objective world of a society or sector of it." While paraenesis at times patterns itself on important elements of primary socialization, nevertheless, it is for the most part secondary socialization that occurs later in the life of an individual after

---

[89]Ibid., 249. For examples see Perdue, 249-250.
[90]Ibid., 249-250.

childhood when he joins social groups or is elevated to new social roles.
Paraenesis, then, is a means by which an individual is introduced to the group's
or role's social knowledge, including especially norms and values pertaining to
group or role behavior, internalizes this knowledge, and makes it the basis for
both behavior and the meaning system by which he interprets and orders
his world.[91]

As this quote indicates, Perdue discusses the social function of paraenesis in
highly theoretical terms. His discussion draws heavily upon modern social
theory, but it does not sufficiently consider ancient Greco-Roman society.
I agree that the primary function of paraenesis is socialization, but this
process must be primarily understood from the society that produced a
paraenetic document rather than modern social theory.

   Greco-Roman society was an hierarchical society. Esteem and
reputation, not only by one's peers and superiors but also by one's
inferiors, were highly sought after. Socialization involved performing
one's duties, discharging one's responsibilities, and relating to others so one
could attain δόξα. An extended discussion of Cicero regarding this subject
demonstrates that attainment of δόξα was the objective of socialization and
thus of paraenesis in his society. He comments in the following:

The highest, truest glory depends upon the following three things: the affection,
the confidence, and the mingled admiration and esteem of the people. Such
sentiments, if I may speak plainly and concisely, are awakened in the masses in
the same way as in individuals. But there is also another avenue of approach to
the masses, by which we can, as it were, steal into the hearts of all at once. But
of the three above-named requisites, let us look first at good-will and the rules for
securing it. Good-will is won principally through kind services; next to that, it is
elicited by the will to do a kind service, even though nothing happen to come of
it. Then, too, the love of people generally is powerfully attracted by a man's
mere name and reputation for generosity, kindness, justice, honor, and all those
virtues that belong to gentleness of character and affability of manner. And
because that very quality which we term moral goodness and propriety is pleasing
to us by and of itself and touches all out hearts both by its inward essence and its
outward aspect and shines forth with most luster through those virtues named
above, we are, therefore, compelled by Nature herself to love those in whom we
believe those virtues to reside. Now these are only the most powerful motives to
love—not all of them; there may be some minor ones besides. Secondly, the
command of confidence can be secured on two conditions: (1) if people think us
possessed of practical wisdom combined with a sense of justice. For we have
confidence in those who we think have more understanding than ourselves, who,

---

[91]Ibid., 251.

we believe, have better insight into the future, and who, when an emergency arises and a crisis comes, can clear away the difficulties and reach a safe decision according to the exigencies of the occasion; for that kind of wisdom the world accounts genuine and practical. But (2) confidence is reposed in men who are just and true–that is, good men–on the definite assumption that their characters admit of no suspicion of dishonesty or wrong-doing. And so we believe that it is perfectly safe to entrust our lives, our fortunes, and our children to their care. Of these two qualities, then, justice has the greater power to inspire confidence; for even without the aid of wisdom, it has considerable weight; but wisdom without justice is of no avail to inspire confidence; for take from a man his reputation for probity, and the more shrewd and clever he is, the more hated and mistrusted he becomes. Therefore, justice combined with practical wisdom will command all the confidence we can desire; justice without wisdom will be able to do much; wisdom without justice will be of no avail at all.

. . . .

The third, then, of the three conditions I named as essential to glory is that we be accounted worthy of the esteem and admiration of our fellow men. While people admire in general everything that is great or better than they expect, they admire in particular the good qualities that they find unexpectedly in individuals. And so they reverence and extol with the highest praises those men in whom they see certain pre-eminent and extraordinary talents; and they look down with contempt upon those who think they have no ability, no spirit, no energy. For they do not despise all those of whom they think ill. For some men they consider unscrupulous, slanderous, fraudulent, and dangerous; they do not despise them, it may be; but they do think ill of them. And therefore, as I said before, those are despised who are "of no use to themselves or their neighbors," as the saying is, who are idle, lazy, and indifferent. On the other hand, those are regarded with admiration who are thought to excel others in ability and to be free from all dishonor and also from those vices which others do not easily resist. For sensual pleasure, a most seductive mistress, turns the hearts of the greater part of humanity away from virtue; and when the fiery trial of affliction draws near, most people are terrified beyond measure. Life and death, wealth and want affect all men most powerfully. But when men, with a spirit great and exalted, can look down upon such outward circumstances, whether prosperous or adverse, and when some noble and virtuous purpose, presented to their minds, converts them wholly to itself and carries them away in its pursuit, who then could fail to admire in them the splendor and beauty of virtue?

. . . .

Those three requisites, therefore, which were presupposed as the means of obtaining glory, are all secured by justice: (1) good-will, for it seeks to be of help to the greatest number; (2) confidence, for the same reason; and (3) admiration,

because it scorns and cares nothing for those things, with a consuming passion
for which most people are carried away.[92]

As Cicero's extended discussion demonstrates, the attainment of δόξα was
the primary social objective for privileged individuals in this society. As
his treatment also demonstrates, this objective was also the primary
objective of ethical conduct and thus of paraenesis. The state or attainment
of δόξα for Cicero depends upon the attainment of the affection,
confidence, admiration, and esteem of the people. This state of δόξα was
achieved by good conduct. Ethical conduct was therefore meant to lead to
δόξα, and this state was the primary objective of the socialization effected
by paraenesis in Greco-Roman society.

This notion was so pervasive that the cynic philosopher Teles stated
there are two roles that all people are called upon to play in life: ἔνδοξος
and ἄδοξος.[93] In his collection of letters, Stowers quotes letter 3057 from
the *Oxyrhynchus Papyri* collection; this letter states that the goal of its
advice is to be well spoken of and not to be reproached as indicated in the
following excerpt:

> I don't want you, my brothers, to quarrel for my sake or for anyone else's;
> indeed I pray for concord and mutual affection to maintain itself in you, so that
> you can be beyond the reach of gossip and not be like us: experience leads me to
> urge you to live at peace and not to give others a handle against you. So try and
> do this for my sake too–a favour to me, which in the interim you'll come to
> recognize as advantageous [to you as well].[94]

In discussing the paraenetic, model letter of Libanius, Stowers explicitly
identifies the objective of paraenesis to be a good reputation:

> The actual advice in Libanius' model letter is gnomic and unexceptional, as the
> author indicates paraenesis should be. The motivation for the advice is to be well
> spoken of and not reproached. Libanius believes that paraenesis concerns

---

[92]Cicero, *De Officiis* 2.9-11. Walter Miller, trans., *Cicero: De Officiis*, The Loeb
Classical Library (Cambridge: Harvard University Press, 1975), 198-207.

[93]Teles, *On Circumstances* 52h. Text and translation in Edward N. O'Neil, *Teles
(The Cynic Teacher)*, Society of Biblical Literature Texts and Translations 11 (Missoula,
Montana: Scholars Press, 1977), 58-59.

[94]Stowers, *Letter Writing*, 98.

those basic and unquestioned patterns of behavior which are sanctioned by honor and shame.[95]

Pliny in writing to Maximus refers to a social truism that asserts it is far more shameful to lose a reputation than not to win one.[96] All of these examples demonstrate that paraenesis, which inculcates ethical conduct, was meant to lead to a state of δόξα.

Since the objective of paraenesis was socialization, which for this society meant the attainment of δόξα, the author of the paraenesis in 1 Peter has a perplexing problem. The acceptance of these rules of conduct by the Christian community has not led to a state of δόξα but just the reverse. They are maligned as evil doers (2:12; 3:16-17). They are reproached (4:14). They suffer persecutions (2:19-21; 3:14; 4:1, 12-13, 19; 5:9-10). The realization of the expected δόξα has not occurred. In fact, the recipients' former "δόξα" has been eroded, and they are now being perceived as shameful (2:12; 4:4).

This problem sets up the rhetorical situation for the author of 1 Peter and explains the unique paraenetic feature of eschatology not only in his letter but also in Christian paraenesis in general. Koester and Malherbe have arrived at different conclusions regarding the use of eschatology in Christian paraenesis. In a brilliant article, Koester demonstrates that in writing 1 Thessalonians Paul creates a new genre known as the Christian letter. He states in this article:

> It is difficult to classify 1 Thessalonians according to any of the known genres of ancient letters. Paul seems to use the form of the private letter. . . . But one searches in vain for analogies among private letters which have such extensive and elaborate thanksgiving sections, let alone the lengthy moral and eschatological instructions.[97]

He goes on to say, "In the case of the 'instructions' it is still possible to cite the philosophical moral epistle as an analogy or parallel; but no analogies exist in letters of any kind for the eschatological admonitions which are found in 1 Thess. 4:13--5:11."[98] He argues that the eschatological material

---

[95]Ibid., 94.
[96]Pliny, *To Maximus* 8.24.
[97]Koester, "1 Thessalonians," 35.
[98]Ibid., 39.

became the distinctive mark of a new genre, the Christian letter.[99]
Malherbe provides a needed corrective to Koester's position, saying:

> Koester is, of course, correct so far as the content of the eschatological material is
> concerned. But when it is observed that the eschatological statements function to
> comfort Paul's readers (4:18; 5:11), the absoluteness of his claim must be called
> into question. Paul is not providing eschatological instruction to inform his
> readers, but to console those who were grieving. In doing so, Paul's direction
> exhibits a number of similarities to themes found in the letter of consolation, a
> well-known epistolary genre in antiquity. To the Church Fathers, who knew the
> classical genres, this section of the letter appeared close to a consolatory epistle.
> Consolation was conceived of as belonging to paraenesis, and the letter of
> consolation was discussed in epistolographic handbooks in terms which reflected
> its paraenetic character.[100]

According to Malherbe, eschatological elements could and did function
within the genre of paraenesis.

The author of 1 Peter has resorted to eschatological ideas in his
paraenesis to resolve this problem of a non-realization of δόξα. He adopts
an apocalyptic scheme that is summarized in 5:10, "But the God of all
grace who called you into his eternal glory in Christ Jesus, after you have
suffered a little while, shall restore, support, strengthen, and establish
you." He affirms that the paraenesis or ethical conduct to which God has
called the readers does lead to a state of δόξα, but there will be a short
period of suffering before the δόξα will be realized. He illustrates this
truth by appealing to the paradigm, Jesus. He mentions the death of Jesus
and the giving of δόξα to Him through the resurrection (1:21). He
mentions the sufferings of Jesus and the δόξα that is about to be revealed
(5:1). Reminding his readers that the sufferings in Christ and the δόξα
after these sufferings were announced beforehand by the prophets and by
those who had announced the Gospel (1:10-12), he points out that the non-
realization of δόξα and the experiences of suffering bring benefits. These
benefits include praise, glory, and honor at the revelation of Jesus Christ
(1:6-7); the glorifying of God in the day of visitation (2:12); benefit with
God (2:19-20); blessedness (3:14); cooperation with the will of God
resulting in good works (4:19); and vindication by God Himself (5:9-10).

---

[99]Ibid., 40, says, "In 1 Thessalonians, as well as in later Christian letters, the
eschatological section became the most distinctive mark of the new genre."

[100]Malherbe, "First Thessalonians," 254-255.

The conduct recommended in the author's paraenesis does in fact lead to δόξα as a paraenesis should but only after a short period of suffering and illusory ἀδοξία has been endured.

1 Peter therefore evidences the paraenetic social function of socialization whose primary objective in this society is the attainment of δόξα. However, if this paraenesis is to be persuasive, it must resolve the problem that the conduct it is advocating has not led to a state of δόξα but just the reverse. The eschatological material in this document functions rhetorically to resolve this problem and persuade the readers to continue to follow the conduct prescribed. This problem and its resolution clearly demonstrates that 1 Peter belongs to the paraenetic genre.

Paraenesis utilized many means in order to attain this primary function of socialization. The previous discussion of the objective of paraenesis addressed the question: What did paraenesis attempt to do? The following discussion of the means responds to the question: How did paraenesis attempt to do it? Three of these means will now be discussed since they further demonstrate that 1 Peter fits within the paraenetic genre.

The first and most prominent means of paraenetic socialization is the utilization of persuasion and dissuasion. In paraenesis, someone is encouraged to pursue or not pursue a course of action in order to arrive at a state of δόξα. In his definition of paraenesis, Malherbe points to this important tool saying, "Paraenesis is moral exhortation in which someone is advised to pursue or abstain from something."[101] In his description of the paraenetic style, Pseudo-Libanius also mentions this tool of paraenesis. He says in his epistolary handbook, "The paraenetic style is that in which we exhort someone by urging him to pursue something or to avoid something. Paraenesis is divided into two parts, encouragement and dissuasion."[102] Similarly, Pseudo-Demetrius describes the admonishing letter, saying, "The admonishing type [νουθετητικός] is one which indicates through its name what its character is. For admonition is the instilling of sense in the person who is being admonished, and teaching him what should and should not be done."[103]As all of these authors indicate, an important

---

[101]Malherbe, *Moral Exhortation*, 124.

[102]Libanius, *Epistolary Styles*. Text and translation in Malherbe, "Epistolary Theorists," 62-63.

[103]Pseudo-Demetrius, *Epistolary Types*. Text and translation in Malherbe, "Epistolary Theorists," 32-33.

means used by paraenesis to achieve socialization was persuasion and dissuasion.

Paraenetic persuasion often assumed the form of recommendation of particular practical rules by which daily life could be regulated. Seneca plainly illustrates this tendency in *Epistle* 94:

> That department of philosophy which supplies precepts appropriate to the individual case, instead of framing them for mankind at large–which, for instance, advises how a husband should conduct himself towards his wife, or how a father should bring up his children, or how a master should rule his slaves–this department of philosophy, I say, is accepted by some as the only significant part, while the other departments are rejected on the ground that they stray beyond the sphere of practical needs–as if any man could give advice concerning a portion of life without having first gained a knowledge of the sum of life as a whole![104]

Pseudo-Isocrates' *Address to Demonicus* also makes this fact plain. He states the means of his paraenesis as follows:

> Therefore, I have not invented a hortatory exercise [παράκλησιν], but have written a moral treatise [παραίνεσιν]; and I am going to counsel you on the objects to which young men should aspire and from what actions they should abstain, and with what sort of men they should associate and how they should regulate their own lives. For only those who have travelled this road in life have been able in the true sense to attain to virtue–that possession which is the grandest and the most enduring in the world.[105]

This recommendation of practical rules as a form of persuasion is also illustrated by the paraenesis in the generals' speeches where practical conduct for their troops is being urged. Thus, one of the ways whereby paraenesis persuaded and dissuaded was the recommendation of practical rules of conduct by which daily life could be regulated.

Paraenesis only recommended practical rules of conduct that were generally accepted. It did not discuss controversial issues, such as the meaning of moral terms: *good, evil, right,* or *wrong.* Paraenesis assumes the meaning of these terms to be understood, and a discussion of the meaning of these terms belongs to a different department of philosophy as Seneca notes, "Virtue is divided into two parts–into contemplation

---

[104]Seneca, *Epistle* 94.1. Translation by Gummere, 10-11.

[105]Pseudo-Isocrates, *To Demonicus* 5. Translation by Norlin, 6-7.

[*contemplationem*] of the truth and conduct [*actionem*]. Training [*institutio*] teaches contemplation, and admonition [*admonitio*] teaches conduct."[106] Paraenesis deals with generally accepted rules of conduct, not controversial issues that require contemplation. Isocrates notes that paraenetical discourses are not useful for treating material outside the circle of accepted belief. He says in an important passage:

> But the truth is that in discourses of this sort we should not seek novelties, for in these discourses it is not possible to say what is paradoxical or incredible or outside the circle of accepted belief; but, rather, we should regard that man as the most accomplished in this field who can collect the greatest number of ideas scattered among the thoughts of all the rest and present them in the best form.[107]

Thus, in its attempt to persuade and dissuade, paraenesis only recommends principles of conduct that are generally accepted and uncontroversial.

This tenet implies that paraenesis is more of a reminder of what one ought or ought not to do than an introduction to new rules of conduct.[108] Seneca explicitly explains this feature of paraenesis, stating:

> People say: "What good does it do to point out the obvious?" A great deal of good; for we sometimes know facts without paying attention to them. Advice is not teaching; it merely engages the attention and rouses us, and concentrates the memory, and keeps it from losing grip. We miss much that is set before our very eyes. Advice is, in fact, a sort of exhortation. The mind often tries not to notice even that which lies before our eyes; we must therefore force upon it the knowledge of things that are perfectly well known.[109]

Pliny's *Letter to Maximus* reiterates this feature of paraenesis:

> Pliny to his own Maximus, greeting. I know you need no telling, but my love for you prompts me to remind you to keep in mind and put into practice what you know already, or else it would be better for you to remain ignorant. Remember that you have been sent to. . . .[110]

---

[106]Seneca, *Epistle* 94.45. Translation by Gummere, 40-41.

[107]Isocrates, *To Nicocles* 41. Translation by Norlin, 62-63.

[108]Aune, *Literary Environment*, 191, says, "Paraenesis is so familiar that it is often presented as a 'reminder' (Seneca, *Letters* 13.15; 94.21-25; Dio Chrysostom, *Oration* 17.2, 5; 1 Thessalonians 4:1-2; 2 Thessalonians 3:6; Philippians 3:1)."

[109]Seneca, *Epistle* 94.25. Translation by Gummere, 26-29.

[110]Pliny, *Letters* 8.24. Translation by Radice, 72-73.

So the practical rules of conduct recommended by paraenesis serve more as a reminder than an impartation of new ideas.

As an aid to the memory, paraenesis attempts to organize these principles and rules so that the mind can more easily grasp them. Seneca comments on the function of paraenetical precepts, "In the first place, they refresh the memory; in the second place, when sorted into their proper classes, the matters which showed themselves in a jumbled mass when considered as a whole, can be considered in this way with greater care."[111] He continues to speak concerning organization:

> Moreover, there are certain things which, though in the mind, yet are not ready to hand but begin to function easily as soon as they are put into words. Certain things lie scattered about in various places, and it is impossible for the unpracticed mind to arrange them in order. Therefore, we should bring them into unity, and join them, so that they may be more powerful and more of an uplift to the soul.[112]

Organization is an important device in paraenesis and serves as an aid to the memory. Memory permits paraenesis to recommend practical rules of conduct that are well known and generally accepted, and these rules are recommended as a form of persuasion and dissuasion. Persuasion and dissuasion provide paraenesis with its principal means for achieving socialization, the attainment of δόξα.

1 Peter utilizes the paraenetic means of persuasion and dissuasion in order to achieve socialization as Anton Vögtle asserts particularly in regard to the Virtue and Vice Lists. He says in his study of these lists:

> The vice lists of the Petrine letters serve paraenetic purposes. In 1 Peter 2:1 the apostle selects vices that should be abstained from. In 4:15 he selects vices of which Christians could be accused before public judges but of which they should not be accused. In 4:3 he selects those pagan vices that the Christian has left behind with his entrance into Christendom and into which they should not fall back.[113]

In 1 Peter the recipients are urged to act or not act in certain ways so that they can attain not fleeting glory but eternal glory. In his attempt to

---

[111]Seneca, *Epistle* 94.21. Translation by Gummere, 24-25.

[112]Seneca, *Epistle* 94.29-30. Translation by Gummere, 30-31.

[113]Anton Vögtle, *Die Tugend- und Lasterkataloge im Neuen Testament*, Neutestamentliche Abhandlungen 16 (Münster: Aschendorff, 1936), 12.

persuade and dissuade, the author recommends practical rules for daily conduct that are not new instructions for the Christian communities but are familiar rules that the communities had already accepted (1:12). He attempts to recommend these practical rules of conduct by reminding the communities of what they already know and by organizing these rules so that they might be easily grasped by the mind.[114] The author of 1 Peter is using this primary paraenetic means of persuasion and dissuasion in order to effect socialization. Not only in its objective but also in its means for attaining this objective, 1 Peter corresponds to the paraenetic genre.

Besides persuasion and dissuasion, the paraenetic genre also utilizes statements of consolation as a means of effecting socialization. Seneca cites Posidonius to prove that persuasion, consolation, and encouragement, in addition to "precept-giving," are necessary to produce virtue and right conduct in a person. He quotes from Posidonius, "Posidonius holds that not only precept-giving [*praeceptionem*], there is nothing to prevent my using this word, but even persuasion [*suasionem*], consolation [*consolationem*], and encouragement [*exhortationem*], are necessary."[115] This fact can also be demonstrated from the discourses that have already been mentioned. The discourse of Phormio in Thucydides began with a long section of consolation and encouragement before precepts were given. Consolation is therefore a means assumed by paraenesis for attaining socialization.[116]

Since I have already noted that several eschatological statements in 1 Peter serve a consolatory purpose, I will not reiterate them here. Suffice it to say that the statements of encouragement in 1 Peter also indicate it employs paraenetic means in order to accomplish its objective.

---

[114]The earliest document that comments on 1 Peter is 2 Peter 3:1. The author of 2 Peter claims that in both letters [ἐν αἷς] he has attempted to raise the sincere mind of the readers to remember the words of the prophets and the command of the Lord. He claims to have accomplished this goal by reminding [ἐν ὑπομνήσει] them. This author clearly understands that 1 Peter employs "reminding" as the primary means of accomplishing its goal.

[115]Seneca, *Epistle* 95.65. Translation by Gummere, 98-99.

[116]Stowers, *Letter Writing*, 96, says, "Paraenetic letters are generally dominated by encouraging types of exhortation, although words of admonition or mild rebuke here and there could be appropriate. Consolatory sections are also frequently parts of these complex letters of exhortation."

The final means used by paraenesis to achieve socialization is the establishment of group identity. Perdue comments about this aspect of paraenesis:

> Finally, in cases of entrance into a group, paraenesis plays an important part in the establishment of group identity and cohesion during the process of socialization. In the general social setting in which paraenesis is often given, the individual is about to enter or recently has entered a new social group. In order for any group to exist, definite boundaries must be constructed which demarcate the group and its distinctive social world from other groups with differing social worlds. Thus, paraenesis presents a group ethic designed to maintain a clear differentiation between in-group and out-group. In bringing about group identity and cohesion, a number of strategies may be followed, but one that sometimes is used is conflict.[117]

Thus, paraenesis proposes that one will attain δόξα if he/she joins or maintains his/her standing in a particular group.

1 Peter very definitely uses this paraenetic means. Numerous names are applied to the group to which the author writes. They are *elect strangers* (1:1), *obedient children of the Father* (1:14-17), *a spiritual temple* (2:5), *the people of God* (2:9-10), *strangers and aliens in this world* (2:11), *free men yet slaves of God* (2:16), and *beloved* (2:11; 4:12). They belong to a brotherhood that is experiencing conflict with the larger social world (5:9). Scattered throughout the letter are references to this conflict and the ensuing suffering of the author's group. These references form an essential strategy on the part of the author to establish group identity and cohesion. According to the author, attainment of δόξα depends upon one's allegiance to and membership in this group. Group membership provides the author of 1 Peter with a powerful means of effecting socialization among his readers.

Assessment

At the beginning of this chapter, I set out to determine the genre of 1 Peter by applying the genre determiners of literary form and social context established by Klaus Berger. We can now conclude that 1 Peter is a paraenesis. Its literary form corresponds to the paraenetic genre. The prescriptive speech, especially the imperatives with their supporting

---

[117]Perdue, 255.

participles, are a basic indication that it belongs to a paraenesis. In addition to the prescriptive speech, other literary indicators that place 1 Peter in the genre of paraenesis are motivational statements for conduct, moral examples, antitheses, and paraenetic terms. In both its literary form and social context, 1 Peter corresponds to paraenesis. The correspondence of 1 Peter's social setting with the paraenetic social setting demonstrates that it belongs to the paraenetic genre. It completely reflects the social setting of paraenesis. A "preceptor," Peter, who is separated from his readers, writes to them after they have already been incorporated into the group but are experiencing adversity, exhorting them to stand firm by reflecting upon their initiation into the group and the glorious future awaiting them. It is this social setting that conclusively identifies 1 Peter as a paraenesis. In addition to the social setting, the social function also conforms to paraenesis. It reflects the primary paraenetic objective of socialization by attempting to effect $\delta\delta\xi\alpha$ in the lives of the recipients. In this regard 1 Peter has an unusual problem and attempts to resolve it by an appeal to eschatology. 1 Peter utilizes all the means for effecting socialization including persuasion and dissuasion, consolation, and establishment of group identity. In every way, 1 Peter conforms to the genre of paraenesis.

Although Berger established two genre determiners, he thinks that one or the other of them will be the primary determiner of the genre. If a genre requires a distinctive and consistent literary structure, then the literary form becomes the basic genre determiner. If the literary structure of a genre is fluid, the primary determiner is the social context, even if the genre has several recurring literary features. Since the paraenetic literary elements do not occur in fixed-static patterns or compositional structures but are used selectively and randomly by the ancient authors of paraeneses, the social context, not the literary form, is the fundamental paraenetic genre determiner.

Because the primary genre determiner of paraenesis is social context instead of literary form, the identification of 1 Peter as a paraenesis does not resolve its compositional structure. The literary features of paraenesis are helpful in analyzing the individual elements in a paraenetic document, but they do not explain how they are arranged and put together nor how the entire document is composed since the paraenetic genre adopts many compositional devices and assumes many different compositional structures. Therefore, each individual paraenetic document must be analyzed in order to ascertain the compositional devices used by the author.

Before initiating an analysis of the compositional devices and structure of 1 Peter in the next chapter, I must survey some paraenetic compositional devices that have been suggested by previous scholarship.

The Composition of Paraenesis

Paraenetic compositional structure has not received as much attention as has the nature and function of paraenetic materials. Martin Dibelius, the pioneer in New Testament paraenesis, is partially responsible for this neglect. He identified four literary features of paraenesis:

> The first feature is a pervasive eclecticism which is a natural consequence of the history and nature of paraenesis, since the concern is the transmission of an ethical tradition that does not require a radical revision even though changes in emphasis and form might occur. . . . A second, often noted characteristic of Jas is the lack of continuity. This, too, is explained by the literary character of paraenesis. Often enough a continuity of thought cannot be demonstrated in the above-mentioned paraenetic literature. . . . Associated with this feature is yet another characteristic of paraenetic literature: the repetition of identical motifs in different places within a writing . . . what was transmitted combined was left combined, and therefore, there were certain obstacles to the arrangement of the materials according to thought. . . . Finally, there is one other feature which Jas shares with other paraenetic literature: the admonitions in Jas do not apply to a single audience and a single set of circumstances; it is not possible to construct a single frame into which they all fit.[118]

Observing the series of imperatives or imperatival equivalents, Dibelius described paraenesis as a series of precepts or admonitions strung together like beads on a string.[119] His analogy led subsequent scholars to the conclusion that it was futile to search for compositional structure in paraenetic materials. His explanation that these precepts were connected by catchword connections or the undiscernible selection of the author satisfied scholars who then focused almost entirely on the "beads," the individual

---

[118]Dibelius, *James*, 5-11.

[119]Ibid., 6, says, ". . . the stringing together of saying after saying is the most common form of paraenesis." Even his definition of paraenesis reveals this conception. On page 3 he says, "By paraenesis we mean a text which strings together admonitions of general ethical content."

precepts and smaller paraenetic forms.[120] Three compositional forms have been studied. These include the two-ways schema, ethical lists--including virtue and vice lists as well as household and station codes--, and topoi. Because the two-ways schema is not well developed in 1 Peter,[121] my discussion will focus on the ethical lists and the topoi.

Ethical Lists

Virtue/Vice Lists

The composition of ethical lists uses the same devices as non-ethical lists. Anton Vögtle distinguishes between the asyndetic and the polysyndetic list. He says, "As in length and content, they also vary in asyndetic and polysyndetic stringing of elements."[122] Siegfried Wibbing agrees with Vögtle but offers some important modifications of the latter's basic position. He comments in the following:

> If one closely examines the New Testament virtue/vice lists, then it is evident that they alternate between asyndetic and polysyndetic arrangement of individual elements. In addition, some series deviate from these established traditional forms. These deviations arise from the attempt of individual authors to make an emphasis or a structure with a more stylistic speech.[123]

Wibbing cites 2 Corinthians 6:6 and 1 Timothy 4:12 where each member of the series is introduced by a preposition as examples of deviations to the normal asyndetic or polysyndetic lists. He also refers to 1 Timothy 1:9

---

[120]Ibid., says, "Although there is no continuity in the thought in such a string of sayings, there are formal connections. The best known device for an external connection in paraenetic literature is the *catchword*: one saying is attached to another simply because a word or cognate of the same stem appears in both sayings."

[121]There is implicit reference to the two ways in 1 Peter. The Christian way of life is distinguished from the life of the non-Christian. The two-ways form is not well represented in 1 Peter because the references to the non-Christians' way of life are only briefly mentioned while the Christian way of life is discussed at length. For paraenetic documents that utilize the two ways schema, see *Didache, Epistle of Barnabas*, and The Sermon on the Mount [especially Matthew 7:13-14].

[122]Vögtle, 13.

[123]Siegfried Wibbing, *Die Tugend- und Lasterkataloge im Neuen Testament,* Beihefte zur Zeitschrift für die Neutestamentliche Wissenschaft 25 (Berlin: Verlag Alfred Töpelmann, 1959), 78-79.

where two polysyndetic members are joined to the other double members asyndetically, to Ephesians 4:2, which introduces the first and third members with a preposition, and to Philippians 4:8, which has six members introduced by ὅσα and two by εἴ τις.[124] In spite of these deviations, he asserts that most of the New Testament lists follow one of the two normal forms of lists with the asyndetic form predominating.[125]

Vögtle proceeds to discuss seven compositional characteristics of these lists in the New Testament that are as follows:

1. The vices are related by associative connections.
2. Rising and falling series: (a) from more serious to less serious [Romans 1:29; Ephesians 5:3; compare 1 Corinthians 6:9; 1 Peter 4:15]; (b) from less serious to more serious [compare 2 Timothy 3:2].
3. The notions that designate the more external acts follow upon the notions that express the attitudinal sins.
4. The explication ensues from a more general notion [a summarizing notion of a sin-group or of the entire catalogue is named at the beginning] to more special notions [compare Romans 1:29: πᾶσα ἀδικία begins the catalogue; Ephesians 5:4: αἰσχρότης is analyzed into two special forms; further 1 Timothy 1:9; also 2 Timothy 3:2] or vice versa [compare Colossians 3:5; Ephesians 5:3].
5. In most catalogues, the arrangement of Galatians 5:19 could be found: (a) sexual sins, (b) sins against the religious order, (c) against neighborly love, (d) sins of intemperance.
6. Only in one case does Paul make use of a previous arrangement: In the catalogue of 1 Timothy 1:9, it is easy to see at least beginning with the fourth element the order of the Decalogue as determinative for the arrangement.
7. Rhetorical considerations that could be affecting the order and selection of ideas are only clearly in two catalogues [Romans 1:29; 2 Timothy 3:2]. . . .[126]

Although Wibbing agrees with these compositional features, he does not think there is an all-inclusive arrangement principle for the New Testament lists.[127] He explains his position below:

---

[124]Ibid., 79-80.

[125]Ibid., 81.

[126]Vögtle, 15-16. J. Rendel Harris, "The Influence of Philo upon the New Testament," *Expository Times* 37 (1926): 565-566, cites inclusio as the literary structure of the vice list in 2 Timothy 3:2-4. Hans Dieter Betz, *Lukian of Samosata und das Neue Testament*, Texte und Untersuchungen 76 (Berlin: Akademie-Verlag, 1961), 194, states that a major difference between Lucian and the New Testament in the use of ethical lists is that Lucian is more interested in the rhetorical effect rather than the paraenetic rules themselves while in the New Testament, this interest is reversed.

[127]Wibbing, 81.

Thus, the result is that apart from isolated lists, one cannot establish a particular unified structure ordered according to logical viewpoints. This conclusion corresponds to what was said above regarding the form so that the looser form and the unsystematic stringing together of elements belong together in the construction.[128]

He notes there is no uniformity of content nor of number of members in these lists.[129] McEleney also concludes regarding the vice lists in the Pastoral Epistles:

> Thus the variations in the vice lists of the Pastorals suggest that no specific and detailed list circulated as an *Urkatalog* which one might hopefully yet discover or at least reconstruct as a source for the materials here, but rather that certain influences and themes present in the literature of antiquity illumine the background from which the author drew these lists.[130]

Thus, each list must be individually analyzed to determine which compositional features it exhibits.

Vögtle lists only one virtue list (3:8) and three vice lists (2:1; 4:3, 15) in 1 Peter.[131] He does not analyze this virtue list in 1 Peter in detail stating only that it is made up of five members drawn primarily from Christian and Jewish sources.[132] The list is easily identified as an asyndetic list, but other compositional features are difficult to ascertain. Rhetorical devices like homoioteleuton may be influencing the arrangement and selection of adjectives and participles with the -ες sound dominating. However, a more significant issue that neither Vögtle nor Wibbing have addressed is the relationship of this virtue list to its context. It concludes the household code that began in 2:11, and it appears to continue in verse nine with the antithetical participles ἀποδιδόντες and εὐλογοῦντες. The failure of these scholars to address the contextual issue points out the pervasive problem in paraenetic compositional analysis that I have already noted. Attention has been given almost exclusively to the compositional

---

[128]Ibid., 86.

[129]Ibid., 81-86.

[130]Neil J. McEleney, "The Vice Lists of the Pastoral Epistles," *The Catholic Biblical Quarterly* 36 (1974): 217.

[131]Vögtle, 1. Wibbing, 78, agrees with Vögtle.

[132]Vögtle, 47, 188.

structure of the individual elements or forms without integrating these elements into the whole.

The three vice lists in 1 Peter encounter the same difficulty. The internal literary devices are easily ascertained, but their relationship to the larger context has not been resolved. Two of them (2:1; 4:15) are polysyndetic while only one (4:3) is asyndetic. The asyndetic list in 4:3 reflects the compositional device of the juxtaposition of similar notions since several terms such as excessive feasting and drinking allude to capitulating to the physical desires. The list in 2:1 may reflect a catechetical form that Selwyn calls *deponentes*, renunciation of certain sins viewed as incompatible with the new life.[133] The items in the catalogue of 4:15 appear to come from two different backgrounds as Selwyn notes, "Our author has passed from his catalogue of legal crimes to the social nuisance of interfering in other men's business and professing to put them to rights."[134] Although previous scholarship has made a contribution to identifying and analyzing virtue and vice lists, a serious problem remains regarding how these lists are integrated into larger paraenetic documents and how they function.

Household/Station Codes

A particular type of list that has received considerable attention since the important monographs of Alfred Seeberg, Martin Dibelius, and Karl Weidinger is the household or station code.[135] Wibbing says, relating the Haustafeln to the virtue and vice lists:

---

[133]Selwyn, *1 Peter*, 393-400. This notion had already been stated by Vögtle, 45, who said that these elements came from a store of tradition that listed sins to be avoided (ἀποτίθημι) like Ephesians 4:31; Colossians 3:8; James 1:21; and 1 Clement 13:1. See also Philip Carrington, *The Primitive Christian Catechism* (Cambridge: Cambridge University Press, 1940), 32-33, 47-49, 61-63.

[134]Ibid., 225.

[135]Alfred Seeberg, *Der Katechismus der Urchristenheit* (Leipzig: A. Deichert, 1903). Martin Dibelius, *Geschichte der urchristlichen Literatur* 2 (Berlin: Walter de Gruyter, 1926). Karl Weidinger, *Die Haustafeln, ein Stück urchristlicher Paraenese*, Untersuchungen zum Neuen Testament 14 (Leipzig: J. C. Heinrich, 1928). For a recent evaluation of the research on Haustafeln, see David L. Balch, "Household Codes," in *Greco-Roman Literature and the New Testament*, ed. David E. Aune, Society of Biblical Literature Sources for Biblical Study 21 (Atlanta, Georgia: Scholars Press, 1988), 25-50.

Now the difficulty lies in this: the virtue and vice lists as they confront us in their New Testament context unite in themselves the various elements of these traditions. In the lists related to the virtue and vice lists, the Haustafeln occupy a unique place in regard to this problem because they form an established uniform whole in the tradition. Their form and content are particularly unmistakable because of their purpose. The persons and also their duties were established by the circle encompassing the family: man, woman and children, masters and slaves [compare Ephesians 5:22f.; Colossians 3:18f.]; the parents should engage themselves in reciprocal love and their children should be obedient to them. The schema of such Haustafeln is demonstrated in the tradition by a relatively uniform form.[136]

Schrage more accurately defines the Haustafel as follows:

Under Haustafeln, I understand, as is customary, those paraenetic pieces whose form stands out from the otherwise freer, disorderly, eclectic series of New Testament exhortations by consistency and distinct disposition and whose content seeks to order the relationships of various groups.[137]

Thus, the Haustafeln exhibit a more or less fixed form and are sometimes called station codes, ethical lists that treat various stations of people and their duties.[138]

David Verner has thoroughly analyzed the compositional structure of the Haustafeln. He identifies three characteristics of the Haustafeln schema.[139] The first relates to the structure of the individual exhortations that he describes as follows:

---

[136]Wibbing, 77.

[137]Wolfgang Schrage, "Zur Ethik der neutestamentlichen Haustafeln," *New Testament Studies* 21 (1975): 2.

[138]David Schroeder, "Lists, Ethical," *Interpreters Dictionary of the Bible, Supplement* (Nashville, Abingdon, 1976), 546. This term *station code* was introduced by H. von Campenhausen, *Polykarp von Smyrna und die Pastoralbriefe* (Heidelberg: Carl Winter, 1951.)

[139]Balch, "Household Codes," 36-40 criticizes Verner's schema. On pages 36-37 he says, "Verner's thesis is doubly problematic. First, the definition of the 'schema' is ambiguous at both 'essential' points: a) the address may be either direct or indirect, and b) the imperative may be one of several grammatical forms. . . . Second, the characterization of the household management topos as an external influence and the 'schema' as an internal, Christian development over-emphasizes the uniqueness of the latter." Balch argues that the schema for individual exhortations in the household codes is not unique to Haustafeln but can be found in other paraenetical forms such as the Jewish wisdom literature and the Greek diatribe. Although Balch's criticism is valid, it does not detract

Firstly, there is an address [usually in the plural] to a group of persons
representing a certain social station [αἱ γυναῖκες, οἱ δοῦλοι, etc.]. Secondly,
there is an imperative, variously expressed with imperative proper, infinitive or
participle, and often accompanied by an object in the appropriate case. Thirdly,
there is an amplification, which is typically expressed as a prepositional phrase,
although other forms are used as well, especially the form μὴ [οὐ] . . .
ἀλλά. . . . The amplification either defines the imperative more fully [typically
as an adverb of manner] or provides a general motivation for it. Finally, there is a
reason clause providing motivation, theological justification, etc., which is
typically introduced by γάρ, ὅτι, or εἰδότες ὅτι. The reason clause may be
expanded into a paragraph.[140]

He applies this compositional scheme for the individual exhortations to
1 Peter 2:18f. The address is expressed by οἱ οἰκέται and the imperative
by ὑποτασσόμενοι. The antithesis, οὐ μόνον . . . ἀλλὰ καί, provides the
amplification, and the reason or motivation is expressed by τοῦτο γάρ,
which introduces a paragraph.[141] All of the individual exhortations in the
Haustafel in 1 Peter correspond to this scheme outlined by Verner.

The second characteristic of the Haustafeln scheme identified by
Verner pertains to the phenomenon that the exhortations do not occur
alone, but in series with other exhortations of the same type. He says, "The
link between exhortations is typically expressed with the connectives καί,
ὁμοίως, and καὶ ὁμοίως. These connectives are especially likely to link
together reciprocally related exhortations."[142]

In 1 Peter the four elements of the Haustafel are slaves, wives,
husbands, and everyone. Except for the last item, these are linked together
by ὁμοίως. Thus, the Petrine Haustafel exhibits this second schematic
characteristic identified by Verner.

Verner's third characteristic of the Haustafel scheme involves
development in several areas. The "reason-clauses" undergo development

---

from the fact that Verner's observation that this schema is used in the individual
exhortations of Haustafeln is correct and helpful.
    [140]Verner, 87. The essentials of this structure were first identified by James E.
Crouch, *The Origin and Intention of the Colossian Haustafel*, Forschungen zur Religion
und Literatur des Alten und Neuen Testaments 109 (Göttingen: Vandenhoeck & Ruprecht,
1972), 10.
    [141]Verner, 88.
    [142]Ibid.

especially in the direction of expansion. Thus the "reason-clause" in 1 Peter 2:18f. becomes an entire paragraph. In a similar direction, the "amplifications" become lengthier especially by the antithetical device *οὐ ... ἀλλά*. Another development involves the insertion of other exhortations among the individual exhortations of the Haustafel. Sometimes the individuals are addressed directly and at other times indirectly. Finally, greater liberties are taken with the basic schema. Groups of individuals are either added or taken away from the basic scheme.[143] The basic scheme can be modified, adapted, or even ignored.[144] This last feature has led Schrage to say that the Haustafel has no rigid schema but rather a form that could be altered in many ways.[145] Since its form fluctuated, Karris correctly stated that the listing of duties is the essential element of the Haustafel.[146]

1 Peter also reflects this third characteristic of Haustafeln identified by Verner. It develops and adapts the Haustafel scheme in several ways. One of the ways it alters the Haustafel scheme is by shifting the persons addressed. Following Thraede's suggestion, Balch convincingly argued that the Haustafel schema originated from the topos, "Concerning Household Management."[147] He cited Aristotle's *Politics* 1.1259.37-39 where three reciprocal relationships are discussed: masters and slaves, husbands and wives, and fathers and children. In 1 Peter this basic scheme is abbreviated, addressing only slaves, wives, and husbands. In 5:1-5 the community groups of elders and young men are even substituted for these pairs. 1 Peter also expands this basic scheme by concluding each of these codes with exhortations to all (3:8; 5:5).

---

[143]Ibid., 89.

[144]Ibid., 106-107.

[145]Schrage, "Zur Ethik," 3.

[146]Robert Joseph Karris, "The Function and Sitz im Leben of the Paraenetic Elements in the Pastoral Epistles" (Ph.D.diss., Harvard Divinity School, 1971), 87.

[147]Balch, passim but especially 9f. Klaus Thraede, "Ärger mit der Freiheit. Die Bedeutung von Frauen in Theorie und Praxis der alten Kirche," in *Die Beziehung von Mann und Frau als Frage an Theologie und Kirche*, ed. Gerta Scharffenorth (Berlin: Burckhardthaus, 1977), 131-181. See also Thraede, "Zum historischen Hintergrund der 'Haustafeln' des NT," in *Pietas*, Festschrift für Bernhard Kötting, ed. Ernst Dassmann and K. Suso Frank, Jahrbuch für Antike und Christentum 8 (Munich: Aschendorff, 1980), 359-368.

This development is not unique to 1 Peter, but it is shared by other Christian Haustafeln. Verner comments about the Haustafel in Polycarp's *Letter to the Philippians* 4:2--6:1:

> Here, of the three traditional family relationships, only that of husband and wife is addressed, although children are mentioned in the exhortation to wives. At the same time, other groups not traditionally discussed in the topos come into view: widows, deacons, young men, virgins, and presbyters.[148]

Indeed, Goppelt distinguishes between Christian Haustafeln that address societal groups and those that address groups in the community. He refers to the latter as a "Ständetafel," a station or community code.[149] Thus, in 1 Peter the first code in 2:18f. is a Haustafel proper while the second code in 5:1f. is a community or station code that addresses elders and young men. Verner contends that this distinction between the two types of codes is unnecessary.[150] Although it may be formally unnecessary, it is still a useful distinction that highlights the focus of the Haustafel either on societal or communal concerns.

Emphasizing subordination is another way in which 1 Peter altered the Haustafel scheme. Attempting to reconstruct the primitive Christian catechism, Carrington observed the emphasis on subordination in the New Testament Haustafeln. Influenced by Clement, who applied the phrase κανὼν τῆς ὑποτάξεως to this kind of catechetical teaching, Carrington called the Haustafeln, "Codes of Subordination."[151] Kamlah noted the emphasis placed on subordination in these codes, saying:

> It can certainly be said on the one hand that a specific feature of the early Christian Haustafel lies in the command of subordination because in no other similar exhortation such as is found in texts of stoically influenced popular philosophy and hellenistic Judaism is it demonstrated, to say nothing of such a domineering role. If one on the other hand designates it as an early Christian novel creation, he speaks rashly because although it is missing in the non-Christian station

---

[148]Verner, 86.

[149]Leonhard Goppelt, "Jesus und die "Haustafel"-Tradition," in *Orientierung an Jesus*, Festschrift für Josef Schmid, ed. Paul Hoffman (Freiburg: Herder, 1973), 94. This distinction is not original with Goppelt but goes back to Dibelius' commentary on the Pastoral Epistles. See also Karris, 96f.

[150]Verner, 107.

[151]Carrington, 37, 42-43, 49f.

exhortation per se, it can certainly be illustrated in connection with the individual topoi offered there.[152]

After surveying the ancient context for the New Testament Haustafeln, Balch states, "This survey has shown that the origin of the pattern of submissiveness is still problematic."[153] Thus, although the notion of subordination is not unique to 1 Peter, the strong emphasis on it is a peculiar feature of the Christian Haustafel.

Modern scholarship has been unanimous in affirming that the basic notion of the Haustafel in 1 Peter 2:18 is subordination.[154] Balch, who has thoroughly studied the Petrine Haustafel, says, "'Be submissive' might be viewed as the superscript of the whole code (2:13, 18; 3:1, 5; cp. 5:5)."[155] Scholarship has overlooked several problems that arise when submissiveness is designated as the basic notion of the code. First, not every group is exhorted to be submissive.[156] Crouch noted this problem in reference to the Colossian Haustafel. Criticizing Carrington's notion of codes of subordination, he says, "He ignores the fact that one half of the Haustafel in Colossians-Ephesians is not based on the idea of

---

[152]E. Kamlah, "Ὑποτάσσεσθαι in den neutestamentlichen Haustafeln," in *Verborum Veritas*, Festschrift für Gustav Stählin, ed. Otto Böcher and Klaus Haacker (Wuppertal: Theologischer Verlag Brockhaus, 1970), 242. Non-Christian parallels can be found in the lexicons under ὑποτάσσω. See Balch, 98f. for further examples. These non-Christian examples render improbable K. H. Rengstorf's contention that the use of the term, "subordinate," in connection with women is specifically Christian. See his monograph, *Mann und Frau im Urchristentum* (Köln: Westdeutschen Verlag, 1954) and his article, "Die neutestamentlichen Mahnungen an die Frau, sich dem Manne unterzuordnen," in *Verbum Dei Manet in Aeternum*, Festschrift für Otto Schmitz, ed. Werner Foester (Witten: Luther-Verlag, 1953), 131-145.

[153]Balch, 10.

[154]C. Freeman Sleeper, "Political Responsibility According to 1 Peter," *Novum Testamentum* 10 (1968): 275 says, "The author's use of this motif is vividly demonstrated in the section ii 13--iii 12. Here he takes over an independent body of paraenetic material, which is found in various forms in other New Testament literature. The dominant and unifying theme of this traditional material is that of subjection...." J. Ramsey Michaels, "Eschatology in 1 Peter III.17," *New Testament Studies* 13 (1966-1967): 395, says, "The whole section from 1 Pet. ii.13 to iii.9 deals with the principle of subordination in various spheres of human life...."

[155]Balch, 98.

[156]Bo Reicke, "Die Gnosis der Männer nach I. Ptr 3:7," *Neutestamentliche Studien für Rudolf Bultmann*, Beihefte zur Zeitschrift für die Neutestamentliche Wissenschaft 21 (Berlin: Alfred Töpelmann, 1954): 298-299, argues that the husband in this Haustafel is not being exhorted to submit.

submission."[157] So also, in 1 Peter 3:7 the husbands are not exhorted to be subject to their wives, and in 5:1-4 neither are the elders exhorted to be subject. Instead of the basic notion being subordination, the basic notion is that each group is exhorted to appropriately respond according to their station in life. Second, participles, not imperatives as in Colossians 3:18f. and Ephesians 5:22f., form the structure of this Haustafel. Unless one is prepared to identify these as imperatival participles, a finite verb must be found upon which they hang.[158] The imperative ὑποτάγητε does occur in 2:13, but another imperative τιμήσατε (2:17) intervenes between this imperative and the participles beginning in 2:18. The imperative τιμήσατε is thus the most obvious finite verb upon which all these participles hang. *Honor*, not *Be subject*, forms the basic notion of this Haustafel. Given these problems, it is obvious that modern scholarship has not correctly explained the basic notion of the Petrine Haustafel.

Failure to explain the basic notion of the Petrine Haustafel arises from an incorrect assessment of the composition of this Haustafel. As in the virtue and vice lists, advancement has been made in regard to the composition of the individual exhortations, but difficulties remain in regard to the inner relationship of these individual exhortations and in regard to the integration of the Haustafel into its context. Further compositional analysis is needed if both the internal and contextual composition of the Petrine ethical lists including both virtue/vice lists and Haustafel are satisfactorily explained.

Topoi

The final paraenetic compositional form that deserves attention is the *topos*. David G. Bradley first identified this paraenetic form stating, "A topos may be defined as the treatment in independent form of the topic of a proper thought or action, or of a virtue or a vice, etc."[159] He described the determining characteristic of this form as a compositional unit "composed

---

[157]Crouch, 17.

[158]Goppelt, *Petrusbrief*, 172, does identify these as imperatival participles but as I will demonstrate in Chapter 4, he is mistaken and thus ignores the compositional structure of this Haustafel.

[159]David G. Bradley, "The Topos as a Form in the Pauline Paraenesis," *Journal of Biblical Literature* 72 (1953): 240. See also idem, "The Origins of the Hortatory Material in the Letters of Paul (Ph.D. diss., Yale University, 1947), 39.

of more than one sentence dealing with the same subject."[160] He says more specifically:

> Thus, a topos may consist of an aggregation of proverbs or other short teachings on the same topic. In such a case the grouping of the proverbs [if they form a true topos and are not just a collection of sentences] finds unity in the common subject matter. This unity is often strengthened by the use of a recurring word which may serve as a binding element. . . . The key word serves a dual role: it is the name of the subject under discussion, while at the same time it acts, by sight [or sound] to link together the teachings which compose the topos.[161]

According to Bradley, the topics or themes that occasion and determine the topos are widely varied and include friends, sex, money, wine, parents, food, etc. His description of the topos has led Robert Funk to describe the topos as a "moral essay in miniature."[162]

Although widely used, Bradley's notion of topos has been severely criticized. Terence Mullins summarizes the formal criteria set up by Bradley and then offers his own critique:

> The formal elements would thus be only two: (1) it is composed of more than one sentence dealing with the same subject and (2) it often uses a recurring word which may serve as a binding element. The first of these would be the only necessary element and the second would be an optional element. This is, clearly, not an adequate set of criteria for establishing a form.[163]

In place of Bradley's two formal criteria, he proposes three essential elements plus one optional element:

> There are three essential elements: an injunction urging that a certain course of behavior be followed or avoided; a reason for the injunction; and a discussion of the logical or practical consequences of the behavior. An optional element is the citing of an analogous situation to the one dealt with in the Topos.[164]

---

[160]Ibid., "Topos," 243.

[161]Ibid., 243-244.

[162]Robert W. Funk, "The Letter: Form and Style," in idem, *Language, Hermeneutic, and Word of God* (New York: Harper & Row, 1966), 255.

[163]Terence Y. Mullins, "Topos as a New Testament Form," *Journal of Biblical Literature* 99 (1980): 542.

[164]Ibid., 542. Later he discusses refutation as another optional element. See 547.

Obviously, with this more restrictive definition of the topos, Mullins excludes some of the examples included by Bradley. It is not evident, however, that Mullins' critique and proposed solution are valid. His criticism that Bradley's description is too broad, vague, and inclusive is accurate, but his solution has confused the topos with the enthymeme as Aune notes, ". . . thinking to correct Bradley, he defines a form that is really an enthymeme."[165]

John Brunt accepts Mullins' criticisms and adds some criticisms of his own. He is particularly concerned with the term *topos* itself. He expresses this concern in the following:

> Although there can be no doubt that the paraenetic form of admonition identified by Bradley and elaborated by Mullins does indeed exist, it is confusing to call this form a *topos*. This is true in spite of the fact that the term has become widely accepted and is used in a way that is virtually synonymous with any stereotyped, recurring motif. The confusion arises from the use of the term *topos* in ancient classical rhetoric, where it had a quite different [although related] meaning. The element of something that is stereotyped and repeated is present, but the specific reference is to stereotyped arguments and types of appeals that can be applied to specific cases by prosecutors and defense attorneys in courtroom situations. These are called *topoi* by Greek authors and *communes loci* by Latin authors.[166]

Brunt's criticism has been substantiated by the numerous ways modern scholarship understands and uses the term topos. Malherbe comments about this varied usage of the term:

> The term "topos," which in ancient rhetoric described a topic or intellectual theme by which a speaker or writer made an argument plausible, was also applied to stock treatments of moral subjects. Some scholars think of topoi as clichés. . . . Others think of a topos as a treatment of a proper thought or action, or of a virtue or vice, in an independent form larger than a cliché. Still others, recognizing that certain elements occur regularly in the treatment of some subjects, describe topoi as recurring themes.[167]

---

[165]Aune, *Literature*, 223.

[166]John C. Brunt, "More on the Topos as a New Testament Form," *Journal of Biblical Literature* 104 (1985): 496-497.

[167]Malherbe, *Moral Exhortation*, 144.

Brunt concluded that Bradley was not dealing with one form but with a multiplicity of forms and that his imprecise formal criteria could allow almost anything as a topos.[168]

T. Conley states the uselessness of the term *topoi* if it is imprecisely defined. He discusses three broad areas to which the term topoi could refer. The first area includes "commonplaces," which are familiar metaphors, comparisons, similes, exempla, and themes. The second area comprises philosophical topoi, which are familiar themes traceable to some philosopher or school. The third area encompasses dialectical topoi, which go back to the lists collected by Aristotle in his *Topics* and *Rhetoric*. This latter area consists of arguments from etymology, from the lesser to the greater, and from opposites.[169] Although Conley has brought a measure of analytical description, his conception of topos is still very broad and the compositional structure very fluid.

Given these serious criticisms of Bradley's paraenetic topos as a literary form, it is not very useful for determining the compositional structure of 1 Peter. Nevertheless, his description of the topos does provide a compositional principle that may prove useful in a compositional analysis of 1 Peter. The topos establishes that paraenetic literary forms may be composed around a common theme or motif. In the next chapter I shall demonstrate this feature proves to be the key for unlocking the Petrine compositional structure.

Conclusion

In an effort to explain the compositional structure of 1 Peter by an appeal to genre, this chapter began with the attempt to establish by form critical means the genre of 1 Peter. Using the genre indicators of literary form and social context, it was demonstrated that 1 Peter corresponds to the paraenetic genre. Unfortunately, this genre is not determined by a fixed literary form but by its social context. This means that each paraenetic text or document must be individually analyzed in order to establish its literary

---

[168]Brunt, 499-500.

[169]T. Conley, "Philo's Use of Topoi," in *Two Treatises of Philo of Alexandria*, ed. David Winston and John Dillon (Chico, California: Scholars Press, 1983), 172-173.

composition.[170] Although some paraenetic compositional forms have been isolated like the two-ways schema, ethical lists, and topoi and some frequently occurring compositional elements have been noted, research has tended to focus on the "beads," the individual units, rather than the unifying compositional string. Since non-paraenetic compositional elements primarily determine the way these are used in a particular document, a careful analysis of an author's compositional style is necessary. Consequently, a literary analysis of 1 Peter is now in order. This literary analysis must identify the compositional elements used by this Petrine author to structure the body of his letter and demarcate the various sections and subsections.

---

[170]Verner, 125, says, "From the above sampling of paraenetic discourse, it can be concluded that paraenesis is often traditional and that often it is a challenging task to discern in it a coherence of presentation and/or perspective. A given paraenetic text may, however, express its relation to tradition in a variety of ways. Furthermore, both the degree and the means of coherence may vary from one instance to the next. Thus the question of how and to what extent a given paraenetic text reflects a coherent perspective can be answered only by examination of that particular text."

CHAPTER 4

LITERARY ANALYSIS

Literary analyses of 1 Peter are not lacking as Chapter 1 of this dissertation demonstrated. Chapter 1 also called attention to the widely divergent conclusions that these literary analyses have reached. The latest commentary on 1 Peter begins with a statement of Stephen Neill, who reflected on the commentaries of Selwyn and Beare, "Now if two scholars can arrive at such widely divergent results, both on the basis of theoretically scientific methods of study, something must have gone seriously wrong somewhere."[1] Indeed, something has gone wrong in these literary analyses, and that something is method. A careful search for the appropriate method by which the compositional structure of 1 Peter can be explicated must be made. In Chapter 2, I established that the first level of the compositional analysis of 1 Peter should identify the letter formulas. Having done that, everything was explained except the body-middle extending from 1:14 to 5:11. In Chapter 3, I attempted to expose the compositional structure of the body-middle by identifying its genre. Unfortunately, the paraenetic genre to which 1 Peter belongs is not determined by a definite compositional structure. Although specific compositional elements can be isolated, the overall composition cannot be explained by an appeal to its genre. Consequently, a second level of the compositional analysis of this letter is necessary. This second level must devise a method of literary analysis that can explain the compositional structure of the letter-body of 1 Peter. This chapter will devote itself to the development and application of a method of literary analysis appropriate for this document.

---

[1]Stephen Neill, *The Interpretation of the New Testament 1861-1961* (London: Oxford University Press, 1964), 344; quoted in Michaels, *1 Peter*, xxxi.

Development of the Method

General consensus maintains that the literary analysis of W. J. Dalton is the most adequate analysis available. Confirming Dalton's analysis, Édouard Cothenet states, "However, Dalton, inspired by the work of A. Vanhoye on Hebrews, has proposed a sufficient enough plan."[2] David Balch states more optimistically, "The most successful attempt to analyze the plan of 1 Peter is that by Dalton."[3] Chevallier, J. N. D. Kelly, Charles Talbert, and others concur with Cothenet and Balch.[4]

Dalton's analysis adopts the method developed by Vanhoye in his analysis of Hebrews.[5] He summarizes this method in the following:

> Vanhoye suggests six types of indications which reveal the literary structure: prior announcement of the theme, inclusion, link-words, repetition of key words, change from statement to exhortation or vice versa, symmetrical disposition of the matter. These provide the basis for our following exposition.[6]

To these six literary indicators developed by Vanhoye, Dalton adds another devised by Stanislas Lyonnet in his commentary in the Jerusalem Bible.[7] This indicator is the use of Scripture quotation to conclude a section or to develop the thought of a section.[8] Dalton thinks these seven literary indicators provide a sufficient method for analyzing the compositional structure of 1 Peter.

Using this method, his analysis identifies three major sections in the letter. First, 1:3--2:10 treats the dignity of the Christian vocation and its responsibilities. This section is divided into two parts: the Christian vocation, 1:3-25, and responsibilities of the Christian vocation, 2:1-10. Second, 2:11--3:12 deals with obligations of the Christian life. This section

---

[2]Édouard Cothenet, "Les Orientations Actuelles de l'Exégèse de la Première Lettre de Pierre," in *Études sur la première Lettre de Pierre*, ed. Charles Perrot, Lectio Divina 102 (Paris: Cerf, 1980), 26.

[3]Balch, *Wives*, 123.

[4]Chevallier, 129-130; Kelly, 21; Talbert, "Plan," 141 note 1.

[5]Albert Vanhoye, *La Structure Littéraire de L'Épître aux Hébreux*, Studia Neotestamentica 1 (Paris: Desclée de Brouwer, 1963).

[6]Dalton, *Proclamation*, 74 note 12.

[7]Stanislas Lyonnet, *Les Epîtres de Saint Paul aux Galates, aux Romains* (Paris: Cerf, 1953). See also idem, "Note sur le plan de l'épître aux Romains," Recherches de science religieuse 39-40 (1951-1952): 301-316.

[8]Ibid., 76.

breaks into three parts: conduct in the pagan world, 2:11-12, traditional catechesis on various aspects of conduct, 2:13--3:7, and charity, 3:8-12. Third, 3:13--5:11 is concerned with the theme of persecution. This section contains two parts: persecution viewed in calm detachment, 3:13--4:11; and persecution faced realistically, 4:12--5:11.[9]

Almost every scholar who praises Dalton's plan also admits that it is less than adequate. Chevallier thinks Dalton was not as specific as he could have been, and he attempts to remedy this defect in his analysis.[10] As I have already mentioned, Chevallier's analysis is even less satisfactory than Dalton's. After praising Dalton, Kelly warns in his commentary:

> The reader should be warned, however, not to look for clear-cut, confident conclusions. If it is certain that the author drew on conventional outlines [catechetical, liturgical, etc.], it is also certain that they were not verbally fixed, and that he felt completely at liberty to expand or recast them as suited his purposes.[11]

Talbert adds his criticism stating, "Even if the unity of 1:3--2:10 is grasped, there are difficulties with how 2:11--5:11 fits together. This is true even for W. J. Dalton."[12] Even Dalton himself admits that his analysis is deficient. After laying out his outline, he adds, "Not every detail of the plan above will be accepted, but its general lines, probably, will be admitted as objective."[13] Concerning the material following 4:6, he confesses, "What follows in the epistle is not easy to define in terms of a total plan."[14]

Dalton's analysis is deficient for several reasons. First, he is not sensitive to the letter formulas. He fails to distinguish the Blessing Section in 1:3-12 from the body of the letter. His analysis does not account for the body opening in 1:13 nor for the body closing in 5:12. Second, his analysis fails to explicate the unifying theme or compositional device that connects the three major parts of the letter. He cannot explain how the second section, 2:11--3:12, dealing with the obligations of the Christian life,

---

[9]Ibid., 83.
[10]Chevallier, passim.
[11]Kelly, 21.
[12]Talbert, "Plan," 141 note 1.
[13]Dalton, *Proclamation*, 84.
[14]Ibid., 81.

differs from the responsibilities of the Christian vocation in the first section, 1:3--2:10. Neither can he explain how the third section, 3:13--5:11, which deals with persecution, relates to the first two sections. Third, his method of analysis does not derive from the text of 1 Peter but from Hebrews. As my study of the paraenetic genre disclosed, each paraenetic document must be analyzed on its own compositional terms. The author of 1 Peter may or may not have used the compositional devices used by the author of Hebrews. He may have developed other compositional devices altogether. In order to develop an adequate compositional method, the compositional devices that arise in the text of 1 Peter must take precedence over those derived from other texts.

Agreeing that Dalton's identification of compositional techniques is the correct approach, William Schutter adopts his method with several important improvements.[15] First, he is sensitive to the letter formulas in his compositional analysis.[16] Second, he is much more rigorous in his attempt to identify the use of the seven literary indicators identified by Dalton. Third, he completely analyzes the epistle whereas Dalton gave less attention to the compositional structure of the epistle's end. In spite of these improvements, however, Schutter's analysis possesses many of the same deficiencies as Dalton's. Because he does not identify the unifying theme or compositional device that controls the composition of 1 Peter, he is unable to distinguish major from minor transitions, inclusios and link words from simple repetition of words, and major themes from minor ones.[17] Neither can he explain how the various sections are related to one another. Since his method is based upon the literary devices used by the author of Hebrews, he, like Dalton, has not recognized the major compositional devices of 1 Peter. In addition, Schutter analyzes the compositional structure of 1 Peter before he identifies its genre. Consequently, he fails to relate the compositional structure to the genre of

---

[15]Schutter, *Hermeneutic*, 19, note 1, says, "For compositional techniques in 1 Peter see W. J. Dalton, *Spirits*, 74-83, M.-A. Chevallier, 'Structure,' 129-42, and D. L. Balch, *Wives*, 123ff. The studies of Dalton and Chevallier are seriously incomplete, devoting most of their attention to 1.1--2.10, less to 4.12--5.11, and hardly any to 2.11--4.11."

[16]He correctly identifies all the letter formulas except for those associated with the letter-body. For a critique, see Chapter 2 above.

[17]Specific examples will be given below as the compositional analysis of this dissertation interacts with Schutter's work.

the letter. In spite of these deficiencies, he has contributed to the recognition of possible inclusios, link words, key words, transitions, and themes in the letter. His suggestions, however, must be tested by the major compositional features of 1 Peter.

Although the method used by Dalton and Schutter is deficient, it nevertheless provides the appropriate direction for a complete analysis of the letter-body. Their attempt to isolate the compositional devices is the correct approach. Almost all of the devices that they identified are utilized by the author of 1 Peter, but since they were using a method developed for Hebrews, they failed to isolate the major devices used by the author of 1 Peter. I will now attempt to identify these major devices.

The appropriate place to begin to locate compositional devices is in the recognition that the letter-body of 1 Peter is a paraenesis. H. D. Betz made an important observation about paraenetic texts that provides the clue for unraveling the paraenetic compositional structure. He noticed the importance of *ethos* in paraenetic texts, saying:

> Finally, societal units of every kind possess what is called "ethos," a distinguishable but implicit life-style based upon cultural values and represented mostly by attitudes and symbols. This "ethos" functions to identify cultural groups and to set them off from each other.[18]

His observation indicates that in paraenetic texts the exhortation will be tailored to fit the ontological status of the persons addressed. The exhortations given to a company of soldiers preparing for battle will be different from the exhortations given to children preparing for school. Although his observation pertains primarily to collective groups, it also applies to individuals. The exhortations directed to a king will be different from exhortations directed to a pauper since his ontological status is quite different. The description of the ontological status of the reader or hearer of a paraenesis is eminently important for analyzing paraenetic texts since the prescriptions are linked to and determined by this status.

Abraham Malherbe and Kathleen Wicker have described this feature of paraenetic texts in Dio Chrysostom and Plutarch respectively. Malherbe

---

[18]H. D. Betz, "Introduction," in *Plutarch's Ethical Writings and Early Christian Literature*, ed. idem, Studia ad Corpus Hellenisticum Novi Testamenti 4 (Leiden: E. J. Brill, 1978), 2-3.

cites Synesius' *Dio* 1.11, who says that Dio admonished people of all
stations [καθ' ἕνα καὶ ἀθρόους], and then comments:[19]

> His statement is referred to here because of the significance it attains when seen in
> the context of discussions of the need for the philosopher to give attention to
> individuals and to vary his exhortation according to the condition he
> addresses. . . . The desirability of individual and personalized instruction was
> widely recognized.[20]

Wicker articulates this same notion in Plutarch's *Mulierum Virtutes* where
Plutarch affirms the essential unity of virtue but admits that it is expressed
in different ways in the lives of specific individuals (*Moralia* 243D).[21]
Thus, in both Dio Chrysostom and Plutarch, admonitions are linked to the
ontological status of the person addressed.

This correlation of the ontological status with the appropriate
admonitions in paraenetic texts yields two basic types of paraenetic
compositional structures. In the first type, the ontological status and the
admonitions are expressed in two distinct sections of the document.
Konrad Gaiser's study of Plato's *Dialogues* relates them to this type of
paraenesis. He asserts that the Platonic *Dialogues* are primarily interested
in the ontological question of the relationship of the world of forms to the
world of sense experience. It is this content that determines the form of
the dialogues. Occasionally in the dialogues, Plato turns to a concern for
protreptikos or *paraenesis*. His interests shift to a concern for human
behavior. Gaiser argues, however, that this concern is always secondary
and subsumed to the ontological concern, which always determines the
form of the dialogue. He thinks that an increasing concern for correct
human conduct led Plato to first insert paraenesis in the middle of the
speeches and then to move it to the end of the speech where he connected it
with myth, making the paraenesis much more potent.[22] Since Gaiser is able
to isolate two distinct sections dealing with ontological status and

---

[19]Malherbe, "Moral Exhortation," 244 note 31.

[20]Ibid., 244. See page 244 note 32 for a list of other primary sources that
recognize the need of personalized instruction. Malherbe lists the personalized instructions
in 1 Thessalonians, 245-246.

[21]Kathleen Wicker, "*Mulierum Virtutes* (*Moralia* 242E-263C)," in Betz,
Plutarch, 107.

[22]Konrad Gaiser, *Protreptik und Paränese bei Platon*, Tübinger Beiträge zur
Altertumswissenschaft 40 (Stuttgart: Kohlhammer Verlag, 1959), passim.

exhortation, Plato's *Dialogues* clearly belong to the first type of paraenetic structure.

In the second type of paraenetic structure, the ontology and the admonitions are interwoven. Statements of ontological status are joined directly with their appropriate exhortations. The two kinds of material are not relegated to two distinct sections, but ontological statements and admonitions are scattered throughout the document. In documents of this type, careful attention to the ontological statements and their accompanying exhortations provide an essential analytical device.

Turning to 1 Peter, I find that it is composed according to the second type of paraenetic structure. Statements of ontological status are intercalated with their correlative admonitions. This compositional structure has always troubled scholars who approach 1 Peter from a Pauline perspective. Since Pauline letters generally follow the first type of paraenetic compositional structure with distinct sections of ontology and exhortation, scholars have been perplexed that 1 Peter did not follow this scheme.[23] What has long been perplexing, now becomes the basis for understanding the compositional structure of 1 Peter. The ontological statements and their admonitions provide the compositional markers for the sections of 1 Peter.

These ontological statements in 1 Peter are almost exclusively expressed by similes and metaphors.[24] This fact has been largely overlooked because these similes and metaphors have become "frozen," which means they have lost their metaphorical aspect and are now perceived as literal. Albert Katz observes that with continued use metaphors lose their metaphoricity and are no longer perceived as non-

---

[23]Talbert, "Plan," 142-143, correctly recognizes the importance of the ontological ground and the corresponding admonitions for determining the plan of 1 Peter. He says, "Any adequate plan of 1 Peter must reflect the fact that 1:3--2:10 deals with the ground of Christian existence . . . while 2:11--5:11 treats the norms of Christian behavior. . . ." His analysis is faulty because he insists on distinct sections of ontology and exhortation as one finds in Paul. Talbert fails to recognize that 1 Peter intercalates ontological ground with corresponding exhortation.

[24]David R. Olson, "Or What's a Metaphor For?" *Metaphor and Symbolic Activity* 3 (1988): 216, says that the simplest characteristic of a metaphor is a discrepancy between what you say and what you mean.

literal.[25] Commenting on the frequent metaphors in Christian texts, Albert Wifstrand remarks, "All this is familiar to us as we have grown accustomed to these frequent metaphors because of Christianity."[26] With almost two thousand years of usage, the modern scholar cannot "hear" these metaphors as the first readers did nor as the author meant them. The intervening years have dulled our metaphorical ears.

John Elliott's entire approach to 1 Peter is misleading because he insists on reading these metaphors as literal speech.[27] He states that a metaphorical understanding of these terms "has resulted in a serious misconception of the letter as a whole."[28] Because the author refers to the readers as *strangers* and *aliens*, Elliott concludes that the recipients of this letter are disenfranchised peoples, living on the fringes of society. Christians are not citizens or participants in the mainstream of society. The primary objective of the letter is to provide a "home for the homeless." The strategy of the letter is to encourage the readers to remain aliens and not to move into the mainstream of society.[29] The major fallacy in Elliott's study is his assumption that the terms *strangers* and *aliens* should be understood in their literal socio-political meaning. There are many indications in 1 Peter that the recipients were not literally strangers or aliens. Since they are obviously Gentile, the only way to understand the phrase *strangers of the dispersion* in 1:1 is metaphorically.[30] The expectation in 4:4 that the readers would participate in society does not indicate that the recipients were living on the fringes. Despite Elliott's assertion that the sociological status of the recipients was not determined by the redeeming action of God, it is precisely this action that integrated them

---

[25]Albert Katz, and others, "Norms for 204 Literary and 260 Nonliterary Metaphors on 10 Psychological Dimensions," *Metaphor and Symbolic Activity* 3 (1988): 194.

[26]Wifstrand, 172.

[27]David L. Balch, "Hellenization/Acculturation in 1 Peter," in *Perspectives on 1 Peter*, ed. Charles H. Talbert, National Association of Baptist Professors of Religion Special Studies Series 9 (Macon, Georgia: Mercer University Press, 1986), 79-101, has a penetrating refutation of Elliott's view of the social conflict in 1 Peter.

[28]Elliott, *Home*, 129.

[29]John H. Elliott, "1 Peter, Its Situation and Strategy: A Discussion with David Balch," in *Perspectives on 1 Peter*, ed. Charles H. Talbert, National Association of Baptist Professors of Religion Special Studies Series 9 (Macon, Georgia: Mercer University Press, 1986), 61-78.

[30]This was first championed by Steiger. See Chapter 2, pages 45-46, of this dissertation.

into their present sociological status according to 1:3 and 2:9. If these terms are not taken in their literal but their metaphorical meaning, then Elliott's entire argument collapses. I would assert that his failure to appreciate the metaphorical use of these terms "has resulted in a serious misconception of the letter as a whole."[31]

In contrast to Elliott, many scholars have observed the metaphors in 1 Peter. The work of J. D. Schulze is particularly worthy of note. Among the metaphors and similes that he lists are the new birth (1:3, 23), newborn babes (2:2), testing of faith is more precious than gold (1:7), girding up the loins of your mind (1:13), Christ the lamb (1:19) and shepherd (2:25; 5:4), sincere milk (2:2), living stones, spiritual house, holy priesthood (2:5), royal priesthood (2:9), strangers and aliens (2:11), wanderiing sheep (2:25), the secret man of the heart (3:4), good stewards (4:10), and the Devil as a roaring lion (5:8).[32] Schulze has not identified all the metaphors that occur in 1 Peter, but as this list demonstrates, the author of 1 Peter was very fond of them.[33]

Since metaphors and similes are used to express the ontological status of the recipients, they become important compositional indicators. It would be incorrect to assume that every metaphor in the letter is a compositional indicator. Only those metaphors that describe or relate directly to the readers and provide the basis for an exhortation determine the compositional structure. These metaphors not only describe the readers but also determine the exhortations addressed to them. Moreover, metaphor clusters, a series of metaphors connected in ancient thought, become the primary indicators of the major sections of the letter.[34] Thus, the metaphor of the new birth fits well with the child and milk metaphor. Likewise, the metaphor of strangers and aliens is apropos to that of free

---

[31]In his earlier work, *The Elect and the Holy* (Leiden: E. J. Brill, 1966), he does not take these metaphors literally.

[32]Johann Daniel Schulze, *Der schriftstellerische Charakter und Werth des Petrus, Judas, und Jakobus zum Behuf der Specialhermeneutik ihrer Schriften* (Weißenfels: Bösesche Buchhandlung, 1802), 31-32.

[33]L. Radermacher, "Der erste Petrusbrief und Silvanus," *Zeitschrift für die neutestamentliche Wissenschaft* 25 (1926): 289, says, "... the particle ὡς and once καθό are found in it because of a predilection for metaphor."

[34]Paul S. Minear, *Images of the Church in the New Testament* (Philadelphia: The Westminster Press, 1960), uses the terms *metaphor cluster* and *metaphor constellation*. See page 67.

men. By perceiving the movement from one metaphor cluster to another, the major compositional sections of the letter-body can be ascertained. In 1 Peter, therefore, metaphor is the major literary device used to structure the letter-body.

Along with metaphor, the author also uses various transitional devices to mark the structure of the letter. These transitional devices are of two types. One type marks the movement to a major section while the other signals minor movements within a section. These types are not mutually exclusive since a major transitional device in one passage may be used in another passage as a minor transition. The metaphor clusters are indispensable for determining major from minor transitions. Transitional devices in the letter include introductory similes, conjunctions, conditional sentences, disjunctive constructions, asyndetic statements, and conjunctive participles.[35] All of these will be explicitly noted as the analysis proceeds.

Our proposed analytical method is now in place. By using the twin compositional devices of metaphor and transitional markers, the compositional structure and plan of 1 Peter can be uncovered. In the next section of this chapter, I shall apply this method to the letter-body of the document.

Application of the Method

Diaspora--The Controlling Metaphor

The controlling metaphor of 1 Peter is the Diaspora.[36] This metaphor is announced in the prescript and reiterated in the greeting section of 1 Peter. The letter is addressed to *the elect strangers of the Dispersion* in 1:1. In 5:13 *the co-elect in Babylon* send greetings. As Michaels correctly notes, "*Babylon* at the end of the epistle is simply the counterpart to *Diaspora* at the beginning."[37]

---

[35]The "conjunctive participle" is a concept used by Wifstrand, 175-176.

[36]Because of the explicit use of the term *Diaspora*, all commentators recognize the presence of this idea in 1 Peter. Surprisingly, however, none of the commentators have recognized the important role that this metaphor plays in the compositional structure of the document.

[37]Michaels, *1 Peter*, 311.

The term *co-elect* [συνεκλεκτή] in the greetings section is variously interpreted. The term is a nominative feminine singular adjective. The exegetical issue requires that some noun be supplied, at least in thought. The oldest commentaries along with Codex Sinaiticus and the Vulgate add either ἐκκλησία or *ecclesia* depending upon whether the writing is in Greek or Latin.[38] This position is maintained by almost all of the modern commentators but is problematic because the term ἐκκλησία occurs nowhere else in the text of 1 Peter.[39] Some of the post Reformation commentators, as well as Charles Bigg in more recent times, understand the phrase to refer to Peter's wife.[40] This interpretation is given credence by the reference to the author's son in the next phrase. However, the prepositional phrase ἐν Βαβυλῶνι renders this suggestion improbable.[41] The simplest suggestion is to supply ἀδελφότης [brotherhood]. This term was used just four verses previously in 5:9 and therefore is present in the context. Furthermore, the cognate term ἀδελφός [brother] is frequently used in the prescripts and greetings sections of Diaspora correspondence.[42] Another possible suggestion is to supply the term διασπορά [Diaspora] in 5:13.[43] Supplying Diaspora in the greetings section provides for greater

---

[38]See Bigg, 197, for a discussion of the position of the older references.

[39]Michaels, *1 Peter*, 310, says, "Ἐκκλησία, *congregation* [a term never used in 1 Peter] is probably implied here." So also Best, *1 Peter*, 177-178; Beare, *1 Peter*, 184; Brox, *Petrusbrief*, 247; Goppelt, *Petrusbrief*, 350-351; Kelly, 218; Reicke, *1 Peter*, 134; Selwyn, *1 Peter*, 243.

[40]Bigg, 197, translates the phrase, "the fellow-elect woman in Babylon." He explains that the phrase can refer to Peter's wife or to the church. Opting for the former, he says, "Against the metaphorical interpretation it may be argued that ἡ ἐν Βαβυλῶνι is an unprecedented and perhaps impossible phrase for *the Church in Babylon*. Bengel, Mayerhoff, Jachmann, and Alford all understand the phrase to refer to Peter's wife.

[41]Best, *1 Peter*, 177, says, "If it is an actual person she can only be Peter's wife (cf. 1 Cor. 9:5), but it is a strange way to introduce her; we would expect 'with me' rather than 'in Babylon'; she would hardly have been so well-known over so wide an area that such a vague reference would identify her; moreover the 'fellow' of 'fellow-elect' implies 'fellow-elect' with the readers and not with the writer."

[42]See the letters of Gamaliel (I or II?) in J. *Sanh*. 18d; B. *Sanh*. 18d; Tos. *Sanh* 2.6. See also *2 Baruch* 78:2 and 82:1. The letter in Acts 15 from the Jerusalem Assembly utilizes brotherhood terms in its salutation.

[43]I do not think that anyone else has ever suggested this possibility. If διασπορά is supplied, then this letter becomes a communication between the two very different segments of the Jewish Diaspora. Menahem Stern, "Diaspora," *Encyclopaedia Judaica*, vol. 6: *Di-Fo* (New York: Macmillan Co., 1971), 9, says, "Only one large Jewish group, that in Babylonia and in the countries of the Parthian Empire, was outside the sphere of

correspondence with the prescript. The co-elect Diaspora in Babylon sends greetings to those of the Diaspora of Asia Minor.[44] Regardless of whether brotherhood or Diaspora is understood as the ellipsed noun, Michaels' observation that the greetings section provides a counterpart to the Diaspora of the prescript remains valid.

Commenting on the non-Pauline character of the metaphors in the prescript, Goppelt observes their importance for introducing the theme of 1 Peter:

> The recipients are designated with none of the typical pauline expressions, such as ἀγαπητός, κλητός, ἅγιος, πιστός, ἐκκλησία. In comparison with Paul, *1 Peter* has utilized strange designations *for the recipients* which introduces the theme of the letter. This designation also appears in other letters such as James and in the Apostolic Fathers and belongs to the nonpauline tradition: James 1:1 ἐν τῇ διασπορᾷ, *1 Clement*, Polycarp's *Philippians*, and *Martyrdom of Polycarp*'s prescript τῇ ἐκκλησίᾳ τῇ παροικούσῃ.[45]

Although Goppelt correctly observed the importance of the metaphors, he failed to capitalize upon his observation. Instead of focusing upon the conception of the Diaspora as the controlling theme, he emphasized the notion of strangers [παρεπίδημοι] stating, "The designation of the readers as παρεπίδημοι programmatically introduces here the first part (1:3--2:10) and then in 2:11, supplemented by πάροικοι, the second part (2:11--4:11)."[46] Goppelt's failure to correctly assess Diaspora as the controlling theme renders him unable to relate the third part of the letter (4:12--5:11)

Hellenistic or Roman political rule during the greater part of the period and developed its own form of life, which in the course of time influenced Jewry as a whole."

[44]Because the Diaspora metaphor dominates this letter, scholars have probably been too hasty to connect Babylon with Rome as do apocalyptic writings like Revelation 14:8; 17:5, 18; 18:2, *Sibylline Oracles* 4:143; 5:159, and *2 Baruch* 11:1; 67:7. Brox, *Petrusbrief*, 247, cogently argues, ". . . this cryptogram is hardly meant to be taken seriously in its apocalyptic drama because that would harmonize badly with 2:13f. and 1 Peter does not reveal in any passage a reservation against the state and the state is never presented as the one who causes the suffering [= persecution]." This positive attitude toward the state is more characteristic of a Diaspora setting than the setting of those apocalyptic writings that portray Rome as the evil world power that persecutes God's people. The Diaspora setting seriously weakens the attempt to establish the provenance of 1 Peter by equating the term *Babylon* with Rome.

[45]Goppelt, *Petrusbrief*, 76.

[46]Ibid., 79.

to the controlling theme that he identified.[47] Nevertheless, he does identify the compositional significance of the metaphors in the prescript of 1 Peter.[48]

In order to understand how the metaphor of the Diaspora controls the composition of 1 Peter, it is necessary to distinguish between two essential aspects of a metaphor: the image-contributor and the image-receptor.[49] Klaus Berger explains this distinction:

> Since Weinrich, a distinction is made between image-contributor and image-receptor. In the metaphorical predication, "I am the brightly shinning morning-star," (Revelation 22:16), Jesus is the image-receptor and the field of Astronomy is the image-contributor.[50]

Although he does not use this terminology, F. Lau identifies the image-contributor and the image-receptor in 1 Peter as follows:

> Christendom has taken over from Judaism the notion of the Diaspora and the consciousness of living in the Diaspora as well as in the Dispersion. The author of James greets the 12 tribes in the Diaspora (James 1:1) and the author of 1 Peter greets the elect strangers of the dispersion of Pontus and other provinces of Asia Minor (1 Peter 1:1). At bottom lies the thought that the Israel according

---

[47]It is his failure to recognize Diaspora as the controlling metaphor that causes him to misplace 3:13--4:11. He places this subsection in the second major section of the letter rather than taking it as the beginning of the third major section. See the analysis in Chapter 4 of this dissertation.

[48]Heinrich Rendtorff, *Getrostes Wandern: Eine Einführung in den ersten Brief des Petrus*, Die urchristliche Botschaft 20 (Hamburg: Furche, 1951), 18, had already observed the compositional significance of these metaphors in the prescript. He states, "The theme of the entire letter is contained in these first verses: Elect Strangers, preordained homeless in the world because destined for God. The letter wants to do nothing else than to unfold this view of the Christian life." Rendtorff sees the entire letter as an exposition of the Christian life viewed primarily as a life of alienation in the world. He is essentially correct in identifying the position of the readers as strangers and aliens as the overall compositional theme of the letter. His exposition goes awry, however, because, like Bernhard Weiss, he actually uses the theme of hope to explain the letter's composition. See his outline of the letter on pages 7-8.

[49]This distinction was explicated by Harald Weinrich, *Sprache in Texten* (Stuttgart: Klett, 1976), 276-341.

[50]Klaus Berger, *Formgeschichte des Neuen Testaments* (Heidelberg: Quelle & Meyer, 1984), 32.

to the spirit is also strewn among the peoples just as the Israel according to the flesh.[51]

Thus, in the metaphor of the Diaspora utilized by 1 Peter, the Jewish Diaspora is the image-contributor and the Christian community is the image-receptor. The author of 1 Peter took images and concepts from the Jewish Diaspora and applied them to his readers in order to describe their ontological status and their moral obligations.[52] Since the images and concepts taken over from the Jewish Diaspora control the composition of 1 Peter, these images must be carefully analyzed.

The Diaspora images and concepts utilized in 1 Peter fall into two categories: general images that pervade the entire letter and specific images that are limited to particular sections. The general images set up the rhetorical situation, reveal the author's purposes for writing, and lend continuity to the document while the specific images provide the author with the means for accomplishing his purposes and also demarcate the various sections of the letter. The former will now be discussed while the latter will be treated as each section of the letter is explained.

Any study of the images and concepts of the Jewish Diaspora must acknowledge the important caveat articulated by John Collins. He states, "It should be apparent from the foregoing chapters that there was no simple normative definition determining Jewish identity in the Hellenistic

---

[51]F. Lau, "Diaspora," *Die Religion in Geschichte und Gegenwart*, vol. 2: *D-G* (Tübingen: J. C. B. Mohr (Paul Siebeck), 1958), 177.

[52]Elliott, *Home*, 48, states, "The terms *diaspora* (1:1) and *Babylon* (5:13) indicate the similar condition of both Christian addressees and authors. They also express an additional religious-historical dimension of the condition of Christian estrangement in society. Like the words 'elect [visitors of the Diaspora in . . . ,' 1:1] and 'coelect [of Babylon . . . ,' 5:13] they recall, from a religious-historical perspective, the link of the Christian strangers and aliens with both the alienated predicament and the exalted status of God's unique redeemed community. The religious implications of the terms *diaspora* and *Babylon* in no way vitiate the social conditions of the strangers and aliens to whom they are applied. Nor do they suggest or, even less, require that *paroikia, paroikoi* and *parepidemoi* be taken in an exclusively figurative or 'spiritual' sense. To the contrary, their evocative power derives from the fact that now Christians, like God's Israel of old, find themselves in an analogous situation of actual social and religious estrangement and alienation." As this quote demonstrates, Elliott has already recognized the importance of the notion of the Diaspora in the description of the readers' ontological status. Unfortunately he refuses to see the metaphorical dimension of this notion in 1 Peter and its consequent role in the composition of the letter.

Diaspora. There are, however, some persistent tendencies."[53] Collins correctly recognized that the Jewish Diaspora was variously interpreted and described by both Jews and Gentiles. Therefore, the images and concepts selected by the author of 1 Peter may not be substantiated by every surviving source that discusses the Diaspora. Nevertheless, the images and concepts selected by him refer to important tendencies that characterize the Jewish Diaspora.

Any study of the Jewish Diaspora must also acknowledge the limitation of sources. A large number of the surviving sources simply indicate the presence of Jews in a certain locality without providing significant information about their self-conception or life style.[54] A. Stuiber laments this fact:

> Almost nothing is preserved about the history, community organization, theology and liturgy of the varied and rich life of the Diaspora. More numerous witnesses for the local particularities of the Diaspora communities would be especially enlightening.[55]

In spite of this limitation of sources, some valuable literature does survive. Particularly useful are the Prophetic writings of Jeremiah, Second and Third Isaiah, and Ezekiel. These authors were the first to attempt to conceptualize the Exile and dispersion of the Jewish people among the Babylonians. Because their works were widely read throughout the Diaspora, their conceptualizations effected significant tendencies in Diaspora self-understanding. Equally important are the so-called Diaspora Novels. The books of Daniel and Esther and perhaps also the Joseph Saga in Genesis portray and interpret Jewish life in the Diaspora.[56] Also

---

[53]John Collins, *Between Athens and Jerusalem: Jewish Identity in the Hellenistic Diaspora* (New York: Crossroad Publishing Company, 1983), 244.

[54]Because of this characteristic of the surviving sources, many of the studies of the Jewish Diaspora are entirely or almost entirely devoted to the geographical extent of the Diaspora.

[55]A. Stuiber, "Diaspora," *Reallexikon für Antike und Christentum*, vol. 3: *Christusbilt-Dogma* (Stuttgart: Anton Hiersemann, 1957), 977.

[56]Arndt Meinhold, "Die Gattung der Josephsgeschichte und des Estherbuches: Diasporanovelle I," *Zeitschrift für die alttestamentliche Wissenschaft* 87 (1975): 306-324; 88 (1976): 72-93. In the latter article on page 92 he says, "The theme of the genre of the Diaspora Novel of Esther is, as in the Joseph Saga, the portrayal and interpretation of Jewish life in the Diaspora. . . ." Although his identification of the Joseph Saga as a Diaspora Novel may be questionable, both of these books were used in the Diaspora for the

significant are the numerous Jewish apocalypses like *4 Ezra, 2 Baruch, 1 Enoch,* and *Sibylline Oracles.* In addition to these sources, some of the Jewish historical writings like the *Books of the Maccabees* and Josephus as well as Jewish paraenetic writings such as the *Testament of the Twelve Patriarches* provide valuable information about Diaspora life. The Jewish philosopher, Philo, adds his contribution to the understanding of Jewish self conceptions in the Diaspora. From this literature, significant tendencies in the self-conception of Diaspora Jews have been noted by modern scholars attempting to understand the Diaspora.

There are two conceptions of the Diaspora that pervade 1 Peter and consequently function as general images. The first conception arises from the notion that the Diaspora is only temporary and will end with the return of the Jewish people to their homeland. Hans Joachim Schoeps comments on the anomaly of the Diaspora:

> Even though the Jewish form of life in the Galut had been made theoretically possible as a people-of-God-community, the fragmentary character of this life had not been forgotten at any time. The Galut is simply an anomaly. Its conquest is the task, hope, and goal.[57]

As Schoeps has correctly observed, the Jewish people devised theoretical means of coping with the Diaspora in order to maintain their religion. However, they never described the Diaspora as the eternal ideal of Jewish existence. There was a pervasive tendency among the Jews of the Diaspora to view their situation as temporary.

From this notion of the temporal nature of the Diaspora arose the conception that the Diaspora was a road to be traveled, a journey to be undertaken. This conception of the Diaspora described the Jewish people as God's wanderiing people. Yitzhak Baer comments on this conception:

> The surviving Jewish literature from this period frequently classifies history in terms of the rise and fall of empires. The process of atonement consists in

---

purpose he describes. W. Lee Humphreys, "A Life-Style for Diaspora: A Study of the Tales of Esther and Daniel," *Journal of Biblical Literature* 92 (1973): 211-223, had already expressed this purpose for the books of Esther and Daniel.

[57]Hans Joachim Schoeps, "Die Tempelzerstörung des Jahres 70 in der Jüdischen Religionsgeschichte," in idem, *Aus frühchristlicher Zeit* (Tübingen: J. C. B. Mohr (Paul Siebeck), 1950), 175.

Israel's enslavement by the empires and expiatory pilgrimage among the nations; the meaning of this process is immeasurably deepened by the idea that the *Shekhinah* itself takes part in the Galut and also waits for deliverance. And the picture of the suffering servant of God in the fifty-third chapter of Isaiah is already accepted in the Diaspora at this time as the permanent symbol of the sufferings of the Jews in the Galut-which is the meaning given this passage by the Jews of the Middle Ages. . . . The more terrible the suffering of the Diaspora, the more it operates as seed thrown forth in the world for the dissemination of the true faith. Abraham, the primal ancestor of Israel, is the prototype of the pilgrim who wanders through the world to usher *gerim* [proselytes] under the wing of the *Shekhinah.*[58]

Haim Hillel Ben-Sasson observes this same conception in *4 Ezra*:

. . . the author of *IV Ezra* (3:32-34, 6:59) argues with his Creator, asking: "Have the deeds of Babylon been better than those of Zion? Has any other nation known Thee besides Zion? If the world has indeed been created for our sakes, why do we not enter into possession of our world? How long shall this endure?" He is bitter about the fact of "the reproach of the nations" and the profaning of God's name which occurs in the galut (ibid. 4:23-25), but he lays no stress on the physical suffering entailed. Accepting neither the cosmic explanation of the exile, nor the mysteriousness of the ways of the Lord, nor the world to come, which nullify the valuation of the events in this world (ibid. 4:9-10), he seeks to explain the exile as a road of suffering which must be traveled in order to reach the good (ibid. 7:3-16).[59]

Thus, the Diaspora was conceived as a road to be traveled and a journey to be undertaken. Correspondingly, the dispersed Jews were viewed as the wanderiing people of God.

This conception of the Diaspora and of Diaspora existence had a profound influence upon Christian writers as Ernst Käsemann observes in his insightful investigation of Hebrews. He identifies the wanderiing people of God as the principal motif in Hebrews stating:

Finally, this has again made clear that all the utterances in Hebrews culminate in the description of Christ's high priestly office, but take their basis, which

---

[58]Yitzhak F. Baer, *Galut* (New York: Schocken Books, 1947), 12.

[59]Haim Hillel Ben-Sasson, "Galut," *Encyclopaedia Judaica*, vol. 7: *Fr-Ha* (New York: Macmillan, 1971), 277.

supports and purposefully articulates the individual parts, from the motif of the wandering people of God.[60]

He explains this motif as follows:

> It was already explained that in every age faith's wandering must be a march through a zone of conflict and death, and it is clearly shown in the example of Jesus (12:1ff.). Indeed, the visible and invisible do not confront each other in static fashion, but rather as powers contending with each other. Viewed from the world, the church must appear as a band of deserters when it forsakes encampment in an existence where all else is intent on solidarity and total union. So the world's fate will also overtake the church in all its severity. But that God's people traverse this zone of conflict and death for the sake of the Word is taken for a sign of victory (cf. 11:11f., 19, 29f., 33f.) and sonship, which paradoxically enough, and yet with inner necessity, embraces as $\pi\alpha\iota\delta\epsilon\iota\alpha$ the divine instruction in the present distress (12:7ff.).[61]

Käsemann explains the essentially eschatological perspective of this wanderiing saying, "Faith thus becomes a confident wanderiing. Since the past of the $\delta\iota\alpha\theta\eta\kappa\eta$ and the future of the consummation stand firm for it, it finds the power to overcome the earthly present."[62] He further explains why the author of Hebrews chose this motif:

> Hebrews intends to show the Christian community the greatness of the promise given it and the seriousness of the temptation threatening it. For this reason, it sets before its eyes the picture of Israel wandering through the wilderness. From such a type the possibilities of Christian existence can be perceived.[63]

Käsemann's observation and explication of this theme in the Epistle to the Hebrews demonstrates the importance of the conception of the wanderiing people of God for Christian writers.

The author of 1 Peter has also taken over this conception of Jewish Diaspora life in order to portray the Christian existence of his readers.[64]

---

[60]Ernst Käsemann, *The Wandering People of God: An Investigation of the Letter to the Hebrews*, trans. Ray A. Harrisville and Irving L. Sandberg (Minneapolis: Augsburg Publishing House, 1984), 240.

[61]Ibid., 44-45.

[62]Ibid., 44.

[63]Ibid., 17.

[64]In spite of the similarities, there are differences between Hebrews and 1 Peter's conception of the wandering people of God. Goppelt, *Petrusbrief*, 81, notes, "In this eschatological orientation of election and alien existence, Hebrews interpolates two

They have embarked upon an eschatological journey that takes them from their new birth to the eschaton.[65] This journey is graphically described in the blessing section in 1:3-12. Particularly important are verses three to five, which are translated as follows:

> Blessed be the Father-God of our Lord Jesus Christ who according to His great mercy through the resurrection of Jesus Christ from the dead has rebegotten us into a living hope, a hope for an indestructible, incorruptible, and unfading inheritance that has been preserved in the heavens for you who by the power of God are guarded through faith in a salvation prepared to be revealed at the end time.

In these verses their new birth or rebirth [ἀναγέννησις] commences their journey, but their reception of salvation in the eschaton marks their destination. These verses indicate that the new birth has taken place in the past, and the reception of salvation in the eschaton remains in the future.[66] Between these two points lies the present journey in which the travelers encounter manifold temptations that engender grief in them (1:6). Their

---

Hellenistic aspects that 1 Peter does not know: In Hebrews 11:10, 16 the promised inheritance is pictured as the future city that according to Hebrews 12:22 (compare 13:14) is at the same time the already existing heavenly city. Here the conception of homeland and citizenship in the πόλις is connected with the Old Testament apocalyptic expectation of inheritance and the city of God. This feature is lacking in 1 Peter. Also, lacking in 1 Peter is every connection with the conception of the antique-hellenistic dualism that the soul is at home in the heavenly world and therefore is alien to the material earthly world. Hebrews, however, has taken over some features of this dualism."

[65]Goppelt, *Petrusbrief*, 79, says, "From the complex of concepts, 1 Peter and the larger early Christian talk of Diaspora take over essentially only the sociological components: The Christians are a Diaspora as a people who live in small communes strewn among the peoples and await their gathering in the end time. However, the scattering is not here occasioned by judgment but rather through an election that estranges and separates them from the peoples of the world. And the gathering is not the reunification in Jerusalem which is not however described as a homegoing into the heavenly commonwealth (Philippians 3:20), but rather as a future gathering around the Lord whenever believing turns into seeing (1 Peter 1:8). The Diaspora situation is an expression of the eschatological already and not yet, an expression of election and alien existence."

[66]Goppelt, *Petrusbrief*, 106, admittedly articulates sound New Testament theology when he affirms that salvation has both a future and a present orientation. However, the strong emphasis in 1 Peter upon the future orientation of salvation should not be minimized in order to force 1 Peter into "the decisive soteriological point of reference of the New Testament." Goppelt correctly recognizes this future orientation in 1:4-5, 7-8, 9, 13.

present time of testing is contrasted with their joyous arrival at their destination (1:7-9). Their destination has been studied by the Hebrew Prophets of old (1:10), and it was made clear to them that the sufferings [παθήματα] in Christ would be followed by glories [δόξαι] (1:11).[67] This message has now been announced again [ἀνηγγέλη] to the readers by Christian evangelists (1:12).[68] Clearly this blessing section indicates that the author of 1 Peter has taken over the conception of the Diaspora as a journey in order to describe the existence of his readers as the wandering people of God on an eschatological journey.[69]

This general image of Diaspora life pervades 1 Peter. The beginning of their journey is mentioned in several ways. The statements

---

[67]Schutter, *Hermeneutic*, 106-108, discusses the exegetical issue of whether these sufferings and glories exclusively pertain personally to Christ or collectively to His followers. Schutter, 107-108, concludes, "Perhaps the mistake is to assume that the personal and collective frames of reference are somehow fundamentally incompatible with each other. Given the context dominated by a radically eschatological outlook, for example, it would seem plausible that any mention of 'the sufferings destined for Christ' is likely to possess a collective frame of reference that might conceivably take many possible forms. . . . On this view, accordingly, the parallel 'and the glories after these things' may by way of analogy retain both the personal and collective dimensions." Schutter, *Hermeneutic*, 109, proceeds to identify this sufferings/glories schema as the basic hermeneutical orientation of the author of 1 Peter.

[68]Selwyn's view, *1 Peter*, 259-268, that the prophets in verse 10 refers to Christian prophets should be rejected. The problem that occasioned Selwyn's mistake is the lack of the article with προφῆται. The second portion of the Jewish canon is usually designated with the article (Matthew 5:17; 7:12; Luke 16:16). The problem is exacerbated by the articular attributive participle that modifies προφῆται. The lack of the article probably indicates that the author is not thinking only of the prophets in the Jewish scriptures but also of other Jewish prophets as Michaels, *1 Peter*, states on pages 40-41.

[69]In addition to the blessing section, several allusions to this journey motif occur in 1 Peter. "Girding up the loins" (1:13), "being sober" (1:13; 5:8), "being alert" (5:8), "putting off" unnecessary baggage (2:1), and "arming oneself" (4:1) are all necessary preparations for a journey. The danger of encountering wild beasts (5:8) is characteristic of a journey. The term ἀναστροφή [course of life] used throughout the letter semantically relates to journey or travel ideas. Terms like πάροικος and παρεπίδημος were used to refer to the transient status of the Jewish wanderers in the Dispersion and also allude to the journey image in 1 Peter. The notion of Christ as a shepherd to whom Christians have returned [ἐπιστρέφω] (2:25) and whom they now follow [ἐπακολουθέω] (2:21) are descriptions of the Christian journey. The notion that Christians are coming [προσέρχομαι] to the "living stone" (2:4) in order to build a temple is very similar to the journey image in 1 Enoch. Just as God's call precipitates the return journey from Exile and dispersion, so also in 1 Peter God's call (1:15; 2:9, 21; 3:9; 5:10) initiates the present Christian journey.

that God called them (1:15; 2:21; 3:9; 5:10) as well as statements about their redemption (1:18) and new birth (1:23) all allude to the beginning of their journey. The author mentions their destination as the grace that will be brought to them at the revelation of Jesus Christ (1:13), growing into salvation (2:2), the inheritance of a blessing (3:9), rejoicing at the revelation of Christ's glory (4:13), their exaltation (5:6), and their establishment by God (5:10). In between this beginning and destination is the time of their sojourn (1:17; 2:11; 4:2; 5:10). Thus, the image of the people of God on a journey pervades 1 Peter.

This general image of Diaspora life not only pervades 1 Peter but also sets up the rhetorical situation. The author does not focus undue attention upon the past beginning or future destination of their journey. Rather, his concern is with their present travel between these two points. This concern is expressed by the term $\dot{a} v a \sigma \tau \rho o \phi \dot{\eta}$ [course of life or conduct], which occurs several times in 1 Peter.[70] In 1:15 the author exhorts his readers to be holy in their entire conduct. In 1:18 their present conduct is contrasted with their former foolish conduct. The author is concerned with their good conduct among the Gentiles (2:12; 3:2, 16) and the good conduct of Christian wives toward their unbelieving husbands (3:1). In fact, the entire paraenesis of the letter-body is designed to explicate the conduct or course of life appropriate for the eschatological travelers.[71] This concern for appropriate conduct comprises one of the author's two main purposes for writing his letter. In this way, the Diaspora image of the wanderiing people of God sets up the rhetorical

---

[70]Georg Bertram, "$\sigma \tau \rho \acute{\epsilon} \phi \omega$," in *Theological Dictionary of the New Testament*, vol. 7: Σ, ed. Gerhard Friedrich (Grand Rapids: Wm. B. Eerdmans Publishing Co., 1971), 715, discusses the broad range of meanings attached to the term $\dot{a} v a \sigma \tau \rho \acute{\epsilon} \phi \omega$. These meanings include *to convert*, *to bring back*, *to gather*, *to behave*, and *to walk*. The neglect of the commentators to place emphasis on this word is surprising since it occurs as many times in 1 Peter as in the rest of the New Testament. W. C. van Unnik, "The Redemption in 1 Peter 1:18-19 and the Problem of the First Epistle of Peter," in *Sparsa Collecta: The Collected Essays of W. C. van Unnik*, vol. 2, ed. J. Reiling, G. Mussies, and P. W. van der Horst, Supplements to Novum Testamentum, 30 (Leiden: E. J. Brill, 1980) is an exception. On page 28 he says in regard to the use of $\dot{a} v a \sigma \tau \rho o \phi \dot{\eta}$ in 1 Peter, "That this word was of special significance for 1 Peter emerges from the fact that it appears thirteen times in the New Testament, six of which are in this epistle [see also 1:17, the verb]."

[71]Van Unnik, "Redemption," 31, says, "How must they behave in this world, where they are like exiles? That the author was particularly concerned with this $\dot{a} v a \sigma \tau \rho o \phi \dot{\eta}$ appears from the frequent use he makes of the word."

situation allowing the author to address his concerns and persuade his readers to direct their lives according to his recommendations.

The second conception of the Diaspora that pervades 1 Peter and thus functions as a general image is the danger of assimilation to the pagan environment and the consequent defection from the Jewish faith. Collins states, "The basic problem in the Jewish Diaspora was how to maintain the Jewish tradition in an environment dominated by Gentiles. . . . The very juxtaposition of diverse beliefs challenged the plausibility of minority views."[72] Collins describes this experience as *dissonance* explaining:

> Where dissonance is present there is inevitably pressure to reduce or eliminate the dissonance. Perhaps the simplest way to do this was by abandoning Judaism altogether. Philo's nephew, Tiberius Julius Alexander, is the most notorious example. There were Jews who exercised this option, but they were always a minority. The majority sought ways to reduce the dissonance while remaining Jewish but without rejecting Hellenistic culture.[73]

Although not using the term *dissonance,* Schürer had earlier observed this same conception of the Diaspora experience stating:

> The Jews though scattered throughout the ancient world, maintained their religious identity for the most part with remarkable tenacity. There were of course cases of defection to paganism or syncretism. . . . Such traces of syncretism however never acquired the same extent or significance as with other religions of the East. On the whole, the resistant attitude of Judaism in the face of other religions remained a continuing characteristic.[74]

This conception of the Diaspora as a dangerous place where assimilation to paganism and defection from Judaism takes place pervades 1 Peter and functions as a general image in the document.[75]

The use of this conception of the Diaspora as a general image in 1 Peter reveals the second of the author's main purposes for writing. As already discussed, the author conceives of his readers on an eschatological

---

[72]Collins, *Athens*, 2.

[73]Ibid., 9.

[74]Emil Schürer, *The History of the Jewish People in the Age of Jesus Christ (175 B.C.—A.D. 135)* vol. 3.1, ed. and trans. Geza Vermes, Fergus Millar, and Martin Goodman (Edinburgh: T. & T. Clark, 1986), 138.

[75]Of course, as I will explain below, 1 Peter uses this image not because of concern with defection from Judaism but because of concern over possible defection from Christianity.

journey. They have been rebegotten in the past and look forward to a glorious destiny, but in the present they experience dissonance. As in the Jewish Diaspora, this dissonance could lead the readers to be scandalized [σκανδαλίζω] and to defect [ἀφίστημι] from this new religion that has not brought them δόξα but trials and grief. The author is concerned that his readers may not complete the journey upon which they have set out but may defect to their pagan environment. Defection from Christianity provides the author of 1 Peter with a second purpose for writing his letter.

The problem that our author addresses was a chronic one in the new fledgling religion. Adherents were quickly won but soon scandalized by dashed expectations. Many New Testament texts address this problem. In the Passion Narrative, the disciples are scandalized when their hopes for Jesus came to nothing (Mark 14:27, 29). This scandal resulted in their being scattered (Mark 14:27) and denying Jesus (Mark 14:31). In the Parable of the Sower, the new adherents of the faith are scandalized because of tribulation [θλίψις] and persecution [πειρασμός] (Mark 4:17). In the Lucan parallel (Luke 8:14), these adherents fall away [ἀφίστημι] in the time of trial [πειρασμός]. In the context of trial and persecution in Luke 22:31-34, Jesus prays that Peter's faith might not fail [ἐκλείπω]. Other passages like 1 Timothy 4:1 and Hebrews 3:12 also attest to Christian defection. In addition to these biblical texts, Pliny's letter to Trajan indicates that defection was a problem in Christianity. In this letter he mentions those who were brought before him with the accusation that they were Christians. He describes one group as follows:

> Others who were named by that informer at first confessed themselves Christians, and then denied it; true, they had been of that persuasion but they had quitted it, some three years, others many years, and a few as much as twenty-five years ago. They all worshiped your statue and the images of the gods, and cursed Christ.[76]

This is the problem that the author of 1 Peter addresses.

Our author responds to this problem by the rhetorical strategy of suppression. Only once does he mention any of the terms for scandal or

---

[76]Pliny, *Letters* 10.96. William Melmoth, trans., *Pliny: Letters*, vol. 2, The Loeb Classical Library (Cambridge, Harvard University Press, 1963), 402-403.

defection mentioned above.[77] Instead, he emphasizes antonyms to these
notions, such as hope (1:13, 21; 3:15), sobriety and realistic assessment of
the situation (1:13, 18; 2:7, 15, 19-21; 3:9, 13; 4:7, 12; 5:6, 8), and
steadfastness (1:21; 5:9, 10, 12). He stresses these antithetical notions
because he attempts to move the mind of his readers away from the notions
of scandal and defection to the notions of hope, sobriety, and steadfastness.
Mentioning the former notions, even in a negative manner, would have
reinforced these notions in the mind of his readers. His rhetorical strategy
is to suppress these undesirable responses and emphasize their antonyms.

Our author also responds to the problem of scandal and defection by
use of the twin paraenetical aspects of ontology and the morality ensuing
from it. Repeatedly in the letter-body, he mentions who his readers are
and the conduct expected of them. His description of who they are and a
corresponding morality is constantly contrasted with the unbelievers and
Gentiles and their alternative morality. The believers' ontology and
morality as God's elect people (2:9-10) are contrasted with who they were
formerly, people behaving stupidly out of lust and desire. In 1:14-15 they
are described as obedient children who conduct themselves in a holy
manner. In 2:11-12 they are described as strangers and aliens who put
away fleshly desires and maintain good conduct. The Gentiles, on the other
hand, irrationally malign them as evil doers, but on the Day of Visitation
the Gentiles will be proven wrong. In 4:1-5 the author's readers live by
God's will, not by the Gentiles' counsel. Their good conduct is contrasted
with the debauchery and blasphemy of the Gentiles. The author argues that
if his readers defect, they join this other group that adheres to a very
different morality. By contrasting the superiority of Christian ontology
and morality to its pagan counterpart, the author hopes to persuade his
readers not to be scandalized and defect but to continue on their
eschatological journey "hoping in the favor that will be bestowed upon
them at the revelation of Jesus Christ (1:13)." His primary objective is to
encourage them to stand fast for this favor and thus attain their
destination (5:12).

---

[77]In 2:8 he uses the noun σκάνδαλον. In this context the term does not refer to
Christians but to unbelievers who have rejected Christ, a group that the Christians should
definitely not want to fall into.

In his response to the problem of dissonance, the author of 1 Peter shares many characteristics with other Diaspora authors. Schürer summarizes the purpose and strategy of the Jewish Prophetic-Apocalyptic Pseudepigrapha in the following manner:

> Most of these writings were occasioned by times of particular distress and hardship, or by the low circumstances of the people in general. It was the contradiction between ideal and reality, between promises which the Jews believed they had received from God, and their present subjugation and persecution by Gentile powers; it was this contradiction that induced the authors to write. Even when there was no immediate hardship or oppression, a pessimistic assessment of affairs still constituted the motive for writing. The existing situation, the present condition of the chosen people, stood in glaring contrast to their true destiny. A complete revolution must come, and soon. Such is the conviction expressed in all these writings. They therefore owe their inception on the one hand to a gloomy appraisal of the present time, and on the other to a very energetic faith in the nation's glorious future. And their purpose is to awaken and animate this faith in others. It is not a question of despairing, but of holding fast to the belief that God will lead his people, through all the misfortunes which he sends to test and purify them, to brightness and glory. This faith is to comfort and encourage the people in the suffering of the present time.[78]

Schürer's description of the purpose and strategy of these Diaspora documents indicates that the author of 1 Peter shares many characteristics with them. He is concerned about their present suffering and grief and the dissonance between the present and the promised future. He attempts to strengthen their faith that God will take care of them (5:6) and bring them through their present struggles (5:10). Although he shares a similar purpose and design, the author of 1 Peter obviously does not incorporate into his writing the specific apocalyptic content of these documents summarized by Schürer.[79]

As the foregoing discussion indicates, the conceptions of the Diaspora as a journey to be undertaken and as a dangerous place where assimilation to paganism and defection from the true faith takes place

---

[78]Schürer, vol. 3.1, 243. The documents that he is summarizing are *4 Ezra, Apocalypse of Abraham, Chronicles of Jeremiah, Daniel, Ethiopic Book of Enoch,* and the *Assumption* or *Testament of Moses.*

[79]Michaels, *1 Peter,* xlvi, identifies the genre of 1 Peter as "an apocalyptic Diaspora letter to Israel." His identification of the genre should be rejected. The letter is eschatological, not apocalyptic. See Goppelt, *Petrusbrief,* 311-314.

pervade 1 Peter and function as general images setting up the rhetorical situation and revealing the author's purposes for writing.   The author conceives of his readers on an eschatological journey that began with their new birth or election and terminates in the eschaton. He does not focus on the past beginning nor on the future destination. His purpose for writing is rather to explicate the conduct appropriate for his readers on their journey.[80] His purpose is also to encourage them to continue their journey and not to defect to paganism. In the body-opening (1:13), body-closing (5:12), and body-middle (1:14--5:11), the author of 1 Peter recommends fitting conduct and responds to the problem of defection by attempting to lift the mind of his readers away from scandal and defection to sobriety, steadfastness, and faith.[81]

After having examined these two general images of the Diaspora that pervade 1 Peter, the specific images of the Diaspora that are limited to individual sections must now be discussed. Whereas the general images reveal the rhetorical situation and the purposes of the letter, the specific images provide the author with the means for accomplishing his purposes and also indicate the various sections of the letter-body. These specific images along with their related concepts form metaphor clusters and will be treated in greater detail in as much as they function as the compositional indicators for the letter-body.

The metaphors in 1 Peter's body-middle fall into three metaphor clusters that determine the three major sections of the body-middle. The specific images around which these metaphor clusters are built are announced in the prescript (1:1). The letter is addressed to the elect strangers of the Dispersion [ἐκλεκτοῖς παρεπιδήμοις διασπορᾶς].[82] The first metaphor cluster is built around the image of the elect people of God

---

[80]Since the letter is a paraenesis, it should not be assumed that the recommended conduct was unknown to the readers. As Chapter 3 of this dissertation stated, a paraenesis does not recommend new or controversial moral rules. Rather, it recommends rules that are known and accepted.

[81]In 2 Peter 3:1-4, the earliest commentary on 1 Peter, the author says that he has attempted in both letters [ἐν αἷς] to raise [διεγείρω] the mind [διάνοια] of his readers to remember the words of the prophets and not to be scandalized by scoffers who question the promise of the parousia.

[82]I think Beck, 29-30, 151-152, and 180-181, was the first to recognize the compositional importance of these descriptive terms in the prescript. See page 13, note 34, in Chapter 1 of this dissertation.

and contains metaphors pertaining to the house of God (1:14--2:10). The second metaphor cluster is composed of metaphors that group around the notion of strangers and aliens (2:11--3:12). The third metaphor cluster is determined by the concept of the Diaspora as a place of suffering (3:13--5:11). All three of these metaphor clusters are related through the overarching and controlling metaphor of the Diaspora.[83] Each of these metaphor clusters must now be carefully examined.

The First Metaphor Cluster (1:14--2:10):
The Elect Household of God

In an important monograph about this section of 1 Peter entitled *The Elect and the Holy*, John Elliott has correctly identified some important themes in this section. Election and holiness receive repeated treatment. Schutter maintains that these themes are expressed in the compositional inclusio of this passage:

> When looking for clues as to the organization of 1.13--2.10 between the transition (1.13) and afterthought (2.10), a kind of inclusion can be seen that relates start and finish: τὸν καλέσαντα . . . τοῦ ὑμᾶς καλέσαντος (1.14f./2.9). Because the technique of inclusion conventionally functions to identify the main emphasis of any given passage, it is therefore reasonable to take God's call to holiness' as the rubric under which the several parts of the body-opening line up.[84]

Although Schutter has correctly identified the major inclusio of this passage, he has not correctly interpreted its meaning. Neither in 1:14-15 nor in 2:9 is it stated that God's call is to holiness. Rather, God's call is expressed by an aorist participle that emphasizes its past, not present nature, and refers to the readers' election.[85] Michaels accurately states,

---

[83]Michaels, *1 Peter*, 6, says, ". . . the terms ἐκλεκτοί, παρεπίδημοι, and above all διασπορά, appear to be expressions of a Jewish consciousness arising out of the Jewish experience."

[84]Schutter, *Hermeneutic*, 52. I have already discussed above Schutter's mistake in identifying this section as the body-opening of the letter.

[85]Best, *1 Peter*, 86, comments on the word *called* in 1:15, "The word expresses the strong belief of the early Christians that God had chosen and destined (1:1f) them to be his people." Best has correctly connected this word with the term *elect* in 1:1. Selwyn, *1 Peter*, 167, accurately perceives that the word called in 2:9 refers to "a description of the change from heathenism to Christianity."

"Peter mentions the divine 'calling,' a corollary of divine election. . . ."[86]
It is election that enables these readers to become the people of God [λαὸς
θεοῦ] (2:10). It is as the people of God that holiness becomes an important
attribute to be attained and maintained. Thus, God's call is not specifically
to become holy but to become the people of God who should of course be
holy. Although holiness and election are important themes in this passage
as Elliott has noted, election, not holiness, is the dominant theme as the
inclusio identified by Schutter, and correctly interpreted, demonstrates.

In addition to the inclusio, the theme of election is maintained
throughout this passage. Election is presupposed in 1:18 where the
readers' redemption from the vain way of life inherited from their
forefathers is mentioned. It is also in view in 1:20 where foreknowledge
of Christ is affirmed. It is closely related to the readers' new birth
referred to in 1:23. The term *elect* occurs in 2:4, 6, and 9. In the first two
occurrences it refers to Christ and in the latter to the readers. As already
discussed, election effects the transformation of the 'no people' [οὐ λαός]
into the 'people of God' [λαὸς θεοῦ] (2:10).

Throughout this passage, this transformation is viewed as a result of
the new birth or rebirth brought about by God's election.[87] The author has

---

[86]Michaels, *1 Peter*, 111.

[87]Many attempts have been made to ascertain the origin of the conception of the
new birth. An older but still useful treatment of the concept is that of Joseph Dey,
ΠΑΛΙΓΓΕΝΕΣΙΑ: *Ein Beitrag zur Klärung der religionsgeschichtlichen Bedeutung von Tit
3,5*, Neutestamentliche Abhandlungen 17.5 (Münster: Aschendorff, 1937). He traces its
use in philosophical, nonphilosophical, and religious circles. The two most frequently
suggested origins for the conception in 1 Peter are the Mystery Religions and Judaism.
Perdelwitz is the chief proponent for the Mystery Religions' background for the new birth
according to Dey, 156. W. C. van Unnik has proposed the strongest argument for the
Jewish background. In his article on redemption in 1 Peter 1:18-19, pages 40-41, he says,
"So far the result of my investigation is this: the text is about a conversion from the pagan
world to Christianity and something is being said in connection with a sacrifice and its
condition. . . . The question now is: where do we find a sacrifice mentioned in connection
with the conversion from one way of life to another? . . . There is only one case of
conversion from paganism where this happened: conversion from paganism to Judaism,
and the proselyte's sacrifice." Van Unnik's position is weakened by the lack of evidence
for this sacrifice. Schürer, vol. 3, 173, thinks that this sacrifice was practiced in Second
Temple Judaism but admits that definite proof is lacking. In spite of this difficulty,
van Unnik's argument is very persuasive and more adequately than others explains several
features of this text like the antithesis of φθαρτοῖς and τιμίῳ and the question of how blood
can be more lasting than silver or gold. See especially pages 48-52. Regardless of which
origin is accepted, Dey, 156, correctly observes that the concept of the new birth was taken

already informed his readers that their new birth is a result of God's great mercy (1:3).[88] Now, as those who have been reborn, he describes them as obedient children (1:14) who call God father (1:17). He refers to the brotherhood into which they have been born (1:22) and calls them newborn babes [ἀρτιγέννητα βρέφη] (2:2). Since this new birth results from God's election, election is implied in all of these references to the new birth.

This theme of election and its corollary, the elect people of God, are prevalent in the Jewish Diaspora.[89] Collins comments, "It is true that nearly all the Diaspora literature assigns a special place to the covenantal people."[90] The Jews of the Diaspora considered themselves to be the elect people of God.[91] The author of 1 Peter takes this prevalent Diaspora

---

up by the Christian tradition and was available to Christian writers in its Christian rather than its pagan or Jewish contexts. In his excellent discussion of the new birth in 1 Peter, Goppelt, *Petrusbrief*, 94-95, points out the distinctively Christian features. He says, "The resurrection of Jesus, however, effects the new birth only in connection with two factors that are mentioned as causes in other passages. According to 1 Peter 1:23 and James 1:18, people are reborn through the word of God, the message of Jesus Christ, particularly of his resurrection, and according to Titus 3:5 and John 3:5, through baptism." Goppelt finds the closest parallels to new birth in 1 Peter in the Qumran materials. See page 94.

[88]Dey, 151, compares 1 Peter 1:3 with Pauline conceptions. He says, "Also, in other points the interpretation corresponds to pauline thought: the act of God proceeds from His mercy (κατὰ τὸ πολὺ αὐτοῦ ἔλεος); the goal is our salvation [5 εἰς σωτηρίαν] that will be apparent only at the end of time (5)."

[89]This positive assessment of Jewish self-understanding in the Diaspora is offset by the negative assessment of their ontological status by pagan authors. For a list of these negative characteristics see Dora Askowith, *The Toleration of the Jews Under Julius Caesar and Augustus* (New York: Columbia University, 1915), 70-98. For further literature dealing with pagan conceptions of the Jews, see Schürer, vol. 3.1, 150, note 1.

[90]Collins, *Athens*, 168.

[91]Kelly, 40, says, "Similarly chosen was the epithet regularly used by the Jews to express their conviction that God had singled them out from all nations to be His special people (e.g. Dt. iv.37; vii.6; xiv.2; Ps. cv.6; Is. xiv.4). In Maccabean times and later the growing consciousness of living in a hostile environment strengthened this conviction (e.g. Jub. ii.20); at Qumran, too, the sectaries regarded themselves as God's elect (e.g. 1QS viii.6; xi.16; 1QpHab. x.13)." Also Best, *1 Peter*, 70, says, "Israel believed itself to be chosen, selected or elected by God (Hos. 11:1; Ezek. 20:5; Isa. 41:8f; 51:2; Ps. 105:43). This belief was emphasized in the inter-testamental period, e.g. the faithful in *1 Enoch* are known as 'the elect' (cf. 1QS 8:6; 11:16). The early Christians, viewing themselves as the people of God, realized also that they had been 'chosen' by God to be so. Here [1:2] the thought is closely linked to verse 1: it is because they are 'chosen' by God that they are now exiles of the dispersion in the world."

theme and applies this designation to his readers.[92] His readers in their
Diaspora sojourn on their eschatological journey are none other than the
elect people of God. Thus, the primary theme of this section fits in with
and is derived from the overarching and controlling theme of the Diaspora.

The author of 1 Peter has chosen to develop these themes of election
and the elect people of God by selecting metaphors pertaining to the house
of God [οἶκος τοῦ θεοῦ].[93] The conception and description of the chosen
people as a house is prevalent in the Hebrew Scriptures and is frequently
used to refer to the people in exile.[94] John Elliott, among others, has
perceived the importance of this concept for 1 Peter. He says, ". . . the
oikos tou theou functioned as the chief integrative concept of 1 Peter."[95]
As we shall see, Elliott incorrectly ascribes this concept to the entire letter
since it only functions to organize the metaphors in the first section of the
body-middle as Lohse has correctly perceived.[96] Thus, the first metaphor
cluster in the body-middle arises from the concept of the house of God

---

[92]This designation for Christians had already been taken over by the Christian
tradition and consequently the author of 1 Peter was not the first to describe Christians as
the elect people of God.

[93]Fortunately, the author of 1 Peter usually uses a concise descriptive term for the
metaphor cluster he is employing in each major section of the epistle. In this section,
however, the descriptive term does not occur until 4:17 where it is stated that it is time to
begin the judgment with the house of God [οἶκος τοῦ θεοῦ]. Then the author makes a
metaphorical connection between this phrase and his readers. Apart from the discussion of
this metaphorical connection in 1:14--2:10, the connection in 4:17 is unexpected and needs
clarification. The use of this phrase to refer to the readers in 4:17 clearly indicates that the
author has already made this connection in 1:14--2:10. Goppelt, *Petrusbrief*, 311, astutely
recognizes the connection between 4:17 and 1:14--2:10. He says, "The οἶκος τοῦ θεοῦ is
in the first place the temple in the Old Testament passage cited--Ezekiel 9:6 reads: 'My
Sanctuary.' For the author of 1 Peter, however, it is the community according to the
metaphor in 2:5. In 4:17b οἶκος τοῦ θεοῦ is transcribed: 'first upon us' [πρῶτον ἀφ'
ἡμῶν]." The lack of the descriptive term for the metaphor cluster in this section does not
pose a serious problem for my analysis because metaphor clusters are identified by
observing metaphors that belong together, not by simply looking for specific descriptive
terms for a metaphor cluster. Of course, the author's use of a concise descriptive term
greatly facilitates the identification of a metaphor cluster, but the use of such a term is
necessary neither in the construction of a metaphor cluster nor in its identification.

[94]See Ezekiel 3:4, 17; 37:11; 39:25; 36:19.

[95]Elliott, *Home*, 270.

[96]See Lohse, "Parenesis," 48 who says, "The entire passage 1:3--2:10 is
dominated by the idea of the holy people of God, to which the Christians now belong."

[οἶκος τοῦ θεοῦ] and is used to describe the nature of the readers in the Diaspora as the elect people of God.

The term οἶκος carries a double meaning, both of which provide material for the metaphors in this section of the body-middle of 1 Peter.[97] In one sense, οἶκος refers to the house or building that provided living quarters for the family. Although there were probably many different types of domiciles in the Roman Empire, two basic types gained prominence in the cities: private mansions [domi] and multi-storied apartment houses [insulae].[98] In 1 Peter there is no mention of either of these two basic types because the οἶκος that is mentioned belongs to God and therefore qualifies as a temple.[99] Several related images cluster around

---

[97]Bertil Gärtner, *The Temple and the Community in Qumran and the New Testament* (Cambridge: University Press, 1965), 21, says, "The word 'house' has of course a double meaning: on the one hand *building*, on the other *family*, *dynasty*." Friedrick Ohly, "Haus III (Metapher)," in *Reallexikon für Antike und Christentum*, vol. 13 (Stuttgart: Anton Hiersemann, 1986) comments on the widespread and variable use of the house-metaphor in the ancient world. On pages 906-907 he says, "To the human, the house in which he enters the world, lives, and dies ought to be most familiar. The linguistic projection of the experience of the house familiar to the human into the unfamiliarity of his existence in the world [nature, society, spiritual world] in the form of the application of the house-metaphor to the cosmos [including heaven and the underworld] and nature; to the body and body parts like head and heart; to the systems of society like state and church; to innate religious and ethical qualities; to the actions of the intellect in philosophy, theology, and other disciplines, not the least to poetry, establishes the house, thanks to its antiquity and continuance, ubiquity and variability, as one of the most frequently selected metaphor-contributors in the world of antiquity and of early Christianity. . . ."

[98]Verner, *Household*, 57.

[99]J. Goetzmann, "House," in *The New International Dictionary of New Testament Theology*, vol. 2: *G-Pre*, ed. Colin Brown (Grand Rapids: Zondervan Publishing House, 1971), 247, says, "Used with God's name, *oikos*, as in secular Gk., means the temple, the sanctuary: *oikos theou* [house of God] or *oikos kyriou* [house of the Lord]. Both expressions are common." Georg Klinzing, *Die Umdeutung des Kultus in der Qumrangemeinde und im Neuen Testament*, Studien zur Umwelt des Neuen Testaments 7 (Göttingen: Vandenhoeck & Ruprecht, 1971), 192, note 5, says, "In connection with sacrifice and priesthood, 1 Peter 2:5 can only mean the temple by the phrase, 'spiritual house.'" Elliott's argument that οἶκος does not refer to the temple is not convincing. See idem, *Elect and Holy*, 157f. See the refutation of his position by Ernest Best, "1 Peter II 4-10—A Reconsideration," *Novum Testamentum* 11 (1969): 280f. I agree with Gärtner, *Temple*, 73, who says, "This οἶκος πνευματικός, in a context in which are also mentioned priests, sacrifices and the 'corner stone,' can hardly refer to anything but the temple." Recognizing the close connection between the temple-metaphor and the house-metaphor, Ohly, 958-959, states, "Jesus' word about the temple of his body (John 2:21)

the notion of οἶκος as a temple. Otto Michel notes many of these saying, "The series of concepts: heavenly temple, holy priesthood, acceptable sacrifices, fuses and intermingles. . . ."[100] Goetzmann details other images that adhere to this notion:

> Given the figurative use of the terms, it was inevitable that many related concepts and images would be introduced to elucidate the truth concerning the Christian community which is expressed in the phrase "the house of God." There is the idea of the foundation (1 Cor. 3:10-12; Eph. 2:20; 2 Tim. 2:19), of Christ as the corner stone (Acts 4:11; Eph. 2:20; 1 Pet. 2:4) and Christians as living stones (1 Pet. 2:5), of the pillars (1 Tim. 3:15) and above all the temple (1 Cor. 3:16f.; 6:19; 2 Cor. 6:16; Eph. 2:21).[101]

Thus, the meaning of οἶκος as a residence or building and particularly as a temple provides much of the material for the metaphors in this section of 1 Peter.

In addition to the meaning of house or building, οἶκος also acquired the meaning of household and referred to the family that inhabited the house.[102] This concept of οἶκος was extremely important for Hellenistic

---

pioneered a far-reaching personalization and spiritualization of the Jewish sacred temple cult so that in Christendom the temple-metaphor and the house-metaphor for the body of the faithful could vary."

[100]Otto Michel, "Οἶκος," in *Theological Dictionary of the New Testament*, vol. 5: Ξ–Παα, ed. Gerhard Friedrich (Grand Rapids: Wm. B. Eerdmans Publishing Co., 1970), 127.

[101]Goetzmann, 249. Gärtner, *Temple*, 27, says, "To the same complex of ideas surrounding the temple belong such images as 'the precious corner-stone,' 'the tested wall' and the foundations which 'shall not be shaken and shall not be removed from their place'; these form an exegesis of Isa. xxviii 16 and belong to the imagery with which late Judaism surrounded the 'stone' on which the Ark of the Covenant rested in the 'Holy of Holies.'" Ohly, 909, discusses the field of metaphors associated with the term *house* and specifically cites the keystone as belonging to this complex of ideas.

[102]J. Gaudemet, "Familie I (Familienrecht)," *Reallexikon für Antike und Christentum*, vol. 7 (Stuttgart: Anton Hiersemann, 1969), 304, says, "Οἶκος designates the resident community of a household to which also the slaves belonged. . . ." After commenting on the historical treatment of the term house as a building in the first article and as a theological concept in the second article on Haus in the *Reallexikon für Antike und Christentum*, Ohly, 910-911, states, "Areas of the House-Semantic like the use of house as a designation for family, race, tribe, people, and country remained in the background because an admixture of the metaphorical area and the historical area would have blurred the threshold between metaphor and concept." Clearly, Ohly recognizes the use of the term *house* to refer to the family.

society. It was the basic socio-political unit. J. Gaudemet distinguishes between two types of families in Greco-Roman society, saying:

> As in Greece, so also in Rome, two types of families are encountered. A larger association in which the basic unity of the members relates to a common origin that can be real or fictional to which the members of the union attribute significance. This unity is established through bonds of an economic, religious, perhaps political, sometimes aristocratic type. Another very much smaller union is limited to the marital relations of parents and their children. . . .[103]

It is the former type of family that is represented in 1 Peter. This conception of the οἶκος as a family composed of members who have specific roles and responsibilities along with the conception of οἶκος as a house dominates the constellation of metaphors in this first section of the body-middle of 1 Peter.

Metaphor-Obedient Children

The first metaphor arising from the notion of οἶκος is the description of the readers as obedient children in 1:14. This metaphor, introduced by ὡς, provides the transition from the body-opening to the body-middle, legitimates the exhortation to be holy, and controls the material in verses fourteen to sixteen.[104]

Obedience was a fundamental obligation for the children of the Hellenistic household.[105] Epictetus says, "To be a son is to regard all one's possessions as the property of the father, to obey the father in all things, never to blame him before anyone, to support him with all one's

---

[103]Gaudemet, 302.

[104]A similar use of an introductory simile as a transitional device is found in 2:16. See below.

[105]Gaudemet, 340-341, states, "The relationship between parents and children is treated in both parallel passages of the letters to the Ephesians (6:1, 4) and to the Colossians (3:20-21): The children ought to be obedient to the parents [and not only to the father], however, 'in the Lord.'" A. Lumpe and H. Karpp, "Eltern," in *Reallexikon für Antike und Christentum*, vol. 4 (Stuttgart: Anton Hiersemann, 1959), 1192, state, "Throughout the entire Greek literature the exhortation is extended to show reverence and obedience to the parents." Several examples are then cited. Later when discussing the Roman family, they say, "From the family order sketched above, it follows that among the Romans respect and obedience to the parents was a self evident duty of the children." Again, several examples are then cited. For examples from the New Testament, see columns 1205-1206.

power."[106] Obedience demands that children in the household carry out the commands of the father. In verse sixteen, our author quotes a command of the readers' father through the new birth, "You shall be holy because I am holy." If his readers are obedient children, they must fulfill this command and be holy. Thus, the description of the readers as obedient children substantiates the exhortation to be holy.[107]

Since these readers are not natural children, but children by the new birth, the exhortation to be holy is given further specificity by an allusion to this experience.[108] The new birth has effected their total transference from one *familia* to another.[109] The participial antithesis in verses fourteen and fifteen, μὴ συσχηματιζόμενοι ταῖς πρότερον ἐν τῇ ἀγνοίᾳ ὑμῶν ἐπιθυμίαις ἀλλὰ [συσχηματιζόμενοι] κατὰ τὸν καλέσαντα ὑμᾶς ἅγιον [as you do not conform to your former ignorant desires but as you conform to the holy *father* who called you], describes the change in the readers' status effected by the new birth and provides the specific context in which the exhortation to be holy should be carried out. In this context, the command to be holy means to conform to the nature of their newly acquired father and to undo the character formation of their former

---

[106]Epictetus, *Dissertationes* II.10,7. Citation in Gottlob Schrenk, "Πατήρ," in *Theological Dictionary of the New Testament*, vol. 5: Ξ–Πα, ed. Gerhard Friedrich (Grand Rapids: Wm. B. Eerdmans Publishing Co., 1970), 949. See also Homer's *Iliad* 15.197ff. where sons and daughters must obey their fathers without qualification. See also Musonius Rufus 16.24 who says, "To be sure, *disobedience* and the *disobedient person* are terms of shame. . . ." Text and translation by Cora E. Lutz, "Musonius Rufus: The Roman Socrates," *Yale Classical Studies* 10 (1974): 102-103.

[107]Weiss, *Lehrbegriff*, 40 stated, "Exhortations to a holy life (1:14-16) and to a conduct in the fear of God (1:17-21) are motivated in an entirely analogous manner through the child metaphor in which we approach the creator of our new life."

[108]Michaels, *1 Peter*, 57, correctly suggests, "Yet it is possible that the word τέκνα was chosen for its own sake as well as for idiomatic or stylistic reasons. Peter may have been suggesting that the readers of his epistle were τέκνα ὑπακοῆς by virtue of the 'new birth' God had granted them (v. 3) and therefore possessed the privileges of addressing God as 'Father (v. 17).'"

[109]Because both adoption and new birth effected the transfer of an individual from an old *familia* to a new one, these terms were not always clearly distinguished in antiquity. Commenting on the adoption of Heracles as reported in Diodorus Siculus 4.39, Joseph Dey, 128, notes, "Here adoption is conceived as a new birth as the procedure itself and the explanation about it that Diodorus gives certainly show." Dey, 128-131, gives other examples to illustrate the compatibility of the conceptions of adoption and the new birth.

familia.[110] This exhortation is perfectly understandable in the context of the new birth.

This segment of the body-middle containing the first metaphor is concluded by a scripture quotation, which Dalton has already described as a compositional feature of this document.[111]

Metaphor-Children under a New Pater Potestas

The second metaphor in the οἶκος-cluster begins in verse seventeen and extends through verse twenty-one. It is introduced in verse seventeen by a conditional clause that functions as a minor transitional device.[112] The end of this metaphor's dominance is marked by the disjunction of the two accusatives, θεόν and τὰς ψυχάς, which conclude verse 21 and begin verse 22 respectively.

This metaphor specifically describes the readers as children who call God, "Father," and who have been redeemed [λυτρόω] from the vain conduct inherited from their former *familia* [πατροπαραδότος].[113] This metaphor relies heavily upon the notion of a family as a group of people who have originated from a common father. Discussing the definition of family in the Roman jurist, Ulpian, Gaudemet comments as follows:

> Under family would also be understood all the descendents of a common progenitor. Family in a narrow sense applies when the group still stands under the authority of this progenitor. Family in a broad sense applies when some of its

---

[110]Nils A. Dahl, "Das Volk Gottes," *Skrifter utgitt av det norske Videnskaps-Akademi: Historisk-Filosofisk Klasse* 1.2(1941):87; reprint, *Das Volk Gottes* (Darmstadt: Wissenschaftliche Buchgesellschaft, 1963), states, "The people of the end-time are holy, purified from all sin and freed from all sin (Ps Sal 17, 22f. 32, 41; Jub 4, 26; 50, 5; I Hen 10, 22; 39, 6; 49, 2; 69, 29; 91, 17; 92, 5; II Bar 73, 4; Test Levi 18; Judae 24; Or Sib V 431 etc.)."

[111]Dalton, *Proclamation*, 78, says, "The second part of ch. 1 begins with an exhortation to holiness. . . . This development reaches its climax and end with the Old Testament citation calling for the imitation of God's own holiness (1:16)."

[112]White, *Form*, 28, says, "Conditional clauses . . . are employed with a variety of meaning in the body-middle and thus indicate transitional force in a variety of ways. Though they sometimes mark a major movement to a new subject, more often they are used for minor shifts, i.e., the transition to a new but minor subject or to the development of the present subject."

[113]The ability to call God father is a result of their new birth as Michaels, *1 Peter*, 57, correctly suggests.

members have grown up, become independent, and have established a
separate home.[114]

In 1 Peter 1:3 God is designated as the *Stammvater* who has rebegotten the
author and his readers. As the rebegotten children of God, the readers
now belong to God's family and may address God as Father.

Francis Lyall describes the composition of an *οἶκος*. "The household
therefore consisted of the father, his wife, children [either natural or
adopted], their children and wives if any, and the slaves."[115] In this family
structure, the father or dominant male exercised complete control. In his
extended treatment of *οἶκος*, Verner describes the role of the father:

> At the head of the *familia* stood the *pater familias*, who possessed almost
> unlimited power over wife, children, and slaves. . . . The paternal authority
> [*patria potestas*] of the *pater familias* was almost unlimited. He had the power of
> life and death over his children. . . . The *pater familias* had sole right of
> proprietorship over all property held by members of his family. . . .[116]

A. Lumpe states, "The father of the house [*pater familias*] possessed an
almost unlimited power over his children [*patria potestas*]."[117] Given this
degree of control, members of the family were obligated to respect the
father. Musonius Rufus describes the deference owed the father:

> For, as a student of philosophy he will certainly be most eager to treat his father
> with the greatest possible consideration and will be most well behaved and gentle
> in his relations with his father he will never be contentious or self willed, nor
> hasty or prone to anger; furthermore, he will control his tongue and his appetite
> whether for food or for sexual temptations, and he will stand fast in the face of
> danger and hardships; and finally with competence in recognizing the true good,
> he will not let the apparent good pass without examination. As a result he will
> willingly give up all pleasures for his father's sake, and for him he will accept all
> manner of hardships willingly.[118]

---

[114]Gaudemet, 320.

[115]Francis Lyall, *Slaves, Citizens, Sons: Legal Metaphors in the Epistles* (Grand
Rapids: Zondervan Publishing House, 1984), 126.

[116]Verner, *Household*, 33-34.

[117]Lumpe, 1194.

[118]Musonius Rufus, 16.70. Text and translation in Lutz, 104-105.

This absolute power of the *pater familias* known as the *pater potestas*, obligated the family members to respect the father.[119]

This concept of the *pater potestas* provides the basis for the exhortation in this passage. Since the newborn child's father has absolute power over him/her, the appropriate attitude for the child to assume is respect and reverence toward his/her new father.[120] Thus, our author summons his readers in verse seventeen to conduct themselves in reverence [ἐν φόβῳ] if they exercise their privilege of calling God, "Father."

The writer intensifies this summons in several different ways. First, he places the intensifier καί before the protasis of the conditional sentence in verse seventeen. This position of καί means that the apodosis must take place if the protasis occurs.[121] If the readers call God, "Father," they must conduct themselves in reverence. Second, the writer intensifies his summons to reverent conduct by referring to their new father as one who judges impartially according to performance not status. Since their father is not an indulgent, spoiling father, the readers **must** conduct themselves in reverence and not rely on their position as children to act in any manner they please. Third, he intensifies his call to a reverent life by reference to the enormous price connected with their new birth. Their new birth was not procured by money but by the precious blood of Christ. Reflection upon this price should predispose the readers to give heed to the author's summons to reverent conduct. In these three ways, the writer intensifies his exhortation to reverence.

The author of 1 Peter concludes this passage by stating the result of the manifestation of Christ and the price He paid for their new birth. At the end of verse twenty-one, he says the result of all this is so that his

---

[119]Gaudemet, 331, warns against the misconception that the father was a tyrant with no responsibilities. He says, "The *pater familias* is however no tyrant with unlimited power. He is the agent of the union that he rules. He must exert his special prerogatives in the interest of the union."

[120]Ibid., 340, he notes, "Provided that Jesus indicates that respect is owed to the parents (Matthew 19:19), he does not insist on the authority of the father (Matthew 21:28-29; Luke 15:11-12."

[121]Smyth, 537, says, "Καί εἰ commonly implies that the conclusion must be true or must take place even in the extreme, scarcely conceivable, case which these words introduce." Blass, 190, says that conditional sentences introduced by εἰ καί require no special remarks since they function the same in the New Testament period as in the classical period.

readers' faith and hope might be in God. This aspect of the author's thought relates to the new birth because the newborn child can only place his/her expectation, confidence, and hope in his/her new *pater familias* who holds complete power and authority over him/her.

Metaphor-Children in a New Brotherhood

The third metaphor of the *οἶκος*-cluster extends from verse twenty-two to the end of Chapter 1. Like the first two metaphors, this metaphor also arises from the readers' new birth. The readers are now members of the *familia Dei* and gain not only a new father but also new siblings. Through this new birth, they enter into a new brotherhood. Love is the appropriate relational attitude toward one's siblings.[122] Lyall says, "The household . . . was bound together by the natural familial bonds of feeling and love."[123] Thus, on the basis of the metaphor of the brotherhood, the author exhorts his readers to love one another.

In this passage, two circumstantial participles, ἡγνικότες [having purified] and ἀναγεγεννημένοι [having been rebegotten], provide the context in which the command for brotherly love should be understood.[124] The first participle, ἡγνικότες, describes the readers' purification from hypocritical brotherly love. By obeying the truth, which refers to their acceptance of the Gospel message, the readers are prepared for unhypocritical brotherly love. In a familial situation, it is possible for a child to *play-act* and only pretend to love his/her siblings. Greco-Roman society recognized widespread failure in attaining love in familial relations. Betz comments on Plutarch's essay pertaining to brotherly love:

---

[122]See Plutarch's essay on περὶ φιλαδελφίας in his *Moralia* 478-492. See also the introduction and discussion of this essay by Betz, "De Fraterno Amore," passim, but particularly page 232, where he says, "We can assume that the family ethics upon which his essay is based was widely shared in antiquity, including, to an extent, Judaism and primitive Christianity. Plutarch spells out what other writers simply presuppose as commonly shared morality or life experience. Therefore, his essay is of great value not only for the understanding of Hellenistic ethics, but also all ancient ethics, including OT, Judaism, and Christianity. In biblical literature, terms and concepts related to "brotherly love" appear again and again. Their meaning is rarely discussed because its knowledge could simply be presupposed."

[123]Lyall, *Slaves*, 126.

[124]Goppelt, *Petrusbrief*, 129, states that these participles are not used imperatively, but circumstantially as motivations for the imperative.

The crisis of family relations, of which Plutarch speaks so pessimistically at the end of the first chapter of his essay, is reflected also in ECL. Both Plutarch and primitive Christianity admit that the natural bonds do not hold, given the pressures of the times. Both recognize that a religious bond must undergird the natural status of brotherhood if a lasting and proper relationship between brothers is to be achieved. Plutarch despairs when he looks at his own people.[125]

The religious bond that Betz describes is provided by the second participle, ἀναγεγεννημένοι, in verse twenty-three. The writer states that his readers' brotherhood is not based on a common natural origin from a transitory seed, but their brotherhood is based on a common spiritual origin from an eternal seed.[126] They have been constituted brothers by a regenerative process guaranteed by the enduring word of the living and enduring God.[127] Thus, their brotherhood is more real, genuine, and lasting than brotherhoods based on physical descent. Given this conception of their brotherhood, our author advocates that they love one another strenuously [ἐκτενῶς]. It is clear that the two circumstantial participles in this passage provide important perspectives from which the command to love should be understood.

As I have demonstrated, the metaphor of brotherhood dominates this passage. It provides the basis and rationale for the author's exhortation for

---

[125]Betz, "De Fraterno Amore," 233-234.

[126]Ibid., 233, he says, "Brothers in Christian families were related to each other not only 'by nature,' but as Christians."

[127]Eugene A. LaVerdiere, "A Grammatical Ambiguity in 1 Pet 1:23," *Catholic Biblical Quarterly* 36 (1974): 89-94, argues that the participles in 1:23 go with λόγου not θεοῦ by comparing this phrase to the preceding prepositional phrase ἐκ σπορᾶς φθαρτῆς ἀλλὰ ἀφθάρτου. Διὰ λογοῦ gives the instrument while ἐκ σπορᾶς gives the source. He speaks about the relationship of the two nouns, σπορᾶς and λόγου, on page 92, "Such a relationship of the two substantives would normally imply a similar relationship between their respective attributes." LaVerdiere offers no proof for this statement and, therefore, his assessment that the participles in 1:23 go with λόγου rests only on an assumption. In his grammatical analysis, he failed to identify the rhetorical figures utilized by this phrase. Hyperbaton, and more precisely interchained hyperbaton, is the rhetorical figure used here. Λόγου and θεοῦ, though grammatically linked, are separated by ζῶντος while ζῶντος and μένοντος, though linked grammatically, are separated by θεοῦ. The purpose of an interchained hyperbaton is to place each and every word in emphasis. The participles can go with either λόγου or θεοῦ, and in the absence of any clear grammatical indication, the author probably intended for them to go with both as Beare supposed. See his commentary, page 112. Thus, the participles are connected with λόγου and θεοῦ with equal emphasis.

his readers to love one another. It is linked to the two preceding metaphors by the conception of the new birth. This passage concludes with a scripture quotation (1:24-25), which is a common literary device used by this author.

Metaphor-Newborn Babies

The passage that contains the fourth metaphor of the οἶκος-cluster begins in 2:1 and extends to verse three. It is introduced by the inferential particle οὖν and the conjunctive participle ἀποθέμενοι.[128] This passage is concluded by a scripture quotation in verse three as is customary with this author.

This fourth metaphor of the οἶκος-cluster also arises from the new birth of the readers. In 2:2 the author describes them as newborn babies [βρέφη]. In contrast to the three previous metaphors, this metaphor does not focus upon the familial relations but instead emphasizes the growth following the new birth. The concept of the growth of newborn babies forms an important and distinguishing aspect of this metaphor. Clearly, newborn babies is a conception that arises from the institution of the οἶκος, and, therefore, is an appropriate metaphor for the author to use in this first section of the body-middle.

The metaphor of newborn babies substantiates the author's exhortation to desire the pure spiritual milk.[129] Just as newborn babies desire their mother's milk, this author calls his readers to desire the pure spiritual milk. He wants his readers to desire this milk so that they may grow up into salvation.

The author's summons to desire this milk is conditioned by the circumstantial participle in verse one and the protasis in verse three. He calls upon his readers to desire the milk after they have put away all evil, all guile, hypocrisies, envyings, and all evil speakings. It is interesting that

---

[128]See Wifstrand, 175-176, for a description of this type of participle.

[129]Scholars have exerted much effort to determine what our author meant by *pure spiritual milk*. The various positions are outlined by Michaels, *1 Peter*, 86f. On page 88 he concludes that *pure spiritual milk* refers to Christian instruction necessary for the believer to grow up into salvation. Goppelt, *Petrusbrief*, 134, says, "The *mother's milk* is in early Christianity as in its cultural environment a common metaphor for spiritual nourishment that imparts life."

all of these vices are lacking in newborn babies.[130] Although babies may have the potential for all of these vices, they are not actively engaged in them at birth. The most prominent desire of a newborn baby is for its mother's milk. Thus, the author of 1 Peter implies that his readers can only desire this milk after they have put away all of these vices. The protasis in verse three further specifies the condition under which the readers may desire this milk. The statement, "If you have tasted that the Lord is good [χρηστός]," provides the specific condition for desiring the milk. This statement assumes that the readers have already tasted, and, like a newborn baby, they liked what they tasted. This pleasant taste should drive them to desire more of the milk that will enable them to grow up into salvation.

Metaphor-Living Stones

The fifth and last metaphor of the οἶκος-cluster begins in 2:4 and ends in 2:10.[131] It is introduced by a conjunctive participial phrase in verse four and concluded by extended scripture quotation and midrash in verses 6-10.

This metaphor describes the readers as living stones that are being fashioned into a temple.[132] This metaphor of the temple or house of God

---

[130]There is a discussion in antiquity concerning the innocence of children that is explained by Albrecht Oepke, "Παῖς," in *Theological Dictionary of the New Testament*, vol. 5: Ξ-Πα, ed. Gerhard Friedrich (Grand Rapids: Wm. B. Eerdmans Publishing Co., 1970), 646-647. On page 651, he says, "The Church emphasizes esp. the innocence of the child."

[131]This passage has been thoroughly analyzed by Elliott, *Elect and Holy*, passim. See the critique of Elliott in Best, "Reconsideration," passim.

[132]The imagery of the living stone or stones continues to mesmerize scholars as they attempt to describe the meaning that this image conveys. Elliott, *Elect and Holy*, 26f., discusses and references the various positions that have been taken in regard to this image. I would suggest that it may refer to the natural rock on the temple mount that served as an altar. In *Wars of the Jews* V.5.6, Josephus describes it as follows: "Before this temple stood the altar, fifteen cubits high, and equal both in length and breadth; each dimension was fifty cubits. The figure it was built in was a square, and it had corners like horns; and the passage up to it was by an insensible acclivity. It was formed without any iron tool, nor did any such tool so much as touch it at any time [Whiston's translation]." In *Against Apion* 1.22, he further describes this altar, "There is a square altar, not made of hewn stone, but composed of white stones gathered together. . . ." J. C. Plumpe, "*Vivum saxum, vivi lapides*: The Concept of 'Living Stone' in Classical Antiquity," *Traditio* 1 (1943): 1-14, has pointed out that several Roman poets have used this image to refer to rock in its natural state, embedded in the earth. R. J. McKelvey, *The New Temple: The*

has obvious relations with the concept of the *οἶκος* as a building. Menahem Haran explains the implications of the phrase *house of God*:

> Further, the term *house of God* clearly designates the institution's primary function, which was exactly what the term implies–a house for the god, his dwelling place. Just as every temporal king, and indeed any man, has his own domicile, so the divine king, in whose shadow the community finds protection, has a residence of his own. And in this dwelling place, just as in every luxurious house, the master of the residence is provided with all his "needs": bread set on the table, incense for smell, lamps for light, meat-, grain-, and drink-offerings presented on the outer altar–the altar which in the fossilized cultic language is still referred to as "the Lord's table" (Ezek 44:16; Mal 1:7). In this dwelling place, moreover, the master of the residence has his own servants, the priests, who care for his necessities and keep the house in order.[133]

Although very different from the previous children metaphors that arose from the notion of *οἶκος* as family, this metaphor of the community as the house or temple is appropriate to this section since it arises from the idea of the *οἶκος* as the building that houses the family.[134]

This metaphor is closely connected grammatically and semantically with the preceding metaphor of newborn babies.[135] Because of the relative

---

Church in the New Testament, Oxford Theological Monographs (Oxford: Oxford University Press, 1969), 127, says, "In ancient thinking a 'living' stone was one that had not been hewn or broken and which, therefore, retained its numinous power." Given this conception of a *living stone*, it is very likely this image arises from the altar on the temple mount that was composed of a large natural rock to which smaller unhewn rocks were added.   For a further discussion of this image, see R. J. McKelvey, "Christ the Cornerstone," *New Testament Studies* 8 (1962): 352-359.

[133]Menahem Haran, "Temple and Community in Ancient Israel," in *Temple in Society*, ed. Michael Fox (Winona Lake: Eisenbrauns, 1988), 17.

[134]This notion of the community is used elsewhere as Philipp Vielhauer, *Oikodome*, Theologische Bücherei 65 (München: Chr. Kaiser, 1979), 138, notes, "Another instance is the thought of the community as a temple that also occurs at other times in the New Testament. As in Paul, so it is also used here not primarily in the sense of a building but rather as a collective designation under the point of view of holiness. The meaning in Ephesians is different where the real heavenly building is designated as a temple." Vielhauer, 138, has correctly noted the metaphorical use of the image here, stating, "The double meaning of *οἶκος* as house and as house community makes the allegory possible and perhaps occasions the designation of Christians as 'living stones.'"

[135]A later text, *The Shepherd of Hermas, Similitude* 9:29-30, calls the stones that are being taken from the mountain to build the tower or temple *innocent babes*. This document describes these innocent babes as being free from evil. Thus, this document

pronoun ὅν in verse 4, the passage that contains the metaphor of living stones is grammatically subordinate and dependent upon the passage that contains the metaphor of newborn babies. Also, the protasis of the conditional sentence that contained the previous metaphor was placed after the apodosis, and the term *Lord* was positioned as the last element in that protasis so that an essential association could be made between the term *Lord* and the participial phrase that introduces the metaphor of the readers as living stones. The Lord, whom the readers had tasted in the previous metaphor, is the same Lord upon whom they, as living stones, are fashioned into a temple for God.

Semantically, both of these metaphors are linked by the notion of growth.[136] Just as the growth of the body can be described in construction terms, so also the construction of a building can be referred to as growth.[137] Otto Michel cites Philo, who uses construction terms to discuss the growth of the body:

---

makes an explicit connection between the innocent babies and the stones that compose the temple. If the author of this document is not relying directly upon 1 Peter, he is probably relying upon a tradition he holds in common with 1 Peter. Since it contains more developed details, it is unlikely that the metaphor in *Similitude* 9 predates 1 Peter.

[136]Best, "Reconsideration," 281, says, "Commentators have often been puzzled by the sudden change of metaphor between 1 Pet. ii 1-3 [growth] and ii 4f. [building]. But these two conceptions are found together in the tradition at 1 Cor. iii 1-17 [cf. especially iii 9 where the transition is made; it recalls 1QS viii 4ff.] and Eph. ii 21 [where the temple is said to grow]." McKelvey, *Temple*, 98, concurs with the position of Best. McKelvey says, "The designation of the Christian community as the temple of God at 1 Cor 3:16-17 is prepared for by the use of the allegory of the building in verses 9-15, which, in turn, is introduced by the figure of the field under cultivation in vv. 5-9." A planting or plantation is another growth metaphor associated with the building metaphor. See Klinzing, 55, who cites many primary texts to support this association.

[137]Vielhauer, 74-75, notes the traditional connection of the building and agricultural metaphors in 1 Corinthians 3:5-17, saying, "And now he characterizes the community as God's possession with the double image: you are God's field, God's building. The cultivated field remains in the images. It is the field that the servants had planted and watered and it is God's possession. With the second image, Paul leaves behind this comparison. This transition from planting to building is not very astounding because the connection of both images is traditional. In the Old Testament and Judaism, in the Greek and Hellenistic worlds, in Philo and Gnosis, this connection is present. It is not an arbitrary creation of the apostle." Vielhauer, 78-79, explains how the images of the plantation and the building are used in this passage, saying, "As he had designated his relationship to Apollos in the image of planting and watering, so he designates his relationship to the Corinthians and their teachers in the image of foundation and

In *Leg. All.*, 2,6 he compares the leading part of the soul with the total soul, and uses as an analogy the relation of the heart to the body. It is formed before the whole body, "like a basic pillar or the keel of a ship," and on it the rest of the body is built [οἰκοδομεῖται τὸ ἄλλο σῶμα]. Here the term οἰκοδομεῖσθαι seems to be a stock image.[138]

Obviously, growth is the common conception that links the metaphor of the temple (2:4-10) with the metaphor of the body (2:1-3).[139]

   This connection of building and body terminology by the conception of growth occurs in the New Testament, especially in Ephesians. Commenting about Ephesians 4:16, Philip Vielhauer says, "The goal, in certain respects, identical with the building up of the body, is the growth of the body."[140] Ephesians 4:16 clearly links body terminology with building terminology. Vielhauer explains the connection of this terminology in Ephesians 4 by the groundwork laid in Ephesians 2. His explanation is as follows:

---

superstructure. . . . As the laying-a-foundation metaphor pertains to his proclamation, so the building-upon metaphor pertains to the teaching and the work metaphor to the teachings of those teachers." As Vielhauer has correctly perceived, the common denominator between these two metaphors is growth and development. Just as plants grow from the planting, so also buildings grow from the foundation. Vielhauer, 72-100, recognizes that the building metaphor with its notions of inception and growth is a favorite Pauline metaphor, describing his missionary activity.

   [138]Michel, "Οἰκοδομέω," 138. In addition to this reference, he cites many others.

   [139]Gärtner, *Temple*, 88, articulates yet another connection between 2:1-3 and 2:4-10. He says, "The passage in 1 Peter ii dealing with the temple, the priesthood and sacrifices also began with an exhortation to all Christians to avoid malice, guile, insincerity, envy and slander. This purity is an element in the Church's growing up in Christ until it becomes the 'new' temple, ii. 1-3. This combination of the demand for moral purity and the concept of the holiness of the 'new' temple was decisive for the temple symbolism of Qumran; it became no less a part of the New Testament description of the Church as the temple of God." McKelvey's suggestion that the metaphors of temple and body are linked because the temple housed the rock, which was conceived to be the *navel of the earth*, is interesting. In his article, "Christ the Cornerstone," he says, "A common expression for the *ebhen shetiyyah* [foundation stone] was *navel of the earth*. . . . This conception of the stone as the point from which the world grows received particularly fine expression under the image of the fountain or watering-place." The same conception is also found at Delphi. Also see McKelvey, *Temple*, 203.

   [140]Vielhauer, 133.

Ephesians 2:11-18 contained the discourse that the creation of a new man is intended through the unification of Jew and Gentile and reconciliation with God. . . . This new man as the totality of those reconciled through Christ bound in unity is the Church, the Body, whose head is Christ--in what sense will become clear in the exegesis of Ephesians 4. This notion of the new man very probably plays into the image of the church as a building and occasions the selection of 'to grow' as indeed the church in Ephesians is conceived as a personal essence and also here as a building consisting of men. Thereby, it is also understandable in so far as 'in Christ the entire building being fitted together grows' and in so far as Christ can function as the keystone for the building.[141]

Vielhauer recognizes the incompatibility of growth terminology with an inorganic process, concluding that the essential significance of this terminology when applied to buildings is to emphasize that the building is still not complete but in a state of development. He states the following:

Aὔξειν or respectively αὔξανειν equal to 'to grow' is almost always a description of an organic process or of a process that we would call organic in contrast to a mechanical process although antiquity, at the very least the New Testament, does not know our notion of organic as a self evident development according to an immanent conformity. For the New Testament, the 'Organic' is a miracle. In the mechanical process of building, the term 'to grow' is strange. One thing is however clear: With 'to grow' it is expressed that the building is still not complete but rather is still in process.[142]

Thus, the notion of development and growth is the essential connection between body and building terminology according to Vielhauer. In addition to Vielhauer, Gärtner also correctly notes the connection between the temple and the body in Ephesians 2. He says in his important study:

Another element in the development of this doctrine in the early church is the connection between the two images "temple" and "body." It has been correctly pointed out that these come into contact in Eph. ii 20-22. . . . It is evident that the concepts of the temple and the body were united at a very early stage in the traditions.[143]

---

[141]Ibid., 121.

[142]Ibid., 121.

[143]Gärtner, *Temple*, 140-141. The community is described as a temple and as children in 2 Corinthians 6:14--7:1. If this passage is Pauline, then the connection between temple and body was made very early. Even if the passage is not genuine, this connection was made before the Pauline letters were collected and began to be widely circulated. For a discussion of the genuineness of this passage see Hans Dieter Betz, "2 Cor 6:14--7:1: An

Noting the close connection between these two metaphors, Gärtner explicitly says, "The temple building is said to be a living being, capable of growth."[144] As these passages from Ephesians demonstrate, the connection of body and building terminology by the conception of growth is not unusual in the New Testament.

Relying on this conception of growth and the description of his readers as living stones, our author exhorts his readers to allow themselves to be built into a spiritual house so that a holy body of priests[145] might offer spiritual sacrifices acceptable to God through Jesus Christ.[146] Elliott argues that this passage states facts and contains no exhortation. He argues that οἰκοδομεῖσθε is indicative rather than imperative saying, "The descriptive character of these verses indicates that the two initial verbs προσερχόμενοι (v. 4a) and οἰκοδομεῖσθε (v. 5a) are to be understood as indicatives rather than imperatives."[147] His arguments are not as convincing as the arguments he cites that indicate these verbs should be understood as imperatives:

> From (1) the participial imperative ἀποθέμενοι (2:1), (2) the similarity of sentence structure in vv. 1f. and 4f. [ἀποθέμενοι . . . ὡς ἀρτιγέννητα βρέφη . . . ἐπιποθήσατε followed by final ἵνα/προσερχόμενοι . . . ὡς λίθοι ζῶντες . . . οἰκοδομεῖσθε followed by a final infinitive], and (3) the position of vv. 4-10 within preceding and succeeding paraenesis one might assume that both verbs should be treated as imperatives.[148]

Anti-Pauline Fragment?" *Journal of Biblical Literature* 92 (1973): 88-108. He concludes that the theology of this passage is not only non-Pauline but also anti-Pauline.

[144]Gärtner, *Temple*, 103.

[145]Both Elliott, *Elect and Holy*, 66-67 and Ernest Best, "Spiritual Sacrifice," *Interpretation* 14 (1960): 273-299, argue that ἱεράτευμα does not mean *priesthood* but *body of priests*. On page 233, Elliott says, "'Ιεράτευμα means 'body of priests.' It does not mean 'priesthood' which is rather the equivalent of ἱερατεία, a more static and abstract term."

[146]McKelvey, *Temple*, 129, comments, "The acceptability of sacrifice was a matter of fundamental importance for the ancients, and the reference to it in this text may echo the popular belief that in the eschatological age worship would be pleasing to God (Mal. 3:1-4; *Ps Sol.* 17:32f.)." For Qumran documents that reflect this same perspective, see Gärtner, 20f.

[147]Elliott, *Elect and Holy*, 16-17.

[148]Ibid., 16, note 1. Vielhauer, 140, also thinks that the verb is probably indicative not imperative but offers no supporting argument.

Except for taking the participle as an imperative, I agree with Goppelt, who understands οἰκοδομεῖσθε to be an imperative.[149] He correctly assesses the meaning of οἰκοδομεῖσθε in the following passage:

> The agent [let yourselves be built] suggests perhaps that the community is built not by God but by Christ as the New Testament consistently affirms. This affirmation does not exclude the use of the imperative but rather includes the use of the imperative.[150]

As Goppelt observes, the passive form of this imperative is significant. Blass comments on the passive imperative saying, "The passive in the sense of 'to allow oneself to be . . .' [cf. German *sich lassen*] was common from earliest times: ἀδικεῖσθε 1 Cor 6:7 'let yourselves be wronged' [in the sense of allowing it]."[151] The author of 1 Peter used the passive imperative because of the widespread belief that the new eschatological temple would be built by the Messiah or God.[152] After quoting *1 Enoch* 90:28-29, McKelvey comments, "The temple is said to be erected by God himself. Its newness, size, magnificence, and difference from the former temple are emphasized."[153] He also cites *Sibylline Oracles* 5:424, which reads, "He [the Messiah] made a giant tower touching the very clouds and seen of all."[154] Thus, the passive imperative in this passage indicates that the author summons his readers to provide the materials and give their consent, but the temple of which he speaks is built by the Messiah or God.

This conception of the religious community as a temple or sanctuary has many parallels in the Qumran documents.[155] Gärtner explains this phenomenon:

---

[149]Goppelt, *Petrusbrief*, 141, says, "The new subject is introduced with the participle intended as an imperative."

[150]Ibid., 144.

[151]Blass, 165.

[152]Vielhauer, 138-139, says, ". . . it is very possible, indeed very probable, that originally the conception of the eschatological temple, spoken of by *Ethiopic Enoch* 91:13 and *Jubilees* 1:17 lay at the base of the collective designation, 'Temple,' 'House of God'. . . ."

[153]McKelvey, *Temple*, 29.

[154]Ibid., 19.

[155]Hans Wenschkewitz, "Die Spiritualisierung der Kultusbegriffe: Tempel, Priester und Opfer im Neuen Testament," *Angelos* 4 (1932): 126, thought that the transference of the notion of temple to the body or community was derived from Stoicism.

The transference of the complex of ideas from the temple to the community may
have been facilitated by the fact that even in the OT, Israel was sometimes spoken
of as 'the house of God.' The people are described as a 'house,' thus providing a
parallel to the ideology of the Qumran community in speaking of itself as 'the
house of God,' the true temple.[156]

In these documents, many of the ideas associated with the literal temple are
sequestered and pressed into the service of this metaphor. The *Manual of
Discipline* 9:3-6 provides an excellent illustration of this transference
of ideas:

> When these things obtain in Israel, as defined by these provisions, the Holy Spirit
> will indeed rest on a sound foundation; truth will be evinced perpetually; the guilt
> of transgression and the perfidy of sin will be shriven; and atonement will be
> made for the earth more effectively than by any flesh of burnt offerings or fat of
> sacrifices. The 'oblation of the lips' will be in all justice like the erstwhile
> 'pleasant savor' on the altar; righteousness and integrity like that free-will offering
> which God deigns to accept. At that time, the men of the community will
> constitute a true and distinctive temple—a veritable holy of holies—wherein the

---

However, the discovery of the Dead Sea Scrolls provide a much better parallel to this
phenomenon. Gärtner, 78, says, "The resemblance between Qumran and 1 Pet. ii is so
striking at this point that we are compelled to assume the existence of some common
tradition." See Klinzing, 192, note 4, for a list of several works that discuss parallels
between 1 Peter and Qumran. Ohly, 1042-1043, has a very good discussion of the house-
metaphor in the New Testament and Qumran documents.

[156]Gärtner, *Temple*, 21. On page 29f., he refers to the following documents that
refer to the community as temple: 1QS ix 3ff.; 1QS v 5f.; viii.4f.; x 18; 1QH vi 25f.; and
4QFlor. After scrutinizing each of these texts, Elisabeth Schüssler Fiorenza, "Cultic
Language in Qumran and in the NT," *The Catholic Biblical Quarterly* 38 (1976): 165,
qualifies Gärtner's list of passages that equate community with temple. She says, "The
notion of the community as the temple of the endtime is found only in 1QS, CD and
perhaps 4QFlor, but not in 1QH, 1QM or the other fragments." Allan J. McNicol, "The
Eschatological Temple in the Qumran Pesher 4QFlorilegium 1:1-7," *Ohio Journal of
Religious Studies* 5.2 (1977): 133-141, further limits the list. He argues that
4QFlorilegium does not refer to the temple as a community but to the literal eschatological
temple in the future. This entire debate is only marginally pertinent to this dissertation since
some of these texts from Qumran undeniably refer to the community as a temple as
Klinzing, 88, correctly concludes. On page 89, he says, "When the community designates
itself as the temple, it expresses by that designation essential conceptions of its
self understanding."

priesthood may fitly foregather, and a true and distinctive synagogue made up of laymen who walk in integrity.[157]

As the *Manual of Discipline* illustrates, the community assumed the liturgy of the temple and performed that liturgy with greater precision and effectiveness than the liturgy of the literal temple. The entire sacrificial system of the temple is appropriated by the community that performs these sacrifices in their purest form by its moral and righteous life.[158]

Many, but not all, of these ideas are present in the metaphor in 1 Peter.[159] The author exhorts his readers to allow themselves to be built into a spiritual house, i.e., temple,[160] so that a holy body of priests might

---

[157]Theodor H. Gaster, trans., *The Dead Sea Scriptures* (Garden City: Doubleday, 1976), 63.

[158]For a discussion of other texts from Qumran see Gärtner, *Temple*, 44f. See Klinzing, 93-105, for a possible explanation for this notion at Qumran. This notion of cultic acts being replaced by moral action is not limited to Qumran. Seneca, *Epistle* 95.50, says, "Would you win over the gods? Then be a good man. Whoever imitates them is worshipping them sufficiently." Text and translation in Gummere, vol. 3, 90-91. McKelvey, *Temple*, 44-45, recognizes the same trend in Diaspora Judaism. He says, "This trend found fruitful soil in Diaspora Judaism, since it was very largely cut off from worship at Jerusalem. *Every sacrifice as a fragrant offering is a small thing, and all fat for burnt offerings to thee is a very little thing, but he who fears the Lord shall be great forever* (Judith 16:16). Again, *When the Lord demands bread or candles or flesh or any other sacrifice, then that is nothing; but God demands pure hearts* . . . (Slav. En. 45:3). *What is the highest form of glory? And he said, 'To honor God, and this is done not with gifts and sacrifices but with purity of soul and holy conviction.'* (Letter of Aristeas 234). . . . The mood of the period we are now studying is well illustrated by Ben-Sira: *He who keeps the law makes many offerings; he who heeds the commandments sacrifices a peace offering* (Ecclus. 35:1)."

[159]Klinzing, 194-195, correctly observes that the notion of the substitution of the temple formed by the Christian community for the temple in Jerusalem is not specifically stated in Christian documents but only implied. In contrast, this substitution is explicitly expressed in the Qumran documents. Many of these ideas associated with the temple had already been appropriated by Christian writers before 1 Peter and continued to be used after this document was written. Ohly, 949, says, "The spiritualized-intensified metaphorization in the New Testament of the occurrence of temple, house, and building that is actual in the Old Testament, especially through Paul, as well as the exposition of biblical references to buildings according to the spiritual sense in Christian exegeses opened up to the metaphorical language bequeathed to Christianity from Antiquity a broad field of theologically packed house-metaphors. . . ."

[160]Commenting on the quotation of Psalm 118:22 in Mark 12:10, Vielhauer, 57-58, says, "Should the image be explained further so that along with it the 'future temple' (*Theological Dictionary of the New Testament*, vol. 4, 278), 'the notion of a sanctuary devoted to God without likeness' would refer to the community of the end-time? Should

offer sacrifices acceptable to God through Jesus Christ.[161] The participle
προσερχόμενοι in verse four provides the context in which the author's
exhortation is to be observed.[162] As his readers come to the living stone,
they are to allow themselves to be built into a spiritual house. The
scripture quotations that conclude this passage reinforce the author's
exhortation.[163] They affirm that the temple the readers are forming is the
true temple because it is founded upon the chosen rock, Jesus Christ. In
verses nine and ten, the author quotes scriptures that had previously been
applied to the old Israel, and he now applies them to the new Israel.[164]
These scriptures confirm that the readers should allow themselves to be
built into this spiritual house because as such they are God's true

---

the image also be explained further so that the image of the divine plantation is placed next
to the image of the divine building? Certainly the community has taken over this
explanation, for example, 1 Peter 2:3-10." Vielhauer concludes that the context of Mark 12
does not support the notion of the community but expresses the Messianic character of
Jesus. He reaches the same conclusion about the quotation in Acts 4:11 and says that
1 Peter 2:7 introduces a new nuance.

[161]Since our author does not specify the nature of these sacrifices, many studies
have attempted to speculate on what the author meant. A. Feuillet, "*Les sacrifices spirituels*
du sacerdoce royal des baptisés (1 P 2, 5)," *Nouvelle revue Théologigue* 96 (1974): 704-
728, proposes that the sacrifices refer to the voluntary imitation of the sacrificial offering of
Christ, the suffering servant. See the articles by E. Ferguson, "Spiritual Sacrifice in Early
Christianity and Its Environment," *Aufstieg und Niedergang der römischen Welt* II, 23.2
(1980): 1151-1189 and D. Hill, "'To Offer Spiritual Sacrifices' (1 Peter 2:5): Liturgical
Formulations and Christian Paraenesis in 1 Peter," *Journal for the Study of the New
Testament* 16 (1982): 45-63. See also McKelvey, *Temple*, 129, who concurs with
Feuillet and Gärtner, *Temple*, 84-85.

[162]Best, "Spiritual Sacrifice," 281, says, "Thus προσέρχεσθαι carries here its full
significance and refers to the approach of the priest to God."

[163]McKelvey, *Temple*, 125, concurs, "*You are a chosen race, a royal priesthood, a
holy nation, God's own people. . . . Once you were no people, but now you are God's
people* (2.9). The words form the conclusion of a string of Old Testament quotations
which is intended to reinforce the paraenesis in the earlier part of the section (vv. 4-5)."

[164]Best, "Reconsideration," 278, says, "To summarize: in vv. 4-5 Peter sets out
the nature of the church using [as we shall see] an imagery which was common to the early
Christian tradition and which serves to contrast the church with the OT people of God; he
then confirms this with OT quotations in vv. 6, 7; with that of v. 7 and the words of v. 8
he moves his argument to consider the position of those who reject Christ; finally in vv. 9-
10 he goes on to show the continuity between the new and the old Israel." Klinzing, 195,
says, "Both the Christian and the Qumran communities understand themselves as the
eschatological people of God and take upon themselves the corresponding Old
Testament attributes."

community, which performs their divine task of declaring the wonderful deeds of their God.[165]

The metaphor of the community forming a temple lends credence to the author's exhortation and provides the theme that controls the various ideas expressed in this passage. This metaphor is closely related to the previous metaphor of newborn babies and fits well into the οἶκος-cluster of metaphors.

Assessment

The preceding discussion has demonstrated that this first section of the body-middle's composition is controlled and determined by the conception of the οἶκος. The dual meaning of this term as *family* or *house* gives rise to all five of the compositional-determining metaphors in this section of the letter.[166] These five metaphors that describe the ontological status of the readers permit the author to make various kinds of exhortations to them. Each of these exhortations are intimately connected with, and supported by, the appropriate metaphor. The exhortation to be holy is legitimated by the description of the readers as obedient children. Given the new *pater potestas* under which the readers now live, the exhortation to reverent conduct is appropriate. The summons to love one another is required because the readers find themselves in a new *familia*, part of a new

---

[165]McKelvey, *Temple*, 130, says, "The new cult, thus offered, will declare the wonderful deeds of him who called you out of darkness into his marvelous light (v. 9). That is to say, the church is commissioned to do the task which Israel failed to do. . . . Our author suggests, the new temple, raised now at the end of the times, is for the purpose of witnessing to the saving act of God in Christ." Best, "Spiritual Sacrifice," 279, recalls that one of the primary functions of priests is to declare the righteous deeds of God.

[166]Goppelt's analysis of 1:13--2:10 is seriously deficient. He does not recognize that 1:13 forms the body opening. Neither does he recognize the various sections of metaphor and corresponding paraenesis. He divides this section into three subsections based upon the exhortations in 1:13, 22 and 2:5. He does not fully explain why he selects these exhortations as being compositionally significant while ignoring 1:15, 17 and 2:2. He states, *Petrusbrief*, 110, "Both of the imperatives in 1:13, 22 together with the present imperative in 2:5 thematicize the call to enduring membership in the community. They designate the three subsections of this passage." His failure to observe the correlation of metaphor and exhortation is illustrated on page 110 by the fact that he understands 1:13-21 to be stating the imperatival implications of the indicatives of 1:3-12. As I have shown, 1:3-12 states the context for the letter and the imperatives in 1:13-21 arise from their corresponding metaphors, not the indicatives of 1:3-12.

brotherhood. The command to desire the pure spiritual milk is
appropriately situated within a description of the readers as newborn
babies. The author's exhortation to his readers to allow themselves to be
built into a spiritual house for God is understandable given the description
of the readers as living stones forming a new temple. Thus, these five
metaphors taken from the conception of the οἶκος determine the subsections
of the first section of 1 Peter

In order to understand how these subsections relate to each other, the
relationship of these metaphors must be considered.[167] The first three
metaphors relate to the concept of the new birth and the consequent
familial relations (1:14-25) whereas the last two relate to the growth
subsequent to the new birth (2:1-10). These considerations indicate that the
first three metaphors and the last two metaphors form two distinct
subsections. Furthermore, the first subsection can be divided into two
parts because the first two metaphors are concerned with the newborn's
relationship with the father (1:14-21) while the third metaphor is

---

[167]Failure to recognize these metaphors is the essential error of Schutter,
Hermeneutic. Although he correctly identifies each of the subsections by his method of
literary analysis, he is unable to correctly relate them to one another. He summarizes his
position on p. 52 saying, "The first sub-unit (1.14-6) introduces the theme in terms of Lev.
19.2, setting the imitation of divine holiness in strict opposition to conformity with the kind
of conduct that had typified the addressees' former lives. The second (1.17-21) goes
behind the commandment to the God who uttered it, enjoining upon the addressees specific
attitudes commensurate with his holy character as revealed in the story of salvation,
'reverence,' 'faith,' and 'hope.' And this triad is foundational to a fourth attitude promoted
in 1.22-5, one directed this time not towards God but fellow Christians, 'love.'
Afterwards, 2.1-3 resumes the topic of conduct antithetical to the way of holiness in order
to enlarge upon those forms especially inimical to the loving fellowship just emphasized.
The fifth sub-unit (2.4-9) erects a veritable edifice of cultic imagery to bring the body-
opening to an exalted conclusion . . . ." He incorrectly states that 1:14-16 introduces
holiness as the controlling theme of the passage. As my analysis has shown, election and
its corollary, the new birth, is the controlling theme. He mistakenly bases the third
subsection on the second by stating that the triad of reverence, faith, and hope in the second
subsection is foundational to the attitude of love promoted in the third subsection. He does
not see the connection of the fourth and fifth subsections. His statement that the fifth
subsection brings this section to an exalted conclusion by recalling the privileges that
belong to those who have answered God's call fails to recognize that privileges have either
been explicitly stated or implied in each subsection of this passage. Thus, my analysis
confirms the subsections identified by Schutter but disproves his conception of their
relationship to one another as well as his identification of the controlling theme of
this passage.

concerned with the newborn's relationship to siblings (1:22-25). Considering the relationship of these metaphors to one another permits the subdivision of the first section of 1 Peter. Thus, the preceding discussion of the οἶκος-cluster of metaphors leads to the following outline of this section of the body-middle:

The Οἶκος-Cluster
The Elect Household of God
(1:14--2:10)

1. Οἶκος-metaphors arising from the new birth and consequent familial relations (1:14-25)

    1.1. Metaphors relating the newborn to the Father (1:14-21)

        1.1.1. Metaphor-obedient children: Be holy (1:14-16)

        1.1.2. Metaphor-children under a new *pater potestas*: Be reverent (1:17-21)

    1.2. Metaphor-children in a new brotherhood: Love one another (1:22-25)

2. Οἶκος-metaphors arising from the conception of growth (2:1-10)

    2.1. Metaphor-newborn babies: Desire spiritual milk (2:1-3)

    2.2. Metaphor-living stones forming a new temple: Allow yourselves to be built (2:4-10)

By using the concept of the οἶκος in this first section of the body-middle, the author has attempted to accomplish his twin objectives of explicating conduct befitting his readers on their journey and of encouraging them to continue their journey and not to defect.[168] He has

---

[168]Sander, xl, provides a likely explanation for the predestination theme prevalent in 1 Peter 2:7-8 in relation to the author's stated objective in 5:12. She says, "The emphasis on predestination which is so strong in the Qumran community leads to the certainty of its members that they will, indeed, be in the *lot* [גורל] of God in the end-time, i.e. that they will be saved and not in the *lot* of Belial. The office or station of the sectarians is to stand firm in that *lot*. . . . It is probable that the early Christian community

described his readers as belonging to a new family, the family of God. The people making the eschatological journey are none other than the elect family of God. Those who belong to this family through the new birth have obligations as family members to conduct themselves in holiness, reverence, and love on their journey. To defect from the Christian faith would mean abandonment of this family with all its rights and privileges. The ethical conduct that finds appropriate expression in this family loses its frame of reference if the family is abandoned. The author has described his readers as children growing into salvation and as stones growing into the temple of God. Defection means they cut themselves off from the milk that enables them to grow into salvation, and they exclude themselves from the true temple of God. More importantly, defection would remove them from the protection of this family's God.[169] Since our author is using a rhetoric of suppression, he does not explicitly mention any of these negative consequences but leaves the reader to draw his/her own conclusions. He will continue this rhetorical approach in the following section composed around the παρεπίδημος-cluster of metaphors.

The Second Metaphor Cluster (2:11--3:12):
Aliens in this World

In 2:11--3:12 the author of 1 Peter selects another specific image of the Diaspora as the basis for another metaphor cluster. The metaphor cluster in this section arises from the author's description of his readers as aliens in this world [παρεπίδημος/πάροικος]. The metaphor cluster that dominates this section is intimately related to the οἶκος-cluster that precedes.[170] This

---

shared this hope and felt that they through Christ would indeed be among those saved, the elect. In 1 Peter 5:12 it is possible that there is an injunction to stand firm in this *lot*."

[169]Verner, 28, says, "The οἶκος was also a religious unit. Everyone who became a part of it passed into the service and under the protection of its gods."

[170]Bernhard Weiss, *1 Peter*, A Commentary on the New Testament, vol. 4: *Thessalonians-Revelation* (New York: Funk and Wagnalls, 1906), 275, correctly identified the metaphor cluster in this section although he did not correctly identify the extent of the section carrying it through 4:6. He says, "The Second Principal Part of the Epistle discusses the relation of the readers to the Gentile world around them, in the midst of whom they live. As citizens of the kingdom of heaven, they really do not any longer belong to this world, but as pilgrims they merely enjoy the privileges of hospitality among

connection is explicitly stated in 1:17. K. L. Schmidt comments on this verse:

> Christians, then, are to understand their life, their ἀναστρέφεσθαι on earth as a παροικία [sojourn], and they are to pay heed to the exhortation: ἐν φόβῳ τὸν τῆς παροικίας ὑμῶν χρόνον ἀναστράφητε [Conduct yourselves in reverence during the time of your sojourn], 1 Pt. 1:17.[171]

Since God's family is away from its *patria*, it falls into the legal category of alien; and this legal concept provides the basis for the metaphor cluster in this section.[172]

The author of 1 Peter derives this metaphorical notion of his readers as aliens in this world from the experience of the Jewish Diaspora. By and large, the Jews lived in the Diaspora as aliens. He describes his readers with two specific Diaspora terms: παρεπίδημος and πάροικος.[173] Goppelt comments on these terms, "Both ideas are made clear by the reference to the model of the Diaspora."[174] Stählin also comments on the use of these terms in 1 Peter:

---

a foreign people; and are like strangers, who only for the time being have taken lodging at a place. As such they must not accept the customs of life that are in vogue around them."

[171]K. L. Schmidt, "Πάροικος," in *Theological Dictionary of the New Testament*, vol. 5: Ξ-Πα, ed. Gerhard Friedrich (Grand Rapids: Wm. B. Eerdmans Publishing Co., 1970), 852.

[172]Demosthenes' *Oration Against Eubulides* defends Euxitheus from the charge that he was an ἀπολίτης. In order to establish the citizenship of Euxitheus' mother, Demosthenes reasons in section 34, "If she were an alien, they should have examined the market-tax roles and shown that she paid the alien's tax and from what country she came. . . ." Schmidt, 29, explains the figurative application of this institution in early Christianity, "To express this thought there developed in the language of Christianity a kind of constitutional terminology. In the NT, as in Philo (esp. *Cher.*, 120; *Gig.*, 61), the Stoic categories πόλις and πολιτεία are applied to the heavenly and earthly world, and in apocalyptic expectation these are fused with the city of God. . . . When a person becomes a believer, then he moves from the far country to the vicinity of God. His former outlawry is replaced by civil rights in heaven. But this also means migration from the world to a place distant from the world. There now arises a relation of reciprocal foreignness and estrangement between Christians and the world."

[173]Bigg, 90-91, says that παρεπίδημος is very applicable to Jews in the Dispersion.

[174]Goppelt, *Petrusbrief*, 80.

Christians are in the world as a ξένον ἔθνος. . . . Hence they cannot κατοικεῖν in this alien world. They can only παροικεῖν, "reside as less privileged aliens," or strictly παρειπδημεῖν, "sojourn temporarily as foreigners without rights" (1 Pt. 2:11; 1:1, 17). . . . For this distinctive position of Christians in the world the NT finds prototypes . . . especially in the Jewish Dispersion, whose characteristic terminology was richly used by the NT in its new sense-one aspect of the appropriation of Jewish perogatives by the new Israel.[175]

Thus, both of the terms descriptive of the readers' alien status are drawn from Diaspora terminology.

Schürer describes the position of Jewish Diaspora communities, "In most areas, however, the position of the Jewish communities is perhaps more comparable with that of other associations of immigrants from the Near East. Jews, like Phoenicians and Egyptians, lived as aliens within a foreign city."[176] He continues his description a little later:

In most of the ancient cities of Phoenicia, Syria and Asia Minor, as in Greece itself, immigrant Jews certainly occupied the position of aliens (non-citizens). Their communities were corporations of foreigners, recognized by the city and granted certain rights, but their members did not enjoy citizenship and therefore took no part in the conduct of city affairs.[177]

The fact that Jews lived in the Diaspora as aliens provides the basis for the author's conception of his readers as aliens living in the Diaspora (1:1).

Either the author of 1 Peter took over these terms from the Jewish Diaspora and modified them, or he received them in their modified form from the Christian tradition. Stuiber articulates the Christian development of these terms:

For Jewish Christian Addressees, the term Diaspora was taken in its usual Jewish meaning. For Gentile Christians, the term Diaspora can only pertain in a developed meaning. Just as for the Diaspora Jews Jerusalem is their native city, so the Christians have the Jerusalem above (Galatians 4:26) as well as their essential citizenship in heaven (Philippians 3:20) and they live as παρεπίδημοι of the Diaspora or as πάροικοι. Already in the Jewish terminology, Diaspora and

---

175Gustav Stählin, "Ξένος," in *Theological Dictionary of the New Testament*, vol. 5: *X-Pa*, ed. Gerhard Friedrich (Grand Rapids: Wm. B. Eerdmans Publishing Co., 1970), 30-31.

176Schürer, vol. 3.1, 113.

177Ibid., 126.

παροικία are correlative terms. He who lives in the Diaspora can only be in his dwelling place a πάροικος.[178]

The author of 1 Peter uses these Diaspora terms in accord with Christian tradition to describe his readers as non-citizens of this world who, nevertheless, live in this world.

The author describes his readers as παροίκοι [resident aliens] and παρεπίδημοι [visiting aliens] in 2:11.[179] Although commentators frequently understand both of these terms as synonyms,[180] they are not, but these terms represent different categories of aliens. W. Dittenberger quotes an inscription that differentiates between the various peoples inhabiting a city. The inscription refers to three categories of inhabitants: (1) πολῖται [citizens], (2) ἄλλοι οἱ κατοικοῦντες τὴν πόλιν [others who settle down in the city], and (3) οἱ παρεπιδημοῦντες ξένοι [visiting strangers].[181] In this inscription, κατοικοῦντες and παρεπιδημοῦντες refer to two different categories of aliens. The former term refers to alien settlers while the latter term designates alien visitors.[182] Plato makes a similar societal division in his discussion of the laws relating to the harvest of fruit. He describes stipulations relating first to the citizen, then to the slave, the resident alien, and the visiting alien.[183] Thus, πάροικοι and παρεπίδημοι are not synonyms but describe two basic classes of aliens, the resident alien and the visiting alien. When these two terms are used together as they are

---

[178]Stuiber, 974.

[179]Schmidt, "Πάροικος," 842, distinguishes between these two terms, "The πάροικος is not a παρεπίδημος, who lives in a place for only a short time, but a resident alien, who has his domicile with or among the natives, having no civil rights but living under the common protection." Commenting on the verb παρεπιδημέω, Walter Grundmann, "Δῆμος," in *Theological Dictionary of the New Testament*, vol. 2: Δ–H, ed. Gerhard Kittel (Grand Rapids: Eerdmans Publishing Company, 1964), 64, says, "Παρεπιδημέω means 'to stay in a place as an alien' with the suggestion of transitoriness. . . . This gives us the meaning of παρεπίδημος, namely, 'one who is [temporarily] resident in a place as an alien.'" Commenting on the verb παροικέω, Schmidt, states, "The verb παροικεῖν means (a) 'to dwell beside' and (b) . . . 'to be a resident alien,' of a foreigner who dwells somewhere without national rights."

[180]Selwyn, *1 Peter*, 169, says, "Peter has used both terms earlier. . . . Both terms are almost identical. . . ."

[181]W. Dittenberger, ed., *Orientis Graecae Inscriptiones Selectae* (Hildesheim: G. Olms, 1960), 339, 29.

[182]For further examples of this distinction, see Stählin, 30, note 203. This same distinction between these two terms is also maintained in the lexicons.

[183]Plato, *Laws*, 8.844e-845d.

in 2:11, they form a figure of speech known as hendiadys and express the concept, non-citizen.[184] Both of these terms describe the alien status of the Jew in the Diaspora and by transference, the metaphorical alien status of the Christian in this world.

In 2:16 the author describes his readers as ἐλεύθεροι [free men], a term closely associated with the terms παρεπίδημος/πάροικος and indicative of the Jewish Diaspora experience. Because of the significant theological tradition behind this term, many commentators deny it has any political connotation in this passage.[185] However, I argue it does have political connotations in this context that contains political terms drawn from the Diaspora and discusses various groups of aliens. Ἐλεύθερος and δοῦλος describe the two basic categories of individuals in this society.[186] Both the παρεπίδημος and the πάροικος fall in the category of ἐλεύθερος, not δοῦλος, and the Jews of the Diaspora were by and large free men. As Reinach notes, the unfortunate Jews who entered the Diaspora as slaves were usually freed quickly. He explains as follows:

> On the other hand, during the wars of the third and second centuries BCE, thousands of Jews were made captives and reduced to slavery, passing from owner to owner and from land to land until their enfranchisement. This enfranchisement indeed usually occurred very soon, it being precipitated by the fact that, through their unswerving attachment to their customs, they proved inefficient servants. Besides, owing to the close solidarity which is one of the lasting traits of the Jewish race, they had no difficulty in finding coreligionists who were willing to pay the amount of their ransom.[187]

Except for isolated incidents and the special circumstances following the insurrections under Vespasian and Trajan, almost all Jews lived as free men

---

[184]B. Kübler, "Peregrinus," *Paulys Real-Encyclopädie der classischen Altertumswissenschaft*, ed. Wilhelm Kroll, vol. 19: *Pech-Petronius* (Stuttgart: J. B. Metzler, 1937), 639, says, "The *peregrinus* is not only the foreigner but also the one who has his place of habitation in the land when he does not have Roman citizenship. The antonymn to *peregrinus* is *citizen*." Schmidt, "Πάροικος," 845, notes a similar hendiadys in Hebrew. He says, "It is noteworthy that often, as in Gn. 23:4; Lv. 25:23, 35, 47; Nu. 35:15, the terms גֵּר and תּוֹשָׁב form a single concept." Grundmann, 65, cites LXX Gn. 23:4 where παρεπίδημος is used with πάροικος in reference to the resident alien.

[185]Michaels, *1 Peter*, says, "Peter has in mind not political or social freedom, but freedom in Christ. . . ."

[186]Gaius, *Institutes*, 1.9.

[187]Theodore Reinach, "Diaspora," *The Jewish Encyclopedia*, vol. 4: *Chazars-Dreyfus* (New York: KTAV Publishing House, 1906), 560.

in the Diaspora. It was only as free men that the terms παρεπίδημος and πάροικος technically applied.[188] Our author in 2:16 likens his readers to free men and thus fills out the concept of παρεπίδημος/πάροικος, which he introduced in 2:11 by the hendiadys, *resident aliens and visiting aliens.*

In addition to these terms that arise from the Jewish experience of the Diaspora, the function of the domestic code that comprises a significant portion of this section also emphasizes the author's interest in describing the alien status of his readers. David L. Balch, who has engaged in the most exhaustive study of this domestic code, concludes that such codes were used for one of two purposes. On the one hand, spokespersons of the political establishment employed them to encourage good citizenship. On the other hand, various non-citizen groups used them as propaganda to refute the charge that they were subverting the morals of society.[189] He assigns the code in this section of 1 Peter to the latter purpose.[190] For him, this code is apologetic and urges Christians to exemplary behavior in order to refute the slanders of their antagonists in the larger society.[191] His conclusion that this code functions as propaganda for a non-citizen group concurs with my contention that this section is composed around the concept of Christians as aliens in this world.

I conclude that the composition of this section of the letter (2:11--3:12) is dominated by the metaphor cluster of aliens in this world. This compositional structure is demonstrated by each of the metaphorical descriptions of the readers. All of these metaphors are drawn from the Jewish experience of the Diaspora. The function of the domestic code, which serves to legitimate the actions of these non-citizens, is further evidence that the metaphor cluster of aliens controls this section.[192] Each of the metaphors of this cluster must now be examined to determine the extent of its control and the admonition ensuing from it.

---

[188]Kübler, 639, says, "The peregrinus is the free man who is not a roman citizen."

[189]Balch, *Wives*, 61-63.

[190]Ibid., 81f.

[191]Ibid., 87-88, he says that the code contains behavior demanded by the governor even of aliens.

[192]Elliott's contention, along with others, that the content of 1 Peter is accurately described as an ethics for exiles is not entirely correct. *Non-citizen* not *exile* is the determining theme for this section. The non-citizen theme only controls this section, not the entire letter. See Elliott, "Rehabilitation," 251.

Metaphor-Resident and Visiting Aliens

The first metaphor in verse 11 describes the readers as resident and visiting aliens. This metaphor is introduced by the vocative, $\dot{a}\gamma a\pi\eta\tau o\acute{\iota}$, which functions here as a major transitional device introducing this section.[193] This metaphor gives rise to two admonitions: *abstain from fleshly desires* (2:11) and *submit to every human creature* (2:13).[194] The termination of the control of this metaphor is signaled in 2:16 by the introductory simile that introduces the next metaphor. Thus, the metaphor of resident and visiting aliens controls the material from 2:11-15.

The two admonitions that ensue from this metaphor are expressed in different ways. The first is expressed by an infinitive complement construction: $\pi a\rho a\kappa a\lambda\hat{\omega}\ \dot{a}\pi\dot{\epsilon}\chi\epsilon\sigma\theta a\iota\ \tau\hat{\omega}\nu\ \sigma a\rho\kappa\iota\kappa\hat{\omega}\nu\ \dot{\epsilon}\pi\iota\theta\nu\mu\iota\hat{\omega}\nu$ [I exhort you to abstain from fleshly desires]. The second is expressed by an imperative: $\dot{\nu}\pi o\tau\dot{a}\gamma\eta\tau\epsilon\ \pi\dot{a}\sigma\eta\ \dot{a}\nu\theta\rho\omega\pi\dot{\iota}\nu\eta$ [Submit to every human creature]. The participle $\dot{\epsilon}\chi o\nu\tau\epsilon$s in verse 12 connects with the imperative, not the infinitive construction, because it is nominative, not accusative. This participle, like the other participles in 1 Peter, provides the context in which the readers are to carry out the command expressed by the imperative. As they maintain good conduct among the provincials,[195] they are to submit to every human creature.

Both of these admonitions have been variously interpreted. Wilhelm Brandt discusses the meaning of $\dot{\epsilon}\pi\iota\theta\nu\mu\dot{\iota}a\iota\ \sigma a\rho\kappa\iota\kappa a\dot{\iota}$:

> The segregation pertains rather to the $\dot{\epsilon}\pi\iota\theta\nu\mu\dot{\iota}a\iota\ \sigma a\rho\kappa\iota\kappa a\dot{\iota}$. The $\dot{\epsilon}\pi\iota\theta\nu\mu\dot{\iota}a\iota$ are the forces of the world from which the strangers and sojourners have separated (1:14). The segregation from the surrounding world is not amicable or peaceable.

---

[193]White, "Form," 29, says, "The vocative is employed intermittently during the Roman period, as a means of making major transitions in all three body-sections. . . . Its use is extended, in addition, to all the points in the body where major transitions occur." Our author uses the vocative for minor transitions as well. See 2:18; 3:7, and 4:12.

[194]Weiss, *Lehrbegriff*, 44, correctly noted the relationship of this metaphor to the exhortation. He says, "This consequence is even greater when we see how the entire series of admonitions that follow are placed under this viewpoint and motivated by the character of the Christians as strangers and pilgrims." Because he fails to recognize the topos of the non-citizen, he extends the influence of this metaphor beyond the passage it actually controls.

[195]This translation of $\dot{\epsilon}\theta\nu o$s captures the meaning of the term in the context of resident and visiting aliens.

In Petrine terms, the ἐπιθυμίαι struggle against the *essence* of man that God has designated for σωτηρία; namely, the ψυχή.[196]

In contrast to Brandt's theological interpretation, Balch provides a social interpretation of this admonition stating, "Roman society typically suspected foreign, Eastern cults of being associated with sexual immorality, and so Christians are exhorted to 'abstain from the passions of the flesh' (2:11) in a context concerned with the opinions of outsiders."[197] As these two different interpretations indicate, the precise meaning of ἐπιθυμίαι σαρκικαί, from which the readers are admonished to abstain, is debated.

No less debated is the meaning of κτίσις in the second admonition in verse 13. The most common translation for this term is *institution* proposed by Walter Bauer, who says, ". . . κτίσις is also the act by which an authoritative governmental body is created. . . . It is probably also the result of the act, *the institution* or *authority* itself 1 Pt 2:13."[198] S. Légasse rejects this interpretation, saying:

> A good number of exegetes, in fact most, do not hesitate to enrich their Greek vocabulary by translating the term κτίσις by *institution* (especially governmental), *instance*, or some other such analogous term. . . . But that meaning . . . is not attested anywhere. Besides this meaning agrees badly with the context that speaks of persons, not institutions. In non-biblical Greek, κτίσις primarily signifies the foundation of a town or house. In the Septuagint, its meaning is always *creature* or *creation* in reference to God. It is this biblical meaning with its human connotation that asserts itself here. . . .[199]

---

[196]Wilhelm Brandt, "Wandel als Zeugnis nach dem 1. Petrusbrief," in *Verbum Dei manet in Aeternum*, Festschrift für Otto Schmitz, ed. Werner Foerster (Witten: Luther-Verlag, 1953), 12. A similar interpretation is taken by Stählin. On page 30, he says, "Each πόλις has its own νόμος. The Christian must live according to that of his city. . . . The alien goods of earthly possession and the alien desire of ἐπιθυμίαι σαρκικαί are not fitting for πάροικοι καὶ παρεπίδημοι (1 Pt 2:11) who hope one day to return εἰς τὴν ἰδίαν πόλιν."

[197]Balch, *Wives*, 86. Stählin, 31, interprets similarly in another place, "The Christian, even though he has learned to regard the world as a foreign land, is always in danger of making it his homeland and treating as ἴδια the things of the world which ought to be ἀλλότρια for him. Here, then, constant vigilance is required. In particular, the ways and means of the world should not find entry into the Christian community."

[198]Bauer, 456.

[199]S. Légasse, "La Soumission aux autorités d'après 1 Pierre 2. 13-17: Version spécifique d'une parénèse traditionelle," *New Testament Studies* 34 (1988): 380-381.

Légasse concludes that the readers are being exhorted to submit to every human being.[200] The reference to the king and his representative provides the author with an example of what he means.

Amid the maze of interpretations of these two admonitions, there is a simpler explanation. Both of these admonitions stem from the same metaphor of resident and visiting aliens. People in these categories were always thought of as guests of the provincials.[201] Schmidt says, "Legally the alien resident is according to the current view sacrosanct as a guest."[202] Two incidents in the reign of the Emperor Claudius illustrate this fact. The first incident is his banishment of the Jews from Rome. Since they were there as guests of the Romans, they could be expelled.[203] The second incident relates to the tension between the Alexandrians and the Jews to whom Claudius responded with his *Letter to the Alexandrians*.[204] In that letter he recognized that the Jews were living in a city not their own, but he exhorted the Alexandrians to show a forbearing and hospitable [πραέως καὶ φιλανθρώπως] attitude toward the Jews.[205] In his recommendation for the resolution of the problem in Alexandria and in his banishment of the Jews from Rome, Claudius operated from the perspective that the Jews were guests in their host city.[206]

It is this treatment of the aliens as guests that explains the two exhortations in this passage. In good paraenetic style, these two admonitions stipulate something to be avoided and something to be done. Together they form a balanced statement of the duties of aliens who are

---

[200]Michaels, *1 Peter*, 124, adopts the same view.

[201]Because of their proverbial ξενηλασία [a measure for keeping foreigners out of the country], the Spartans are disparaged while the hospitable Athenians are praised.

[202]Schmidt, "Πάροικος," 846.

[203]Lyall, *Slaves*, 57, says, "In terms of Roman law the ordinary Jew was an alien, a *peregrinus*." Stählin, 6-7, comments, "Even up to the imperial period, the alien was theoretically without protection or rights . . . and only by acquiring a *patronus* could he enjoy legal protection. As aliens had no legal rights, so . . . they were often excluded from cultic fellowship and troublesome aliens might be deported at any time."

[204]A. S. Hunt and C. C. Edgar, trans., *Select Papyri*, vol. 2, The Loeb Classical Library (Cambridge: Harvard University Press, 1977), 78-89.

[205]Stählin, 18, relates the importance of this term for hospitality. He says, "The Greeks mention as the motive for hospitality, along with religion, their natural sympathy and φιλανθρωπία."

[206]The question of Jewish citizenship in the Diaspora and particularly in Alexandria is variously understood. Some scholars argue that they possessed citizenship, others that they did not. For a discussion of this issue see Schürer, vol. 3, 126-137.

treated as guests. Cicero describes the obsequious attitude required of aliens as follows, "As for the foreigner or the resident alien, it is his duty to attend strictly to his own concerns, not to pry into other people's business, and under no condition to meddle in the politics of a country not his own."[207] As a guest, aliens must mind their own business and control their desires, or they will arouse the envy of the provincials, who could retaliate with an attitude of ὕβρις [aggravated personal assault].[208] When Herod and Agrippa toured Asia Minor, they encountered many Jews who complained of mistreatment by the provincials. Nicolas, speaking before Agrippa for the mistreated Jews of Ionia, explicitly says, "And although we have done splendidly, our circumstances should not arouse envy, for it is through you that we, in common with all men, prosper."[209] Part of the source of the mistreatment was the fact that the Jewish guests had prospered and had incurred the envy and hence assault of the provincial residents of Ionia. In addition to controlling their desires, guests were expected to submit or give way to their hosts since they had no claim to any rights.[210] Stählin explains, "The foreigner who was originally denied all rights found rich compensation in the primitive custom of hospitality."[211] Since the alien as guest lacked any rights, Greco-Roman society placed

---

[207]Cicero, *De Officiis*, 1.125. Miller, *Cicero*, 126-127.

[208]The attitudes and behavior of aliens are expressed in Euripides, *Suppliants*, 888-900. He describes Parthenopaeus, "The fourth was huntress Atalanta's son, Parthenopaeus, unmatched in goodlihead: Arcadian he, but came to Inachus, and lived his youth at Argos. Fostered there, first, as beseems the sojourner in the land, he vexed not [λυπηρός], nor was jealous [ἐπίφθονος] of the state, nor was a wrangler, whereby citizens or aliens most shall jar with fellow-men; but in the ranks stood like an Argive born, fought for the land, and, whenso prospered Argos, rejoiced, and grieved when it went ill for her; of many a man, of many a woman loved, yet from transgression did he keep him pure." Arthur S. Way, trans., *Euripides*, vol. 3, The Loeb Classical Library (Cambridge: Harvard University Press, 1962), 570-571.

[209]Josephus, *Jewish Antiquities*, 16.41. Ralph Marcus and Allen Wikgren, trans., *Josephus: Jewish Antiquities*, The Loeb Classical Library (Cambridge: Harvard University Press, 1980), 224-225.

[210]Otto Hiltbrunner, D. Gorce, and H. Wehr, "Gastfreundschaft," in *Reallexikon für Antike und Christentum*, vol. 8: *Fluchttafel-Gebet I* (Stuttgart: Anton Hiersemann, 1972), 1061, says, "A stranger is without rights." Likewise, Kübler, 643, states, "In every nation of the ancient world, the stranger was basically without rights." For a discussion of the laws affecting aliens see E. Weiss, "Fremdenrecht," *Paulys Real-Encyclopädie der classischen Altertumswissenschaft*, ed. Wilhelm Kroll, *Supplement* 4: *Abacus-Ledon* (Stuttgart: J. B. Metzler, 1924), 511-516.

[211]Stählin, 17.

him/her under the direct protection of a god. Zeus Ξένιος was considered
the one who protected the oppressed foreigner.[212] For this protection the
alien or guest is obligated to express respect and gratitude toward the god
and his host. In the same speech of Nicolas, the Jews are described as
living a manner of life that is not hostile [ἀπάνθρωπος] to others and does
not force [βιάζω] others to give up their manner of life.[213] As this
discussion indicates, the notion of aliens as guests provides the context in
which both of the admonitions in this passage should be understood. These
exhortations are closely connected, forming a balanced paraenetic statement
of actions that aliens, perceived as guests, should avoid and emulate. They
should curb their desires and submit to everyone as proper guests should.

The conception of aliens not only explains the admonitions in this
passage, but it also accounts for the other material. Verses twelve and
fifteen allude to the mistreatment of the aliens by the provincials. This
problem was chronic in the Roman Empire as indicated by the large
number of Jews, who appealed to Herod and Agrippa as they traveled
through Asia Minor.[214] In a situation of mistreatment, an alien's only hope
lay in his/her appeal to a higher authority as the appeals to Herod and
Agrippa demonstrate.[215] Since this society generally believed that divine

---

[212]Ibid., 16, Stählin says, "All other religions to some degree placed the stranger
under the direct protection of the deity. The Greeks said that Zeus avenges the stranger.
Hence those who fear the gods will be gracious to strangers."

[213]Josephus, *Jewish Antiquities*, 16.42, 47.

[214]Ibid., 16.16f.

[215]In the Jewish Diaspora, a positive relationship developed between the Jews and
their overlords. E. Mary Smallwood, *The Jews Under Roman Rule From Pompey to
Diocletian*, Studies in Judaism in Late Antiquity 20 (Leiden: E. J. Brill, 1981), 140-143,
specifically discusses the travels of M. Vipsanius Agrippa and Herod the Great through
Asia Minor in 14 BCE The Jewish communities frequently appealed to them for help. See
Josephus, *Antiquities*, 16.27-65. Smallwood, 124, discusses the rationale for the
preferential treatment of the Jews by the Roman overlords and the consequent beneficent
attitude taken toward them. She explains, "In dealing with a religious minority which
would countenance neither compromise nor assimilation and which was liable to be at
loggerheads with its Gentile host, Rome was faced with the alternatives of suppression on
the one hand and on the other toleration with the corollary of active measures to protect the
sect from Gentile molestation. The normal Roman attitude towards foreign religions was
one of toleration, provided that they appeared to be both morally unobjectionable and
politically innocuous. Judaism with its high moral code and non-subversive character
fulfilled the criteria for permitted survival, and received toleration on an ad hoc basis in the
late republic in the form of exemption from specific Roman requirements which caused
religious embarrassment, followed by positive protection under the charter of Jewish

protection was accorded the alien and that the king was the divine representative, the king and his representatives became the guarantors of the alien's rights.[216] This notion is stated in verses thirteen and fourteen where the king is described as one who holds his authority under the Lord [$ὑπερέχω$]; and his representative, the governor, is sent to punish evildoers and to praise do-gooders. Given this state of affairs, our author constantly assumes throughout this passage that his readers are maintaining good conduct.[217] As long as they behave well, the readers can expect their Lord's protection, which is mediated through the king and his representatives. Since the divine power is responsible for defending the alien, anyone who mistreats the alien is stupid [$ἄφρων$] (2:15).[218] In his *Treatise on Exile*, Plutarch states that only the foolish [$ἄφρονες$] treat the stranger badly.[219] Our author states that it is God's intention to silence this

---

religious liberty formulated by Julius Caesar and reiterated by Augustus." This preferential treatment led the Jews to frequently appeal to the Roman ruler for help against the oppressive actions of the locals.

[216]Stählin, 10, says, "As in Greece, this law is fundamentally religious, for the one who guarantees the protection of aliens is God, who loves the stranger, and as His vice-regent the king." Plato, *Laws*, 729e, states that since the stranger is devoid of associates and family, he is more pitied by men and gods.

[217]W. C. van Unnik, "Die Rücksicht auf die Reaktion der Nichtchristen als Motiv in der altchristlichen Paränese," in *Judentum Urchristentum Kirche*, Festschrift für Joachim Jeremias, ed. Walther Eltester, Beihefte zur Zeitschrift für die neutestamentliche Wissenschaft 26 (Berlin: Verlag Alfred Töpelmann, 1960; reprinted in, *Sparsa Collecta: The Collected Essays of W. C. van Unnik*, vol. 2, Supplements to Novum Testamentum 30, Leiden: E. J. Brill, 1973, 307-322), 221-234, has demonstrated that consideration of the reaction of the non-Christian played an important role in early Christian paraenesis. Brandt, 10-25, argues this exemplary conduct was never meant to supplant the preached word but only to remind the unbeliever of the word that he had heard and rejected.

[218]Stählin, 5, recognizes the importance of treating the stranger well. He states, "In the old lists of vices, esp. in connection with judgment in the underworld, maltreating the $ζένος$ comes just after ungodliness and impiety vis-à-vis parents, and in the popular philosophy in the Hell. period $τὸ καθῆκον πρὸς ζένοις$ has an assured place." Plutarch, *On Exile* 607 says, "But *exile* is a term of reproach. Yes, among fools, who make terms of abuse out of *pauper*, *bald*, *short*, and indeed *foreigner* and *immigrant*. But those who are not carried away by such considerations admire good men, even if they are poor or foreigners or exiles." Phillip H. de Lacy, trans., *Plutarch's Moralia*, vol. 7, The Loeb Classical Library (Cambridge: Harvard University Press, 1984), 564-567. See also Hiltbrunner, 1071-1072, where paradigmatic Old Testament examples of treating strangers well are listed.

[219]Plutarch, *De Exilio*, 2.607a.

misguided slander of the foolish provincials by the good works of the slandered.[220] Clearly, all of the material in verses eleven to fifteen is determined by the metaphor of resident and visiting aliens.

Metaphor-Free Men

The metaphor of resident and visiting aliens gives way in verse sixteen to the metaphor of free men. This metaphor is introduced by an introductory simile that functions as a minor transitional device. Our author has previously used an introductory simile as a major transitional device in 1:14. Here, however, the simile provides only a minor transition because this section is linked to the previous section by the notion of the alien as I have already demonstrated. There is only one admonition that ensues from this metaphor: *honor all* (2:17). All the other material in this section is only an explication of this command. This section, which is dominated by the metaphor of free men, is concluded in 3:10-12 by a scripture quotation as Dalton has already established.[221]

In verse sixteen, the description of the readers as free men is followed by the qualifying attributive participles ἔχοντες and ὄντες.[222]

---

[220]Floyd V. Filson, "Partakers with Christ: Suffering in First Peter," *Interpretation* 9 (1955): 400-412, maintains that the sufferings in 1 Peter are social, not official. He says on page 401, note 1, "My own conclusions are (1) that the letter does not necessarily reflect imperial persecution, (2) that it probably reflects popular hostility which on occasion was able to use local authorities to trouble the Christians." On the basis of my analysis of this section, I agree with his contention. For a different perspective, see Horst Goldstein, "Die politischen Paränesen in 1 Petr 2 und Röm 13," *Bibel und Leben* 14 (1973): 88-104. By comparing the political paraenesis of Romans 13 with 1 Peter 2, he concludes that the Petrine passage reflects a diminishing confidence in Caesar and an increasing skepticism about the Roman political machine. He uses these conclusions to argue that 1 Peter was written in response to the persecutions under Domitian. Against Goldstein, I would argue that different literary contexts and not different historical situations cause the differences between these two documents.

[221]Dalton, *Proclamation*, 80-81.

[222]The participle ὄντες has been ellipsed, and this ellipsis has caused many commentators to understand the phrase ἀλλ ὡς θεοῦ δοῦλοι as an antithesis to ὡς ἐλεύθεροι. This understanding is incorrect on grammatical grounds. The phrase ὡς ἐλεύθερος is equivalent, not antithetical, to ὡς θεοῦ δοῦλοι. The phrase ὡς θεοῦ δοῦλοι is antithetical to the phrase μὴ ἔχοντες as the antithesis set up by μή . . . ἀλλα indicates. The participle ἔχοντες following μή indicates the need for a participle following ἀλλα in order to maintain the parallelism of this antithesis. Since the verb εἰμι can be ellipsed at any time and especially in cases of parallelism, the ellipsed participle is ὄντες.

These participles should not be confused with circumstantial participles. Since these participles are preceded by the conjunction καί, which connects them with ἐλεύθεροι, they modify this noun and do not attach to the imperative in verse seventeen. The noncircumstantial aspect of these participles is also indicated by the fact that ὡς precedes each of them. This verse should be translated, *As free men, and not as free men who hold their freedom as a pretext for evil but as free men who are slaves of God. . . .*

These qualifying participles address a pervasive problem in Greco-Roman society when *freedom* was defined as doing what one wants.[223] This conception of freedom as unrestrained individual liberty posed a problem.[224] J. Blunck describes this problem, "The constant danger is rejection of the law in the name of a misconceived freedom that is purely arbitrary since it is willing to grant itself more freedom than it is willing to grant to others."[225]   F. Stanley Jones discusses the perception of this problem in Plato and Euripides. Concerning Euripides' *Alcestis*, 677-678, 681-684, and 690, Jones comments as follows:

---

[223]For a discussion of this problem, see F. Stanley Jones, *"Freiheit" in den Briefen des Apostels Paulus: Eine historische, exegetische und religionsgeschichtliche Studie*, Göttinger Theologische Arbeiten 34 (Göttingen: Vandenhoeck & Ruprecht, 1987), 80; Dieter Nestle, "Freiheit," *Reallexikon für Antike und Christentum*, vol. 8: *Fluchtafel-Gebet I* (Stuttgart: Anton Hiersemann, 1972), 270; and Samuel Vollenweider, *Freiheit als neue Schöpfung: eine Untersuchung zur Eleutheria bei Paulus und in seiner Umwelt*, Forschungen zur Religion und Literatur des Alten und Neuen Testaments 147 (Göttingen: Vandenhoeck & Ruprecht, 1989), 30-31. The classic formulation of this understanding of freedom is by Epictetus. In *Discourses* 4.1.1, he says, "He is free who lives as he wills, who is subject neither to compulsion, nor hindrance, nor force, whose choices are unhampered, whose desires attain their end, whose aversions do not fall into what they would avoid." Text and translation by W. A. Oldfather, trans., *Epictetus*, vol 2, The Loeb Classical Library (London: William Heinemann, 1928), 244-245.

[224]Kurt Niederwimmer, "Ἐλεύθερος," in *Exegetisches Wörterbuch zum Neuen Testament*, vol. 9: Ἀαρων–Ἐνώχ, ed. Horst Balz and Gerhard Schneider (Stuttgart: Kohlhammer, 1980), says, "Correspondingly, the obtained freedom must be guarded against the danger of falling back into legalism (Galatians 2:4; 5:1) as well as against the danger of antinomianism (Galatians 5:13)."

[225]J. Blunck, "Freedom," in *The New International Dictionary of New Testament Theology*, vol. 1: *A-F*, ed. Colin Brown (Grand Rapids: Zondervan Publishing House, 1975), 715. See Hans Dieter Betz, *Galatians*, Hermeneia (Philadelphia: Fortress Press, 1979), 271-274, for a discussion of the problem of the abuse of freedom in Galatians 5:13. See page 255, note 24, for literature on freedom.

This contrast to an ostensible Greek freedom is scarcely accidental. On the contrary, it is to be assumed that Euripides here struggles against a popular conception that understands freedom to be individual. Since the free decision of Alcestus was asserted in the fable, it is very possible that Alcestus gives evidence of the origin of the Euripidean theme of free-will sacrificial death: It has originated from the struggle against a freedom understood as individual freedom.[226]

By the addition of these two qualifying participles, our author quells the possibility that his description of the readers as free men might be misconstrued. The readers are compared to free men who do not use their freedom as a means for evil but who recognize that they are slaves of God.[227] Jones notes similar attempts to curb the abuse of freedom in Plato and Euripides, stating:

> Instead of freedom, Plato wanted to introduce "slavery to God" as the ideal where *God* is like *law*. Just as the tendency to compensate for satiation with freedom through a new duty is seen in Plato, so also, prior to Plato, Euripides had undertaken to connect freedom and duty in a dialectical unity.[228]

Although Plato and Euripides lived in the fourth and fifth centuries BCE, Jones demonstrates that the problem and solutions articulated by them were still influential in the first century.[229] This discussion of the abuse of freedom indicates that the author of 1 Peter added these two qualifying participles [ἔχοντες and ὄντες] in verse sixteen in order to avoid a misunderstanding of his description of the readers as free men. They are not free to live as they please, but they are free to perform their duties.[230]

---

[226]Jones, 50.

[227]Goppelt, *Petrusbrief*, 187, recognizes this notion in Paul. He states, "That only the slave of God is a free man and that hence freedom cannot be a pretext in order to live to oneself terminologically and factually brings Paul to mind ... (Romans 6:22) ... (Galatians 5:13; as well as 1 Corinthians 9:19)."

[228]Jones, 48. For an extended discussion of the notion of slavery to God in Plato, see Dieter Nestle, *Eleutheria: Studien zum Wesen der Freiheit bei den Griechen und im Neuen Testament*, vol. 1: *Die Griechen*, Hermeneutische Untersuchungen zur Theologie 6 (Tübingen: J. C. B. Mohr (Paul Siebeck), 1967), 89-101.

[229]Jones, 51-53.

[230]Ibid., 48, Jones states, "If the history of the term *freedom* is surveyed in antiquity, a certain uneasiness with this notion is observed. In these cases, the aspect of duty receives stronger emphasis."

This concept of freedom as communal responsibility rather than individual license is more Roman than Greek. Hans Dieter Betz comments on this distinction in 1 Corinthians:

> Paul's letters to the Corinthians document that moral and communal anarchy was indeed a possibility inherent in the Pauline gospel. The slogan πάντα μοι ἔξεστιν expressed this concept of freedom in a way impossible to misunderstand. As we have suggested before, Paul acted like a Roman when he did not accept the "typically Greek" slogan and concept of freedom. His Corinthian correspondence is almost entirely preoccupied with his attempts to interpret Christian freedom as communal and ethical responsibility.[231]

A little later Betz comments again, "Paul's concept of freedom, oriented to the community and to law and obedience, as opposed to the Gnostics who say πάντα μοι ἔξεστιν, also reflects a Roman feeling and mentality rather than a Greek. Paul is not a Greek individualist."[232] Like Paul, the author of 1 Peter reflects the Roman conception of freedom as communal responsibility. Also like Paul, he regards the Greek conception of freedom as individual license to be an inappropriate understanding of freedom. For the author of 1 Peter, the free man behaves responsibly in his society.

On the basis of this free-men metaphor, the author exhorts his readers to honor all. This attitude recognized the position and rights of people both above and below the free man.[233] This attitude is the proper attitude of the free and is therefore required among the free.[234] After asserting the freedom of his readers in an earlier part of his epistle, Paul exhorts his readers in Romans 13:7 to render the obligation to whomever it is due; to whom honor, honor. The free man is free to render his social

---

[231]Hans Dieter Betz, *Paul's Concept of Freedom in the Context of Hellenistic Discussions about the Possibilities of Human Freedom*, Protocol of the Colloquy of the Center for Hermeneutical Studies in Hellenistic and Modern Culture 26 (Berkeley, California: The Center for Hermeneutical Studies in Hellenistic and Modern Culture, 1977), 11.

[232]Ibid., 38. See also pages 2-3 for further information about the Greek and Roman conceptions of freedom.

[233]Sverre Aalen, "Honor," in *The New International Dictionary of New Testament Theology*, vol. 2: *G-Pre*, ed. Colin Brown (Grand Rapids: Zondervan Publishing House, 1975), 50-51, says, "Τιμή in this culture recognizes the position and rights of people both above and below one's legal standing."

[234]Jones, 124, notes several Hellenistic authors who affirm that freedom is only possible if one does one's duty. See also Vollenweider, 82-85, who discusses this Stoic concept of freedom.

obligations. Thus, on the basis of this metaphor, our author summons his readers to honor all; that is, to recognize the position and rights of others.

Everything that follows in verse seventeen and in the remaining part of this passage is an explication of the exhortation to honor all that is expressed by the aorist imperative τιμήσατε.[235] The three present imperatives that follow in this verse indicate they are subsidiary ideas of the command to honor all.[236] E. Bammel comments on the New English Bible's translation of this verse:

> The new English translation renders the verse: 'give due honor to everyone: love to the brotherhood, reverence to God, honor to the sovereign.' This rendering makes 'give due honor to everyone' the heading and the main clause to which the three other clauses are subordinated.[237]

---

[235]My analysis proves Kamlah, 237-243, and Balch, *Wives*, 98, among others, to be completely mistaken in their contention that the exhortation to *be submissive* provides the superscript of the whole code. This exhortation occurs in the previous subsection dominated by the metaphor of aliens and, therefore, cannot function as the superscription of the code contained in this subsection dominated by the metaphor of free men. The admonition to *honor all* serves as the superscription of this section. As far as I can ascertain, John Owen, the translator and editor of Calvin's *Commentaries of the Catholic Epistles* is the first in more recent times to correctly recognize the composition of this passage. In an editor's note on 1 Peter 3, he says, "The construction of the whole passage, beginning at the 17th verse of the last chapter, and ending at the 12th of this [for at the 13th of this, he resumes the subject he left off at the end of the 16th of the last] deserves to be noticed. 'Honor all,' is the injunction which he afterwards exemplifies as to servants, wives, and husbands; for the construction is 'Honor all–the servants being subject, & c.–in like manner, the wives being subject, & c.–in like manner, the husbands, cohabiting according to knowledge, giving honor, & c.' Then follows this verse in the same form, 'and finally, all being of one mind, sympathizing, loving the brethren, compassionate, friendly-minded [or humble-minded], not rendering, & c.' And thus he proceeds to the end of the 12th verse." See idem., trans., *Commentaries on the Catholic Epistles by John Calvin* (Edinburgh: T. Constable, 1855), 101, note 1.

[236]Theophylact, 1216, renders 1 Peter 2:16 in this manner, "Πάντας τιμήσατε, τὴν ἀδελφότητα μὲν ἀγαπῶντες, τὸν δὲ θεὸν φοβούμενοι, τὸν βασιλέα τιμῶντες. [Honor all by loving the brotherhood, by fearing God, by honoring the king.]" He renders the present imperatives as present participles, clearly demonstrating that he considers them to be subordinate to the aorist imperative τιμήσατε. Goppelt, *Petrusbrief*, 187, note 46, is absolutely incorrect in asserting, "Just as the twice repeated ὡς in verse 14, so also the thrice repeated ὡς in verse 16 has a causal meaning. The subject and predicate is ὑποτάγητε in verse 13."

[237]E. Bammel, "The Commands in 1 Peter 2:17," *New Testament Studies* 11 (1965): 279. He summarizes almost all of the positions that commentators have taken in regard to this verse. He disagrees with the New English Bible's rendering. He argues that the verse is constructed in the form of a chiasmus because of the repetition of the same verb

By citing specific instances in which honor is to be conferred, these three present imperatives explicate the exhortation to honor all.

The participles that begin in 2:18 and extend throughout the remainder of the passage give specific contexts and recommendations for the conferment of honor and thus continue to explicate the command to honor all.[238] Slaves give honor by submitting with all respect to their masters (2:18-25).[239] Wives render honor by submitting to their husbands (3:1-6). Husbands show honor to their wives by cohabiting with them according to knowledge (3:7). Finally, everyone shows honor by being likeminded, sympathetic, loving of brothers, good-hearted, humbleminded, and by not repaying evil with evil but instead blessing (3:8-9). In all of these specific contexts and situations, the author describes how honor should be conferred.

Each of these subsections is designated by important compositional features. In each instance, a vocative introduces the subsection, and in each subsection except the last, a concluding simile is employed. These vocatives serve as minor transitional devices between these subsections. The first subsection (2:18-25), which deals with servants, begins with the vocative οἱ οἰκέται (2:18) and concludes with the simile *you were wandering like sheep* (2:25). The second subsection (3:1-6) treats the relationship of wives toward husbands. This subsection is introduced by the vocative γυναῖκες and ends with a reference that they have become children of Sarah.[240] The third subsection (3:7), describing how a husband

---

in the first and fourth members. His argument is weakened because the second and third members do not have the same verb. His proposal of a chiasmus does not resolve the problem of the change in the tenses of the imperatives. For these reasons, his proposal should be rejected.

[238]Although he designates these participles as imperatival, Balch, *Wives*, 97, is troubled by the notion of an imperatival participle and admits that it is an unusual construction in Greek. My analysis does not understand these participles to be imperatival but circumstantial, describing circumstances that attend to the imperative statement *honor all*.

[239]1 Timothy 6:1 affirms that slaves owe their masters all honor. Similar to 1 Peter, Titus 2:9-10 refers to the duty of slaves to submit to their masters.

[240]Elliott, *Home*, 250, note 92, says, "The reference to Abraham and Sarah in 1 Pet. 3:5-6 may well have been intended as an example of *oikos* life in a *paroikia* situation."

shows honor to his wife, begins with the vocative οἱ ἄνδρες and concludes with the simile *as co-heirs of the grace of life*. In the last subsection (3:8-12), the vocative πάντες opens the passage, and the adverbial phrase τὸ δὲ τέλος indicates this is the last subsection in this section. A scripture quotation (3:10-12) concludes not only this subsection but also the entire section that began in 2:11.

The adverb ὁμοίως is also an important compositional feature of this passage. It occurs in the second (3:1) and third (3:7) subsections. Over sixty years ago, Radermacher noted that this adverb was used in the composition of lists and referred, not to the item before it, but to the head of the list.[241] This is the function of ὁμοίως not only in this code but also in other Christian codes.[242] Titus 2:1-10 contains a station code that is constructed similarly to the code in 1 Peter. It begins with a statement, *But you, speak* [imperative] *what is fitting for sound teaching. . . .* What follows is a succession of infinitives that are clearly subordinate to this opening statement and express the actions and attitudes fitting for sound doctrine. In this list, four groups of people are mentioned: aged men, aged women, young men, and slaves. Although ὁμοίως does not occur, a similar adverb, ὡσαύτως, does occur. Its position in the list is significant; it occurs with all members of the list except the first and last. The function of the adverb is not to refer to the preceding member of the list but to refer each member of the list to the opening statement in Titus 2:1. This function of ὁμοίως in 1 Peter confirms that each situation addressed in these subsections relates to the command to *honor all* in 2:17.

Assessment

These compositional features and transitional devices, along with the metaphors and their corresponding admonitions, demonstrate that the concept of aliens in this world dominates and controls the composition of

---

[241]Radermacher, 290-291.

[242]This observation would have greatly strengthened Bo Reicke's argument that *according to knowledge* in 3:7 does not refer to the subordination of the husband to the wife. He operates under the assumption that ὁμοίως refers to the element preceding and thinks that the construction could imply that men, like women, are being exhorted to submission. Although he correctly concludes that this is not the case, his extended argument is unnecessary if the function of ὁμοίως is correctly understood. See idem, "Gnosis," 296-304.

this second section of the body-middle. By comparing his readers to resident and visiting aliens, the author of 1 Peter exhorts them to curb their appetites (2:11) and submit to everyone (2:12-15). By comparing them to free men, he exhorts them to render honor to everyone (2:16-17). Utilizing a station code, he then specifies situations and contexts in which they are to confer honor (2:18--3:9). He then concludes this section with an extended scripture quotation that contains several allusions to aliens (3:10-12). This scripture quotation speaks of the blessing to which God has called them. This blessing is the protection that God Himself affords the alien who behaves well. This παρεπίδημος/πάροικος-cluster of metaphors indicates the following outline for this section:

The παρεπίδημος/πάροικος-Cluster
Aliens in this World
(2:11--3:12)

1. The παρεπίδημος/πάροικος-metaphor of aliens (2:11-15): Abstain from fleshly lusts (2:11). Submit to every human creature (2:12-15)

2. The παρεπίδημος/πάροικος-metaphor of free men (2:16--3:12): Honor all (2:17)

    2.1. Slaves, show honor by submitting to your masters (2:18-25)

    2.2. Wives, show honor by submitting to your husbands (3:1-6)

    2.3. Husbands, show honor by co-habitating according to knowledge (3:7)

    2.4. All, show honor by being likeminded. . . . (3:8-12)

As with the οἶκος concept in the first section, the author of 1 Peter continues to draw on Diaspora images to construct his metaphor clusters. Here he has used the concept of the παρεπίδημος/πάροικος in order to describe his readers as aliens in this world. God's people on their eschatological journey are aliens in the world because they are away from their *patria*. He uses this description of his readers to achieve his objective of revealing the behavior they should demonstrate on their journey. Our author states that the conduct arising from their status as aliens will ultimately lead to the glorification of their God (2:12), the praise of rulers (2:14), and perhaps the conversion of others (3:1).

The author also uses this description of his readers as aliens in order to achieve his objective of encouraging them to continue on their journey. On the basis they would forfeit great benefits and good conduct, he continues to assert they should not defect from their new faith. By referring to his readers as aliens, he admits they are in a precarious position. However, our author does not dwell on the negative aspects of their situation; rather he emphasizes the positive. Their vulnerability requires that they behave circumspectly by curbing their appetites and submitting and honoring everyone. This conduct, however, is not shameful but in many ways represents the ideals of Greco-Roman society. Defection would remove them from the status of alien and thus obliterate the rationale for this praise-worthy behavior. Furthermore, as aliens they stand under the direct protection of God. Defection would remove them from the most secure protection available to them. Continuing his rhetoric of suppression, our author does not specifically state any of these negative aspects. He continues to persuade by extolling the positive benefits that Christianity has brought to his readers. As in this section, he continues to extol the benefits of Christianity in the next section of the body-middle that is dominated by the concept of the sufferers of the Dispersion [οἱ πάσχοντες τῆς διασπορᾶς].

The Third Metaphor Cluster (3:13--5:11):
The Sufferers of the Dispersion[243]

The third section of 1 Peter (3:13--5:11) has proven to be the most difficult section to analyze in terms of a compositional plan. Concerning this section, Dalton admits, "What follows in the epistle is not easy to

---

[243]The exact phrase οἱ πάσχοντες τῆς διασπορᾶς does not occur in 1 Peter. However, the verb πασχεῖν [to suffer] occurs repeatedly, especially in this section. In 5:9 the author states that this suffering takes place in the world [τὰ αὐτὰ τῶν παθημάτων τῇ ἐν τῷ κόσμῳ ὑμῶν ἀδελφότητι ἐπιτελεῖσθαι]. Michaels, *1 Peter*, 301, comments, "The meaning of ἐν τῷ κόσμῳ is not simply that the brotherhood is 'in the world' [where else would it be?], but that it is spread throughout the world [cf. διασπορᾶς, 'scattered,' in 1:1]." Thus, although the exact phrase does not occur, it appropriately describes the contents of this section.

define in terms of a total plan."[244] Indeed, Weiss, who correctly identified some of the most important metaphors in the first two sections, is completely lost in this section.[245] Even Schutter repeatedly comments on the difficulties associated with an analysis of this passage. Regarding 3:13--4:11, he says, "The organization of the second part of 1 Peter's body-middle is not quite so obvious. . . ."[246] He also states, "The nature of the relationship of the eschatological climax, 4.7-11, to the foregoing is comparatively more problematic still."[247] Recognizing that 5:1-11 does not fit well into its context, he reasons as follows, "Like the Pauline letter, 1 Peter seems to have a paraenesis section, 5.1-11, at least on this view it is easy to explain the relatively artificial relationship these verses have to the immediate context, as well as the distinctively ad hoc nature of the contents."[248] As the perspectives of Dalton, Weiss, and Schutter illustrate, the third section of 1 Peter is difficult to analyze.

The problematic compositional structure of this section is further illustrated by Schutter's analysis. He breaks 3:13--5:11 into three sections: 3:13--4:11, 4:12-19, and 5:1-11. In his analysis 3:13--4:11 forms the second part of the body-middle with 2:11--3:12 forming the first part.[249] The body-closing extends from 4:12 to 4:19 and 5:1-11 represents a closing paraenetic section.[250] Schutter divides this material into three sections even though he admits that the material possesses a common theme. He identifies the theme of 3:13--4:11 as righteous suffering.[251] Commenting on 4:12-19, he says, "The impression is therefore difficult to resist that 4:12-19 is composed of three sub-units joined together in tandem behind the theme of righteous suffering. In this respect the body-closing unites itself completely with the body-middle."[252] If the body-closing (4:12-19)

---

[244]Ibid., 81.

[245]Weiss, *1 Peter*, 289, says, "The Third Principle Part of the letter contains an exhortation concerning the life to be led within the Christian communion." He does not begin the third section until 4:7. Thus, he incorrectly includes 3:13--4:6 with the second section.

[246]Schutter, *Hermeneutic*, 59.

[247]Ibid., 71.

[248]Ibid., 26.

[249]Ibid., 59.

[250]Ibid., 26.

[251]Ibid., 67-71.

[252]Ibid., 76.

"unites itself completely" with the second part of the body-middle (3:13--4:11), this material should not be separated into two different major sections but should be included in the same major section. Schutter's basic argument for making this major separation of the material in 3:13--4:11 and 4:12-19 is that, as in the letters of Paul, a body-closing should come before the concluding paraenesis section in 5:1-11. He explains his division of the letter-body:

> More striking still is the affinity of 1 Peter's body with that of the Pauline letter. Its natural divisions correspond neatly to the tripartite body of the Pauline letter, body-opening (1:13--2:10), -middle (2:11--4:11), and -closing (4:12--5:11). . . . The last principal transition in 1 Peter's body (4:12) proceeds by means of a vocative [ἀγαπητοί] with asyndeton, a common occurrence in Paul's letters, and reiterates reassurance. Finally, 1 Peter shares with the Pauline letter the use of eschatological periods to conclude various parts of its body (esp. 4.7-11, 17-19, 5.10-11). . . . Like the Pauline letter, 1 Peter seems to have a paraenesis section, 5.1-11. . . .[253]

Schutter's demonstration of the division of the letter-body is weak because he assumes these are "natural divisions" that need little substantiation, and he does not interact with scholars who would contest his division of the letter-body.[254] As I have already established earlier in Chapter 2, the body-closing is found in 5:12. Therefore, Schutter is incorrect in his identification of 4:12--5:11 as the body-closing. Consequently, his separation of 3:13--4:11 from 4:12-19 on the basis that 4:12-19 forms the body-closing is a mistake. This mistake in his analysis illustrates the difficulties encountered in uncovering the compositional plan of this section of 1 Peter.

The problem with this section is also illustrated by the diverse manner in which it has been treated by recent commentators. Goppelt, like Schutter, places 3:13--4:11 in the same major section as 2:11--3:12. He then identifies 4:12--5:11 as a separate major section.[255] He also admits, however, that 4:12--5:11 carries on the theme of suffering contained in

---

[253]Ibid., 25.
[254]The most he does is to state in footnote 26 on page 25 that his division of the letter-body is against the analyses of F. W. Danker and W. J. Dalton.
[255]See his outline of the contents of the letter on page 8.

3:13--4:6.[256] This same major division is made between 4:11 and 4:12 by Michaels[257] and those commentators who adhere to partition theories.[258] In contrast, Selwyn and Best perceive a major break at 3:13 and identify the major sections as 2:11--3:12 and 3:13--4:19.[259] Kelly also accepts this major break at 3:13 but, like Dalton, continues the major section from 3:13--5:11.[260] The diverse treatment of 3:13--5:11 by these commentators highlights the basic problems of determining the major sections and the controlling themes of this passage.

The resolution of these problems and the explanation of the compositional structure of this passage lie in recognizing that the overarching metaphor in 1 Peter is the Diaspora. Just as the first section (1:14--2:10) and the second section (2:11--3:12), describing the readers as the elect household of God and aliens, focused on metaphors and images drawn from the Diaspora, so also this third section (3:13--5:11) describes the readers using descriptions and experiences arising from the Diaspora.

The metaphor cluster in 3:13--5:11 arises from the conception of the Diaspora as a place of testing, tribulation, and persecution of God's people.[261] The origins of the Jewish Diaspora are found in the forced exile of the Jewish people from their homeland. A prophecy recorded in Jeremiah 32:37-38, 42 reveals the negative appraisal of the Exile. It records God saying:

> Behold, I will gather them from all the countries to which I drove them in my anger and my wrath and in great indignation; I will bring them back to this place, and I will make them dwell in safety. For thus says the Lord: Just as I have brought all this great evil upon this people, so I will bring upon them all the good that I promise them.[262]

---

[256]Goppelt, *Petrusbrief*, 293, remarks about 4:12--5:11, "The passage again goes into the suffering of Christians within society that has already been explained paraenetically in 1:6f.; 2:18-25; and 3:13--4:6."

[257]Michaels, *1 Peter*, xxxvii.

[258]See Chapter 1 for a discussion of these commentators and their theories.

[259]Selwyn, *1 Peter*, 5. Best, *1 Peter*, 131.

[260]Kelly, 24.

[261]See the discussion above about the Diaspora as a dangerous place where assimilation could occur.

[262]Revised Standard Version.

The notion of punishment is echoed in Second Isaiah 40:2 where it is said that in the Exile God's people have received double for all their sins. Second Isaiah describes the Exile as a furnace of affliction (48:10). Ezekiel 12:15 states that the purpose of the dispersion is not simply to punish the people but to teach them that Yahweh is God. These texts clearly indicate that the Exile was a time of tribulation and affliction for God's people.

It is difficult to determine just how much this appraisal of the Exile as the punishment and affliction of God's people influenced the conception of the Diaspora.[263] Some texts, however, indicate the persistence of this appraisal of the Exile in the descriptions of the Diaspora. These texts present a description of the Diaspora situation of their author's time in terms of the situation of the Exile. The author of the *Testament of Asher* (7:2-3) describes the experience of the dispersed Jewish people of his day using an exilic context:

> For I know that you will sin and be delivered into the hands of your enemies; your land shall be made desolate and your sanctuary wholly polluted. You will be scattered to the four corners of the earth; in the dispersion you shall be regarded as worthless, like useless water, until such time as the Most High visits the Earth.[264]

The author of *2 Baruch* includes in his work a letter to the exiles that is clearly intended for dispersed Jews following the destruction of the Temple in 70 CE. He says in this letter:

> Therefore, I have been the more diligent to leave you the words of this letter before I die so that you may be comforted regarding the evils which have befallen you, and you may also be grieved with regard to the evils which have befallen your brothers, and then further, so that you may consider the judgment of him who decreed it against you to be righteous, namely that you should be carried away into captivity, for what you have suffered is smaller than what you have done, in order that you may be found worthy of your fathers in the last

---

[263]It should not be forgotten that by and large the Jews faired very well in the Diaspora. Philo and Josephus both mention positive aspects of the Diaspora. The Jewish faith is spread and the Jewish people are protected from being annihilated by a single blow.

[264]Text in M. de Jonge, *Testamenta XII Patriarcharum* (Leiden: E. J. Brill, 1970), 66. Howard Clark Kee, trans., "*Testaments of the Twelve Patriarchs*," in *The Old Testament Pseudepigrapha*, vol. 1: *Apocalyptic Literature and Teataments*, ed. James H. Charlesworth (Garden City: Doubleday and Company, 1983), 818.

times. . . . My brothers, therefore I have written to you that you may find consolation with regard to the multitude of tribulations.[265]

These texts indicate that the Diaspora, like the Exile, was a time of tribulation in which God's people suffer afflictions as a punishment for their sins.

Not all of the texts that envision the Diaspora as a place of suffering attribute the affliction to punishment for sins. Esther, Daniel 1-6, and *Joseph and Asenath* are notable examples. Collins explains these texts:

> Tension between Jew and Gentile in the Diaspora was not, of course, a new phenomenon. Perhaps the most characteristic product of the eastern Diaspora in the Hellenistic age was the so-called *Diasporanovelle* represented by Esther and Daniel 1-6. These tales envisaged situations in which exiled Jews were threatened with mortal danger, but in the end were dramatically delivered. Like many other Hebrew and Aramaic writings these stories were translated into Greek in the Ptolemaic period and so were available as models for Egyptian Judaism.[266]

He comments on *Joseph and Asenath*:

> The story of chapters 22-29 is evidently paradigmatic of Jewish-Gentile relations in the Egyptian Diaspora, although it is by no means a simple historical allegory. The benevolence of the sovereign is assumed. . . . Yet there are powerful forces, high at court, which are hostile to the Jews. . . .[267]

These texts treat the danger and suffering of the Jews in the Diaspora not as a punishment for sins but as a result of the hatred and envy of some of the provincials where the Jews were living. Regardless of the cause, there was a tendency to view the Diaspora as a dangerous place where Jewish people could be called upon to suffer simply because they were Jewish.[268]

---

[265]2 *Baruch* 78:5; 82:1. A. F. J. Klijn, trans., "2 *(Syriac Apocalypse of) Baruch*," in Charlesworth, *Apocalyptic*, 648-649.

[266]Collins, *Athens*, 87.

[267]Ibid., 90-91.

[268]Victor Tcherikover, *Hellenistic Civilization and the Jews*, trans. Simon Applebaum (New York: Atheneum, 1985), 357-377, has an excellent discussion of the anti-Semitism endured by the Jews in the Diaspora. He summarizes his discussion, "Thus the two peoples faced each other without being able to achieve mutual understanding. Anti-Semitism was the external expression of this lack of understanding. Its growth was not coincidental, but was bound up with the Jews' actual situation outside their homeland, since they had built their public life on the basis of Jewish tradition and neither desired nor were able--even had they wished--to reconcile Jewish monotheistic doctrine with Greek

Heinrich Schlier identifies suffering as a basic characteristic of Israel as God's chosen people. In the following he elaborates upon this idea:

> This term [θλῖψις], which is so common and which has so many senses in the LXX, acquires its theological significance from the fact that it predominantly denotes the oppression and affliction of the people of Israel or of the righteous who represent Israel. To be sure, we never find the general statement that θλῖψις necessarily belongs to the history of Israel as the people chosen and guided by God. Yet Israel does in fact constantly experience θλῖψις in its history, and it is aware that this θλῖψις is significant in the history of salvation. The oppression in Egypt, which is called θλῖψις in Ex. 4:31 (cf. 3:9), and the affliction of the exile, for which θλῖψις is used in Dt. 4:29 (cf. 28:47ff.), are both events of salvation history.[269]

Schlier correctly characterizes Israel as a suffering people who endure affliction. As we have seen, this characteristic is not only true for Israel in the Hebrew Scriptures, but it is also true for the Jewish people in the Dispersion.[270]

The author of 1 Peter recognizes this conception of the Diaspora as a place of suffering and affliction, and in this third section of his letter (3:13--5:11), he builds a metaphor cluster around the notion of his readers as sufferers in the Diaspora.[271] He begins in 3:13 by posing a rhetorical question that asks who is able to harm the readers if they have become

---

culture based on polytheism. The two fundamental anti-Semitic accusations-atheism [contempt of the gods] and misanthropy [hatred of mankind]-grew directly from this fundamental antagonism. And after hatred of the Jews had taken root among the Greeks, it was not difficult to interpret all Jewish observance in a malicious manner and make Jews frauds, knaves and shedders of innocent blood."

[269]Heinrich Schlier, "Θλίβω," in *Theological Dictionary of the New Testament*, vol. 3: Θ-Κ, ed. Gerhard Kittel (Grand Rapids: Wm. B. Eerdmans Publishing Co., 1970), 142.

[270]Ethelbert Stauffer, *New Testament Theology*, trans. John Marsh (London: SCM Press, 1955), 331, says, "The people of God is the martyr nation among the Gentiles (Psa. 73.3ff.; 78.1ff.; 79.9ff.; 82.3ff.; Jdth. 9.8; Isa. 42.1 LXX; AEn. 85ff.; 89.59ff.; iv Ezra 3.27ff.; MEx. on 20.23; SB, II, 284)."

[271]Schlier, "Θλίβω," 143, notes that the connection of Christian suffering with the suffering of the Old Testament people of God is characteristic of the New Testament as a whole and not just of 1 Peter. He says, "According to the understanding of the New Testament, however, θλῖψις is also necessary. . . . The constant tribulation of Israel in the Old Testament has become the necessary tribulation of the Church in the New Testament. The former is thus an indication of the latter."

zealots of the good [ζηλωταὶ τοῦ ἀγαθοῦ].[272] This rhetorical question posed in 3:13 is not fully resolved until 5:10 where the author affirms that God will restore them after their time of suffering. Our author takes the position that no one is able to harm his readers ultimately if they have become zealots of the good, but in the present, sufferings and afflictions are not only a possibility (3:14) but also a reality (4:12). This third section of 1 Peter is delimited by the rhetorical question in 3:13 that raises the issue of suffering and the final resolution of that issue in 5:10.[273]

Metaphor-Righteous Sufferers

The first metaphor in this cluster describes the readers as sufferers on account of righteousness or as righteous sufferers [3:14 εἰ καὶ πάσχοιτε διὰ δικαιοσύνην].[274] Because this metaphor occurs first in this section, it is introduced by the major transitional marker καὶ τίς, which designates the apodosis of a conditional sentence. The author of 1 Peter has used a conditional sentence as a transitional marker before.[275] This metaphor controls this subsection (3:13--4:11) and provides the basis for the paraenesis down to the benediction in 4:11.

---

[272]Goppelt, *Petrusbrief*, 231, says, "The introductory question, 'Who is able to harm you?' introduces the new theme of conflict. This theme of suffering stands in the background (1:6f.; 2:12, 15, 19f.; 3:9) but now is specifically stated." Although Goppelt recognizes the introduction of a new theme here and states that it is related in a "polar" way to the previous theme of socially correct conduct, he, nevertheless, states that a new major section of the letter does not begin here. Goppelt makes this mistake in his compositional analysis because he fails to perceive the shift in metaphor from the aliens of the Diaspora in the previous section to the sufferers in the Diaspora in this section. See Appendix 2 for a discussion of the exegesis of the phrase ζηλωταὶ τοῦ ἀγαθοῦ.

[273]The inclusio of πάσχοιτε in 3:13 and παθόντας in 5:10 also indicates the extent of this third section of the letter as Dalton, *Proclamation*, 81-82 has already observed.

[274]Schutter, *Hermeneutic*, 67-73, identifies the theme of 3:13--4:11 as righteous suffering. He states on page 68, "The next unit carries forward the theme of righteous suffering. . . ." He astutely notes the connection of this section with the preceding section's concluding scripture quotation. On page 67, he says, "Such a favorable reading of the relationship between the psalm and 3:13-7 is made the more plausible by the likelihood of the psalm's association with persecution and martyrdom in Jewish tradition. It is a largely neglected fact that IV Macc. 18.15 singles out Ps. 34 among a handful of classic OT texts applicable to the righteous sufferer. . . ." More generally, Goppelt, *Petrusbrief*, 8, identifies the theme of this section as "readiness to suffer in society on account of the good."

[275]See 1 Peter 1:17.

The rhetorical question in 3:13 articulates a basic conviction regarding the suffering of the righteous. Brian Beck describes this conviction when commenting about *Wisdom* 1-5:

> It is surprising that, among the surviving early Jewish documents that deal with the sufferings of the righteous, more attention has not been given by commentators to *Wisdom* 1-5 . . . especially in the section 1:16--3:9. These paragraphs depict the persecution of the righteous [ὁ δίκαιος] by the irreligious. . . . They intend to prove false his claim to have God for his father and protector, not recognizing that the righteous are in the hands of God beyond death. . . . The ungodly consider the death of the righteous to be his end, but in truth he is with God (*Wisdom* 3:2f; 4:6ff.). It is not fully clear whether deliverance occurs at the moment of death or later (3:7ff.), but in either case there is a contrast between the plight of the sufferer and the immortality of which he is assured.[276]

Beck's description documents the conviction that a righteous man could not ultimately be harmed.[277] This conviction expressed in the rhetorical question in 3:13 introduces the metaphor of the righteous sufferer.

The introduction of the metaphor of the righteous sufferer is continued in 3:14 by reference to another conviction regarding the righteous sufferer. He is blessed [μακάριος].[278] J. A. Sanders comments on this belief:

---

[276]Brian E. Beck, "*Imitatio Christi* and the Lucan Passion Narrative," in *Suffering and Martyrdom in the New Testament*, Studies Presented to G. M. Styler, ed. William Horbury and Brian McNeil (Cambridge: Cambridge University Press, 1981), 45.

[277]Beare, *1 Peter*, 137, explains, "But the thought of 'harm' is capable of being understood in a deeper sense. Men may undergo suffering, and yet not be 'harmed.' In this ultimate sense, the only real 'harm' is that which touches the inner life, attacking the integrity of the personality; and when one's life is devoted to goodness and to God, it does not lie in the power of man so to harm it." After surveying ancient Jewish literature that discusses the suffering of the righteous, Karl Theodor Kleinknecht, *Der leidende Gerechtfertigte: Die alttestamentlich-jüdische Tradition vom "leidenden Gerechten" und ihre Rezeption bei Paulus*, Wissenschaftliche Untersuchungen zum Neuen Testament 13 (Tübingen: J. C. B. Mohr (Paul Siebeck), 1984), 163, states, "In ever new variations, a particular master structure, thoughts and thought forms, encountered us, and almost all the texts studied with all the distinctiveness of their contexts and their communicative interests resonated the basic conception that God renders to the humbled, suffering righteous his healing, rescuing צדקה."

[278]Berger, *Formgeschichte*, 146, notes the importance of the markarism for the paraenesis. He says, "What meaning the marcarism has for the suffering paraenesis is discernable. In 3:14 it is placed next to the rhetorical question and also in 4:14 to a central passage [compare in addition the prominent marcarism in Matthew 5:10-12; Luke 6:22f.]."

Far more prominent, however, was the belief that afflictions carried with them corresponding compensations which tended to offset the pain and hardship suffered. In the Bible God's restoration of a glorious Israel was often promised after calamities endured by the nation (cf. Lev. 26:40ff., Deut. 30, Jer. 30, Ezek. 33-37, *et al.*), and the individual who found himself in the throes of distress could be counted as fortunate because of compensating rewards to follow upon his suffering (cf. Ps. 94:12, Job 5:17, cp. Luke 24:26, Heb. 2:10, 1 Peter 3:14, 4:14, and Matt. 5:10).[279]

The blessedness of the righteous sufferer is expressed in a conditional sentence in 3:14 that begins with *ἀλλά*. This *ἀλλά* is very significant because it indicates that the author is introducing an exception to the previous statement that his readers could not be harmed.[280] This exception is expressed by a conditional sentence that admits suffering as a possibility in the lives of his readers.[281] The construction *εἰ καί* indicates that the

---

For a discussion of the Beatitudes in relation to the tradition of the righteous sufferer, see Kleinknecht, 168-169.

[279]Jim Alvin Sanders, *Suffering as Divine Discipline in the Old Testament and Post-Biblical Judaism*, Colgate Rochester Divinity Bulletin 28 (Rochester, New York: Colgate Rochester Divinity School, 1955), 109.

[280]Smyth, 632, says, "After a negative clause, or a question implying a negative answer, *ἀλλά*, or more commonly the colloquial *ἀλλ' ἤ*, may mean except." Selwyn, Goppelt, and Best do not even comment on this term. Michaels, *1 Peter*, 185, incorrectly states, "The purpose of this connective is not to set up a contrast to the assurance of 'no harm' in v 13, but actually to reinforce that assurance." Kelly, 141, correctly asserts, "This verse is closely tied to the preceding one, where he has in effect declared, 'No one can possible hurt you if you are devoted to goodness.' Now, as if conscious that this may sound [as it is] unrealistic, he qualifies his statement by adding, 'Nevertheless, if your devotion to goodness should land you in trouble, you should count it a privilege.'"

[281]Beare, *1 Peter*, 136-137, 162, interprets the optitive *πάσχοιτε* as referring to a remote contingency. According to him, the situation of suffering envisioned here is different from the situation of 4:12f. Goppelt, *Petrusbrief*, 234, correctly argues against Beare saying, "However, he leaves open the possibility as in verse 17 that such suffering enters in by formulating the statement with the rare and for that reason particularly striking optative: *εἰ καί πάσχοιτε*. He emphasizes the candor of the situation in order to protect the community from fatalistic resignation and to effect courage in it toward positive conduct in the sense of the basic statements posed in 2:12. If this kerygmatic purpose is seen, then a situation different from the 'must' in 1:6 (compare 2:21; 4:12) will not be reconstructed from the optative." Kelly, 140-141, and Brox, *Petrusbrief*, 158, argue for a similar view of the optative. Brox comments, "If the optative is in fact intended more strictly to be a condition, then it is not, however, the case that suffering for Christianity represents altogether only a future possibility or that by leading a good life it could be avoided.

suffering of the readers is not a hindrance to their blessedness.[282] This blessedness is a characteristic of the righteous sufferer. The author of 1 Peter uses this conviction that the righteous sufferer is blessed along with the conviction that the righteous sufferer could not be harmed to introduce the metaphor of the righteous sufferer.

According to Klaus Berger, the first exhortation to arise from the metaphor of the righteous sufferer is adapted from the tradition of Jewish martyr-paraenesis. He identifies three perspectives in this tradition. The first perspective instructs concerning the correct and false fear. He explains this perspective as follows:

> A distinct tradition of martyr-paraenesis is closely defined semantically and formally: a) In the background stand to be sure the wisdom and prophetic predictions about the correct and the false fear like Proverbs 7:1a LXX ["Fear the Lord . . . fear no other except Him"]; Isaiah 8:12-13 ["You should not fear what the people fear and you should not be terrified of it. The Lord Sabaoth, you

---

Rather, possibly just because the letter has an indefinite circle of addressees from which it supposes obviously a general situation of persecution. . . . To derive a situation without present suffering from the optative in 3:14, 17 is therefore incorrect because harm is not only persecution but also according to 2:13--3:7 the daily allotment of social discrimination . . . so that, as the letter wants to say, suffering is always acknowledged." The explanation of Maximilian Zerwick, *Bibical Greek*, Scripta Pontificii Instituti Biblici 114, trans. Joseph Smith (Rome: n.p., 1963), 110-111, is cited by many of the more recent commentators. He says, ". . . in 1 Pet 3,14 . . . and again in verse 17 . . . the condition is expressed as a theoretical possibility rather than as an envisaged eventuality, although St Peter well knows that in fact such sufferings are eminently probable in the Christian life, and indeed perhaps already a reality for his readers."

[282]The protasis of this conditional sentence begins with εἰ καί. Smyth, 538, comments on this construction, "Εἰ καί commonly admits that a condition exists [granting that], but does not regard it as a hindrance. The condition, though it exists, is a matter of no moment so far as the statement in the principle clause is concerned." The formulation of this conditional sentence implies that the experience of suffering is of no hindrance to the blessedness expressed in the apodosis. This notion of the blessedness of the one who suffers on account of righteousness goes back to a saying of Christ contained in the Beatitude in Matthew 5:10 as most of the commentators note. Wolfgang Nauck, "Freude im Leiden: Zum Problem einer urchristlichen Verfolgungstradition," *Zeitschrift für die neutestamentliche Wissenschaft und die Kunde der älteren Kirche* 46 (1955): 68-80, isolates a brief persecution form using Matthew 5:11f.; Luke 6:22; 1 Peter 1:6; 4:13f.; and James 1:2, 12. This persecution form brings suffering and joy together and may be stated in basic form as follows: Blessed are you when you are persecuted; Rejoice, you will be rewarded. See also J. L. Villiers, "Joy in Suffering in 1 Peter," *Neotestamentica* 9 (1975): 64-86.

should hold Him to be hallowed. He should be your fear and your terror."] In the context, this refers to the fear of hostile peoples.[283]

In this perspective the martyr-paraenesis instructs the recipient to have no fear except for the Lord. The only appropriate fear is the fear of the Lord. In contrast to this first perspective of martyr-paraenesis, the second is formulated negatively containing exhortations not to fear sinners or the wicked. Berger illustrates this perspective:

> The exhortation to not fear before sinners in the Enoch paraenesis is important. For example, 1 Enoch 95:3: "You righteous ones, fear not the sinners because the Lord will deliver them again into your hands" [Compare 96:1: "You righteous ones, hope because the sinners will soon perish before you"]. In the context the sinners are described as violent.[284]

In this second perspective, the recipients of the paraenesis are exhorted not to fear the wicked because they will soon perish. The third perspective in the tradition of martyr-paraenesis admonishes devotion to God as creator and contempt for those who only think they can kill. Berger explains this perspective in the following:

> Already directly in the context of an account of martyrdom, the seven brothers say to one another in 4 Maccabees 13:13-15: "With the whole heart let us devote ourselves to God who gave us our souls and give our bodies as a bulwark for the Law. (14) Let us not fear the one who thinks he could kill. (15) Because the soul's toil and peril that is kept in eternal tribulation is great for those that have transgressed the command of God."[285]

This perspective that God as creator is the only one who can ultimately determine life and death, as well as the first two perspectives, is important to the tradition of Jewish martyr-paraenesis.

Berger asserts that the exhortations in 1 Peter 3:14-16 are constructed according to the two-fold structure of the first perspective of Jewish martyr-paraenesis that instructs concerning the correct and false fear. He states his position as follows:

---

[283]Berger, *Formgeschichte*, 145.
[284]Ibid.
[285]Ibid.

In the formation of the positive half ["Fear rather..."] the New Testament
texts transcend the Jewish expressions. These comply formally, however, to the
two part expressions under (a) discussed above. That is particularly pertinent to
1 Peter 3:14 where the first part is taken from Isaiah 8:12 but the second,
corresponding structurally to the positive part, is constructed with new content
["but hold the Lord Christ to be hallowed in your hearts," compare Isaiah 8:13:
"You should hold the Lord Sabaoth to be hallowed"]. Thus, Isaiah 8:12
following has been drawn from martyrdom and has been Christianized.
Similarly, the positive half of the exhortation in Matthew 10:28b and Luke 12:5
has been formed in the sense of the fear of the Lord. Thus, form criticism shows
an interplay of a word for word appropriation of Old Testament and Jewish
passages and a new formation of analogous structure.[286]

Although there may be problems with Berger's term *martyr-paraenesis*,[287]
he has correctly placed the exhortations in 1 Peter 3:14-16 within the
context of the Christian appropriation of the suffering of the righteous
person in ancient Israelite faith.[288]

---

[286]Ibid., 146.

[287]The context of 1 Peter 3:14-16 and the several passages from the Hebrew
Scriptures that Berger cites are not specifically situations of martyrdom but of suffering and
persecution of the righteous in general. Berger's term is also problematic because of the
uncertainty of how far back the second century Christian concept of martyr can be pushed.
Karl Holl, *Gesammelte Aufsätze zur Kirchengeschichte*, vol. 2: *Der Osten* (Tübingen: J.
C. B. Mohr (Paul Siebeck), 1928; reprint, Darmstadt: Wissenschaftliche Buchgesellschaft,
1964) and Hans von Campenhausen, *Die Idee des Martyriums in der Alten Kirche*
(Göttingen: Vandenhoeck & Ruprecht, 1936) maintain that the term *martyr* is used in the
New Testament with its second century meaning. In contrast, Ernst Günther, "Zeuge und
Märtyrer," *Zeitschrift für die neutestamentliche Wissenschaft* 47 (1956): 145-161, holds
that the second century martyr church first created the title from biblical views and
concepts. Norbert Brox, *Zeuge und Märtyrer*, Studien zum Alten und Neuen Testament 5
(München: Kösel, 1961), 233, rejects both of the previous views. He states, "If one held
on the other hand that the martyr's church had first formed the title from the biblical views
and concepts, as Günther does, then one falls into the embarrassment of not being able to
provide substantiation." Brox makes this statement after dismissing Holl and
von Campenhausen's view that the term *martyr* is used in the New Testament. He
dismisses this view by arguing that 50-60 years passed after the writing of the New
Testament until we have proof that the term *martyr* was used. Thus, Brox reaches the
negative conclusion that neither position is tenable.

[288]Situations of suffering and martyrdom should be understood within the broader
category of the suffering of the righteous. Brox, *Zeuge*, 232, comes close to this position
when discussing the relationship between the suffering witness and the martyr. He says,
"Only in the necessity that the witness must experience suffering and persecution is the
purely external similarity between these concepts, witness and martyr, shown, without the
cleft between both concepts being spanned through an evolutionary-history explanation."
Brox does not think that the latter is possible. Kleinknecht, 122-123, states, "Since the

Admonitions regarding correct and false fear were important to the righteous sufferer. The notion of the righteous sufferer often occurs in the Psalms, which emphasize the sufferer's relationship to God and the persecutor.[289]   Artur Weiser comments on Psalm 34 quoted in 1 Peter 3:10-12:

> (Psalm 34:15-17) The Old Testament always sees behind every moral demand made upon man the will of God, who in the eyes of the sinners is their enemy, but in the eyes of the righteous is their friend and helper in adversity. (18-22) With this last thought, the worshipper once more reverts to his own experience and in his statement concerning the suffering of the righteous throws out a hint that he by no means advocates a 'naïve superficial belief in retribution' nor conceives of happiness in life as consisting in an 'easy life' for the godly in the customary sense. The true happiness of a godly life consists in the nearness of God and in the living experience of his help and not in being spared suffering and affliction. On the contrary, suffering is an essential part of the life of the righteous, and only he who is brokenhearted and crushed in spirit will experience what the nearness of God and his help can really come to mean. The fact that God does not forsake the godly forever but preserves him from utter despair and from the complete destruction of his existence (v. 20), is the blessed experience of the presence of God and of communion with him, a communion which is granted to the God-fearing man at the very time of his suffering, whereas the godless, left to his own devices, breaks down in his adversity and perishes.[290]

---

martyr texts and the conceptions contained in them are doubtless important for the Jewish and early Christian explanations of suffering, certainly in the scholarship they are often seen as constitutive for the explanation of the suffering of Christ and of Christian suffering, it is in each case necessary to explain the relationship of these texts and conceptions to the tradition of the suffering righteous." In what follows he explains the relationship of martyr texts to the tradition of the righteous sufferer.

[289]Schlier, "θλίβω," 142-143, says, ". . . there is also in the Psalms the affliction of righteous individuals whose sufferings have paradigmatic significance. Great tribulation is only to be expected by the righteous: πολλαί αί θλίψεις τῶν δικαίων· ψ 33:19 (4 Macc. 18:15). They walk ἐν μέσῳ θλίψεως (ψ 137:7). They know all about the ἡμέρα θλίψεως, the καιρός θλίψεως (ψ 36:39; 49:15; 76:2). In constant hostility and persecution by their enemies [οί θλίβοντες,ψ 3:1: 12:4; 22:5], in sickness and mortal peril (ψ 65:11; 70:20), . . . God is also the one who hears their prayers and delivers them out of their distress, ψ 9:9; 31:7; 33:6, 17; 36:39f.; 53:7; 58:16; 90:15." See Kleinknecht, 24-33, for a discussion of these Psalms. For him these Psalms with their relationship structure of suppliant, Yahweh, and enemy indicate that the oldest articulation of suffering before God in the Hebrew Scriptures arises from the situation of affliction by enemies.

[290]Artur Weiser, *The Psalms: A Commentary*, The Old Testament Library (Philadelphia: The Westminster Press, 1962), 299.

Psalm 22 is another example that presents the relationship of the sufferer to God and his persecutors. In verses twelve and eighteen, the Psalmist discusses his state of anxiety because of the fear of his enemies. In verses nineteen to thirty-one, the Psalmist's tone changes as he begins to focus upon his relationship to God.[291] In a potential or actual situation of suffering, the righteous sufferer needed the admonition not to fear his/her persecutors but to fear God.

Two circumstantial constructions in verses fifteen and sixteen that describe contexts of persecution or peril modify the admonitions concerning the correct and false fear in the preceding verses. The first circumstantial construction is the adjective $\H{\epsilon}\tau o\iota\mu o\iota$ [prepared] and the second is the participle $\H{\epsilon}\chi o\nu\tau\epsilon$s [holding or maintaining]. The former indicates that the readers are to exercise the correct fear while being prepared to give an apology in every situation of interrogation.[292] The latter portrays the context of maintaining a good conscience with meekness and fear while being spoken against and reviled.[293] The purpose of maintaining a good conscience and conduct is so that the revilers [$\kappa\alpha\tau\alpha\iota\sigma\chi\upsilon\nu\theta\hat{\omega}\sigma\iota$] may be shamed.[294] In good paraenetic style, these circumstantial constructions contrast contexts of word and deed. Both of the contexts described by these circumstantial constructions, as well as the attitudes ascribed to the readers, are apropos to the conception of the righteous sufferer as one who witnesses to his/her devotion to God and

---

[291]See ibid., 223-226. Kleinknecht, 31, comments on the function of psalms that portray the relationship structure of supplicant, Yahweh, and enemy. He says, "The psalm has the function to induce the restoration of this intact structure. This is brought about by the Yahweh › supplicant relationship proving the supplicant › Yahweh relationship as positive and revealing the Yahweh › enemy relationship as negative."

[292]G. W. H. Lampe, "Martyrdom and Inspiration," in Suffering and Martyrdom in the New Testament, Studies presented to G. M. Styler, ed. William Horbury and Brian McNeil (Cambridge: Cambridge University Press, 1981), 122-125, discusses the Christian confession in situations of accusation and its connection with the prophets.

[293]Beck, 31, says, "It is a natural feature of the literature of martyrdom to insist that the victims are innocent of any real crimes and are being punished only for their religious loyalty or because their persecutors are activated by supernatural malice (cf. Daniel 6:4f.; 3 Macc. 3:1-10; 1 Peter 2:19f.)."

[294]Ibid., 31-32, he says, "In some descriptions of martyrdom the sufferings of the victims are described in horrific detail; his endurance is thereby emphasized, and its effect on his persecutors and onlookers is noted. They are amazed at his courage, and [in the later literature, at least] may even be provoked to remorse."

maintains a good conscience and conduct in the face of interrogation and persecution.

In 3:17 a *better-proverb* or *Tobspruch* follows these circumstantial constructions and confirms the truth of the preceding statements.[295] This proverb is almost always interpreted in the light of 2:20 as a social truism from the ancient world.[296] Michaels, however, correctly notes the different contexts of these verses. He differentiates between the two contexts in the following manner:

> If 3:17 is merely a generalized repetition of 2:20, it appears almost tautological in a way in which 2:20 does not. The statement that suffering for doing good is "better" than suffering for doing evil, is all too easily reduced to saying merely that good is better than evil! In fact, something essential to the meaning of 2:20 has been lost: i.e., the emphasis on "endurance" [ύπομενεῖτε], and the distinction between endurance that has merit [when one suffers unjustly] and endurance that has no merit [when one suffers for actual wrong committed]. Thus, 2:20 has a point, but 3:17 appears to have none. . . . In the synoptic tradition, the *Tobspruch* is characteristically used to set forth eschatological alternatives. It is "better" to enter the kingdom of God minus an eye or a limb than to escape such mutilation and be sent away to eternal fire. . . . If 1 Pet 3:17 is read as a *Tobspruch* of this kind, it yields a coherent meaning: it is "better" to suffer in this life at the hands of persecutors for doing good, than at God's hand on the "day of visitation" for doing wrong [for the thought, cf. Matt 10:28].[297]

According to Michaels' interpretation, 3:17 confirms the preceding circumstantial constructions by stating a basic conception of the righteous sufferer who suffers according to the will of God. Indeed, submission to the will of God is an essential characteristic of the righteous person.[298]

---

[295]Goppelt, *Petrusbrief*, 238, says, "The admonition to counter discrimination by a positive apologetic is substantiated as the γάρ shows in that the slogan developed at the beginning in verses 13 and 14a is modified again."

[296]Ibid., 238, he says, "The statement is a sentence spoken in the Wisdom style that is transmitted in similar form already since Socrates (Plato, *Georgias*, 508C). It generalizes what was said to the slaves in 2:20. . . ."

[297]Michaels, *1 Peter*, 191-192.

[298]Gottlob Schrenk, "Δίκαιος," in *Theological Dictionary of the New Testament*, vol. 2: *Δ–H*, ed. Gerhard Kittel (Grand Rapids: Wm. B. Eerdmans Publishing Co., 1968), 189, says, "With reference to men who do God's will, δίκαιος is used in the OT sense of the patriarchs [Abel: Mt. 23:35; Hb. 1:14; cf. 1 Jn. 3:12] and saints of the OT [Lot: 2 Pt. 2:7, cf. 8] who stand out from the world with its wicked works. Together with the saints who render full obedience to God, the main representatives of the earlier

Because of future retribution, it is better to suffer according to the will of God as a righteous person than to become one of the unrighteous.

The author of 1 Peter gives a Christological substantiation for the *Tobspruch* expressed in verse seventeen. In verses eighteen to twenty-two, he records a kerygmatic description of Christ's death, resurrection, and ascension that is heavily influenced by the notion of the righteous sufferer.[299] Schutter explains the theme of this kerygmatic statement as follows:

> The next unit carries forward the theme of righteous suffering through a link-word πάσχειν/dπέθανεν (3.17/18), and a key-word, 'Christ' (3.15, 16/18), correlated with yet another source-item, what is generally accepted as a kerygmatic/creedal formula, a version of which appeared earlier in 2.21. From its association there with Is. 53, and a possible echo of 53.11 (LXX), it also approximates to an iterative allusion to that OT text.... Hence, the compositional method begun in 3.13, which correlates formal source-materials with the psalm quotation to develop the theme of righteous suffering, seems to continue unbroken through 3.18b.[300]

Schutter has correctly observed the primary theme of righteous suffering in this kerygmatic statement concerning the passion and resurrection of Jesus.

---

period are the prophets: Mt. 13:17; 23:29, cf. Mt. 10:41 and the αἷμα δίκαιον of innocent martyrs (Mt. 23:35)."

[299]For a discussion of the literature that interprets Christ's Passion in the tradition of the righteous sufferer, see Kleinknecht, 177-192. On page 177, he remarks, "How strongly the Synoptic Passion narratives are connected to the psalms of the righteous sufferer was seen at all times and was made fruitful for the interpretation of these reports in various ways." Goppelt, *Petrusbrief*, 240, correctly observes, "Accordingly, the following aspects about the salvation effect of the suffering death of the righteous ensues for the passage: (Verse 18) his constant presentation to God; (Verses 19-20a) his salvation proclamation to the spirits in prison; (Verses 20b-21) the salvation effected by him from the commencing judgment through baptism; additionally, (Verse 22) his Lordship over the powers. This is no fixed systematic outline. It is rather a sequence of traditional conceptions and forms standing through association that desires to place in view the universal effect of salvation that arises from the suffering death of the righteous. Thus, the passage in its paraenetic context wants to portray an exemplary model less than the other two [previous Christological passages]. The suffering of the righteous is expressly recognized as unique (Verse 18). So much the more, these expositions want to win over [the readers] to the having and taking part in this way of blessing and thus support the blessing of the sufferers on account of righteousness (3:13-17)."

[300]Schutter, *Hermeneutic*, 68.

The Passion of Jesus determined the understanding of righteous suffering in early Christianity. Otto Michel states, "At the center of the view of suffering in early Christianity stands the Passion Narrative of Jesus."[301] Eduard Lohse connects the passion of Jesus with the tradition of the righteous sufferer in the following statement:

> It [Christian preaching] has adduced . . . the testimony of Scripture: "The Messiah died for our sins in accordance with the scriptures." In this appeal to "the scriptures" what was doubtless intended was primarily a reference to those passages which deal with the suffering and death of the righteous one, who has to endure misery and persecution at the hands of the wicked. Christians repeatedly connected Psalm 22, 31, and 69 with the account of Jesus' passion. The clearest reference, however, was to the suffering of God's Servant in the fifty-third chapter of the Book of Isaiah.[302]

Thus, appropriating the Jewish tradition of the righteous sufferer, Jesus became the paradeigma of righteous suffering for early Christian thought.[303]

This understanding of Jesus' passion as the paradeigma of the righteous sufferer explains the function of this kerygmatic statement in 1 Peter 3:18-22. The statement confirms the *Tobspruch* that it is better to suffer according to the will of God while doing good than doing evil. Christ suffered righteously even to the point of death, but God intervened in His death raising Him to life (3:18), removing Him to heaven (3:19, 22), and seating Him at His right hand after subordinating angels, authorities,

---

[301]Otto Michel, "Leiden im NT," in *Die Religion in Geschichte und Gegenwart*, vol. 4: *Kop-O* (Tübingen: J. C. B. Mohr (Paul Siebeck), 1960), 297-298.

[302]Eduard Lohse, *History of the Suffering and Death of Jesus Christ*, trans. Martin O. Dietrich (Philadelphia: Fortress Press, 1967), 8-9.

[303]Jesus' Passion becomes even more determinative for the later Christian understanding of martyrdom. Hans Werner Surkau, *Martyrien in jüdischer und frühchristlicher Zeit* (Göttingen: Vandenhoeck & Ruprecht, 1938), 135, says, "It has already been expressed that in the early Christian martyrdoms the Passion Narrative exerted a distinctive influence so that we must observe two formative moments in Christian Martyrdoms: Jewish thoughts and reports of martyrs and the Passion Narrative. In the literature the influence of the Passion has been mostly overlooked until now as also the effect of Jewish thoughts were much less strongly recognized." Similarly Ethelbert Stauffer, "Märtyrertheologie und Täuferbewegung," *Zeitschrift für Kirchengeschichte* 52 (1933): 547-548, states, "Early Christendom has made the work of Christ plain with the categories of martyr theology and has understood the fate of the martyr from the fate of Christ. However, it has not therefore included Christ in the circle of martyrs. It has rather placed the martyr under the marks of Christ's experience."

and powers to Him (3:22). This vindication of the righteous sufferer and the salvation benefits provided by His suffering (3:18) confirm the *Tobspruch* in 3:17.

A new subsection begins in 4:1 with the minor transitional marker οὖν. This subsection continues the exhortation arising from the metaphorical description of the readers as righteous sufferers. In contrast to the previous section, however, the exhortation is cast in terms of a military metaphor describing the mental equipment needed by the righteous sufferer.[304] In 4:1 the author exhorts his readers to arm themselves [ὁπλίσασθε] with the ἔννοια of Christ. Several exegetical issues in this verse must be resolved before the relationship of this subsection to the compositional structure of the larger section can be correctly understood.[305]

The first issue is the meaning of the verb πάσχω in the genitive absolute Χριστοῦ παθόντος and the participial phrase ὁ παθών.[306] This verb can either refer to suffering in general or to death.[307] Theophylact favors the latter meaning when he comments on the participial phrase "ὁ

---

[304]Michaels, *1 Peter*, 225, says, "The exhortation proper is a military metaphor [ὁπλίσασθε, 'arm yourselves'], somewhat reminiscent of 1:13, with its call to prepare oneself mentally for action." Dalton, *Proclamation*, 241, associates this metaphor with a baptismal context, saying, "One recalls the baptismal exhortation of Rom 6:13: 'Do not yield your members as instruments [ὅπλα] of wickedness, but yield yourselves to God as men who have been brought from death to life, and your members to God as instruments [ὅπλα] of righteousness.' Another theme which throws light on 1 Pet 4:1a is that, found also in baptismal exhortation, of 'putting on' Christ, the new man, Christian virtues."

[305]Selwyn, *1 Peter*, 208, says, "Verse 1 is one of the most important, as it is one of the most difficult, verses of this whole section."

[306]It is grammatically possible for Χριστοῦ to hang on ἔννοια and for παθόντος to modify Χριστοῦ. In this case, the phrase Χριστοῦ παθόντος would not be a genitive absolute. Nevertheless, since this phrase occurs first in its sentence and since ἔννοια is already modified by αὐτῇ, it is best to understand the phrase as a genitive absolute as almost all commentators do.

[307]Best, *1 Peter*, 150, questions the meaning of this verb in the genitive absolute, "Is this to be understood in the general sense that Jesus endured suffering throughout his life or in a more particular sense as referring to his death alone?" Wilhelm Michaelis, "Πάσχω," in *Theological Dictionary of the New Testament*, vol. 5: Ξ-Πα, ed. Gerhard Kittel (Grand Rapids: Wm. B. Eerdmans Publishing Co., 1970), 905, recognizes both meanings in classical Greek. He says, "Already very common in Hom. (Il., 5, 567; 11, 470 etc.) is the expression πάσχω τι, 'some evil overtakes me,' also the euphemism παθεῖν τι, 'to die.'" On page 918-919, he states that this verb in 1 Peter 2:21, 23; 4:1 refers to the death of Christ.

παθὼν ἀντί τοῦ ὁ ἀποθανών [*he who suffered* instead of *he who died*]."[308] Goppelt also favors the latter meaning when he comments on the genitive absolute "This statement takes over the distinctive catch word of 3:18: 'Christ has . . . suffered, . . . died in the flesh.'"[309] Thus, on the basis of the context, both of these commentators understand πάσχω to refer to death.

The second issue is the meaning of ἔννοια. Dalton describes the possibilities, "The noun ἔννοια is used in various ways in profane Greek, ranging from a purely intellectual meaning of 'thinking,' 'notion,' 'idea,' to that of 'intention.'"[310] Michaels prefers the latter meaning and interprets ἔννοια as referring to the intention or resolve that Christ brought to his moment of crisis.[311] On the other hand, Goppelt prefers the former meaning. He states, "Ἔννοια is here not the 'intention,' rather as in the wisdom language of Proverbs the 'understanding,' which produces a corresponding behavior described here in verse two."[312] Because the author is not exhorting the readers to suffer or to endure martyrdom, Goppelt's explanation of ἔννοια is preferable to Michaels'.[313] The author exhorts his readers to arm themselves with the understanding that results in the behavior described in verse two and following.

The third issue is the content of ἔννοια. Best outlines the possibilities, "Does this [ἔννοια] refer backwards to 'Christ suffered in the flesh' or forwards to 'whoever has suffered . . . sin?'"[314] The resolution of this issue rests upon the function of the ὅτι clause. There are two possibilities. One possibility is that ὅτι meaning *that* introduces a clause that states the content of ἔννοια. Windisch proposes this possibility stating, "The ἔννοια, 'the discerning understanding' Proverbs 23:19; 3:21; 1:4, not

---

[308]Theophylact, 1236.

[309]Goppelt, *Petrusbrief*, 268. Michaels, *1 Peter*, 225, as well as the majority of commentators, takes a similar position on the meaning of this verb in 4:1.

[310]Dalton, *Proclamation*, 241. Dalton prefers the former meaning.

[311]Michaels, *1 Peter*, 225.

[312]Goppelt, *Petrusbrief*, 267.

[313]Dalton, *Proclamation*, 243, says, "If the readers of 1 Peter were face to face with martyrdom, then possibly we could find a more satisfactory meaning of 4:1b by understanding 'suffer in the flesh' as the martyr's death. But as this is by no means the situation portrayed in the letter, there is no point in considering such a hypothesis further."

[314]Best, *1 Peter*, 151.

'resolve' or 'disposition,' finds its exposition in the ὅτι-statement."[315] The meaning would then be, "Arm yourselves with the same understanding that he who has died in the flesh has ceased from sin." Goppelt argues against this possibility, proposing a second alternative. He reasons as follows:

> Although it is philologically possible, the ὅτι cannot be translated with "that" and the clause be understood as a paraphrase of the contents of the ἔννοια that is parallel to the preceding, because the expression "he has ceased from sin" cannot be related to Christ. On the other hand, the clause fits meaningfully into the context if it is understood as a general substantiation and is placed in parenthesis.[316]

For Goppelt, the ὅτι clause does not give the content of the ἔννοια, but stands as a parenthetical statement giving the substantiation for the exhortation to arm oneself with the ἔννοια. Since, for both Windisch and Goppelt, the ὅτι clause is important for understanding the content of ἔννοια, the function and meaning of this clause must be examined before the content of ἔννοια can be determined.

Goppelt admits that it is philologically possible for the ὅτι clause to function as a statement of the content of ἔννοια. However, he rejects this possibility because the clause implicates its subject in the practice of sin and consequently cannot take Christ as its antecedent. Goppelt's argument is untenable for two reasons. First, the verb πέπαυται [has ceased] can be understood in such a way as to avoid the implication that Christ practiced sin.[317] Second, early Christian tradition did understand Christ's death as a termination of His involvement with sin. Dalton explains this tradition:

> A far more fruitful line of investigation is opened up by a comparison of our text (1 Peter 4:1) with St. Paul's classic treatment of baptism in Rom 6:3-11. In a section parallel to 1 Pet 4:2-5 the Christian is urged to abandon sin: "Let not sin therefore reign in your mortal bodies, to make you obey their passions . . . but

---

[315]Windisch, 73. Best, *1 Peter*, 151; Kelly, *1 Peter*, 166; and Moffatt, 146, hold a similar view.

[316]Goppelt, *Petrusbrief*, 268.

[317]E. A. Sieffert, "Die Heilsbedeutung des Leidens und Sterbens Christi nach dem ersten Briefe des Petrus," *Jahrbücher für deutsche Theologie* 20 (1875): 371-440 and August Strobel, "Macht Leiden von Sünde frei? Zur Problematik von 1. Petr. 4, 1f.," *Theologische Zeitschrift* 19 (1963): 412-425, both take Christ as the antecedent of ὁ παθών and then argue for a meaning of πέπαυται that does not indicate that Christ had committed sin. Michaels, *1 Peter*, 227-229 favorably discusses their positions.

yield yourselves to God." The basis for this life of renunciation of sin and loyalty to God is expressed by both writers in terms which are very close. Paul insists on the central role of the death of Christ into this death the Christian enters by baptism: "Do you not know that all of us who have been baptized into Christ Jesus were baptized into his death?" He justifies the statement that, by baptism, the Christian is freed from the slavery of sin by a sentence which runs like a proverb: "For he who has died is freed from sin" [ὁ γὰρ ἀποθανὼν δεδικαίωται ἀπὸ τῆς ἁμαρτίας]. This statement applies directly to the Christian, but, with a remarkably bold expression, Paul goes on to speak of Christ in a way which brings Him also under this proverb: "The death, he died he died to sin, once for all."[318]

By this comparison of 1 Peter 4:1 with Romans 6:3-11, Dalton cogently implies that the ὅτι clause in 1 Peter 4:1 is a proverbial statement that can apply to Christ as well as to Christians.[319] In addition to this passage in Romans, Michaels cites Hebrews 9:28 as an expression of this tradition in early Christianity. He comments on this verse:

"So Christ, having been offered up once [ἅπαξ] to bear the sins of many, will appear a second time *apart from sin* [χωρὶς ἁμαρτίας] to bring salvation to those who wait for him." The distinction is not that Christ, once sinful, is now sinless, but that the purpose of his first coming was to deal with human sin, and that now, with that purpose accomplished, he has nothing more to do with sin. . . . In 1 Peter, therefore, it is not surprising to find that Christ, having "gone to heaven" at God's right hand and with angels subject to him, is also said to be "through with sin."[320]

For these two reasons Goppelt's argument is untenable, and it is best to take the function of the ὅτι clause as an expression of the content of ἔννοια.[321]

Since the ὅτι clause expresses the content of the ἔννοια, the meaning of this clause must be ascertained. Although Goppelt incorrectly identifies the function of the ὅτι clause, he correctly ascertains its meaning. He discusses four different meanings of the ὅτι clause, "because he who has

---

[318]Dalton, *Proclamation*, 244.

[319]Michaels, *1 Peter*, 226-227, argues persuasively, "Similarly, there is in the present passage a specific antecedent for the anonymous participial expression, ὁ παθὼν σαρκί, or 'he who suffered in the flesh.' It is, of course, the phrase Χριστοῦ . . . παθόντος σαρκί, 'Now that Christ has suffered in the flesh,' in v 1a. The parallel is unmistakable, and the natural conclusion is that the second participle, like the first, refers to Jesus Christ."

[320]Ibid., 228.

[321]So Best, *1 Peter*, 151; Kelly, 166; and Dalton, *Proclamation*, 240.

suffered in the flesh has ceased from sin."[322]   First, the cognitive-
psychological understanding states that righteous suffering documents the
break with sin. Goppelt rejects this view because $\pi\alpha\theta\acute{\omega}\nu$ means *to die*, not
to suffer in general. Second, the gnomic understanding holds that the
statement expresses the general truth that through suffering the flesh is
mastered and sin removed. He dismisses this view because in Christian
theology humans are freed from sin through Christ, not suffering. Third,
the baptismal understanding conceives of death to sin through baptism with
Christ (Romans 6:2; Colossians 2:11). Goppelt admits that the baptismal-
paraenesis context of this passage supports this view. Nevertheless, he
rejects this view arguing that the Petrine theological conception of
suffering, death, and cessation from sin differs from the Pauline position.
Fourth, the anthropological understanding posits that the dead are free
from sin (Romans 6:7). Goppelt prefers this view, explaining:

> This clause does not proclaim what is done by Christ in baptism, rather it
> substantiates it. . . . According to 2:24 Christ died for us, "so that we died to
> sin but live to righteousness." As there that paraenetic kerygma was inferred
> from Jesus' death, so here this anthropological teaching is inferred.[323]

The anthropological truism that the dead are free from sin thus becomes
the basis for the baptismal truism that those who have died with Christ in
baptism are free from sin. Although death with Christ is usually associated
with baptism in the New Testament, Goppelt is correct in his contention
that this clause should be understood as an anthropological truism rather
than a baptismal truism. The clause does not mean that one who has died
with Christ in baptism is free from sin, but that one who has died is free
from sin.[324]   Goppelt correctly understands that the $\H{o}\tau\iota$ clause states this
anthropological truism even though he fails to perceive that the function of
this clause is to state the content of the $\H{\epsilon}\nu\nu o\iota\alpha$.

---

[322]Goppelt, *Petrusbrief*, 269-270.

[323]Ibid., 269-270. On page 271 Goppelt states, "The call to this understanding is
developed in our passage directly from the suffering of Christ (verse 1a), not from a
baptismal event, although the broader context is baptismal paraenesis. Also Paul traces this
conviction once directly back to Jesus' death (2 Corinthians 5:14) and another time to its
mediation through baptism (Romans 6:2)."

[324]Kelly, 168-169, argues on contextual grounds that the $\H{o}\tau\iota$ clause should be
understood in baptismal terms. However, Goppelt's interpretation is superior because he
takes into account both the context and the actual wording of the clause.

Having determined the function and meaning of the ὅτι clause, the content of ἔννοια can now be stated. Ἔννοια is the insight or understanding that one who has died has ceased from sin. This insight or understanding can apply to Christ as well as to the Christian. Thus, the third exegetical issue in 1 Peter 4:1 has been resolved.

With the resolution of these exegetical issues, 1 Peter 4:1 can be interpreted. The author exhorts his readers, "Since Christ suffered in the flesh [i.e, died], arm yourselves with the same understanding that one who has suffered in the flesh [i.e. died] has ceased from sin."[325] This anthropological truism applies to Christ's actual death and to the readers' metaphorical death. Although the author does not explicitly state here that his readers have died with Christ in baptism like Romans 6:8, he does articulate the resultant attitude of this conception.[326] From 1 Peter 2:24, it is clear that he already conceives of his readers as dead to sin but alive to righteousness.[327] Therefore, the author now exhorts them to arm themselves with the same understanding of Christ's death that one who has died has ceased from sin.

This interpretation of 4:1 permits an understanding of the relationship of this subsection (4:1-7a) to the compositional structure of the

---

[325]Goppelt's interpretation of 1 Peter 4:1 is inconsistent with his contention that the ὅτι clause substantiates the exhortation to arm oneself rather than states the content of ἔννοια. He interprets 1 Peter 4:1 according to the latter function of the ὅτι clause. Goppelt, *Petrusbrief*, 270, says, "Thus, the essential meaning of verse 1b comes to the fore: Arm yourselves with the same understanding of Christ who placed Himself under the faith-conviction that His flesh, His mortal human nature must be subjected to suffering because it only then ceases from sinning when it is judged through a suffering death."

[326]Michaelis, 922-923, interprets 1 Peter 4:1 as follows: "In 4:1 ... the ὅτι clause ... in so far as it applies to Christians, ... should not be referred to their sufferings (3:14, 17). In analogy to Christ's παθεῖν σαρκί, which is mentioned just before and in which πασχεῖν means 'to die,' it refers to their death, i.e., in baptism (cf. 3:21). The similarity to R. 6:7 ... and to the context of this verse is very plain. In dying Christ, too, accepted the will of God (cf. 4:2). If Christians arm themselves with the same ἔννοια, they, too, will in the future live only to God, R. 6:11. The transferred use of πασχεῖν [σαρκί] with reference to baptism ... is possible only on the basis of the usage παθεῖν = 'to die.' Moreover it is difficult to explain unless we assume the influence of the thought of R. 6 which Paul regarded as common to primitive Christianity."

[327]Schutter, *Hermeneutic*, 70, notes the relationship of 4:1 with 2:24b. He states, "Nevertheless, 4.1 does have a point of contact with 2.21 in the form of a similar emphasis on Christ's example ... and its 'death to sin' trope clearly recalls 2.24b, ταῖς ἁμαρτίαις ἀπογενόμενοι."

larger section (3:13--4:11).[328]   The purpose or result of arming oneself
with the same ἔννοια as Christ is exposed in 4:2 as living during the
remaining time in the flesh by the will of God and not by the desires of
men.[329] This antithesis, which expresses the positive and negative sides of
righteous conduct, is characteristic in discussions of the righteous
person.[330] The righteous person lives by the will of God and abstains from
libertinism.[331] Gottlob Schrenk comments on the term δίκαιος in regard to
the Messiah, "The Messiah is called righteous because His whole nature and
action are in conformity with the norm of the divine will."[332] He continues
his discussion:

> When δίκαιος is applied as a Messianic designation, the term is first used . . . to
> describe the piety of Jesus in fulfillment of the will of God. This corresponds to
> the OT usage. . . . In 1 Jn. 2:29; 3:7 there is advanced against libertinism the
> fact that those who belong to the δίκαιος, as Jesus is called, must give evidence
> of righteous conduct.[333]

As Schrenk correctly states, the righteous Messiah and those who belong to
Him live by the will of God and avoid libertinism. Whereas, the previous
subsection discussed the appropriate fear for the righteous person,
this subsection lays out the negative conduct to be avoided by the
righteous sufferer.

The conduct that the readers as righteous sufferers are to avoid is
generally described as the counsel of the Gentiles [βούλημα τῶν ἐθνῶν] in
4:3 and as dissipation [ἀσωτία] in 4:4. This counsel is set in direct contrast
to the will of God and is specifically described by the vice list that

---

[328]Goppelt, *Petrusbrief*, 271, says, "The exegesis of the complex first verse is
confirmed through the final clause of result in the second verse to which it aims: He who
relinquishes the flesh in the developed understanding is free for the rest of the time in the
flesh from its jurisdiction. 'The remaining time in the flesh' is the earthly lifetime
after baptism."

[329]The construction in 4:2 is εἰς τὸ . . . βιῶσαι. According to Blass, 207, this
construction denotes purpose or result.

[330]Abraham Cronbach, "Righteousness in the OT," in *The Interpreter's Dictionary
of the Bible*, ed. George Arthur Buttrick, vol. 4: *R-Z* (Nashville: Abingdon, 1962), 85-86,
cites numerous Jewish texts from 200 BCE to 100 CE that discuss the positive and negative
qualities constituting righteousness.

[331]See the discussion above on 1 Peter 3:17.

[332]Schrenk, "Δίκαιος," 186.

[333]Ibid., 188-189.

follows.[334] Obviously, these are deeds that have no place in the life of the righteous person.[335]

The avoidance of this conduct of dissipation leads to surprise on the part of the Gentiles and a strain in the readers' relationship with them (4:4).[336] Dalton correctly places this reaction of the Gentiles to the righteous conduct of the readers in the context of *Wisdom* 2:12-16. He explains as follows:

> The reaction of the pagans to the Christian way of life expressed in 4:4 has its own interest. We are reminded of the attitude of the wicked to the righteous man described in Wis 2:12-16: "Let us lie in wait for the righteous man, because he is inconvenient to us and opposes our actions. . . . He becomes to us a reproof of our thoughts; the very sight of him is a burden to us, because his manner of life is unlike that of others, and his ways are strange. We are considered by him as something base, and he avoids our ways as unclean."[337]

Thus, the reaction of the Gentiles to the readers' avoidance of dissipating conduct has its parallel in the discussions of the reaction of the wicked to the righteous person.[338]

The use of the concept of judgment in verses five and six to vindicate the righteous conduct of the Christians and to condemn the blaspheming

---

[334]Michaels, *1 Peter*, 230, says, "The βούλημα, or purpose, of the Gentiles echoes the 'human impulses' of the preceding verse and stands in opposition to 'the will of God.'"

[335]This vice list is composed from stock material in the Jewish and Christian ethical tradition. Kelly, 170, comments, "The catalogue of misconduct which follows closely resembles those in Rom. xiii.13f. and Gal. v.19-21 [note the prominence of sexual and alcoholic excesses in all three, and the stress on idolatry here and in Gal. v.20], as well as having points of contact with late Jewish texts (e.g. Ass. Mos. vii.3-10) and the Dead Sea Scrolls (e.g. 1QS iv.9-11). The material is therefore probably stock . . . but is worked up in such a way as to convey a graphic impression of the sexuality, heavy drinking and disorder which were characteristic of many social parties in the towns of Asia Minor in the 1st cent." For a good discussion of each of these vices and their parallels in Jewish and Christian tradition, see Michaels, *1 Peter*, 231-232.

[336]Goppelt, *Petrusbrief*, 273, says, "Along with the opposition of one's own old human existence, the distancing from the manner of life of society causes conflict with the environment. Nonconformity finally occasions conflict between the Christian and society."

[337]Dalton, *Proclamation*, 239.

[338]Cronbach, 90, states, "The righteous are, by word and deed, a reproof to the ungodly, and this the ungodly resent (Wisd. Sol. 2:1-21)." Beck, 45, also observes, "The righteous man is persecuted because he is unlike others and shows up their lives as counterfeit (Wisdom 2:15f). By his constancy in goodness, even under insult and torture, he proves himself ἄξιος τοῦ θεοῦ (3:5); he vindicates his right to be called δίκαιος."

Gentiles likewise relates to the traditional discussion of the relationship between the wicked and the righteous.[339] Again, citing *Wisdom* 2:12-16 as a parallel, Dalton comments as follows:

> As in the case of 1 Pet 4:5, the godless who persecuted and reviled the righteous man will have to stand before the divine Judge: "But the ungodly will be punished as their reasoning deserves, who disregarded the righteous man and rebelled against the Lord. . . . They will come with dread when their sins are reckoned up, and their lawless deeds will convict them to their face." On the other hand, "The righteous man will stand with great confidence in the presence of those who afflicted him, and those who make light of his labours. . . . But the righteous live forever, and their reward is with the Lord; the Most High takes care of them."[340]

According to Dalton, the author of 1 Peter treats the judgment of the blaspheming Gentiles in verse five and then proceeds in verse six to discuss the judgment of the Christians. He comments on the meaning of verse six:

> This larger context is made even more definite by the immediate context of 1 Pet 4:6. The writer is dealing with the vindication of Christians. . . . We have seen from the preceding section that the writer is thinking of those Christians who have heard the preaching of the gospel in their life-time but have since died. He stresses that, for them, the preaching of the gospel was not in vain: although they died, and thus in the eyes of men seemed to be condemned [judged], still the preaching of the gospel will enable them to reach true life, the only life which God acknowledges.[341]

As Dalton astutely observes, the author of 1 Peter makes a contrast between the outcome of the judgment of the blaspheming Gentiles and the Christians that is similar to the contrast between the judgment of the

---

[339]For an extended discussion of the exegetical problems in these two verses, see Dalton, *Proclamation*, 263-277. Kleinknecht, 98, discusses this aspect of judgment in *1 Enoch*, stating, "In contrast to the Daniel Apocalypse, *1 Enoch* lays great weight on the description of the condition of the righteous and of the godless in the final judgment in which a reversal of circumstances takes place: the godless will be given over to revenge at the hand of the righteous; they will not enter into the future age while the righteous partake of it through the resurrection or transformation."

[340]Ibid., 239.

[341]Ibid., 271-272.

unrighteous and the righteous. To the Gentiles the judgment is ominous, but for the Christians there is hope.[342]

Given this context of judgment, the function and meaning of the statement πάντων δὲ τὸ τέλος ἤγγικεν in verse seven is largely misunderstood. Goppelt translates and interprets this statement:

> *The end of all things has come near.* . . . With the indication of the near end of all things in verse seven, the new passage distances itself from the previous grappling with the environment and one's own old human existence. This new passage seeks to activate the life which remains through this time, namely; the inner life of the community.[343]

Almost all modern commentators agree with Goppelt in translating this statement as the end of all things has drawn near.[344] They also understand this statement as the beginning of a new section of paraenesis based upon this statement.[345] In comparison to Goppelt, Theophylact provides a more cogent explanation saying, "'But the end of all is drawing near.' That is, the end of all who have been justified both the living and the dead. For in the Second Coming the end which has been kept for each shall be accomplished."[346] Theophylact's interpretation is an improvement over

---

[342]Kleinknecht, 98-99, discusses the future fate of the righteous and the unrighteous following the judgment in *1 Enoch.* After portraying the negative circumstances of the unrighteous, he describes the circumstances of the righteous as follows, "The situation of the righteous in the comming age is likewise described at length: on one hand negatively, no affliction and distress; on the other hand positively, a glorious lot, a stage of life without end, life in the light of the Son and of eternal life, peace with God, partaking of the tree of life, light, joy, peace, and heirs of the land. The righteous will receive wisdom. They will have table fellowship with the Son of Man and will be clothed with the garment of the glory of God. They will shine as the stars--here certainly occurs an expansion to all of the righteous of the particular glorification of the משכילים of Daniel 12."

[343]Goppelt, *Petrusbrief,* 278.

[344]So Beare, *1 Peter,* 157; Best, *1 Peter,* 158-159; Bigg, 172; Brox, *Petrusbrief,* 201-204; Kelly, 176-177; Michaels, *1 Peter,* 243-246; Moffatt, 152-153; Schutter, *Hermeneutic,* 71; Wand, *1 Peter,* 112-113; and Windisch, *Petrusbrief,* 75. Reicke, *1 Peter,* 121, translates "For all, however, the end is near." His translation correctly implies that the "all" refers to people, not things. Nevertheless, he is ambiguous in his explanation as to whether the "all" refers to people or things. Selwyn, *1 Peter,* 216, correctly links this statement with the preceding discussion of judgment.

[345]An exception is Holzmeister, 362-370, who connects this statement with verses five and six and begins the new subsection at 4:7b.

[346]Theophylact, 1240.

Goppelt's for three reasons. First, he takes πάντων as a masculine referring to the groups of people that the author of 1 Peter mentioned in the previous verses. This understanding is better than taking it as neuter referring to things. The author has not been talking about things, but about people. Second, the previous verses intimated that all, both the righteous and unrighteous, are coming to judgment. According to Theophylact's interpretation, this statement in 4:7a concludes this discussion of judgment and does not abruptly introduce a new idea.[347] Third, the author of 1 Peter has never introduced a new section with the conjunction δέ, but prefers the conjunction οὖν. The οὖν in 4:7b indicates that this statement introduces the new subsection, not 4:7a.[348] Thus, Goppelt and almost all modern commentators have misunderstood the function and meaning of this statement. It refers to the final judgment of all people and concludes this subsection.

In view of the preceding discussion, a new subsection begins in 4:7b and extends to the benediction in 4:11. The paraenesis in this subsection continues to discuss the mental equipment needed by the righteous sufferer as well as the behavior befitting him/her. Schutter correctly relates this subsection to the preceding as follows:

> Of greater material significance for the relationship between 4.1-6 and 7-11, however, is the possibility the latter is completing a pattern initiated by the former. In 4.2f. a bold antithesis is set out between living in accordance with God's will or with "human passions," that is, "the will of the nations" [4.3, τὸ βούλημα τῶν ἐθνῶν]. What their will entails is then listed in a series of hedonistic and idolatrous corporate practices, but nothing more is said about what the will of God entails beyond the way the *abstinentes* can be seen to come to expression in the "death to sin" idea. One must wait for 4.7bff. to learn what kind of corporate behavior God expects from Christians in the meantime characterized above all by a temperate, self-sacrificing life-style and true worship. Thus 4.7-11 may be taken as intended to bring out the other side of the antithesis after a fashion that has an immediate formal parallel in the antithesis which the transition from 4.1 to 4.2 presupposes.[349]

---

[347]Thus, Schutter's problem with the abrupt entrance of an eschatological section is resolved. See Schutter, *Hermeneutic*, 71.

[348]The disjunction of ἤγγικεν and σωφρονήσατε also indicates that the new subsection begins in 4:7b, not 4:7a.

[349]Schutter, *Hermeneutic*, 71-72.

Whereas the previous subsection laid out the practices that the righteous sufferer should avoid, this subsection subsequently proposes the positive practices to be emulated.

This understanding of the context of the paraenesis in this subsection transcends the positions taken in the commentaries. Commentators relate this subsection to the community paraenesis in Romans 12; 1 Thessalonians 5:1-10; and James 5:7-20.[350] What they have failed to observe is that the paraenesis in these passages has close affinities with discussions of the righteous person. In particular, the passage in James that, according to Goppelt, is the closest parallel to the passage in Peter cites the prophets, Job, and Elijah (James 5:10-11, 17) as examples to emulate. All of these were considered to be outstanding paragons of righteousness in the ancient world.[351] This close affinity of the paraenesis to discussions of the righteous person is not surprising because the characteristics of the righteous person were often stated in contrast to their wicked environment. In a similar fashion, the characteristics urged upon the community in these passages are stated in contrast to the pagan environment in which the community exists. Although the paraenesis in 1 Peter 4:7b-11 is clearly community paraenesis, it is drawn from the conception of the positive attributes of the righteous person.

The author begins with an exhortation to be sane [$\sigma\omega\phi\rho\sigma\nu\dot{\eta}\sigma\alpha\tau\epsilon$] and sober [$\nu\dot{\eta}\psi\alpha\tau\epsilon$] for prayers. The two imperatives continue the mental metaphor of 4:1.[352] Particularly the latter, with its emphasis on sobriety, stands in stark contrast to the conduct of the Gentiles described in verse

---

[350]Selwyn, *1 Peter*, 375-382, and Kelly, 176-182, emphasize the Thessalonian parallels. Goppelt, *Petrusbrief*, 280-281, states that the passage in James is the closest parallel.

[351]Cronbach, 90, states, "Certain individuals have been outstanding for righteousness: . . . Job (Aristeas Fragment 11), . . . Elijah (Apocal. Esd. 5:22; Apocal. Sophonias 14:3). . . ." Schrenk, 189, remarks, "With reference to men who do God's will, $\delta\dot{\iota}\kappa\alpha\iota\sigma$ is used in the OT sense of the patriarchs . . . who stand out from the world with its wicked works. Together with the saints who render full obedience to God, the main representatives of the earlier period are the prophets: Mt. 13:17; 23:29. . . ."

[352]Michaels, *1 Peter*, 245, asserts, "The two verbs are almost synonymous here in meaning. Their common emphasis on mental alertness and clear thinking recalls 1:13, where Peter in similar fashion urges mental preparedness. . . . Here Peter drops the metaphor of girding oneself and substitutes for it the verb $\sigma\omega\phi\rho\sigma\nu\epsilon\hat{\iota}\nu$, 'to think clearly' or 'to keep one's head.'"

three [οἰνοφλυγίαι, κῶμοι, πότοι].³⁵³ This contrast between the conduct of the righteous and the Gentiles is the primary context for the exhortation here, not the eschatological need for watchfulness and prayer (Mark 14:38 and parallels) as many commentators assert.³⁵⁴ Cronbach states, "Characteristic of the righteous is recourse to prayer."³⁵⁵ Prayer as a characteristic of the righteous was previously mentioned in 1 Peter 3:12, where it was affirmed that God is attentive to their prayers. This exhortation to prayer expresses an essential practice of the righteous and stands at the head of a list of practices appropriate to the righteous person.

The list continues with a series of participles and adjectives that give the circumstances in which the exhortation to mental preparedness for prayer should be carried out. Each of these circumstances describes practices that relate to characteristics of the righteous person. The first group of circumstances discussed in verses eight and nine describes the practice of love and hospitality. Both of these practices are characteristics of the righteous person. Cronbach's long list of characteristics pertaining to the righteous person include "benevolence (*Tob.* 1:3; 14:11; Eccles. 7:10; 40:24); love of neighbor (*Jub.* 7:20; 20:2); compassion for the poor and weak (*Asmp. Moses* 11:17; *Test. Benj.* 4:4); . . . kindness toward all one's kindred (*Jub.* 31:3)."³⁵⁶ In the judgment scene in Matthew 25:31-46, acts of hospitality and charity distinguish the righteous from the cursed.³⁵⁷ The last group of circumstances discussed in verses ten and eleven pertain to the faithful discharge of the duties arising from one's χάρισμα. Schrenk comments on the duties of the righteous in the Greek and Jewish traditions:

> If in the rest of the Greek world a man is δίκαιος who satisfies ordinary legal norms, fulfilling his civic duties in the most general sense, here [in the LXX] the

---

³⁵³Selwyn, *1 Peter*, 140.

³⁵⁴So among others, Beare, *1 Peter*, 157; Best, *1 Peter*, 159; Bigg, 172; Goppelt, *Petrusbrief*, 282; Kelly, 177; and Michaels, *1 Peter* 245-246. The author of 1 Peter does recognize the need for watchfulness in the eschatological context of 5:8.

³⁵⁵Cronbach, 86.

³⁵⁶Ibid., he lists many more characteristics. For a discussion of the characteristics of the righteous person in Philo and Josephus, see Schrenk, "Δίκαιος," 183.

³⁵⁷Schrenk, "Δίκαιος," 190, states, "The δίκαιοι in the last judgment in Mt. 25:37, 46 are those who have attained to true δικαιοσύνη by practicing love in unconscious acts of kindness to the Son of Man."

δίκαιος is the man who fulfils his duties towards God and the theocratic society, meeting God's claim in this relationship.[358]

Thus, both groups of circumstances in this list describe practices that relate to characteristics of the righteous person.

In verses ten and eleven, the connection of the duties arising from one's χάρισμα to the righteous person is enhanced by the metaphor of the good steward [ὡς καλοὶ οἰκονόμοι]. Moffatt summarizes the use of this metaphor in the Christian tradition saying, "The house-steward distributed the rations and pay regularly to his fellow-slaves. Jesus had used the figure (Luke xii.42), and so had Paul (I Corinthians iv.1), for the responsible duty of exercising one's gifts in the service of the church."[359] In Luke 16:8 the unfaithful steward is called a steward of unrighteousness. This passage implies that a good steward, a righteous steward, will responsibly discharge his duties and assignments. The author of 1 Peter uses this conception of the righteous steward to urge his readers to responsibly discharge the duties arising from their χάρισμα.

This subsection that began in 4:7b concludes in verse eleven with a doxology. This doxology does not conclude the entire letter as the commentators who subscribe to the partition theory advocate. L. G. Champion states, "It must also be noticed that many sections of *Paränese* are closed either with a benediction or a doxology."[360] He discusses numerous texts, including Philippians and 2 Thessalonians, that contain several benedictions or doxologies within the paraenetic sections. Thus, the doxology in 1 Peter 4:11 functions like doxologies in other paraenetic letters and only concludes this subsection of the letter.

Having now discussed each of the subsections, the compositional structure of 3:13--4:11 can be explained. The entire passage responds to the notion of the readers as sufferers in the Dispersion by treating suffering from the perspective of the righteous sufferer. The author of

---

[358]Ibid., 185.

[359]Moffatt, 154.

[360]L. G. Champion, *Benedictions and Doxologies in the Epistles of Paul* (Oxford: Kemp Hall Press, 1934), 30. Champion's position was reaffirmed by Robert Jowett, "The Form and Function of the Homiletic Benediction," *Anglican Theological Review* 51 (1969): 18-34. On page 34 he says, "Finally, it is important to examine the role of these benedictions in their contexts within the epistles. Each unit in Thessalonians stands at the end of a major section of the letter, summarizing it and bringing it to conclusion."

1 Peter describes his readers as sufferers on account of righteousness or as righteous sufferers (3:14). This metaphor controls this subsection (3:13--4:11) and provides the basis for three subsections of paraenesis. In 3:13-22 the author exhorts his readers to maintain the correct fear and to sanctify Christ as Lord when suffering. In 4:1-7a he admonishes them to abstain from unrighteous practices and in 4:7b-11 to emulate righteous practices. This third subsection of paraenesis is concluded by a doxology that also functions to conclude the larger section arising from the metaphor of the righteous sufferer. Thus, the metaphor of the righteous sufferer dominates the material from 3:13--4:11 and functions as the first metaphor in the cluster built around the notion of sufferers in the Dispersion.

Metaphor-Partners in Sufferings and Glory

In 4:12 the author proceeds to the second metaphor of this metaphor cluster by describing his readers as partners in the sufferings and the glory of Christ (4:13; 5:1). The transitional device introducing this subsection is the vocative $\dot{\alpha}\gamma\alpha\pi\eta\tau o\acute{\iota}$ in 4:12. Many exegetes following Bengel's lead understand this vocative as a major transitional device because the same word is used in 2:11 to mark a major transition.[361] This author uses vocatives, however, both as major (2:11) and as minor (2:18; 3:1, 7) transitional devices. In 2:11 $\dot{\alpha}\gamma\alpha\pi\eta\tau o\acute{\iota}$ marks a major transition because the metaphor cluster changes. In contrast, it designates a minor transition here because the metaphor cluster of the sufferers of the Dispersion continues in this subsection.[362]

The scholars who ascribe to a partition theory emphasize the shift in the attitude toward suffering in 4:12. They argue that prior to 4:12 suffering is treated as only a possibility, but here it is treated as a reality. They posit a shift in historical circumstances as the cause of this change of perspective and consequently partition the letter. This alteration in the attitude toward suffering is not, however, occasioned by a shift in historical circumstances but by a shift in the metaphor. In this section dominated by the idea of sufferers in the Dispersion, the author has treated suffering

---

[361]So Goppelt, *Petrusbrief*, 296, asserts, "The new passage is introduced like 1 Peter 2:11 with the address $\dot{\alpha}\gamma\alpha\pi\eta\tau o\acute{\iota}$, 'beloved.'"

[362]Best, *1 Peter*, 161, correctly explains, "'Beloved:' a new address which comes naturally after the doxology and does not of itself imply a major break at this point. . . ."

under the auspices of the righteous sufferer metaphor (3:13--4:11). The perspective of this metaphor is not one of actual suffering but of prospective suffering. The author instructed his readers in the correct mental attitude and practices they needed in prospect of suffering righteously. The new metaphor that begins in 4:12 is predicated upon suffering. The author can only describe his readers as partners in the sufferings of Christ if they have already participated in suffering. Therefore, the shift in the attitude toward suffering in 4:12 is not an indication of the beginning of a new letter or of a change in the circumstances of the readers but simply an indication that a new metaphor is now being employed.[363]

The controlling metaphor of this subsection has two corresponding aspects. There is the aspect of partners in the sufferings of Christ (4:13) and the aspect of partners in the glory of Christ (5:1). Schutter notes that this sufferings/glory schema is important to the author of 1 Peter:

> What seems reasonably certain nevertheless is that the contrast of "sufferings" and "glories" functions as a kind of schema which helps the author to organize the Scriptural foundations implied by the reference to the prophets, whether they were OT or NT persons. In this respect he is quite traditional, as the NT parallels show.[364]

As Schutter correctly observes, the sufferings of Christ were traditionally correlated with His glory. This correlation is present in Paul's thought as Hauck observes:

---

[363]Although Goppelt, *Petrusbrief*, 294, fails to recognize the inception of a new metaphor in 4:12, he correctly assesses the general tenor of this passage. He states, "This explanation [the Liturgical explanation of Perdelwitz, Windisch, Beare, and Cranfield] of our passage is not exegetically defensible as has been demonstrated. The distinction with the preceding consists not in a new situation, rather in a new aspect of the meaning of suffering. Verse twelve formulates the theme of the passage: 'Do not let yourselves be surprised by the fiery trial among you . . . , as though a strange thing were happening to you.' This statement regarding the situation does not refer to the introduction of a new circumstance but rather to a continuing one. The participles that describe the situation [γινομένῃ, συμβαίνοντος], stand in the present tense, not in the past tense, which would show the inception of an event. The single new contribution to the image of the situation is the comment in Verse 15f.: It can come to an appearance before a judge and there one can already be condemned on account of belonging to Christendom, that is, on account of the name 'Christ'. . . . This comment therefore fits in completely with the previous image of the situation. It is simply a true concretization."

[364]Schutter, *Hermeneutic*, 108.

According to Paul fellowship with Christ also means that the Christian participates in the detailed phases of the life of Christ. . . . Fellowship with Christ means that present participation in one phase, namely, that of humility and suffering, assures us of winning through to participation in the other, namely, that of glory. . . . By participation in Christ's sufferings Paul has hope of analogous participation in His glory (Phil. 3:10; R. 8:17).[365]

This correlation was already stated in 1 Peter 1:11 and now becomes the basis for the metaphor of partners in the sufferings and glory of Christ that controls this subsection.

The phrase τὰ αὐτὰ τῶν παθημάτων in 5:9 forms an inclusio with the phrase τοῖς τοῦ Χριστοῦ παθήμασιν in 4:13 and determines the extent of this subsection. This inclusio has been overlooked by the commentators because of an uncritical interpretation of the phrase τὰ αὐτὰ τῶν παθημάτων in 5:9.[366] Commentators uncritically assume that this phrase refers to the same circumstances of suffering. Hence, Selwyn interprets, "τὰ αὐτὰ τῶν παθημάτων an unusual construction connoting 'the same kinds of sufferings.'"[367] Windisch even postulates a general edict as the occasion that engenders these same circumstances of suffering.[368] The

---

[365]Friedrich Hauck, "Κοινός," in *Theological Dictionary of the New Testament*, vol. 3: Θ–Κ, ed. Gerhard Kittel (Grand Rapids: Wm. B. Eerdmans Publishing Co., 1965), 806. Kleinknecht, 338, observes this same correlation of present suffering and future glory in Romans 8:18-30. He places this correlation in the apocalyptic context of the messianic woes, stating, "Behind the antithesis of present suffering and future glory (Romans 8:18) stands, as we have already seen several times, the apocalyptic opposition of the old age in which sinners fight against God and therefore oppress the righteous as belonging to Him and of the new age brought in by the turning-point of the final judgment in which the righteous will receive the glory coming to them. From this traditional framework, it is completely evident that the text now places the end time woes in view (cf. 8:22), in which the near reality of judgment takes effect and certainly--here the text refers to an Old Testament tradition already dealt with at length--as a reality encompassing the entire creation and pressing forward to the renewal."

[366]It is surprising that even Schutter, *Hermeneutic*, who is careful to identify almost every possible inclusio in 1 Peter, misses this one. He does, however, connect this phrase in 5:9 with the phrase τῶν τοῦ Χριστοῦ παθημάτων in 5:1. He does not even mention that 4:13 contains the same phrase as 5:1. His faulty literary analysis based upon his mistaken application of epistolary formulas explains the reason he misses this inclusio.

[367]Selwyn, *1 Peter*, 238.

[368]Windisch, *Petrusbrief*, 80, states, "The παθήματα prove not to be simply all sorts of personal harassments and defamations, rather also official persecutions. One would almost be inclined to presuppose a general edict."

point of this phrase, however, is not that Christians suffer in similar circumstances or in a similar fashion, but that their various sufferings belong to the sufferings of Christ. Michaelis correctly observes this distinction in a parallel phrase in 2 Corinthians. He explains as follows:

> According to 1:6 the Corinthians themselves, both then and at other times, were subject in fact to specific παθήματα. The τὰ αὐτὰ παθήματα does not mean that the circumstances were exactly the same. These are the same afflictions because for both Paul and the Corinthians they are τὰ παθήματα τοῦ Χριστοῦ.[369]

A little later, Michaelis states in regard to the phrases about suffering in 1 Peter 1:11; 4:13; 5:1; and 5:9, "The meaning is thus the same as in 2 C. 1:5."[370] According to Michaelis, this phrase in 1 Peter 5:9 refers to the sufferings of Christ. The Christian brotherhood throughout the world shares the same sufferings because they are the sufferings of Christ.[371] Thus, the references to sharing in the sufferings of Christ in 4:13 and 5:9 identify one aspect of the controlling metaphor of this subsection and form an inclusio that binds the subsection together.

Another important inclusio that marks out this subsection is the use of δόξα in 4:13 and 5:10. Although this term occurs in both of these verses, the specific treatment of the metaphorical notion of partners of the glory of Christ occurs in 5:1-5 where the actual phrase ὁ δόξης κοινωνός is found. This inclusio as well as the previous one determines the limits of this subsection and identifies one of the two aspects of the metaphor of partners in the sufferings and glory of Christ. Both aspects of this metaphor control the material in this subsection (4:12--5:11) and permit the author to continue to address the issue of suffering.[372]

---

[369]Michaelis, 931.

[370]Ibid., 934.

[371]Compared to the other commentators, Best, *1 Peter*, 175, has the most accurate interpretation of this phrase. He states, "We need to note also that the word translated 'suffering' is plural in the Greek [it is the same word as in 4:13; 5:1] and in each case we can render 'of the sufferings,' i.e. of the Messianic woes. The woes have to be completed [the word rendered 'required' carries this overtone of meaning] and this is being accomplished by Peter's readers and by the brotherhood throughout the world (cf. Col. 1:24); when the woes are complete the Parousia will take place."

[372]Kelly, 183-184, relates this subsection (4:12--5:11) to the preceding in the following manner: "This paragraph develops and reinforces the theme of suffering which came into the open as early as i.6f. and has been central from iii.13 onwards, reiterating the promise that those who inflict it are already marked out for destruction. . . . The close

The first aspect of this metaphor controls the material in 4:12-19 and is expressed by the phrase καθὸ κοινωνεῖτε τοῖς τοῦ Χριστοῦ παθήμασιν [just as you are partners in the sufferings of Christ] in 4:13. This phrase is variously interpreted. Best outlines and critiques three possibilities:

> (i) "suffer as Christ suffered," cf. 2:20f; Mk 8:34; Jn 15:20; but the word "share" appears to imply much more than the imitation of Christ. (ii) "share mystically in the sufferings of Christ" (cf. Col. 1:24; 2 Cor. 1:5; 4:10; Phil. 3:10); Christians because they have been baptized into the death and resurrection of Christ and are members of his body in their sufferings participate in his suffering. However: (a) it is doubtful if this is the meaning of the Pauline passages cited above; (b) it is even more doubtful if any trace of the Pauline conception of the togetherness of Christians with Christ in his body is to be found in 1 Peter; at 2:20f; 3:17f there is only teaching about the imitation of Christ; (c) it is difficult to fit a "mystical" meaning to "share" when it re-appears in 5:1 [there rendered "partaker"]. (iii) "share in the Messianic woes." The Messianic woes or birthpangs denote a period of trial which the Jews believed would take place before the arrival of the Messiah; he was not himself to suffer in them but out of them the New Age was to be born (Dan. 7:21ff.; 12:1; Joel 2; 2 Esd. 13:16-19; 2 Baruch 25; 68; Jubilees 23:13ff.; Sanhedrin 97a). Christians who believed that the Messiah had already come and would return again transformed this into a belief that they themselves would be involved in these birthpangs immediately prior to that return (cf. Mk 13:9ff.; Rev. 7:14; 12:3ff.; Jn 16:2, 4, 21, 22, 23; 2 Th. 2:3-10). We have already indicated that this idea is present in 1 Pet. 1:5f. It suits the present context which has a strong eschatological orientation; in verse 12 'fiery ordeal' should be understood eschatologically; verse 13 envisages the survival of the readers to the appearance of Christ in glory and their eschatological joy thereat; verse 17 implies that what they suffer is part of God's plan (cf. 3:17) in the inauguration of judgement (cf. 5:10). This view is sustained by: (a) The total eschatological context of the letter in which the end is viewed as coming shortly (1:6, 20; 4:5, 7, 17; 5:10). (b) The literal translation of our phrase is: "share the sufferings of the Christ". . . . Normally "Christ" is used in the NT without the

---

linkage of this section with the foregoing one is confirmed by such touches as the use in both of the same, rather uncommon verb 'be surprised' (iv.4 and 12), the repetition from iv.11 of the idea of glorifying God in iv.16, and the strongly eschatological atmosphere pervading both, with the same threat of judgment (cf. iv.5 and iv.17f.) for the Asian Christian's persecutors." Oecumenius, 574-576, states the theme of this section when commenting on 5:9. He says, "*Knowing the same things of sufferings*. It seems that they to whom Peter is writing were constrained by many tribulations on account of Christ. Therefore, before this and after this, he consoles them. There, he consoles them by the fact that they are partakers of the sufferings of Christ and heirs of the glory about to be revealed. Here, he consoles them by the fact they they do not suffer alone, but with all the faithful throughout the world. The common treatment of those who share in common with each other lightens the burden."

definite article; its addition here suggests that it is used as a title, i.e. "the Messiah," and the phrase would mean: "share the sufferings of the Messiah."[373]

Of the three possibilities, Best opts for the third and interprets the phrase $\kappa\alpha\theta\dot{o}$ $\kappa o\iota\nu\omega\nu\epsilon\hat{\iota}\tau\epsilon$ $\tau o\hat{\iota}s$ $\tau o\hat{\upsilon}$ $X\rho\iota\sigma\tau o\hat{\upsilon}$ $\pi\alpha\theta\acute{\eta}\mu\alpha\sigma\iota\nu$ in the eschatological context of the Messianic woes preceding the End.[374] As Best correctly notes, the conception of these woes was transformed in Christianity because of the Christian belief in two appearances of the Messiah.

Goppelt rejects the apocalyptic position preferred by Best. He states his position in his comments on 4:17:

> For 1 Peter, the $\kappa\alpha\iota\rho\acute{o}s$ is consequently not the time of birthpangs which according to Apocalyptic precede the final judgment (Mark 13:8-13 and parallels) and also bring the persecution of the community (Mark 13:9 and parallels). Rather, it is the particular time, namely, the Endtime, announced by the prophets in which the final judgment itself begins. This time is for the community not one of the final stages of their passage in an outline of an apocalyptic time plan, but with their eschatological existence (1:11f.) is already acknowledged just as the End is already near (4:7). Our passage consequently explains the afflictions befalling the community other than early Christian Apocalyptic. Our letter does not fit in with an apocalyptic view of history in which calculation forces out the possible division of the periods *of history*. Rather, our letter seeks with the help of Scripture meditation from the Old Testament prophets and their view of history to explain *the afflictions of the community*.[375]

By rejecting the apocalyptic background of 1 Peter 4:12-17, Goppelt rejects the position adopted by Best that explains the phrase $\kappa\alpha\theta\dot{o}$ $\kappa o\iota\nu\omega\nu\epsilon\hat{\iota}\tau\epsilon$ $\tau o\hat{\iota}s$ $\tau o\hat{\upsilon}$ $X\rho\iota\sigma\tau o\hat{\upsilon}$ $\pi\alpha\theta\acute{\eta}\mu\alpha\sigma\iota\nu$ from the context of the Messianic woes.

In seeking to exclude the apocalyptic background of 1 Peter 4:12-17, Goppelt has overstated his case.[376] Although 1 Peter does not expose a fully developed apocalyptic scenario, it does not necessarily follow that the

---

[373]Best, *1 Peter*, 162-163.

[374]Schutter, *Hermeneutic*, 107, agrees with Best that the $\pi\alpha\theta\acute{\eta}\mu\alpha\tau\alpha$ $\tau o\hat{\upsilon}$ $X\rho\iota\sigma\tau o\hat{\upsilon}$ cannot be limited to the Passion of Jesus but must also refer to the Messianic woes.

[375]Goppelt, *Petrusbrief*, 311-312.

[376]William Schutter, "I Peter 4.17, Ezekiel 9.6, and Apocalyptic Hermeneutics," in *Society of Biblical Literature 1987 Seminar Papers*, ed. Kent H. Richards, Seminar Papers Series 26 (Atlanta, Georgia: Scholars Press, 1987), 276, quotes a portion of this passage from Goppelt and then comments, "Perhaps the distinction is somewhat overdrawn. . . ."

author rejects all apocalyptic conceptions.[377] The conception of the
Messianic woes as a period of suffering for God's people just prior to the
final consummation was so widespread and prevalent that our author could
include this belief in his eschatological perspective without laying out the
entire apocalyptic scenario.[378] Furthermore, Goppelt's insistence that the

---

[377]Tord Olsson, "The Apocalyptic Activity: The Case of Jamasp Namag," in
Apocalypticism in the Mediterranean World and the Near East, ed. David Hellholm,
Proceedings of the International Colloquium on Apocalypticism (Tübingen: J. C. B. Mohr
(Paul Siebeck), 1983), 27-28, distinguishes among three types of apocalyptic phenomena.
He states, "Much of the discussion of historical influences on Jewish apocalypticism is
confused by the failure to distinguish between apocalypticism and related phenomena. It
would thus be convenient to make distinctions between (1) apocalypticism as a speculative
and verbal activity comprising more or less coherent systems of apocalyptic ideas,
(2) apocalyptic ideas which constitute the above systems but are also found in other
contexts than apocalypticism, and (3) apocalypse as a literary type in which apocalyptic
ideas or systems of ideas are expressed. It should be noted, however, that apocalyptic
ideas and systems of ideas are also communicated in media other than that of the
apocalypse. The distinctions are relevant for the question of historical influence since it
implies that the presence and the spread of apocalyptic ideas are neither restricted to
apocalypticism, nor to apocalypses, and, furthermore, that the presence and spread of
apocalyptic systems of ideas are not confined to apocalypses." As Olsson correctly states,
a work does not have to be an apocalypse in order to contain apocalyptic ideas or systems.
Thus, an apocalyptic scenario can stand behind the ideas in 1 Peter without rendering the
letter as apocalypse. Morton Smith, "On the History of ΑΠΟΚΑΛΥΠΤΩ and
ΑΠΟΚΑΛΥΨIS," in *Apocalypticism in the Mediterranean World and the Near East*, ed.
David Hellholm, Proceedings of the International Colloquium on Apocalypticism
(Tübingen: J. C. B. Mohr (Paul Siebeck), 1983), 15, articulates a similar situation for the
Pauline letters. He outlines the apocalyptic scenario implicit in Paul's letters, but he
disassociates Paul from the later apocalypses. He states, "For Paul, as we know him in his
letters, *ἀποκάλυψις* is the core of his life, but this *ἀποκάλυψις* means 'revelation,' not
'apocalypse,' and this revelation has nothing to do with 'uncovering.' Paul's choice of the
word can be explained neither by its root meaning, nor by its later connection with the
apocalypses. . . . This revelation, as expressed in Paul's gospel, is not only of the
immediate powers of God, but also of his future purposes; it reveals his wrath to the
wicked, to the righteous his justice (Rom 1:17f.) and the things he has prepared for them
(1 Cor 2:10); it is thus a revelation of the long-secret mystery of his will (Rom 16:25).
Because continuing, it is not yet complete-more will be revealed at the end, first the
Antichrist (2 Thess 1:7), the fiery test of what each man has done (1 Cor 3:13), the just
judgment of God against the wicked (Rom 2:5), and the destined glory of the saints (Rom
8:18f.)." Just as in Paul, 1 Peter subscribes to an accepted apocalyptic scenario and
reflects apocalyptic ideas, but it is not an apocalypse.

[378]Schürer, vol. 2, 514, states, "Reference to the last things is almost always
accompanied by the notion, recurring in various forms, that a period of special distress and
affliction must precede the dawn of salvation. It was of course reasonable to suppose that
the way to happiness should lie through affliction. This is also explicitly predicted in the

statement in 4:17 referring to the beginning of judgment dictates that
καιρός must be equated with the last day does not adequately consider the
larger context of this statement.[379] Michaels expressly contradicts Goppelt:

> καιρός ... is defined by the articular infinitive as a time for "beginning" [τοῦ
> ἄρξασθαι], specifically the beginning of judgment [cf. Matt 24:8 par. Mark 13:8,
> "beginning of birth-pangs"]. It is not to be equated [as in Goppelt, 311-12] with
> the joyful "last day" [ἐν καιρῷ ἐσχάτῳ] mentioned as a time of salvation in 1:5,
> nor with the time of vindication mentioned in 5:6. It is a time for judgment, just
> prior to the "end" [i.e., τέλος in the next clause].[380]

Michaels correctly observes that the author simply states that his readers'
afflictions are only the beginning of judgment.[381] The final consummation

---

Old Testament [Hos. 13:13; Dan. 12:1 and elsewhere]. In rabbinic teaching, the doctrine
therefore developed of the חבלי המשיח, the birth pangs of the Messiah which must precede
his appearance [the expression is from Hos. 13:13; cf. Mt. 24:8; Mk. 13.8]." Elisabeth
Schüssler Fiorenza, "The Phenomenon of Early Christian Apocalyptic: Some Reflections
on Method," in *Apocalypticism in the Mediterranean World and the Near East*, ed. David
Hellholm, Proceedings of the International Colloquium on Apocalypticism (Tübingen:
J. C. B. Mohr (Paul Siebeck), 1983), 301, comments on the apocalyptic themes found in
most New Testament writings. She states, "However, motifs and motif-clusters of the
pattern are not only found in materials classified as apocalyptic but in most of the NT
writings. Christian writers seem to have emphasized the following motifs within the motif-
clusters of the apocalyptic pattern. In the motif-cluster, the last times before the
eschatological intervention, (A) the situation of persecution and trial of the community is
stressed. Emphasis is also given to the opponent figures of demonic powers, false
prophets and antichrists. Significant is the rejection of the apocalyptic sign-seeking. In the
second motif-cluster, the divine intervention, (B) the expectation of the parousia and the
coming of the Son of 'Man' for judgment (C) is stressed. The 'day of the Lord' and
judgment are intertwined. Most developed within Christian texts is, however, the last
motif-cluster, the time of salvation (E) [sic]. Here the motifs of Kingdom, exaltation,
resurrection and eternal life, new creation, and the eschatological banquet are especially
developed." All of these apocalyptic motif-clusters identified by Fiorenza are present
in 1 Peter.

[379]Goppelt, *Petrusbrief*, 311, states, " 'O καιρός, the 'time' as a point or period of
time is not defined by the term itself. Hence, it is modified in 1:5 by an adjective, the
coming 'last time,' in 1:11 by a subordinate clause, the predicted time of fulfillment, and
here by an infinitive, although it is used adverbially in 5:6. It is the time in which the
judgment--the absolute expression τὸ κρίμα means the final judgment--begins at the house
of God."

[380]Michaels, *1 Peter*, 270.

[381]Luise Schottroff, "Die Gegenwart in der Apokalyptik der synoptischen
Evangelien," in *Apocalypticism in the Mediterranean World and the Near East*, ed. David

that includes the "End" of the unbelievers is yet to be realized.[382] If, as Goppelt proposes, the final judgment has arrived, the exhortations in 1 Peter would be senseless. However, the author of 1 Peter asserts there is still a little time remaining until the final consummation (5:1, 4, 10). Also, in attempting to disassociate this passage from apocalyptic passages like the Synoptic Apocalypse, Goppelt has overlooked the fact that suffering on behalf of Christ and His name, a prominent feature of the paraenesis of this passage, occurs in those apocalyptic passages as well (Mark 13:9-13).[383] Thus, Goppelt overstates his case. He correctly perceives that 1 Peter does not expound an apocalyptic scenario, but he incorrectly asserts that 1 Peter does not subscribe to early Christian apocalyptic conceptions.[384]

Hellholm, Proceedings of the International Colloquium on Apocalypticism (Tübingen: J. C. B. Mohr (Paul Siebeck), 1983), 726-727, observing that the assessment of present sufferings as the beginning of the end is a characteristic of the Synoptic Apocalypse, states, "In conclusion, it can be said about the eschatological discourse in Matthew and Luke that the distinctive thoughts about the end time encountered in Mark 13 are also expressed here. The present is the beginning of the eschatological woes (Mark 13:8; Matthew 24:8; Luke 21:28). The present is the time of the world wide proclamation of the Gospel (Mark 13:10; Matthew 24:14; Luke 21:24). After the spread of the gospel among the peoples the yearned for end comes. The present is a time of suffering. The suffering of the present is experienced in a societal and political dimension. . . ." 1 Peter shares with the Synoptic Apocalypse this assessment of the present sufferings as the beginning of the end."

[382]Olsson, "Apocalyptic," 36, identifies the periodization of history as a distinctive feature of many apocalypses. He states, "This periodization of history is a distinctive feature of a main type of apocalypses. . . ." In contrast to these apocalypses, 1 Peter does not engage in speculation about the various time periods as Goppelt correctly observes. However, the author of 1 Peter does subscribe to a periodization of history. He asserts that the time for speculation is over (1:10-11) and proclaims that his readers are living in the period of suffering just prior to the end (1:6-7; 4:13; 5:1, 6, 8-10).

[383]Fiorenza, "Apocalyptic," 300, states, "Early Christian writings frequently combine the apocalyptic pattern of eschatological events with paraenesis. Either the apocalyptic pattern is introduced and framed by paraenesis or it is interlaced with hortatory statements. An analysis of Mark 13 par. shows how much the pattern is determined by and used in the context of paraenesis."

[384]Schlier, "Θλίβω," 146, best articulates the eschatological perspective of 1 Peter. He says, "The basic distinction between the Jewish and the Christian understanding of the eschatological θλίψις is to be found, of course, in the fact that this tribulation, which is still future in Judaism, has already begun according to the early Christian view. The great tribulation has already begun. A second distinction is to be found in the fact that eschatological suffering began with the suffering of the Messiah, so that all the suffering of the age is simply a repetition of that which has already taken place in Him. A third

Because he rejects the apocalyptic position, Goppelt is forced to interpret the phrase καθὸ κοινωνεῖτε τοῖς τοῦ Χριστοῦ παθήμασιν in a manner that does not relate to the Messianic woes.   He opts for a soteriological explanation, stating:

> How is this partaking conceived? If one seeks to answer this question from the suffering theology of 1 Peter, then it follows: Earlier it was emphasized that the suffering on account of righteousness (3:14) corresponds in its structure to the suffering of Christ or should correspond (2:21-23; 3:17f.) and that this is established not through imitation, but through his suffering for us leading to righteousness (2:21, 24; 3:18). Hence it follows for our statement: Suffering befalls Christians on account of their Christian existence (4:4, 15f.). Thereupon, they have a part in the suffering of Christ in the first but also implicitly in the

---

distinction is that the manifested eschatological suffering of Christ is experienced by the new people scattered in the world, namely the church. . . ." It could be argued that 1 Peter contains only eschatological, not apocalyptic ideas. Of course, this distinction depends upon one's definition of eschatology and apocalyptic. Neither of these terms have been conclusively defined. Marc Philonenko, "L'apocalyptique qoumrânienne," in *Apocalypticism in the Mediterranean World and the Near East*, ed. David Hellholm, Proceedings of the International Colloquium on Apocalypticism (Tübingen: J. C. B. Mohr (Paul Siebeck), 1983), 212, proposes the following definitions of these terms: "In order to remove this equivocation, we indicate that we mean by 'apocalyptic' a revelation which deals with not only the end of the world, the signs which announce the end, and the catastrophe accompanying it but also the origins of man and the world. Therefore, we distinguish apocalyptic from eschatology which is interested only in the end of man, taken in his individual or collective destiny, and the end of the world. The two concepts of eschatology and apocalyptic are hence blended but not confused. Apocalyptic comprises the materials placed in works about eschatology, but . . . eschatology, being completely confined to the end of man and of the world, does not retrace the problem of origins. There is no eschatology of beginnings. That is to say that an eschatology is possible without an apocalyptic, but that there is no apocalyptic without eschatology." Given Philonenko's distinction between these terms, 1 Peter is both eschatological and apocalyptic. It is concerned with the end (1:5-9, 13; 2:12; 4:7a, 13; 5:1, 10), but there are also statements made about origins. In 1:2 the author refers to election according to the foreknowledge of God the Father. In 1:15; 2:21; 3:9; and 5:10, he refers to his readers' being called in the past. In 1:20 he mentions that Christ was foreknown before the foundation of the world but revealed at the last of times. Thus, although the author of 1 Peter is primarily concerned about the end times, he also mentions events that are more appropriately associated with origins. Although it may be useful in some documents, Philonenko's distinction between eschatology and apocalyptic is difficult to maintain in 1 Peter. As I have demonstrated above, 1 Peter reflects apocalyptic ideas, but it is not an apocalypse.

second way [$\pi\alpha\theta\acute{\eta}\mu\alpha\tau\alpha$ $X\rho\iota\sigma\tauo\hat{v}$, compare 5:1], that is, in the suffering that He suffered (1:11), not as in Paul, that befalls His people on His account.[385]

He explains his position more explicitly as follows:

> The expression $\tau\acute{\alpha}$ $\pi\alpha\theta\acute{\eta}\mu\alpha\tau\alpha$ $X\rho\iota\sigma\tauo\hat{v}$, "the sufferings of Christ," found elsewhere in the New Testament only in Paul designates there the suffering that befalls the apostle and the communities on account of Christ. *This meaning occurs* in 2 Corinthians 1:5 and even also in Philippians 3:10. . . . On the contrary, the sufferings of Christ, $\tauo\hat{v}$ $X\rho\iota\sigma\tauo\hat{v}$ $\pi\alpha\theta\acute{\eta}\mu\alpha\tau\alpha$, in 1 Peter 4:13--5:1 are the Passion of Christ, $\tau\acute{\alpha}$ $\epsilon\acute{\iota}$s $X\rho\iota\sigma\tau\grave{o}\nu$ $\pi\alpha\theta\acute{\eta}\mu\alpha\tau\alpha$ 1,11, according to the expression about the taking part in the $\pi\acute{\alpha}\sigma\chi\epsilon\iota\nu$ of Jesus (2:21-23), which is not encountered in Paul.[386]

Goppelt's soteriological explanation of the phrase $\kappa\alpha\theta\grave{o}$ $\kappa o\iota\nu\omega\nu\epsilon\hat{\iota}\tau\epsilon$ $\tauo\hat{\iota}$s $\tauo\hat{v}$ $X\rho\iota\sigma\tauo\hat{v}$ $\pi\alpha\theta\acute{\eta}\mu\alpha\sigma\iota\nu$ in 1 Peter deprecates the Pauline conception of active participation in the sufferings of Christ in the context of the Messianic woes. Instead, it postulates a passive participation of the readers in the sufferings of Christ. According to Goppelt's explanation, the readers primarily participate soteriologically in the sufferings of Christ in that they are made righteous by his Passion.[387]

Although Goppelt correctly observes that the author of 1 Peter associates more closely than Paul the sufferings of Christ with Christ's Passion, he again overstates his case by attempting to limit the sufferings of Christ to His Passion.[388] The author of 1 Peter does not limit participation in the sufferings of Christ only to the salvation experience of being made righteous by Christ's Passion. There is throughout the letter an active

---

[385]Goppelt, *Petrusbrief*, 297-298.

[386]Ibid., 298, note 7.

[387]Michaelis, 922, completely opposite to Goppelt asserts, "The sufferings of Christians are not here (1 Peter 4:13) derived from the passion of Christ or the necessity of participation in this. What is stated is rather that Christians as $\pi\acute{\alpha}\sigma\chi o\nu\tau\epsilon$s (4:19) do in fact follow in his steps (2:21)."

[388]Ibid., 921, he notes the close relationship between the suffering of Christians and the Passion of Christ in 1 Peter but argues that the relationship is more apparent than real. He says, "If in Paul the question of the relation between the sufferings of Christians and the death of Jesus is very secondary, a first glance at 1 Pt. might give the impression that the author heavily stresses this relation when in 2:19f.; 3:14, 17; 4:1, 15, 19; 5:10 he takes the word $\pi\acute{\alpha}\sigma\chi\omega$, which he uses for the death of Jesus and applies it to Christians. Yet $\pi\acute{\alpha}\sigma\chi\omega$ never means 'to die' in this use, except fig. at 4:1."

aspect to this participation.[389]   Lohse explains this active aspect in the
following manner:

> In this time between the crucifixion and Second Coming of Jesus belongs the
> παθήματα Χριστοῦ. With this expression encountered only in Paul and 1 Peter
> is meant not only the suffering of Jesus in His Passion, but His Passion forms
> the beginning of the eschatological events that come to pass now in the last time in
> the community.   In suffering, in persecutions, Christians have a part in the
> sufferings of Christ (1 Peter 4:13) and know that they stand in the last time. A
> measure is set, however, to suffering and when this is fulfilled, then the Parousia
> occurs. Colossians 1:24 is understood from this concept: "Now I rejoice in my
> sufferings on account of you and fulfill what still lacks in the sufferings of Christ,
> in my flesh for His body, that is, the community." Christ himself has still not
> fulfilled the measure of the eschatological sufferings in His Passion and in that
> which befalls the apostle a further part of the eschatological sufferings are born.
> Thus, the θλίψεις that the apostle has encountered will no more come over the
> community. . . . Participation in the sufferings of Christ is therefore not a
> mystical Passion society that binds the Lord and the community. . . .
> Participation in the sufferings of Christ means more precisely to stand in the
> Eschaton that has arisen with his Passion, his death and resurrection, and strives
> toward its near fulfillment. The suffering of Christ has occurred completely and
> for all time in order to accomplish atonement and to effect forgiveness. The
> suffering of Christ has, however, still not ended after the beginning of the
> Eschaton so that from now on it appears in the suffering of His body,
> the community.[390]

This active aspect explained by Lohse is especially evident in 1 Peter 5:9.
Although Goppelt overlooks the active aspect in his comments on 5:9, he
correctly translates, "In which you know, that the same sufferings are
suffered by your brotherhood in the world."[391]   As demonstrated above,
these sufferings in 5:9 are the sufferings of Christ and the brotherhood
actively participates in them.   Thus, Goppelt's exclusively soteriological

---

[389]Schutter, *Hermeneutic*, 108, note 76, explains the relationship between the
Passion of Christ and the Messianic woes as follows: "That the unthinkable had happened
to God's Anointed might have compelled many to interpret it in terms of the 'Woes,' which
was surely the category closest at hand from an eschatological perspective. . . . And if
such a fate could befall the Messiah, then . . . where would that leave his followers?
Hence it is reasonable to suppose that there was a basis to move directly from a personal
frame of reference in early Christian thinking about the Messianic 'Woes' to a
corporate one."

[390]Eduard Lohse, *Märtyrer und Gottesknecht*, Forschungen zur Religion und
Literatur des Alten und Neuen Testaments 64 (Göttingen: Vandenhoeck & Ruprecht,
1955), 201-202. On page 203, he links this entire discussion to 1 Peter 4:12-19.

[391]Goppelt, *Petrusbrief*, 342.

explanation of the phrase καθὸ κοινωνεῖτε τοῖς τοῦ Χριστοῦ παθήμασιν
should be rejected as an overstatement of the case.

The controlling metaphor of this subsection expressed by the phrase
καθὸ κοινωνεῖτε τοῖς τοῦ Χριστοῦ παθήμασιν [just as you are partners
in the sufferings of Christ] in 4:13 is best explained within the context of
the Messianic woes.[392] The author conceives of the suffering and affliction
of his readers as active participation in the sufferings of Christ (3:13) that
are being accomplished by their brotherhood during the short time before
the final consummation (5:9).[393] Goppelt is correct in asserting that the
author does not engage in apocalyptic speculation about when the final
judgment will occur.[394] For the author, the end is so close that he sees
already in the sufferings of his readers the beginning of the final
judgment.[395] Nevertheless, since there is still a short time of suffering
remaining (5:10), the author exhorts his readers to behavior befitting
partners in the sufferings of Christ.

This metaphor of partners in the sufferings of Christ gives rise to a
number of exhortations. In verse twelve the author admonishes his readers

---

[392]So Best, *1 Peter*, 162-163; Bigg, 103, 176; Kelly, 193-194; Selwyn, *1 Peter*,
128, 300-303; and Michaels, *1 Peter*, 270.

[393]Hauck, "Κοινός," 806, also subscribes to the notion of active participation in the
sufferings of Christ. He explains, "The spiritual union with Christ which characterizes the
whole life and work of Paul is especially described in terms of a spiritual fellowship in
suffering with Him (Phil. 3:10). This is not just a living again of Christ's sufferings. Nor
is it a mere personal conformity. Nor is it a retrospective passion dogmatics. By spiritual
participation in Christ the sufferings of the apostle are a real part of the total suffering
which is laid on Christ (Col. 1:24). By participation in Christ's sufferings Paul has hope
of analogous participation in His glory (Phil. 3:10; R. 8:17). The same thought is picked
up in 1 Peter 4:13 and it is also in the background in 5:1."

[394]Schutter, "1 Peter 4.17," 276 states, ". . . Goppelt is justified to argue that the
author has advanced beyond the understanding of the Messianic Woes as heralds of the
End to one which sees the manifestation of the End itself in at least some of the struggles of
his addresses." Although Goppelt's argument that the End had already arrived correctly
emphasizes the nearness of the End for the author of 1 Peter, it cannot account for the
perspective expressed repeatedly in the letter that the End is still future (1:4-9, 13, 17; 2:2,
12; 3:9; 4:1-2, 13; 5:4, 6, 10). The author of 2 Peter is compelled to exonerate his
predecessor because of a further delay in the Parousia (2 Peter 3:1).

[395]Schutter, "1 Peter 4.17," 284, states, "Astonishingly, the author discloses that
the collective assault against Christians represents nothing less than the start of the Last
Judgment itself."

not to be surprised at the πύρωσις that has happened to them for testing.[396]
Sander comments on πύρωσις:

> As will be seen in the thesis proper, πύρωσις is an eschatological term denoting the end-time trial or ordeal which is expected before the final consummation and revelation of glory. This πύρωσις is for the testing of the church and the vindication of the elect. Thus the situation of πύρωσις has a πειρασμός character.[397]

According to Sander, πύρωσις was an expected eschatological event indicating the immanent consummation of all things and the victory of God's people.[398] Because the πύρωσις was an expected eschatological event, the author exhorts his readers not to be surprised by its occurrence.

Michaels likewise prefers the eschatological meaning of πύρωσις.[399] He uses this eschatological meaning to explain the author's exhortation to his readers not to be surprised at the πύρωσις befalling them, saying:

> ... it is evident from the reference in v 13 to "the sufferings of Christ," and from the allusion in v 14 to Jesus' beatitude on those ridiculed for his sake, that the words and the example of Jesus are the reasons Peter believes a "fiery ordeal" should come as no surprise. If Jesus himself suffered and predicted suffering for

---

[396]Nauck, "Freude," 68-80, sees a connection of 1 Peter 4:12 with *Judith* 8:25-27, which also links πειράζω with πυρόω. He says, "Further, the connection of πειράζειν and πυροῦν with thoughts of joy in suffering is found in James and 1 Peter. Thus, this passage (*Judith* 8:25-27) affords a parallel with πύρωσις πρὸς πειρασμόν (1 Peter 4:12)." This connection of fire and testing becomes popular in early Christian literature being found in 1 Corinthians 3:13, *Didache* 16:5, the fourth vision of the *Shepherd of Hermas*, and the *Martyrdom of Polycarp* 15:2.

[397]Sander, xxvi.

[398]Goppelt, *Petrusbrief*, 297, note 5, notes an important distinction in the use of the term πύρωσις in 1 Peter and Qumran. He states, "This use of the word stands closest to the context in 1 Peter. However, the word itself has a different meaning here than there. Although it is used there as a term for purifying, it is a metaphor in 1 Peter as in Proverbs 27:21 that requires the explanation through testing [πειρασμός], an explanation that never occurs in the Essene texts." In his discussion of this term, he refers to his discussion of 1 Peter 1:6-7 where the purpose of πειρασμοί is stated to be a δοκίμιον. On pages 100-101 Goppelt comments on δοκίμιον, "The genuineness of faith ... is much more costly [πολυτιμότερον] than perishable gold and therefore needs the purification even more." Thus, the notion of purification is not totally excluded from the meaning of πύρωσις πρὸς πειρασμόν in 1 Peter 4:12.

[399]Michaels, *1 Peter*, 260-261, favors Sander's conclusions regarding πύρωσις but admits that she "established no direct lexical link between πύρωσις here and מצרף at Qumran."

his followers, they have no reason to think it strange when his experiences are repeated and his predictions fulfilled (cf. Matt 10:24-25; Luke 6:40; John 13:16; 15:18-21; 16:1-4; 1 John 3:13). Within 1 Peter itself, the inevitability of suffering was intimated already in the εἰ δέον, "must" or "by necessity," of 1:6, based possibly on the conspicuous use of δεῖ, "it is necessary," in the Jesus tradition.[400]

Michaels understands this term to refer to the eschatological necessity of suffering and relates it to the phrase εἰ δέον in 1:6.[401] He comments on this phrase:

> Peter's language recalls Jesus' warning that certain things "must take place [δεῖ γενέσθαι] but the end is not yet" (Mark 13:7; cf. Dan 2:28; Rev 1:1; 4:1; 22:6) or Paul's early reminder to churches in the East that "we must [δεῖ] through many afflictions enter the kingdom of God" (Acts 14:22). Even the sufferings of Jesus Himself were viewed as a divine necessity [cf., e.g., δεῖ in Mark 8:31 and parallels; Luke 17:25; 24:7, 26; John 3:14; 12:34; Acts 3:21; 17:3], and it is entirely appropriate that Peter's first explicit reference to the sufferings of the Asian churches puts these sufferings in a similar framework. It is perhaps because of this widely acknowledged necessity that he later tells his readers not to "be surprised at the fiery ordeal you face . . . as if something strange were happening to you" (4:12).[402]

Thus, Michaels uses the eschatological meaning of πύρωσις to explain the exhortation to the readers not to be surprised at the fiery ordeal befalling them.[403] As an expected and predicted eschatological event (1 Peter 1:11),

---

[400]Ibid., 260.

[401]Selwyn, *1 Peter*, 221, maintains the same view. He says, "And in view of i.6, 7 there can be little doubt that this is the meaning here: a process of refining by fire is going on amongst them for their testing. The word πύρωσις is rare, but occurs in Proverbs xxvii.21 and Did. xvi.5. The eschatological context of the persecution envisaged both in Did. xvi.5 and here may well have prompted the use of the word πύρωσις; for fire played a large part in Jewish expectations of the end (cf. Enoch cii.1, cviii.3, 5. . . ."

[402]Michaels, *1 Peter*, 29.

[403]Goppelt, *Petrusbrief*, 295, explains the background of this exhortation differently. He says, "There is according to an Old Testament, Jewish, early Christian tradition a fundamentally necessary test that proves the faith (verse 12)." He also explains the necessity of this suffering differently. He comments on the phrase εἰ δέον in 1:6 as follows, "This 'must' means in the early Christian tradition God's salvation decision for the Endtime, not a part of a determined plan of history as in Jewish Apocalyptic nor fate as in the Hellenistic environment." Although Goppelt is correct in his assertion that the early Christian tradition did not take over Jewish Apocalyptic conceptions without modification, he is incorrect in his assumption that the Christian belief that they were living in the Endtime made any further eschatological speculation about the periodization of history

suffering, described here as πύρωσις, should come as no surprise to those who are partners in the sufferings of Christ.

The second exhortation to arise from the metaphor of partners in the sufferings of Christ occurs in 4:13. After exhorting his readers not to be surprised by the πύρωσις befalling them, the author exhorts them in a well-constructed paraenetic antithesis, "but rejoice." Goppelt comments regarding the relationship of this exhortation to the metaphor saying, "As verse thirteen brings out in connection to a tradition that is distinguished through the terminology of Paul and yet not directly connected with him, κοινωνία is established with the sufferings of Christ, and is therefore a basis for joy."[404] Although, as Goppelt asserts, Pauline passages such as Romans 8:17; 2 Corinthians 1:5-7; and Colossians 1:24 can be cited as parallels to the thought underlying this exhortation, the closest parallels lie elsewhere.[405] Wolfgang Nauck isolates a brief persecution form using Matthew 5:11-12; Luke 6:22; 1 Peter 1:6; 4:13; and James 1:2, 1:12. This persecution form brings suffering and joy together and may be stated in basic form, "Blessed are you, when you are persecuted; Rejoice, you will be rewarded."[406] In all of these passages containing this persecution form,

---

unnecessary. See H. J. Schoeps, *Paul*, trans. Harold Knight (Philadelphia: The Westminster Press, 1961), 88-125.

[404]Goppelt, *Petrusbrief*, 295.

[405]Ibid., 304, he states, "If verse thirteen with the Pauline 'partaking' refers to the partnership with Christ enclosed in suffering on account of faith whose way the Christ hymns of 1 Peter represent, then the next verse takes up the words of promise from the Jesus tradition for suffering." Goppelt correctly perceives that the next verse (4:14) containing the marcarism is more closely related to Jesus' statements about joy in suffering than this verse (4:13) with its emphasis on partnership in suffering. However, the imperative χαίρετε in 4:13 expressing an exhortation to rejoice in the midst of suffering relates more to the Jesus tradition than to the Pauline. On page 301 Goppelt comments, "The present χαίρετε in Matthew 5:12 agrees with 1 Peter 4:13, not the future χάρητε ἐν ἐκείνῃ τῇ ἡμέρᾳ in the parallel passage in Luke 6:23." In a long excursus on pages 299-304, Goppelt traces the derivation of the conception of joy in suffering on account of Christ back to its Jewish roots.

[406]Nauck, "Freude," 68-80. Although Nauck, 73-76, finds a precedent for this notion of joy in suffering in the Jewish apocalyptic literature, as Michaels, *1 Peter*, 262, says, "Peter's more immediate source is more likely the Jesus tradition in a form close to that found in Matthew 5:12."

Christians are exhorted to rejoice in their suffering.[407]   Michaels
recognizes an important caveat:

> His [the author's] consistent assumption is that the ground of rejoicing is not
> suffering as such, but suffering "unjustly" (2:19), or for doing good (2:20), or
> "in the cause of justice" (3:14), or "for the name of Christ" (v 14), or "for being a
> Christian" (v 16), all of which amount to much the same thing. . . . Not all who
> suffer, but rather those who show themselves faithful in suffering, are invited to
> rejoice, now because they are following Christ's example and in the future
> because they will share his glory.[408]

According to Michaels, the author of 1 Peter exhorts his readers to
rejoice, not because they are suffering, but because they are partners in the
sufferings of Christ. Thus, this exhortation appropriately arises from the
metaphor of partners in suffering.

The recognition that not all suffering is participation in the
sufferings of Christ explains the remaining three exhortations in verses
fifteen, sixteen, and nineteen. Burkhard Gärtner reasons as follows:

> But not all suffering is fellowship with the sufferings of Christ. For suffering to
> be in this category, the apostles and the church must suffer for the sake of their
> office or of their Christian calling; they must suffer as Christians (1 Pet. 4:16),
> unjustly (1 Pet 2:19f.), being regarded not as evildoers or murderers (1 Pet.
> 4:15; Lk. 23:32ff.). . . . True suffering in this sense is called suffering
> 'according to God's will' (1 Pet 4:19). . . .[409]

As Gärtner astutely perceives, each of these admonitions develops from the
description of the readers as partners in the sufferings of Christ.

As this discussion demonstrates, this passage (4:12-19) is dominated
by the description of the readers as partners in the sufferings of the

---

[407]The relationship between joy and suffering in 1 Peter 1:6 differs from 4:13 and
consequently the former should not be included in this persecution form. Michaels,
1 Peter, 262, correctly notes, "The principal difference between the argument here and in
1:6-8 is that instead of urging present faithfulness for the sake of future joy, he is now
weighing present joy in the face of trials against the far greater joy to come. The thought of
joy in suffering, as distinguished from joy after the experience of suffering, is introduced
here for the first time [contrast Nauck, 71-72, who finds an exhortation to present rejoicing
already in 1:6-8]."

[408]Michaels, *1 Peter*, 262.

[409]Burkhard Gärtner, "Suffer," in *The New International Dictionary of New
Testament Theology*, vol. 3: *Pri-Z*, ed. Colin Brown (Grand Rapids: Zondervan, 1979),
724-725.

Messiah. Both the statements and exhortations contained in this passage ensue from this aspect of the metaphor of partners in the sufferings and glory of Christ.

The second aspect of this metaphor, partners in the glory of Christ, determines the next passage in 5:1-5, which is introduced by οὖν in verse one and is concluded by a Scripture quotation in verse five. After identifying himself as a co-elder and witness of the sufferings of Christ, the author describes himself as a partner in the glory about to be revealed. It is clear from verse 4 that this designation applies not only to the author but also to the elders and the entire congregation.[410] This verse indicates that partnership in Christ's glory requires the diligent discharge of the duties He has assigned to each.[411] Thus, the exhortations that arise from this second aspect of the metaphor, partners in the glory of Christ, pertain to the duties of each Christian.

The author presents these exhortations in a community or station code addressing first, elders (5:1-4), then, young men (5:5a), and finally, all (5:5b).[412] Goppelt correctly identifies the testamentary paraenetic form of Acts 20:17-36 and 2 Timothy as the paraenetic background of these exhortations to the elders.[413] He sees Paul's farewell speech in Acts 20 that

---

[410]Goppelt, *Petrusbrief*, 323, also comments on the phrase, "the partner of the glory about to be revealed," saying, "This would pertain to him certainly not different than to all believers according to 4:13, that is, in the future in the Parousia." Michaels, *1 Peter*, 281-282, agrees with Goppelt, stating, "That 'the glory to be revealed' holds a particular reward for elders, and thus, for Peter himself, is clear from v 4, but this does not change the fact that it is also the common hope of the entire Christian community (cf. 1:7, 13; 4:13)."

[411]Goppelt, *Petrusbrief*, 329, points to Luke 12:8f. and Matthew 25:34f. as passages that contain a similar idea. Michaels, *1 Peter*, 287, comments, "The other uses of 'glory' in 1 Peter make it clear, in fact, that the 'crown of glory' promised here is not for elders alone, but for all who share in the Christian hope. The elders will receive their 'crown' like everyone else in the congregation, for doing what they were called to do (cf. 3:9)."

[412]Michaels, *1 Peter*, 277, states, "The section bears comparison, on the one hand, with the household duty codes of 2:13--3:9 and, on the other, with Peter's directives on mutual ministry within the Christian congregations in 4:7-11."

[413]Goppelt, *Petrusbrief*, 318-319, states, "The words to the elders in verses one to four, particularly in verses 2b.c. and three, bring to mind the overseer and deacon images of the Pastoral Letters: 1 Timothy 3:1, 2-7, 8-13; Titus 1:5f., 7-9. The passage as a whole, however, does not resemble in its form those texts and thereby the later church order. Rather, it most resembles the testamentary paraenesis of the apostle to the elders of Ephesus in Acts 20:17-36 and to Timothy in 2 Timothy. Moreover, it has so many topoi in

describes the community as a flock of sheep as particularly pertinent.[414] Indeed, Jewish and early Christian tradition frequently conceived of the duties of community leaders in terms of shepherding and of their communities as flocks.[415] Taking over this tradition, the author of 1 Peter conceives of his readers as a flock of sheep and presents the duties they must perform if they are partners in Christ's glory.

The conception of the community as a flock of sheep is appropriate to the eschatological context of this section of 1 Peter.[416] Commenting on the relationship of the eschatological remarks in Mark 14:27-28 to Deutero-Zechariah, Jeremias states:

---

common with Paul's farewell speech in Acts 20 that the same paraenetic schema must lie behind it as a common tradition."

[414]Ibid., 319, he observes, "The assignment of the elders is described in verse 2a with the same terminology as in Acts 20:28: ποίμνιον ποιμαίνειν, ἐπισκέπτεσθαι. The promise that concludes the instruction to the elders in verse 4 is made with similar terminology as in Acts 20:32, although the 'inheritance' is promised there but the 'crown of glory' here."

[415]Kelly, 199, explains, "For his charge he incorporates a piece of stock exhortation for ministers; it is revealed as such by the contents of 2f., which find close parallels in late Jewish and early Christian literature, and even more by its exceptionally formal structure [cf. esp. the three careful antitheses, with the contrasting adverbs or participial clauses introduced in each case by the same negative and adversative particles]. . . . The thought of God's chosen people as His flock is deeply rooted in the OT (e.g. Ps. xxiii; Is. xl.11; Jer. xxiii.1-4; Exek. xxxiv.1-10); while in Ps. Sol. xvii.45 [1st cent. BCE] the Messiah is represented as 'shepherding the Lord's flock in faith and righteousness.' In the NT the imagery of shepherding is occasionally applied, as here, to the community leaders (Jn. xxi.15-17; Acts xx.28), but only in one place (Eph. iv.11) are they actually designated 'shepherds,' and even here the word is not a fixed title of office. The nearest analogy comes from Qumran, where we read (6QD xiii.9) of the 'mebaqqer,' or overseer, sustaining the people 'as a shepherd his flock.'"

[416]Prophetic predictions of the end time portray God's people as sheep in need of a shepherd. Joachim Jeremias, "Ποιμήν," in Theological Dictionary of the New Testament, vol. 6: Πε-Ρ, ed. Gerhard Friedrich (Grand Rapids: Wm. B. Eerdmans Publishing Co., 1970), 501, summarizes these predictions, ". . . in the time of impending disaster 'shepherd' still occurs as a title for the ruler, but only for the future Messianic son of David. Because the shepherds have refused and become unfaithful, Yahweh will visit them (Jer. 2:8; 23:2; Ez. 34:1-10); He Himself will take over the office of shepherd and gather and feed the scattered flock (Jer. 23:3; 31:10; Ez. 34:11-22; cf. Mi. 4:6f.); He will appoint better shepherds (Jer. 3:15; 23:4) and proclaim: 'I will set up one shepherd over them, and he shall feed them, even my servant David; he shall lead them, and he shall be their shepherd. And I Yahweh will be their God, and my Servant David prince among them; I, Yahweh, promise it,' Ez. 34:23f."

Jesus is the promised Good Shepherd, the "fellow" of God (Zech. 13:7), whom God smites [this is how the πατάξω of Mk. 14:27 must be transl.], i.e., upon whom He causes judgment to fall. The fate of the shepherd involves the scattering of the flock: *qualis rex, talis grex*. In Zech., however, the whole emphasis is upon the cleansing and receiving of the remnant of the flock (13:8f.), and so, too, in Mk. it rests on the promise in v. 28. The fact that the promise of v. 28 is correlative to the prophecy of the passion in v. 27 is perfectly clear once it is realized that the προάγειν continues the shepherd metaphor of v. 27. In other words v. 27 quotes Zech. 13:7b literally, while v. 28 is a free rendering of the contents of Zech. 13:8f. The death of Jesus thus imitates the eschatological tribulation, the scattering (13:7) and decimation (13:8) of the flock, and the testing of the remnant which is left in the furnace (13:9a). But the crisis, the scandal, is the turning point, for it is followed by the gathering of the purified flock as the people of God (Zech. 13:9b) under the leadership of the Good Shepherd (Mk. 14:28).[417]

Thus, 1 Peter's connection of the ideas of God's flock being led by shepherds (5:1-5) and being tried by fire (4:12) is paralleled by the collection of ideas in Deutero-Zechariah.[418] This collection of ideas provides part of the rationale for the connection of this subsection with the previous one.[419]

Utilizing the conception of the community as a flock, 1 Peter describes the elders as shepherds who exercise their rule under the auspices of the Chief Shepherd, who will soon be revealed (5:4).[420] The author exhorts these elders, as shepherds, to shepherd the flock of God among

---

[417]Ibid., 493.

[418]Deutero-Zechariah provides important background material for other notions expressed in 1 Peter. 1 Peter 1:7; 2:10; and 4:12 are paralleled by Zechariah 13:9. 1 Peter 2:25 alludes to ideas expressed in Zechariah 13:7-9.

[419]Of course the major connection is the close correlation of partners in the sufferings (3:13) with partners in the glory (5:1). Schutter, *Hermeneutic*, 79; "1 Peter 4:17," 283; and Michaels, *1 Peter*, 279, suggest that the quote in 1 Peter 4:18 of Ezekiel 9:6 that mentions elders provides the connecting link between this section and the previous one. Although this suggestion cannot be completely ignored, the major connecting link is the correlative notion of partnership.

[420]Best, *1 Peter*, 170-171, explains the use of the term "Chief Shepherd" as follows: "Already at 2:25 Jesus has been described as 'the Shepherd' and now that other shepherds have been introduced it is natural to describe him as 'chief' (Heb. 13:20). The under shepherds are given their reward, the 'crown of glory,' by the chief shepherd.... The use of one image to describe both the ministry of Jesus and that of the leaders of the church shows that the pattern of their ministry is to be that of Jesus' own ministry (Mk 10:42-5)."

them (5:2a). He qualifies this exhortation by the use of three antitheses.[421] They are to lead the flock of God as they give willing, not compulsory oversight according to God's desire (5:2b). Their leadership should be in the context of eager, not greedy oversight (5:2c). They are to lead God's flock in the context of being examples for the flock and not as those who domineer over the part of the flock with which they have been entrusted (5:3). Faithful leadership renders them eligible to receive the crown of glory when the Chief Shepherd appears (5:4).

In verse five, the author continues his exhortation but shifts his attention from the elders to the younger members. In contrast to the elders whom he had admonished as shepherds, he exhorts the younger members as sheep who are responsible to submit to the elders. The exhortation to submit to the elders arises from the conception of a flock. Because the elders are shepherds, the younger members should submit to them as sheep submit to their shepherd.[422]

In the second half of verse five, the author summons all the members of this flock to clothe themselves with humility in respect to one another. Grundmann cites several sources in which humility is predicated of domestic animals. The connection of humility with sheep is explicitly made in the suffering servant passages in Isaiah. Grundmann comments on Isaiah 53:8, saying:

---

[421]Goppelt, *Petrusbrief*, 319, relates these antitheses to the Hellenistic early Christian tradition of the Pastorals rather than to the Palestinian Jewish tradition of Acts 20:18-31. He states, "In verses 2b.c. and three, the type of administration is described by three symmetrically constructed and formulated antitheses that remain a part of church tradition until the present. They call to mind more the episcopal images of the Pastorals than Acts 20. The term αἰσχροκερδᾶς in 5:2 for example recurs in 1 Timothy 3:8 and Titus 1:7 but only regarding content in Acts 20:33f. Behind the antitheses stand not the Jewish tradition but rather the Hellenistic, early Christian tradition."

[422]Ibid., 320, he provides another explanation for the origin of this exhortation to submit. He asserts, "An instruction to the 'young men' in verse 5a stands out according to style and type of content from the preceding. The exegetical problem that the statement presents is largely explained if one observes that it follows the form of the station code. Its transitional particle originates from the logic of the context and is not to be taken with its semantic meaning: As it is formulated there in 3,1 ὁμοίως γυναῖκες . . . , 3,7 οἱ ἄνδρες ὁμοίως . . . , 3,8 τὸ δὲ τέλος πάντες . . . , so here in verse 5a ὁμοίως νεώτεροι . . . [V.5b πάντες δέ . . .]. As there, so also in verse 5a a subordinate partner to another is mentioned: the νεώτεροι and the πρεσβύτεροι, and the former is commanded to submit to the latter." Goppelt's explanation and the metaphorical explanation proposed here are not mutually exclusive but rather supplement one another.

In Is. 53:8 the LXX views the entire fate of the Servant as ταπείνωσις and bears testimony: The ταπείνωσις which he has taken on him removes judgment from him and is the reason for his exaltation full of salvation. This idea has its basis in the original Hebrew. What is summed up as ταπείνωσις in the LXX is to be found in v. 7. The Servant of the Lord is mistreated and he submits. This is illustrated by the sheep which is led to the slaughter and the lamb before its shearers.[423]

Because sheep are imbued with the quality of humility, the author of 1 Peter exhorts all the members of God's flock to clothe themselves with humility.[424] He substantiates this exhortation by quoting Scripture that affirms God gives grace to the humble but resists the proud (5:5b).[425]

In this passage, therefore, the second aspect of the metaphor begun in 4:12 gives rise to paraenesis that treats the duties of those who are partners in Christ's glory. These duties are expressed in a station code in which the community is portrayed as the flock of God. The scripture quotation in verse five concludes this passage.

The final passage (5:6-11) in this subsection does not introduce a new metaphor but brings together both aspects of the metaphor first stated in 4:13. Whereas, partners in the sufferings of Christ dominated the material in 4:12-19 and partners in Christ's glory the material in 5:1-5, both aspects of this metaphor are now brought together as a basis for the exhortations in

---

[423]Walter Grundmann, "Ταπεινός," in *Theological Dictionary of the New Testament*, vol. 8: *Τ-Υ*, ed. Gerhard Friedrich (Grand Rapids: Wm. B. Eerdmans Publishing Co., 1970), 3.

[424]Goppelt, *Petrusbrief*, 320-321, overlooks this metaphorical explanation for the exhortation and provides another. He states, "Not only was the catch word of the concluding exhortation to all in verse 5b, ταπεινοφροσύνη, certainly suggested to the author through the ταπεινόφρονες in the virtue list with which he concluded the station code in 3:8, but it was also transmitted to him through the theme word of the tradition that stands behind the following concluding paraenesis in 5:6-10. It was near at hand for verse 5b most of all through the distinct logion of service of Mark 10:42-44 that always provides a background to paraenesis on community administration. This logion intentionally coincides with the catch word κατακυριεύειν in verse 3." Again, Goppelt's explanation does not exclude the metaphorical explanation adopted here. The former explanation relies on the broader context for this exhortation, but the latter relies on the immediate context of the metaphor.

[425]Ibid., 334, he says, "The call to humility is subsequently justified by a quotation from the Old Testament."

this passage.   In this respect, this passage functions as a concluding paraenesis for this subsection that began in 4:12.[426]

In bringing together both aspects of this metaphor, the author adopts a traditional Jewish and Christian schema of humility or suffering being turned into exaltation. Michaels comments as follows:

> The theme of humility, or humiliation, and exaltation is conspicuous in the OT (e.g., 1 Sam 2:7-8; Isa 1:25; 2:11; 40:4; Ezek 17:24; Job 5:11; Sir 7:11), in the Gospel tradition (not only Luke 14:11 and 18:14; Matt 18:4 and 23:12; but Luke 1:52), and elsewhere in early Christian literature (2 Cor 11:7; Phil 2:8-9; James 1:9; 4:10; cf. also *1 Clem.* 59.3). The coupling of an explicit or implicit command to humble oneself with an accompanying promise of divine exaltation is limited to this verse in 1 Peter, James 4:10, and the sayings of Jesus.[427]

The author had already stated this schema in 4:13 and 5:1, but in each of the passages following these verses; he treated first the sufferings and then the glory, respectively. Here, he treats the schema as a whole.

The author expresses this schema in two sets of exhortation. In verses 6-7, the author exhorts his readers to humble themselves "under the mighty hand of God in order that in time God might exalt them." Kelly explains what the author means by humility, "As always, his attention is concentrated on his readers' afflictions; he is suggesting that, if they accept them humbly as God's providential . . . testing [cf. his teaching in i.6; iii.17; iv.19], they will find themselves vindicated at the last."[428] This exhortation follows the schema by suggesting that after their time of suffering God will vindicate them.   The schema is continued in the exhortation of verses 8-10. After summoning his readers to be alert and to resist their adversary, the Devil, the author reassures them that after a short time of suffering God will restore, establish, strengthen, and settle them. Thus, both sets of exhortation in this passage express the schema of humiliation/exaltation suggested by the metaphor of partners in the sufferings and glory of Christ.[429]

---

[426]Thus, Schutter, *Hermeneutic*, 26, 76, as well as Schnider and Stenger, 84-86, are incorrect in identifying 5:1-11 as the concluding paraenesis.

[427]Michaels, *1 Peter*, 295.

[428]Kelly, 207.

[429]This understanding of the exhortations disproves Kelly's statement that the exhortations in this passage are loosely connected. See Kelly, 207.

In addition to the schema of humiliation/exaltation, the material in this passage also expresses the paraenetic tradition found in James 4:7, 10 that contains the theme, "Comply with God; resist the Devil."[430] Goppelt comments on this tradition in 1 Peter, "The author of 1 Peter has at the same time emphatically emphasized the antithesis through the Old Testament images of 'hand of God' (verse 6) and 'roaring lion' (verse 8)."[431] Goppelt offers no further explanation of how these images, "hand of God" and "roaring lion" fit into the context of 1 Peter. The explanation for the aptness of these images lies in a recognition that the conception of the community as a flock continues in this passage. The author exhorts his readers to humble themselves under the mighty hand of God. As already demonstrated, the exhortation to humility alludes to flock imagery since humility is a characteristic of sheep. The parallel to this exhortation in James 4:10 lacks the image of "the mighty hand of God"[432] as well as the Jesus logion of casting all care upon God.[433] Both the image and the logion are fitting to the conception of God as the shepherd of the flock. Jeremias comments on this conception in the Hebrew Scriptures:

> The application of the shepherd image to Yahweh is embedded in the living piety of Israel. This may be seen from the great number of passages which use the rich shepherd vocabulary for Yahweh and depict God in new and vivid developments of the metaphor as the Shepherd who goes before His flock, who guides it, who leads it to pastures and to places where it may rest by the waters, who protects it with His staff, who whistles to the dispersed and gathers them, who carries the lambs in His bosom and leads the mother-sheep.[434]

This conception suggests that the shepherd is greatly concerned about his sheep. In contrast to the good shepherd, the hireling in John 10:13 is described as one who is not concerned about the sheep [οὐ μέλει αὐτῷ περὶ τῶν προβάτων]. The description of God in 1 Peter 5:7b uses almost the same words to affirm God's concern for the readers. Hence, the image

---

[430]Goppelt, *Petrusbrief*, 335.

[431]Ibid., 335-336.

[432]See Michaels, *1 Peter*, 295. Goppelt, *Petrusbrief*, 336, states, "The hand of God' is an Old Testament image for the mighty acting of God that is brought out covertly by the historical events."

[433]Goppelt, *Petrusbrief*, 337, note 7, discusses this logion.

[434]Jeremias, "Ποιμήν," 487, lists many passages where these concepts may be found in the Hebrew Scriptures.

of humbling oneself under the "hand of God" and the Jesus logion of casting all care upon God continue the conception of the community as a flock of sheep.

Just as humbling oneself under the mighty hand of God and casting all care upon Him are fitting to the image of God as the Shepherd, so it is fitting to conceive of the flock's adversary as a "roaring lion" seeking to devour its prey (5:8). Jeremias asserts, "Along with thieves (Jn. 10:1, 10:8, 10:10), wild beasts, esp. wolves, constituted the danger against which the shepherds, who were always armed, had to protect the flock, Mt. 10:16; Lk. 10:3; Jn. 10:12; Ac. 20:29."[435] Since the image of the wolf is reserved in Christian tradition for human adversaries such as false teachers, the author conceives of his readers' adversary as a lion. The conception of the Devil as a lion has precedents in both Jewish and Christian traditions.[436] Thus, the images of humbling oneself under the mighty hand of God and of the Devil as a roaring lion as well as the Jesus logion fit this passage that conceives of the community as a flock of sheep.

This passage (5:6-11) continues the conception of the community as a flock of sheep and brings together both aspects of the metaphor of partners in the sufferings and glory of Christ. The exhortations in this passage arising from this metaphor reflect the traditional schema of sufferings/exaltation. This passage functions as a concluding section of paraenesis for the subsection that began in 4:12. A doxology in verse eleven concludes this passage.

Assessment

The preceding discussion permits an explanation of the compositional structure of 4:12--5:11. The author continues from the previous subsection (3:13--4:11) the discussion of his readers as sufferers in the Dispersion. Whereas the previous subsection (3:13--4:11) discussed the issue of suffering using the metaphor of the righteous sufferer, this subsection discusses this issue utilizing the metaphor of partners in the sufferings and glory of Christ. In 4:12-19 the author treats the first aspect of this metaphor, partners in the sufferings of Christ. In 5:1-5 he turns to the second aspect of this metaphor, partners in the glory of Christ. In 5:6-11

---

[435]Ibid., 499.

[436]Goppelt, *Petrusbrief*, 339, note 11, cites some of the relevant passages.

he brings both aspects of this metaphor together in a concluding section of paraenesis. The preceding discussion of 4:12--5:11, as well as 3:13--4:11, indicates the following outline for this third section of 1 Peter's letter-body:

The Παθήματα-Cluster
The Sufferers in the Diaspora
(3:13--5:12)

1. Παθήματα-metaphor of the righteous sufferer (3:13--4:11)

   1.1. Do not fear but sanctify Christ as Lord (3:13-22)

   1.2. Arm yourselves with the ἔννοια of Christ (4:1-7a)

   1.3. Be sane and sober for prayers (4:7b-11)

2. Παθήματα-metaphor of partners in the sufferings and glory of Christ (4:12--5:11)

   2.1. Metaphor--partners in the sufferings of Christ:
       Do not be surprised but rejoice (4:12-19)

   2.2. Metaphor--partners in the glory of Christ (5:1-5)

      2.2.1. Elders, shepherd the flock of God (5:1-4)

      2.2.2. Young men, submit to the elders (5:5a)

      2.2.3. All, tie on humility (5:5b)

   2.3. Metaphor--partners in the sufferings and glory of Christ
       (5:6-11)

      2.3.1. Humble yourselves under the Hand of God (5:6-7)

      2.3.2. Be sober, be awake, resist the Devil (5:8-11)

In this third section of the body-middle, the author continues to construct metaphor clusters pertaining to the overarching metaphor of the Diaspora. He recognizes that the Diaspora is often a dangerous and hostile place where God's people suffer and conceives of his readers as sufferers in the Diaspora. The eschatological journey upon which his readers have embarked entails opposition, affliction, and suffering. In order to present the appropriate conduct expected of his readers on this journey and to discourage them from losing heart and defecting, the author describes his readers as righteous sufferers and as partners in the sufferings and glory of Christ. He exhorts them to suffer righteously in order that they might receive the benefits of such suffering, especially vindication at the last judgment. He exhorts them to suffer as partners in the sufferings of Christ so that they might share in His future glory. Continuing his rhetoric of suppression, he does not discuss the ramifications of defection but instead emphasizes the positive benefits accruing from their continued loyalty and adherence to the faith. As his readers exhibit the conduct appropriate to their ontological status, they can expect an end to their Diaspora sufferings and God's restoration as the termination of their journey.

Conclusion

The literary analysis developed and deployed in this chapter is able to explain the compositional structure of the body-middle of 1 Peter. It has identified the compositional devices used by the Petrine author to structure the body of this letter. It indicates there are three main sections that are identified by metaphor clusters drawn from the overarching metaphor of the Diaspora. The first section (1:14--2:10) is constructed by metaphors arising from the notion of the elect household of God. The second section (2:11--3:12) contains metaphors relating to the concept of aliens in this world. The third section (3:13--5:11) develops metaphors relating to sufferers in the Diaspora. This analysis allows for further delineation of these main sections into subsections by observing the individual metaphors of each of these clusters as well as transitional and concluding devices. Finally, this analysis indicates that all of these metaphor clusters contribute to the author's primary objectives of exposing conduct appropriate for his readers on their eschatological journey and of dissuading them from defection while persuading them to steadfast allegiance to the faith.

The deployment of this literary analysis that explains the compositional structure of 1 Peter's body-middle now completes my analysis of the entire letter. My analysis has identified the number, extent, and limit of each of the sections and subsections of the letter. It has also explained the controlling themes of each of these sections and subsections as well as the controlling theme of the letter as a whole. It has resolved the problem of the literary composition of 1 Peter.

CONCLUSION

The problem of the literary character of 1 Peter is a central issue in Petrine studies. This problem complicates both the introductory matters and the exegesis of 1 Peter. Although this problem impinges upon every aspect of Petrine studies, Petrine scholars have been unable to resolve it. Convincing explanations of the compositional structure, literary genre, and thematic motif have not been forthcoming although many proposals have been made.

In this dissertation I have attempted to resolve this problem of the literary character of 1 Peter. In particular I have addressed the issue of 1 Peter's compositional structure. In the process of exposing this structure, two related literary issues, literary genre and thematic motif, also received treatment. A summary of the conclusions reached in regard to each of these three literary issues is now in order.

The major literary genre of 1 Peter is epistolary. Although the document draws on liturgical, paraenetic, and other materials, all of these materials have been modified to fit the epistolary situation and have been placed into an epistolary framework. Therefore, the first level of compositional analysis must identify the letter formulas in 1 Peter as well as their function. Epistolary analysis reveals that 1 Peter exhibits the five basic parts of an ancient letter. The prescript (1:1-2) identifies the sender and addressees. The blessing section (1:3-12) identifies the eschatological context in which the letter is to be read and understood. The letter-body (1:13--5:12) contains the message that the author wanted to communicate to his readers. In particular, the body-opening (1:13) and the body-closing (5:12) indicate that the author intended to encourage his readers to conduct their lives appropriately and not to defect from the Christian faith but to stand firmly in this faith as they expectantly hope for God's intervention.

The greeting section (5:13-14a) and the farewell (5:14b) form the conclusion of this document as in other ancient letters. Epistolary analysis is useful for delineating every part of the compositional structure except the body-middle (1:14--5:11). A more specific determination of genre is needed in order to explicate the compositional structure of this part of the letter.

The specific literary genre of 1 Peter is paraenetic. In both its literary form and social context, 1 Peter corresponds to the paraenetic genre. Unfortunately, this genre does not exhibit a fixed literary form. Therefore, the identification of 1 Peter as a paraenesis does not provide an explanation of its compositional structure. Although specific paraenetic compositional elements can be isolated, the overall composition of the body-middle cannot be explained by the paraenetic genre. Nevertheless, the paraenetic genre is the appropriate place to begin to locate the compositional devices of this document. Because paraenetic texts base exhortation on ontological status, the relationship of ontological status to exhortation is an important compositional device of the paraenetic genre. As a paraenesis, 1 Peter structures the composition of its body-middle by the interplay of the ontological status of its readers with the appropriate exhortations. This observation provides the key to unlock the compositional structure of 1 Peter.

In 1 Peter's description of the ontological status of its readers, metaphors graphically portray their authentic character. Because they describe the ontological status of 1 Peter's readers, these metaphors and their ensuing exhortations provide the basis for a compositional analysis of 1 Peter. By observing the context of these metaphors in other ancient documents and discussions, metaphor clusters can be identified. In these metaphor clusters, certain metaphors persistently occur together because of cultural, logical, and traditional connections. The metaphors in 1 Peter's body-middle fall into three clusters that determine the three major sections of the body-middle. The first metaphor cluster contains metaphors pertaining to the concept of the elect household of God (1:14--2:10). The second metaphor cluster is composed of metaphors that group around the notion of aliens in this world (2:11--3:12). The third metaphor cluster is determined by the concept of sufferers in the Diaspora (3:13--5:11). Recognition of these metaphor clusters, therefore, identifies the major sections of the body-middle. The subsections of the body-middle can be determined by recognizing the movement from one metaphor and its exhortations to another. The recognition of these movements from one subsection to another is aided by transitional and concluding devices, many of which were identified and used for the first time in an analysis of 1 Peter by Dalton. Attention to these metaphor clusters, as well as to the individual metaphors with their exhortations and to these transitional and concluding devices, furnishes an appropriate method by which to analyze the compositional structure of 1 Peter's body-middle. This method of analysis, along with the epistolary analysis mentioned above, indicates the following compositional structure for 1 Peter:

1. The Prescript (1:1-2)
2. The Blessing Section (1:3-12)
3. The Letter-body (1:13--5:12)
    3.1. The Body-opening (1:13)
    3.2. The Body-middle (1:14--5:11)
        3.2.1. The Οἶκος-Cluster, The elect household of God (1:14--2:10)
            3.2.1.1. Οἶκος-metaphors arising from the new birth and consequent familial relations (1:14-25)
                3.2.1.1.1. Metaphor-obedient children: Be holy (1:14-16)
                3.2.1.1.2. Metaphor-children under a new *pater potestas*: Be reverent (1:17-21)
                3.2.1.1.3. Metaphor-children in a new brotherhood: Love one another (1:22-25)
            3.2.1.2. Οἶκος-metaphors arising from the conception of growth (2:1-10)
                3.2.1.2.1. Metaphor-newborn babies: Desire spiritual milk (2:1-3)
                3.2.1.2.2. Metaphor-living stones forming a new temple: Allow

The thematic motif of 1 Peter is provided by the overarching and controlling metaphor of the Diaspora. From the beginning of the letter in 1:1 to its end in 5:13, images and concepts from the Jewish Diaspora dominate the material. The Diaspora provides the author with an image contributor that allows him to describe his readers' ontological status as well as the morality ensuing from that status. The Diaspora provides general images that pervade the entire letter and specific images that are limited to the individual sections of 1 Peter and give rise to the metaphor clusters. It also provides the unifying link among the three metaphor clusters in the letter-body of 1 Peter. Thus, the Diaspora is the thematic motif of 1 Peter.

Pervading the entire letter, two general images drawn from the Diaspora set up the rhetorical situation and reveal the author's twin purposes in writing. The temporal aspect of the Diaspora as a road to be traveled or a journey to be undertaken and the threatening aspect of the Diaspora as a dangerous place pressuring the faithful to assimilate and defect set up the rhetorical situation of 1 Peter. The author conceives of his readers on an eschatological journey. They are enroute from their new birth or election to the eschaton. The journey is difficult and the travelers suffer various trials that engender grief in them. In this rhetorical situation, the author attempts to accomplish two objectives. First, he intends to encourage his readers to engage in a course of life [ἀναστροφή] appropriate for the journey. Second, he wants to dissuade them from not completing their journey by defecting from the faith. The pagan environment through which they are traveling makes their journey difficult. On their eschatological journey, they experience trials and grief. The author is concerned that his readers continue to reflect the noble conduct associated with their calling in spite of opposition. He is also concerned that his readers may not complete their journey but may attempt to reduce or eliminate dissonance by defecting to their pagan environment. Concern about appropriate conduct and defection from Christianity provides the author of 1 Peter with his twin purposes for writing.

The author responds to the rhetorical situation and accomplishes his purposes for writing in the letter-body of 1 Peter by drawing upon Diaspora images. In the body-opening (1:13), he admonishes his readers to hope completely in the grace that will be brought to them at the revelation of Jesus Christ. In the body-closing (5:12), he exhorts them to stand fast for this grace. His objective in these letter parts is to establish his readers in the faith and to discourage them from scandal and defection. In the letter-body (1:14--5:11), he argues on the basis of ontological status and good conduct that they should not defect but rather should more earnestly give allegiance to this religion. He selects three metaphor clusters drawn from Diaspora images and concepts to describe the ontological status of his Christian readers. They are the elect household of God (1:14--2:10), aliens in this world (2:11--3:12), and sufferers in the Diaspora (3:13--5:11).

Each of these clusters demands noble and praiseworthy conduct from the readers corresponding to their ontological status. Because defection removes his readers from their enviable status with its noble conduct, the author argues that they should not defect. Furthermore, he discourages defection by describing the positive benefits accruing from their ontological status. As the elect household of God, the author's readers enjoy the protection of their *pater potestas*. As aliens, they receive the care and attention that God accords individuals in this vulnerable situation in life. As sufferers in the Dispersion, they anticipate God's reversal of their situation. Because defection means the loss of these benefits, the author urges his readers to remain steadfast in the faith. Utilizing a rhetorical strategy of suppression, the author does not specifically mention defection. Instead, he stresses notions antithetical to defection as he attempts to move the mind of his readers away from scandal and defection to hope, sobriety, and steadfastness. Thus, in the letter-body of 1 Peter, the author attempts to respond to the rhetorical situation and to accomplish his purposes of encouraging his readers to behave properly on their journey as well as to complete their eschatological journey by drawing upon images from the Diaspora that provides the thematic motif of 1 Peter.

As these summary conclusions indicate, this dissertation has resolved the literary character of 1 Peter. It has explicated the compositional structure, determined the literary genre, and identified the thematic motif of the letter. The problem explained in the introduction of this dissertation has now been solved.

This solution has implications for the broader world of New Testament scholarship. It indicates that paraenetic texts may not be the desultory musings of an impetuous author, but the skillful construction of a cogent rhetorician. Although there is great diversity in the composition of paraenetic texts, the relationship of ontological status to exhortation is an important feature of paraenetic composition. Perhaps further research that examines the relationship of ontological status to exhortation might be fruitful in the literary analysis of other paraenetic documents.

APPENDIX I

ANALYTICAL TRADITIONS

This appendix contains a table that identifies each scholar who has taken a position on the composition of 1 Peter. This table lists these authors in chronological order and designates the analytical tradition to which they belong. An asterisk indicates that a scholar has made a significant contribution to an analytical tradition to which he did not subscribe. The various analytical traditions, as well as these authors, are discussed in Chapter 1 of this dissertation.

Author   Type of Compositional Analysis

Author	1	2	3	4	5	6
Pamphilus Martyr	x					
Ps. Euthalius	x					
Ps. Oecumenius	x					
The Venerable Bede		x				
Walafridus Strabo		x				
Theophylact	x					
Euthymius	x					

277

	1	2	3	4	5	6
Martinus Legionensis		x				
Desiderus Erasmus	x					
Martin Luther			x			
John Calvin			x			
Benedictus Aretius			x			
Nicolus Serarius			x			
Abraham Calov			x			
Johann Gerhard			x			
Conrad Horneius			x			
Noël Alexandre	x					
Georg Michael Laurentius			x			
George Benson	x					
Albert Bengel				x		
Johann Salomo Semler	x					
David J. Pott	x					
S. F. N. Morus	x					
J. C. W. Agusti				x		

	1	2	3	4	5	6
C. G. Hensler	x					
J. I. Hottinger	x					
W. Steiger	x					
E. T. Mayerhoff		x				
K. R. Jachmann		x				
W. M. L. de Wette		x				
Henry Alford	x					
J. E. Huther				x		
J. C. A. Wiesinger				x		
G. F. C. Fronmüller		*		x		
Theodor Schott				x		
H. Ewald		x			*	
August Bisping				x		
Ludwig Joseph Hundhausen				x		
J. Chr. K. von Hofmann				x		
A Camerlynck				x		
C. F. Keil		*		x		

	1	2	3	4	5	6
Bernhard Weiss				x		
F. W. Bugge				x		
Joh. Martin Usteri				x		
Robert Johnston		x				
Ernst Kühl				x	*	
Karl Burger				x		
Siegfried Goebel				x		
Hermann Couard		x				
Johanis Tobias Beck				x		
Hermann von Soden		x				
F. J. A. Hort				x		
Adolf von Harnack					x	x
J. H. A. Hart					x	
Jean Monnier	x					
W. H. Bennett		x				
Julius Kögel				x		
Charles Bigg	x					

	1	2	3	4	5	6
Hermann Gunkel						x
Revere F. Weidner				x		
Walter Bauer	x					
Hans Windisch (1st edition)	x					
Richard Perdelwitz					x	x
Rudolf Knopf				x		
G. W. Blenkin				x		
Wilhelm Vrede				x		
G. Wohlenberg				x		
W. Bornemann						x
Adolf Schlatter				x		
Oskar Holtzmann				x		
Joseph Felten				x		
Heinrich Rendtorff				x		
Hans Windisch (2nd edition)						x
J. W. C. Wand					x	
Friedrich Hauck				x		

	1	2	3	4	5	6
Urbanus Holzmeister				x		
R. C. H. Lenski				x		
Hans Lilje	x					
P. N. Trempela				x		
Georg Staffelbach		*		x		
Eduard Schweizer	x					
Roland De Pury	x					
F. W. Beare					x	x
E. G. Selwyn			x			
Rudolf Bultmann						x
Pietro De Ambroggi	x					
C. E. B. Cranfield	x					
Peter Ketter				x		
Johann Michl			x			
F. L. Cross						x
E. Lohse				x		
Julian P. Love	x					

	1	2	3	4	5	6
M. E. Boismard				x		*
C. F. D. Moule					x	
A. M. Hunter				x		
Alan Stibbs	x					
Jean-Claude Margot	x					
Karl Hermann Schelkle				x		
Johannes Schneider				x		
Adrienne Speyr	x					
W. C. van Unnik	x					
R. P. Martin						x
Bo Reicke						x
Albert R. Jonsen			x			
G. R. Beasley-Murray					x	x
W. J. Dalton				x		
Ceslas Spicq				x		
A. R. C. Leaney					x	x
J. N. D. Kelly				x		

	1	2	3	4	5	6
Gunther Schiwy				x		
Ernest Best				x		
Max Alain Chevallier			x			
Wolfgang Schrage	x					
Oscar S. Brooks						x
H. J. B. Combrink				x		
Leonhard Goppelt				x		
Norbert Brox	x					
John Hall Elliott				x		
Jean Calloud				x		
Charles H. Talbert				x		
David W. Kendall				x		
Simon J. Kistemaker				x		
J. Ramsey Michaels				x		
William L. Schutter				x		*

APPENDIX II

ZEALOTS OF THE GOOD

The phrase zealots of the good [ζηλωταί τοῦ ἀγαθοῦ] in 1 Peter 3:13 presents an exegetical problem that is resolved by recognizing the overarching metaphor of the Diaspora in 1 Peter. Two basic interpretative positions are possible depending upon whether the phrase is understood in its Greek or Jewish context. Albrecht Stumpff explains the phrase in its Greek context:

> The predominant Gk. use of ζηλόω or ζηλωτής for an ethical attitude [in the special sense] also occurs sometimes in the NT with the sense of 'to strive after something.' Thus ζηλωτής καλῶν ἔργων in Tt. 2:14 and τοῦ ἀγαθοῦ ζηλωταί in 1 Pt. 3:13 both have a good Gk. ring, denoting the consistent and zealous orientation of action to a moral ideal.[1]

As Stumpff correctly recognizes, the Greek context of this phrase emphasizes the pursuit of and a commitment to a moral ideal. Although Goppelt recognizes that this phrase occurs in Jewish and Christian authors, he interprets this phrase in its Greek context, saying:

> The expression 'zealot for the good' frequently used in Hellenistic, Jewish, and Christian language describes the tenacious and entire, nothing short of ardent, standing for the good as it had been required thematically in the preceding part of the letter.[2]

---

[1]Albrecht Stumpff, "Ζῆλος," in *Theological Dictionary of the New Testament,* ed. Gerhard Kittel, vol. 2: *Δ-H* (Grand Rapids: Wm. B. Eerdmans Publishing Co., 1970), 887-888.

[2]Goppelt, *Petrusbrief,* 233.

Goppelt then cites righteousness (3:14), good conduct in Christ (3:16), and doing good (3:17) as developing this theme of moral commitment throughout the passage. It cannot be denied that this passage deals with morality and good conduct, but there is a religious dimension that should not be overlooked. The exhortation in 3:15 is for ardent devotion and commitment to Christ, not simply to a moral ideal. For this reason, the interpretation of this phrase should not be restricted to its Greek context.

W. C. van Unnik and Bo Reicke prefer to understand the phrase in its Jewish context. Reicke explains his position:

> Particularly during the first part of the sixties, there was in Judaism that anti-Roman movement whose adherents were called zealots or 'eager ones,' and who used violence as an instrument of policy to gain their goal of liberty. If, as seems probable, First Peter was written during this period, then the author undoubtedly has in mind these Jewish fanatics and warns against their terroristic methods as he advises the Christians rather to be zealous for what is good. The remarkable expression 'zealots' is best explained in this way.[3]

Reicke's position has been justifiably criticized by Michaels.[4] His position is too speculative and does not have good support in the text of 1 Peter. Van Unnik's position is more tenable. After citing the position of Stumpff mentioned above, he states his contrary position:

> Where ζηλωτής appears in the N.T., however, it means a 'zealot for the Law of the Lord' (Acts xxi 20; xxii 3; Gal. i 14). A strong similarity to this passage can be found in Tit. ii 14, a text the tone of which is very reminiscent of our epistle. Jesus Christ ὃς ἔδωκεν ἑαυτὸν ὑπὲρ ἡμῶν ἵνα λυτρώσηται ἡμᾶς ἀπὸ πάσης ἀνομίας καὶ καθαρίσῃ ἑαυτῷ λαὸν περιούσιον, ζηλωτὴν καλῶν ἔργων [here again we encounter the expression 'a people of [God's] own;' λυτρόω, too, is in keeping with 1 Pet. i 18]. The word ζηλωτής is also used of the proselytes who, like the born Jews, were 'zealots.'[5]

Van Unnik's contention that the readers of 1 Peter were proselytes can lead to a serious misconception and should be rejected. The readers were not proselytes to Judaism, but were Christians. Van Unnik's position is useful, however, in demonstrating that in its Jewish context the phrase *zealots of the good* bears more of a religious connotation than in its Greek

---

[3]Reicke, *1 Peter*, 107.
[4]Michaels, *1 Peter*, 185.
[5]Van Unnik, "Redemption," 65.

context. In its Jewish context, it refers to the ardent adherence to one's religious tradition.

The term ζηλωτής and its cognates are predominantly used in the New Testament in their Jewish, not Greek context. Martin Hengel explains, "The terms are also used in the New Testament to describe the attitude prevailing in Jewish circles."[6] In particular he mentions the Judaizers (Galatians 4:17), the Sadducees (Acts 5:17), the Jews in Pisidian Antioch (Acts 13:45), and the Jews in Thessalonica (Acts 17:5). To this list should also be added the reference to the Jews in Jerusalem in Acts 22:3. In this reference, Paul is described as a zealot of God in his practice of Judaism. In Galatians 1:14, Paul describes himself as a zealot for the traditions of his forefathers.[7] Hans Dieter Betz explains Paul's use of the term here:

> When Paul says he was a ζηλωτής he does not suggest he was a member of the party of the 'zealots,' but rather 'an ardent observer of the Torah.' Such conduct was not extremist or a form of mindless fanaticism, but was in conformity with the contemporary expectations of what a faithful Jew ought to have been.[8]

As Betz's explanation indicates, the term is used to describe Paul's ardent adherence to the Jewish faith expressed in the Torah. It is this context that usually informs the use of ζηλωτής and its cognates in the New Testament.[9]

The one notable exception to the Jewish context for the use of ζηλωτής occurs in Titus 2:14, a verse often associated with 1 Peter 3:13.[10] This association, however, overlooks an important difference between these two verses. The term ζηλωτής is a *vox media* and requires a qualifying genitive construction.[11] This genitive construction can either refer to a person or a thing.[12] The plural genitive ἔργων in Titus 2:14 clearly

---

[6]Martin Hengel, *The Zealots: Investigations into the Jewish Freedom Movement in the Period from Herod I until 70 A.D.*, trans. David Smith (Edinburgh: T. & T. Clark, 1989), 181.

[7]See also Philippians 3:6 where Paul uses the term in a description of his practice of Judaism.

[8]Betz, *Galatians*, 68.

[9]The term is also used in Luke 6:15 and Acts 1:13 to refer to a member of the zealot party.

[10]See Goppelt, *Petrusbrief*, 233, note 5; Best, *1 Peter*, 132; Michaels, *1 Peter*, 185; Kelly, 140; and Selwyn, *1 Peter*, 191.

[11]Stumpff, 877, says, "Ζῆλος as the capacity or state of passionate committal to a person or cause is essentially a *vox media* [i.e., it can be good or bad]."

[12]See the entry, "Ζηλωτής," in Bauer.

indicates that the qualifying genitive construction refers to a thing, not a person, and that the term ζηλωτής in this verse should be taken in its Greek context as a reference to the pursuit of good works ζηλωτὴς καλῶν ἔργων. In contrast, 1 Peter 3:13 qualifies ζηλωτής with a singular adjective in the genitive case [τοῦ ἀγαθοῦ]. This adjective is ambiguous in meaning.[13] It can refer to what is intrinsically valuable or morally good, or it can refer to the inner worth of a person or thing. The former meaning is usually adduced for 1 Peter 3:13. Nevertheless, there are good reasons to accept the latter meaning of this adjective as a description of God. This adjective is frequently associated with God.[14] According to Mark 10:18 and Luke 18:19, God is the only one who is ὁ ἀγαθός. Romans 5:7 says that one would hardly die for a righteous man, but someone might dare to die on behalf of the good [τοῦ ἀγαθοῦ]. In the last part of this statement, Paul is referring to the martyrs who dare to die for God. Τοῦ ἀγαθοῦ is used in Romans 5:7 as a euphemism for the name God. Given 1 Peter's predilection for referring to God with descriptive terms used substantively, the phrase τοῦ ἀγαθοῦ in 3:13 also refers to God.[15] The author describes his readers as zealots of God. The qualifying genitive in 1 Peter 3:13 refers to a person whereas the genitive in Titus 2:14 refers to things. The close association of these two verses should no longer be maintained since the former takes ζηλωτής in its Jewish context while the latter takes it in its Greek context.

The resolution of this exegetical question of the appropriate context for the phrase *zealots of the good* lies in the recognition of the role of the Diaspora in 1 Peter. As I have already established in Chapter 4, the author of 1 Peter uses the Jewish Diaspora as an image contributor to explain the ontological status and corresponding behavior of his Christian readers. Because the Jewish Diaspora is the overarching and controlling metaphor of this letter, it is best to take the phrase zealots of the good in its Jewish context.

---

[13]See the entry, "Ἀγαθός," in Bauer.

[14]Bauer, 2-3, cites several instances.

[15]Michaels, *1 Peter*, 235, details the numerous usages of a descriptive phrase to refer to God in 1 Peter. Commenting on 4:5, he says, "His other uses of attributive participles for a divine being--i.e., not only 'the One who judges' (1:17; 2:23), but 'the One [or Holy One] who called you' (1:15; 2:9; 5:10), 'the One who gave us new birth' (1:3), and 'the One who raised him . . . and gave him glory' (1:21)--refer not to Jesus Christ but to God the Father."

SOURCES CONSULTED

Primary Sources

Dittenberger, W., ed. *Orientis Graecae Inscriptiones Selectae.* Hildesheim: G. Olms, 1960.

Frey, Jean-Baptiste, ed. *Corpus inscriptionum Iudaicarum.* 2 Vols. Sussidi allo studio delle antichità cristiane. Rome: Pontificio instituto di archeologia cristiana, 1936, 1952.

Gaster, Theodor. *The Dead Sea Scriptures.* 3d ed. Garden City, New York: Doubleday, 1976.

Gummere, Richard M., trans. *Seneca.* The Loeb Classical Library. Cambridge: Harvard University Press, 1970.

Hunt, A. S. and C. C. Edgar, trans. *Select Papyri.* The Loeb Classical Library. Cambridge: Harvard University Press, 1977.

Isaac, E., trans. "1 (Ethiopic Apocalypse of) Enoch." In *The Old Testament Pseudepigrapha.* Edited by James H. Charlesworth. Vol. 1: *Apocalyptic Literature and Testaments*, 5-89. Garden City: Doubleday, 1983.

Jonge, M. de. *Testamenta XII Patriarcharum.* Leiden: E. J. Brill, 1970.

Hamilton, Edith and Huntington Cairns, ed. *Plato: The Collected Dialogues.* Bollingen Series 71. Princeton, New Jersey: Princeton University Press, 1985.

Kee, Howard Clark, trans. "Testaments of the Twelve Patriarchs." In *The Old Testament Pseudepigrapha.* Edited by James H. Charlesworth. Vol. 1: *Apocalyptic Literature and Testaments*, 775-828. Garden City: Doubleday and Company, 1983.

Klijn, A. F. J., trans. "2 (Syriac Apocalypse of) Baruch." In *The Old Testament Pseudepigrapha*. Edited by James H. Charlesworth. Vol. 1: *Apocalyptic Literature and Testaments*, 615-652. Garden City: Doubleday and Company, 1983.

Lacy, Phillip H. De, and Benedict Einarson, trans. *Plutarch's Morallia*. The Loeb Classical Library. Cambridge: Harvard University Press, 1984.

Lake, Kirsopp, trans. *Apostolic Fathers*. The Loeb Classical Library. Cambridge: Harvard University Press, 1977.

Lutz, Cora E., trans "Musonius Rufus: The Roman Socrates." *Yale Classical Studies* 10 (1947): 1-147.

Malherbe, Abraham J. "Ancient Epistolary Theorists." *Ohio Journal of Religious Studies* 5.2 (1977): 3-77; reprint, *Ancient Epistolary Theorists*. Society of Biblical Literature Sources for Biblical Study 19. Atlanta, Georgia: Scholars Press, 1988.

Marcus, Ralph, and Allen Wikgren, trans. *Josephus: Jewish Antiquities*. The Loeb Classical Library. Cambridge: Harvard University Press, 1980.

May, Herbert G. and Bruce M. Metzger. *The New Oxford Annotated Bible*. New York: Oxford University Press, 1973.

Melmoth, William, trans. *Pliny: Letters*. The Loeb Classical Library. Cambridge: Harvard University Press, 1963.

Metzger, B. M. "The Fourth Book of Ezra." In *The Old Testament Pseudepigrapha*. Edited by James H. Charlesworth. Vol. 1: *Apocalyptic Literature and Testaments*, 516-559. Garden City: Doubleday, 1983.

Miller, Walter, trans. *Cicero: De Officiis*. The Loeb Classical Library. Cambridge: Harvard University Press, 1975.

Nickelsburg, George W. E., and Michael E. Stone, ed. *Faith and Piety in Early Judaism: Texts and Documents*. Philadelphia: Fortress Press, 1983.

Norlin, George, trans. *Isocrates*. The Loeb Classical Library. Cambridge: Harvard University Press, 1980.

O'Neil, Edward N., trans. *Teles: The Cynic Teacher.* Society of Biblical Literature Texts and Translations 11. Graeco-Roman Religion Series 3. Missoula, Montana: Scholars Press, 1977.

Oldfather, W. A. trans. *Epictetus.* 2 Vols. The Loeb Classical Library. London: William Heinemann, 1928.

Olsson, Bror. *Papyrusbriefe aus der frühesten Römerzeit.* Uppsala: Almquist Wiksell, 1925.

Radice, Betty, and William Melmoth, trans. *Pliny.* The Loeb Classical Library. Cambridge: Harvard University Press, 1969.

Reinhold, Meyer. *Diaspora: The Jews among the Greeks and Romans.* Sarasota, Florida: Samuel Stevens, 1983.

Roberts, W. Rhys, trans. *Aristotle: Poetics; Demetrius on Style.* Loeb Classical Library. Cambridge: Harvard University Press, 1932.

Sanders, E. P., trans. "Testament of Abraham." In *The Old Testament Pseudepigrapha.* Edited by James H. Charlesworth. Vol 1: *Apocalyptic Literature and Testaments,* 871-904. Garden City: Doubleday, 1983.

Smith, Charles, trans. *Thucydides.* The Loeb Classical Library. Cambridge: Harvard University Press, 1951.

Stern, Menahem, ed. *Greek and Latin Authors on Jews and Judaism.* 2 Vols. Jerusalem: The Israel Academy of Sciences and Humanities, 1976.

Tcherikover, Victor A., Alexander Fuks, and Menahem Stern, ed. *Corpus Papyrorum Judaicarum.* 3 Vols. Cambridge: Harvard University Press, 1957-1964.

Thackeray, H. St. J., trans. *Josephus: Jewish War.* The Loeb Classical Library. London: William Heinemann, 1928.

Way, Arthur S., trans. *Euripides.* The Loeb Classical Library. Cambridge: Harvard University Press, 1962.

Secondary Sources

Grammars and Lexicons

Bauer, Walter. *A Greek-English Lexicon of the New Testament and Other Early Christian Literature.* 2d ed. Translated by W. F. Arndt and F. W. Gingrich. Edited by Frederick Danker. Chicago: The University of Chicago Press, 1979.

Blass, F., and A. Debrunner. *A Greek Grammar of the New Testament and Other Early Christian Literature.* Translated by Robert Funk. Chicago: The University of Chicago Press, 1961.

Liddell, Henry George, Robert Scott, and Henry Stuart Jones. *A Greek English Lexicon.* Oxford: Clarendon Press, 1968.

Moulton, James H. *A Grammar of New Testament Greek.* Edinburgh: T. & T. Clark, 1906.

Smyth, Herbert Weir. *Greek Grammar.* Cambridge: Harvard University Press, 1980.

Zerwick, Maximilian. *Biblical Greek.* Translated by Joseph Smith. Scripta Pontificii Instituti Biblici. Rome: n.p., 1963.

Commentaries

Alexandre, Noël. *Commentarius litteralis et moralis in omnes Epistolas Sancti Pauli Apostoli et in VII Epistolas Catholicas.* Paris: T. Bettinelli, 1768.

Alford, Henry. *The Epistle to the Hebrews: The Catholic Epistles of St. James and St. Peter: The Epistles of St. John and St. Jude: And the Revelation.* 4th ed. The Greek Testament 4. Boston: Lee and Shepard, Publishers, 1872.

Alulfus. *De expositione Novi Testamenti.* In *Patrologia Latina.* Edited by J. P. Migne. Vol. 79, 1385-1388.

Ambroggi, Pietro De. *Le Epistole Cattoliche di Giacomo, Pietro, Giovanni e Giuda.* La Sacra Bibbia 14. Torino: Marietti, 1947.

Ammonius Alexandrinus. *Fragmentum in Primam S. Petri Epistolam.* In *Patrologia Graeca.* Edited by J. P. Migne. Vol. 85, 1607-1610.

Aretius Benedictus. *Commentarii in Domini nostri Jesu Christi Novum Testamentum.* Genevae: apud Petrum & Iacobum Chouët, 1607.

Augusti, J. C. W. *Die katholischen Briefe.* Lemgo: Meyersche Buchhandlung, 1801.

Magnus Aurelius Cassidorus. *Complexiones in Epistulis Apostolorum.* In *Patrologia Latina.* Edited by J. P. Migne. Vol. 70, 1361-1368.

Balz, Horst, and Wolfgang Schrage. *Die Katholischen Briefe.* Das Neue Testament Deutsch 10. Göttingen: Vandenhoeck & Ruprecht, 1973.

Barclay, William. *The Letter to the Romans.* The Daily Study Bible Series. Philadelphia: The Westminster Press, 1957.

Barnes, Albert. *Notes, Explanatory and Practical, on the General Epistles of James, Peter, John and Jude.* New York: Harper & Brothers, 1848.

Bauer, Walter. *Die Katholischen Briefe des Neuen Testaments.* Religionsgeschichtliche Volksbücher für die deutsche christliche Gegenwart 1.20. Tübingen: J. C. B. Mohr, 1910.

Beare, Francis Wright. *The First Epistle of Peter.* Oxford: Basil Blackwell, 1958.

Beasley-Murray, G. R. *The General Epistles.* Bible Guides 21. Nashville: Abingdon Press, 1965.

Beck, Johannes Tobias. *Erklärung der Briefe Petri.* Edited by J. Lindenmeyer. Gütersloh: C. Bertelsmann, 1896.

Bede, The Venerable. *Super Epistolas Catholicas expositio.* In *Patrologia Latina.* Edited by J. P. Migne. Vol. 93, 41-68.

_____. *The Commentary on the Seven Catholic Epistles.* Translated by David Hurst. Kalamazoo, Michigan: Cistercian Publications, 1985.

Bengel, Johann Albert. *Gnomon of the New Testament.* Vol. 5. Translated by Andrew Fausset. Edinburgh: T. & T. Clark, 1860.

Bennett, W. H. *The General Epistles: James, Peter, John, and Jude.* The New Century Bible. Edinburgh: T. C. & E. C. Jack, 1901.

Benson, George. *A Paraphrase and Notes of the Seven Catholic Epistles.* London: J. Waugh, 1749.

Best, Ernest. *1 Peter.* The New Century Bible Commentary. Grand Rapids: Wm. B. Eerdmans Publishing Co., 1971.

Betz, Hans Dieter. *Galatians.* Hermeneia. Philadelphia: Fortress Press, 1979.

Bigg, Charles. *A Critical and Exegetical Commentary on the Epistles of St. Peter and St. Jude.* The International Critical Commentary. Edinburgh: T. & T. Clark, 1961; reprint.

Bisping, August. *Erklärung der sieben katholischen Briefe.* Exegetisches Handbuch zum neuen Testament 8. Münster: Aschendorff, 1871.

Blackley, W. L. and James Hawes, ed. *The Epistles (From First Timothy) and the Apocalypse.* 4th ed. The Critical English Testament 3. London: Daldy, Isbister and Co., 1878.

Blenkin, G. W. *The First Epistle General of Peter.* Cambridge Greek Testament for Schools and Colleges. Cambridge: University Press, 1914.

Brox, Norbert. *Der erste Petrusbrief.* Evangelisch-katholischer Kommentar zum Neuen Testament 21. Köln: Benziger Verlag, 1979.

Bullinger, Heinrych. *D. Petri Apostoli Epistolam utramque.* Zürich: Christoph Mense, 1534.

Burger, Karl. *Der erste Brief Petri.* Kurzgefasster Kommentar zu den heiligen Schriften. Nördlingen: C. H. Beck, 1888.

Calov, Abraham. *Biblia illustrata Novi Testamenti.* 2d ed. Dresden: Johann Christoph Zimmermann, 1719.

Calvin, John. *Commentaries on the Catholic Epistles.* Translated by John Owen. Edinburgh: T. Constable, 1855.

Camerlynck, A. *Commentarius in Epistolas Catholicas.* 5th ed. Brugis: Sumptibus Car. Beyaert, 1909.

Carpzov, J. B. *Epistolarum Catholicarum septenarius Graece.* Halae: Vidva Curtius, 1790.

Chrysostomus, Joannes. *Fragmenta in Epistolas Catholicas.* In *Patrologia Graeca.* Edited by J. P. Migne. Vol. 64, 1053-1058.

Clemens Alexandrinus. *Adumbrationes in Epistolas Canonicas.* In *Clemens Alexandrinus.* Edited by Otto Stählin. Vol. 3, 203-206. Die griechischen christlichen Schriftsteller der ersten drei Jahrhunderte 17. Berlin: Akademie-Verlag, 1970.

Couard, Hermann. *Die Briefe des Petrus, Judas und Johannes.* Potsdam: August Stein, 1895.

Cramer, J. A. *Catena in Epistolas Catholicas.* Vol. 8. Oxford: E Typographeo Academico, 1840.

Cranfield, C. E. B. *1 and 2 Peter and Jude.* Torch Bible Commentaries. London: S. C. M. Press, 1960.

_____. *The First Epistle of Peter.* London: S.C.M. Press, 1950.

Crell, Johan. *Commentarius in Primam Petri Apostoli Epistolam.* In *Opera omnia exegetica, didactica et polemica.* Freiburg: I. Philalethius, 1656.

Cyrillus Alexandrinus. *Fragmenta in Epistolas Catholicas.* In *Patrologia Graeca.* Edited by J. P. Migne. Vol. 74, 1011-1016.

Demarest, John T. *A Commentary on the Catholic Epistles.* New York: Board of Publication of the Reformed Church in America, 1879.

Dibelius, Martin. *James: A Commentary on the Epistle of James.* Translated by M. A. Williams. Hermeneia. Philadelphia: Fortress Press, 1976.

Didymus Alexandrinus. *Enarratio in Epistolas Catholicas.* In *Patrologia Graeca.* Edited by J. P. Migne. Vol. 39, 1755-1772.

Eerdman, Charles R. *The General Epistles.* Philadelphia: Westminster Press, 1918.

Elliott, John H. *I-II Peter/Jude.* Augsburg Commentary on the New Testament. Minneapolis: Augsburg Publishing House, 1982.

Erasmus, Desiderius. *Paraphrases in N. Testamentum.* In *Opera omnia.* Vol. 7, 1081-1100. Leiden: Petrus van der Aa, 1706.

Eusebius Hieronymus. *Divina Bibliotheca.* In *Patrologia Latina.* Edited by J. P. Migne. Vol. 29, 877-882.

Ps. Euthalius. *Elenchus capitum septem Epistolarum Catholicarum.* In *Patrologia Graeca.* Edited by J. P. Migne. Vol. 85, 679-682.

Euthymius Zigabenus. *Commentarius in xiv Epistolas S. Pauli et vii Catholicas.* Edited by N. Kalogeras. Athens: Τυποιs Αδελφων Περρη, 1887.

Ewald, Heinrich. *Sieben Sendschreiben des neuen Bundes übersetzt und erklärt.* Göttingen: Dieterichs, 1870.

Felten, Joseph. *Die zwei Briefe des heiligen Petrus und der Judasbrief.* Regensburg: G. J. Manz, 1929.

Fronmüller, G. F. C. *Die Briefe Petri und der Brief Judä.* 2d ed. Theologisch-homiletisches Bibelwerk 14. Bielefeld: Velhagen und Klasing, 1862.

————. *Epistles General of Peter.* Translated by J. Isidor Mombert. New York: Charles Scribner, & Co., 1869.

Gerhard, Johann. *Commentarius super Priorem D. Petri Epistolam.* Hamburg: Sumptibus Zachariae Hertelii, 1709.

Gibson, M. D., trans. *The Commentaries of Isho'dad of Merv.* Horae Semiticae 10. Cambridge: Cambridge University Press, 1913.

Glasgow, Samuel McPheeters. *The General Epistles.* New York: Fleming H. Revell Company, 1928.

Goebel, Siegfried. *Die Briefe des Petrus: griechisch, mit kurzer Erklärung.* Gotha: Friedrich Andreas Perthes, 1893.

Gomarus, Franciscus. *In priorem S. Petri epistolam explicatio.* In *Opera theologica omnia.* Amsterdam: Joannis Janssonius, 1664.

Goppelt, Leonhard. *Der erste Petrusbrief.* Kritisch-exegetischer Kommentar über das neue Testament 11. 8th ed. Göttingen: Vandenhoeck & Ruprecht, 1978.

Gunkel, Hermann. *Die erste Brief des Petrus.* 3d ed. Die Schriften des Neuen Testaments 2. Göttingen: Vandenhoeck & Ruprecht, 1917.

Harms, Louis. *Auslegung der ersten Epistel St. Petri.* Hermannsburg: Missionshausbuchdruckerei, 1869.

Hart, J. H. A. *The First Epistle General of Peter.* The Expositor's Greek Testament 5. Grand Rapids: Wm. B. Eerdmans Publishing Co., 1897.

Hauck, Friedrich. *Die Briefe des Jakobus, Petrus, Judas und Johannes.* 8th ed. Das Neue Testament Deutsch 10. Göttingen: Vandenhoeck & Ruprecht, 1957.

Hensler, C. G. *Der erste Brief des Apostels Petrus.* Sulzbach: T. E. Geidel, 1813.

Hesychius. *Fragmentum in Epistolam I. S. Petri.* In *Patrologia Graeca.* Edited by J. P. Migne. Vol. 93, 1389-1390.

Ps. Hilarius Arelatensis. *Expositio in Epistolas Catholicas.* In *Patrologia Latina.* Edited by J. P. Migne. Supplement 3, 83-106.

Hofmann, Johann Christian Karl von. *Der erste Brief Petri.* Die Heilige Schrift Neuen Testaments 7. Nördlingen: C. H. Beck, 1875.

Holtzmann, Oskar. *Die Petrusbriefe.* Das Neue Testament 2. Gießen: Alfred Töpelmann, 1926.

Holzmeister, Urbanus. *Commentarius in Epistulas SS. Petri et Iudae Apostolorum.* Cursus Scripturae Sacrae 3. Paris: P. Lethielleux, 1937.

Horneius, Conrad. *In Epistolam Catholicam Sancti Apostoli Petri Priorem expositio litteralis.* Braunschweig: Andrea Duncker, 1654.

Hort, F. J. A. *The First Epistle of St. Peter.* Edited by B. F. Dunelm. London: Macmillan and Co., 1898.

Hottinger, J. Iacobus. *Epistolae D. Iacobi atque Petri I.* Leipzig: Libraria Dyckiana, 1815.

Hundhausen, Ludwig Joseph. *Die beiden Pontificalschreiben des Apostelfürsten Petrus.* Vol. 1: *Das erste Pontificalschreiben des Apostelfürsten Petrus* (Festschrift für Pius IX). Mainz: Franz Kirchheim, 1873.

Hunter, A. M. and E. G. Homrighausen. *The Epistle of James, The First and Second Epistles of Peter, The First, Second, and Third Epistles of John, The Epistle of Jude, The Revelation of St. John the Divine.* The Interpreter's Bible 12. Nashville: Abingdon, 1957.

Huther, J. E. *Critical and Exegetical Commentary on the New Testament.* Translated by D. B. Croom. Edinburgh: T. & T. Clark, 1881.

_____. *Kritisch-exegetisches Handbuch über den 1. Brief des Petrus, den Brief des Judas und den 2. Brief des Petrus.* 3d ed. Kritisch-exegetischer Kommentar über das Neue Testament 12. Göttingen: Vandenhoeck und Ruprecht, 1867.

Jachmann, Karl Reinhold. *Commentar über die katholischen Briefe.* Leipzig: Johann Ambrosius Barth, 1838.

Johnstone, Robert. *The First Epistle of Peter.* Edinburgh: T. & T. Clark, 1888.

Keil, Carl Friedrich. *Kommentar über die Briefe des Petrus und Judas.* Leipzig: Dorfeling und Franke, 1883.

Kelly, J. N. D. *A Commentary of the Epistles of Peter and Jude.* Black's New Testament Commentaries. London: A. and C. Black, 1969.

Kelly, William. *The First Epistle of Peter.* London: T. Weston, 1904.

Ketter, Peter. *Hebräerbrief, Jakobusbrief, Petrusbriefe, Judasbrief.* Die Heilige Schrift für das Leben erklärt 16.1. Freiburg: Herder, 1950.

Kistemaker, Simon J. *Exposition of the Epistles of Peter and of the Epistle of Jude.* New Testament Commentary. Grand Rapids: Baker Book House, 1987.

Knopf, Rudolf. *Die Briefe Petri und Judä.* Kritisch-exegetischer Kommentar über das Neue Testament 12. 7th ed. Göttingen: Vandenhoeck & Ruprecht, 1912.

Kühl, Ernst. *Die Briefe Petri und Judae.* 6th ed. Kritisch-exegetischer Kommentar über das Neue Testament. Vol. 12. 5th ed. Göttingen: Vandenhoeck & Ruprecht, 1897.

Laurentius, Georg Michael. *Kurtze Erklärung des ersten Briefs St. Petri.* Halle: Verlegung des Waysenhauses, 1716.

Leaney, A. R. C. *The Letters of Peter and Jude.* The Cambridge Bible Commentary. Cambridge: Cambridge University Press, 1967.

Lenski, R. C. H. *The Interpretation of the Epistles of St. Peter, St. John and St. Jude.* Columbus, Ohio: Luthern Book Concern, 1938.

Lilje, Hanns. *Die Petrusbriefe und der Judasbrief.* Bibelhilfe für die Gemeinde, Neutestamentliche Reihe 14. Kassel: J. G. Oncken, 1954.

Luculentius. *In aliquot Novi Testamenti partes commentarii.* In *Patrologia Latina.* Edited by J. P. Migne. Vol. 72, 857-860.

Luther, Martin. *Epistel Sanct Petri gepredigt und ausgelegt.* In *D. Martin Luthers Werke.* Edited by Paul Pietsch. Vol. 12, 259-399.. Weimar: Hermann Böhlau, 1891.

_____. *Sermons on the First Epistle of St. Peter.* Translated by Martin H. Bertram. In *Luther's Works.* Edited by Jaroslav Pelikan. Vol. 30: *The Catholic Epistles.* Saint Louis: Concordia Publishing House, 1967.

Lyonnet, Stanislas. *Les Epîtres de Saint Paul aux Galates, aux Romains.* Paris: Cerf, 1953.

Margot, Jean-Claude. *Les Épîtres de Pierre.* Genève: Labor et Fides, 1960.

Martin, Ralph P. *James.* Word Biblical Commentary 48. Waco, Texas: Word Books Publisher, 1988.

Martinus Legionensis. *Expositio in epistolam I B. Petri Apostoli.* In *Patrologia Latina.* Edited by J. P. Migne. Vol. 209, 217-252.

Masterman, John Howard Bertram. *The First Epistle of S. Peter.* London: Macmillan and Co., 1900.

Matthaei, Christianus Fridericus. *SS. Apostolorum septem Epistolae Catholicae.* Rigae: Ioannes Fridericus Hartknoch, 1782.

Michaels, J. Ramsey. *1 Peter.* Word Biblical Commentary. Waco: Word Books, Publisher, 1988.

Michl, Johann. *Cartas Católicas.* Comentario de Ratisbona al Nuevo Testamento 8. Barcelona: Herder, 1977.

Michl, Johann. *Die katholischen Briefe*. Das Neue Testament 8.2. Regensburg: Friedrich Pustet, 1953.

Moffatt, James. *The General Epistles: James, Peter, and Judas*. The Moffatt New Testament Commentary. London: Hodder and Stoughton, 1947.

Monnier, Jean. *La Première Épître de l'Apôtre Pierre*. Macon: Protat Frères, 1900.

Moorehead, William G. *Outline Studies in the New Testament*. Pittsburgh: United Presbyterian Board of Publication, 1910.

Morus, S. F. N. *Praelectiones in Jacobi et Petri Epistolas*. Leipzig: Sumptibus Sommeri, 1794.

Ps. Oecumenius. *Commentarii in Epistolas Catholicas*. In *Patrologia Graeca*. Edited by J. P. Migne. Vol. 119, 509-578.

Paterius. *Liber de expositione Veteris ac Novi Testamenti*. In *Patrologia Latina*. Edited by J. P. Migne. Vol. 79, 1097-1100.

Plumptre, E. H. *The General Epistles of St. Peter & St. Jude*. The Cambridge Bible for Schools. Cambridge: University Press, 1879.

Pott, David Iulius. *Epistolae Catholicae*. 2d ed. Göttingen: Henrici Dieterich, 1810.

Pury, Roland De. *Pierres Vivantes*. Paris: Delachaux & Niestlé, 1944.

Reicke, Bo. *The Epistles of James, Peter, and Jude*. The Anchor Bible 37. Garden City: Doubleday & Co., 1964.

Rosenmüller, I. Georg. *Scholia in Novum Testamentum*. 4th ed. Tomus V. Norimberg: Felsecker, 1794.

Sadler, M.F. *The General Epistles of SS. James, Peter, John and Jude*. 2d ed. London: George Bell and Sons, 1895·

Schelkle, Karl Hermann. *Die Petrusbriefe. Der Judasbrief*. 3d ed. Herders Theologischer Kommentar zum Neuen Testament 13.2. Freiburg: Herder, 1970.

Schiwy, Günther. *Weg ins Neue Testament*. Vol. 4: *Nachpaulinen*. Würzburg: Echter-Verlag, 1970.

Schlatter, Adolf. *Die Briefe des Petrus, Judas, Jakobus, der Brief an die Hebräer.* Erläuterungen zum Neuen Testament 9. Stuttgart: Calwer Verlag, 1965.

Schneider, Johannes. *Die Briefe des Jakobus, Petrus, Judas, und Johannes.* 2d ed. Das Neue Testament Deutsch 10. Göttingen: Vandenhoeck & Ruprecht, 1967.

Schott, Theodor. *Der erste Brief Petri.* Erlangen: Andreas Deichert, 1861.

Schweizer, Eduard. *Der erste Petrusbrief.* Prophezei. Zürich: Zwingli-Verlag, 1942.

Selwyn, E. G. *The First Epistle of St. Peter.* London: Macmillan & Co., 1946; reprint, Thornapple Commentaries. Grand Rapids: Baker Book House, 1981.

Semler, Johann Salomo. *Paraphrasis in Epistolam I. Petri.* Halle: Impensis Bibliopolii Hemmerdiani, 1783.

Serarius, Nicolus. *Prolegomena bibliaca et commentaria in omnes Epistolas Canonicas.* Paris: Balthasar Lippius, 1612.

Soden, Hermann von. *Hebräerbrief, Briefe des Petrus, Jakobus, Judas.* 3d ed. Hand-Kommentar zum Neuen Testament 3.2. Freiburg: J. C. B. Mohr, 1899.

Speyr, Adrienne von. *Die katholischen Briefe.* Einsiedeln: Johannes Verlag, 1961.

Spicq, Ceslas. *Les Épitres de Saint Pierre.* Sources Bibliques. Paris: Librairie Lecoffre, 1966.

Staffelbach, Georg. *Die Briefe der Apostel Jakobus und Judas, Petrus und Johannes.* Luzern: Räber, 1941.

Steiger, Wilhelm. *Exposition of the First Epistle of Peter.* Translated by Patrick Fairbairn. Edinburgh: Thomas Clark, 1836.

Steinmeyer, F. L. *Disquisitio in Epistolae Petrinae Prioris.* Berlin: Wiegandt et Grieben, 1854.

Stibbs, Alan M. *The First Epistle General of Peter.* The Tyndale New Testament Commentaries. Grand Rapids: Wm. B. Eerdmans Publishing Co., 1959.

Theophylact. *Expositio in Epistolam Primam S. Petri.* In *Patrologia Graeca.* Edited by J. P. Migne. Vol. 125, 1189-1252.

Trapp, John. *A Commentary on the New Testament.* 1647; reprint, London: Richard D. Dickinson, 1865.

Τρεμπελα, Π. Ν. *Ὑπόμνημα εἰς τὴν πρὸς Ἑβραίοις καὶ τὰς ἑπτὰ Καθολικὰς.* Ἀθῆναι: Ἀδελφότῆς Θεολόγων ἡ Ζωή, 1941.

Usteri, Joh. Martin. *Wissenschaftlicher und Praktischer Kommentar über den ersten Petrusbrief.* Zürich: S. Höhr, 1887.

Vrede, Wilhelm. *Der erste Petrusbrief.* 4th ed. Die heilige Schrift des Neuen Testaments 9. Bonn: Peter Hanstein, 1932.

Walafridus Strabo. *Glossa ordinaria--Epistola 1 Petri.* In *Patrologia Latina.* Edited by J. P. Migne. Vol. 114, 679-688.

Waltemyer, Wm. C. *The First Epistle of Peter.* New Testament Commentary. Edited by Herbert C. Alleman. Philadelphia: The Board of Publication of the United Luthern Church in America, 1936.

Wand, J. W. C. *The General Epistles of St. Peter and St. Jude.* Westminster Commentaries. London: Methuen & Co., 1934.

Weidner, Revere F. *Annotations on the General Epistles of James, Peter, John, and Jude and the Revelation of St. John.* New York: Charles Scribners Sons, 1905.

Weiser, Artur. *The Psalms: A Commentary.* The Old Testament Library. Philadelphia: The Westminster Press, 1962.

Weiss, Bernhard. *A Commentary on the New Testament.* Vol. 4: *Thessalonians to Revelation.* Translated by George Schodde and Epiphanius Wilson. New York: Funk & Wagnalls Co., 1906.

Wesley, John. *Explanatory Notes Upon the New Testament.* Vol. 2: *Romans to Revelation.* 1754; reprint, Grand Rapids: Baker Book House, 1983.

Wette, W. M. L. de. *Die katholischen Briefe.* Halle: Eduard Anton, 1887.

Wiesinger, J. C. A. *Der erste Brief des Apostels Petrus.* Olshausens biblischer Kommentar 6.2. Königsberg: August Wilhelm Unzer, 1856.

Windisch, Hans. *Die katholischen Briefe.* Handbuch zum Neuen Testament 4.2. Tübingen: J. C. B. Mohr, 1911.

Wohlenberg, G. *Der erste und zweite Petrusbrief und der Judasbrief.* 3d ed. Kommentar zum Neuen Testament 15. Leipzig: A. Deichert, 1923.

Wuest, Kenneth. *First Peter in the Greek New Testament.* Grand Rapids: Wm. B. Eerdmans Publishing Co., 1942.

Studies

Books and Dissertations

Askowith, Dora. "The Toleration of the Jews under Julius Caesar and Augustus." Ph.D. dissertation, Columbia University, 1915.

Aune, David E. *The New Testament in Its Literary Environment.* Library of Early Christianity. Philadelphia: The Westminster Press, 1987.

Baer, Yitzhak F. *Galut.* Translated by Robert Warshow. New York: Schocken Books, 1947

Balch, David L. *Let Wives Be Submissive: The Domestic Code in 1 Peter.* Society of Biblical Literature Monograph Series 26. Chico, California: Scholars Press, 1981.

Baltensweiler, Heinrich. *Die Ehe im Neuen Testament: Exegetische Untersuchungen über Ehe, Ehelosigkeit und Ehescheidung.* Abhandlungen zur Theologie des Alten und Neuen Testaments, 52. Zürich: Zwingli Verlag, 1967.

Baron, Salo Wittmayer. *A Social and Religious History of the Jews.* 2 Vols. New York: Columbia University Press, 1966.

Bartlett, John R. *Jews in the Hellenistic World.* Cambridge Commentaries on Writings of the Jewish and Christian World 200 B.C. to A.D. 200 1.1. Cambridge: Cambridge University Press, 1985.

Beasley-Murray, G. R. *Baptism in the New Testament.* London: Macmillan & Co., 1962.

Berger, Klaus. *Formgeschichte des Neuen Testaments*. Heidelberg: Quelle & Meyer, 1984.

Betz, Hans Dieter. *Lukian von Samosata und das Neue Testament: Religionsgeschichtliche und paränetische Parallelen*. Texte und Untersuchungen 76. Berlin: Akademie Verlag, 1961.

————. *Paul's Concept of Freedom in the Context of Hellenistic Discussions about the Possibilities of Human Freedom*. Protocol of the Colloquy of the Center for Hermeneutical Studies in Hellenistic and Modern Culture 26. Berkeley, California: The Center for Hermeneutical Studies in Hellenistic and Modern Culture, 1977.

Bieder, Werner. *Die Vorstellung von der Höllenfahrt Jesu Christi*. Abhandlungen zur Theologie des Alten und Neuen Testaments 19. Zürich: Zwingli Verlag, 1949.

Bjerkelund, C. J. *Parakalô: Form, Funktion und Sinn der parakalô-Sätze in den paulinischen Briefen*. Oslo: Universitetsforlaget, 1967.

Boismard, M. E. *Quatres hymnes baptismales dans la Première Épître de Pierre*. Lectio Divina 30. Paris: Cerf, 1961.

Bonner, Leah. *Sects and Separatism During the Second Jewish Commonwealth*. New York: Bloch Publishing Company, 1967.

Bonsirven, Joseph. *Palestinian Judaism in the Time of Jesus Christ*. Translated by William Wolf. New York: Holt, Rinehart and Winston, 1964.

Brandon, S. G. F. *Jesus and the Zealots*. New York: Charles Scribner's Sons, 1967.

Braun, Herbert. *Das Leiden Christi: Eine Bibelarbeit über den I. Petrusbrief*. Theologische Existenz heute 69. München: Kaiser Verlag, 1940.

Brown, John. *Expository Discourses on the First Epistle of the Apostle Peter*. New York: Robert Carter & Brothers, 1851.

Brown, Raymond E. and Karl P. Donfried, ed. *Peter in the New Testament*. Minneapolis: Augsburg Publishing House, 1973.

Brox, Norbert. *Zeuge und Märtyrer*. Studien zum Alten und Neuen Testament 5. München: Kösel, 1961.

Burgess, Theodore C. *Epideictic Literature.* Studies in Classical Philology 3. Chicago: The University of Chicago Press, 1902.

Calloud, Jean, and Francois Genuyt. *La Première Épître de Pierre: Analyse semiotique.* Lectio Divina 109. Paris: Cerf, 1982.

Campenhausen, Hans von. *Die Idee des Martyriums in der Alten Kirche.* Göttingen: Vandenhoeck & Ruprecht, 1936.

_____. *Polykarp von Smyrna und die Pastoralbriefe.* Heidelberg: Carl Winter, 1951.

Cancik, Hildegard. *Untersuchungen zu Senecas Epistulae morales.* Spudasmata 18. Hildesheim: Georg Olms, 1967.

Carrington, Philip. *The Primitive Christian Catechism.* Cambridge: Cambridge University Press, 1940.

Causse, A. *Les dispersés d'Israël: Les origines de la Diaspora et son rôle dans la formation du Judaïsme.* Études d'histoire et de philosophie religieuses 19. Paris: Félix Ascan, 1929.

Champion, L. G. *Benedictions and Doxologies in the Epistles of Paul.* Oxford: Kemp Hall Press, 1934.

Cohen, Shaye J. D. *From the Maccabees to the Mishnah.* Library of Early Christianity. Philadelphia: The Westminster Press, 1987.

Collins, John J. *Between Athens and Jerusalem: Jewish Identity in the Hellenistic Diaspora.* New York: Crossroad, 1983.

_____. *The Apocalyptic Imagination.* New York: Crossroad Publishing Company, 1984.

Cross, F. L. *1 Peter: A Paschal Liturgy.* 2 ed. London: A. R. Mowbray, 1957.

Crouch, James E. *The Origin and Intention of the Colossian Haustafel.* Forschungen zur Religion und Literatur des Alten und Neuen Testaments 109. Göttingen: Vandenhoeck & Ruprecht, 1972.

Cullmann, Oscar. *Jesus and the Revolutionaries.* Translated by Gareth Putnam. New York: Harper and Row, 1970.

Cullmann, Oscar. *Peter: Disciple, Apostle, Martyr.* Philadelphia: Westminster, 1962.

_____. *The State in the New Testament.* New York: Charles Scribner's Sons, 1956.

Dalton, W. J. *Christ's Proclamation to the Spirits.* Analecta Biblica 23. Rome: Pontifical Biblical Institute, 1965.

Daniélou, Jean. *From Shadows to Reality: Studies in the Biblical Typology of the Fathers.* Translated by Dom Wulstan Hibberd. Westminster: The Newman Press, 1960.

_____. *Sacramentum Futuri: Études sur les Origines de la Typologie Biblique.* Paris: Beauchesne et ses Fils, 1950.

Deichgräber, Reinhard. *Gotteshymnus und Christushymnus in der frühen Christenheit.* Studien zur Umwelt des Neuen Testaments 5. Göttingen: Vandenhoeck & Ruprecht, 1967.

Deissmann, Adolf. *Bible Studies.* Translated by Alexander Grieve. 2d ed. Edinburgh: T. & T. Clark, 1903.

_____. *Light from the Ancient East.* Translated by Lionel R. M. Strachan. Grand Rapids: Baker Book House, 1978.

Delling, Gerhard. *Die Taufe im Neuen Testament.* Berlin: Evangelische Verlagsanstalt, 1963.

Dey, Joseph. *Παλιγγενεσια: Ein Beitrag zur Klärung der religionsgeschichtlichen Deutung von Tit 3, 5.* Neutestamentliche Abhandlungen 17.5. Münster: Aschendorff, 1937.

Dibelius, Martin. *Geschichte der urchristlichen Literatur.* Berlin: Walter de Gruyter, 1926.

Donelson, Lewis R. *Pseudepigraphy and Ethical Argument in the Pastoral Epistles.* Hermeneutische Untersuchungen zur Theologie 22. Tübingen: J. C. B. Mohr (Paul Siebeck), 1986.

Doty, William G. *Letters in Primitive Christianity.* Guides to Biblical Scholarship: New Testament Series. Philadelphia: Fortress Press, 1973.

Dunn, J. D. G. *Baptism in the Holy Spirit.* Studies in Biblical Theology Second Series 15. London: S. C. M. Press, 1970.

Elliott, John H. *A Home for the Homeless: A Sociological Exegesis of 1 Peter, Its Situation and Strategy.* Philadelphia: Fortress Press, 1981.

_____. *The Elect and the Holy.* Supplements to Novum Testamentum 12. Leiden: E. J. Brill, 1966.

Exler, Francis Xavier J. "The Form of the Ancient Greek Letter: A Study in Greek Epistolography." Ph.D. dissertation, Catholic University of America, 1923.

Farmer, William. *Maccabees, Zealots, and Josephus.* New York: Columbia University Press, 1956.

Ferguson, Everett. *Backgrounds of Early Christianity.* Grand Rapids: Wm. B. Eerdman's Publishing Co., 1987.

Fiore, Benjamin. *The Function of Personal Example in the Socratic and Pastoral Epistles.* Analecta Biblica 105. Rome: Biblical Institute Press, 1986..

Foster, Ora Delmer. *The Literary Relations of the First Epistle of Peter.* Transactions of the Connecticut Academy of Arts and Sciences 17. New Haven: Yale University Press, 1913.

Funk, Robert W. *Language, Hermeneutic, and Word of God.* New York: Harper & Row, 1966.

Furnish, Victor P. *Theology and Ethics in Paul.* Nashville: Abingdon, 1968.

Gärtner, Bertil. *The Temple and the Community in Qumran and the New Testament.* Cambridge: Cambridge University Press, 1965.

Gaiser, Konrad. *Protreptik und Paränese bei Platon.* Tübinger Beiträge zur Altertumswissenschaft 40. Stuttgart: Kohlhammer Verlag, 1959.

Gewalt, Dietfried. "Petrus: Studien zur Geschichte und Tradition des frühen Christentums." Ph.D. dissertation, Heidelberg University, 1966.

Ginzberg, Louis. *An Unknown Jewish Sect.* Moreshet Series 1. New York: KTAV Publishing House, 1970.

Gloag, Paton J. *Introduction to the Catholic Epistles.* Edinburgh: T. & T. Clark, 1887.

Goppelt, Leonhard. *Typos: Die typologische Deutung des Alten Testaments im Neuen.* 2d ed. Gütersloh: C. Bertelsmann, 1939.

Grabner-Haider, Anton. *Paraklese und Eschatologie bei Paulus.* Neutestamentliche Abhandlungen 4. Münster: Aschendorff, 1967.

Grant, Michael. *The Jews in the Roman World.* New York: Charles Scribner's Sons, 1973.

Gschwind, Karl. *Die Niederfahrt Christi in die Unterwelt.* Neutestamentliche Abhandlungen 2.3-5 Münster: Aschendorff, 1911.

Gustafson, Henry. "The New Testament's Interpretations of Christian Suffering." Ph.D. dissertation, The University of Chicago, 1967.

Gülzow, Henneke. *Christentum und Sklaverei in den ersten drei Jahrhunderten.* Bonn: Rudolf Habelt, 1969.

Hadot, Ilsetraut. *Seneca und die griechisch-römische Tradition der Seelenleitung.* Quellen und Studien zur Geschichte der Philosophie 13. Berlin: Walter de Gruyter, 1969.

Hare, R. M. *The Language of Morals.* Oxford: Clarendon Press, 1952.

Harnack, Adolf von. *Geschichte der altchristlichen Litteratur bis Eusebius.* Vol. 1: *Die Chronologie der altchristlichen Litteratur bis Eusebius.* Leipzig: J. C. Hinrichs, 1897.

_____. *The Mission and Expansion of Christianity in the First Three Centuries.* Translated by James Moffatt. Gloucester, Mass.: Peter Smith, 1972.

Hartlich, Paulus. *De Exhortationum a Graecis Romanisque.* Leipziger Studien zur classischen Philologie 11 (1889): 207-336.

Hengel, Martin. *Jews, Greeks, and Barbarians.* Translated by John Bowden. Philadelphia: Fortress Press, 1980.

_____. *Judaism and Hellenism.* Translated by John Bowden. Philadelphia: Fortress Press, 1981.

Hengel, Martin. *The Zealots: Investigations into the Jewish Freedom Movement in the Period from Herod I until 70 A.D.* Translated by David Smith. Edinburgh: T. & T. Clark, 1989.

Holl, Karl. *Gesammelte Aufsätze zur Kirchengeschichte.* Vol. 2: *Der Osten.* Tübingen: J. C. B. Mohr (Paul Siebeck), 1928; reprint, Darmstadt: Wissenschaftliche Buchgesellschaft, 1964.

Horsley, Richard A. *Bandits, Prophets, and Messiahs.* San Francisco: Harper and Row, 1988.

Jones, F. Stanley. *"Freiheit" in den Briefen des Apostels Paulus: Eine historische, exegetische und religionsgeschichtliche Studie.* Göttinger Theologische Arbeiten 34. Göttingen: Vandenhoeck & Ruprecht, 1987.

Jost, Wilhelm. *ΠΟΙΜΗΝ: Das Bild vom Hirten in der biblischen Überlieferung und seine christologische Bedeutung.* Gießen: Otto Kindt, 1939.

Jülicher, A. *Einleitung in das Neue Testament.* 7th ed. Tübingen: J. C. B. Mohr (Paul Siebeck), 1931.

Karris, Robert Joseph. "The Function and Sitz-im-Leben of the Paraenetic Elements in the Pastoral Epistles." Th.D. dissertation, Harvard University, 1971.

Kähler, Else. *Die Frau in den paulinischen Briefen.* Zürich: Gotthelf Verlag, 1960.

Käsemann, Ernst. *The Wandering People of God: An Investigation of the Letter to the Hebrews.* Translated by Ray A. Harrisville and Irving L. Sandburg. Minneapolis: Augsburg Publishing House, 1984.

Kim, Chan-Hie. *Form and Structure of the Familiar Greek Letter of Recommendation.* Society of Biblical Literature Dissertation Series 4. Missoula, Montana: Scholars Press, 1972.

Kittel, Bonnie. *The Hymns of Qumran.* Society of Biblical Literature Dissertation Series 50. Chico, California: Scholars Press, 1981.

Kleinknecht, K. T. *Der leidende Gerechtfertigte.* Wissenschaftliche Untersuchungen zum Neuen Testament 2.13. Tübingen: J. C. B. Mohr (Paul Siebeck), 1984.

Klinzing, Georg. *Die Umdeutung des Kultus in der Qumrangemeinde und im Neuen Testament.* Studien zur Umwelt des Neuen Testaments 7. Göttingen: Vandenhoeck & Ruprecht, 1971.

Kögel, Julius. *Die Gedankeneinheit des Ersten Briefes Petri.* Beiträge zur Förderung christlicher Theologie 6. Gütersloh: C. Bertelsmann, 1902.

Koskenniemi, Heikki. *Studien zur Idee und Phraseologie des griechischen Briefes bis 400 n. Chr.* Soumalaisen Tiedeakatemian Toimituksia; Annales Academiae Scientiarum Fennicae 102.2. Helsinki: Akateeminen Kirjakauppa, 1956.

Kroll, Josef. *Gott und Hölle: Der Mythos vom Descensuskampfe.* Studien der Bibliothek Warburg 20. Leipzig: B. G. Teubner, 1932.

Kunkel, Wolfgang. *An Introduction to Roman Legal and Constitutional History.* Translated by J. M. Kelly. Oxford: Clarendon Press, 1966.

Leon, Harry J. *The Jews of Ancient Rome.* The Morris Loeb Series 5. Philadelphia: The Jewish Publication Society of America, 1960.

Lewis, Naphtali, and Meyer Reinhold, ed. *Roman Civilization.* 2 Vols. New York: Harper and Row, 1951.

Lohse, Eduard. *History of the Suffering and Death of Jesus Christ.* Translated by Martin O. Dietrich. Philadelphia: Fortress Press, 1967.

_____. *Märtyrer und Gottesknecht.* Forschungen zur Religion und Literatur des Alten und Neuen Testaments 64. Göttingen: Vandenhoeck & Ruprecht, 1955.

Lundberg, Per. *La typologie baptismale dans l'ancienne église.* Leipzig: Alfred Lorentz, 1942.

Lyall, Francis. *Slaves, Citizens, Sons: Legal Metaphors in the Epistles.* Grand Rapids: Zondervan 1984.

Maier, Johann and Josef Schreiner, ed. *Literatur und Religion des Frühjudentums: Eine Einführung.* Würzburg: Echter Verlag, 1973.

Malherbe, Abraham J. *Moral Exhortation: A Greco-Roman Sourcebook.* Library of Early Christianity. Philadelphia: The Westminster Press, 1986.

Malherbe, Abraham J. *Paul and the Thessalonians*. Philadelphia: Fortress Press, 1987.

_____. *Social Aspects of Early Christianity*. 2d ed. Baton Rouge: Louisiana State University Press, 1977.

Maurach, Gregor. *Der Bau von Senecas Epistulae Morales*. Bibliothek der klassischen Altertumswissenschaft 2.30. Heidelberg: Carl Winter, 1970.

Mayerhoff, Ernst Theodor. *Historisch-critische Einleitung in die petrinischen Schriften*. Hamburg: Friedrich Perthes, 1835.

McKelvey, R. J. *The New Temple: The Church in the New Testament*. Oxford Theological Monographs. Oxford: Oxford University Press, 1969.

Meeks, Wayne A. *The First Urban Christians*. New Haven: Yale University Press, 1983.

_____. *The Moral World of the First Christians*. Library of Early Christianity. Philadelphia: The Westminster Press, 1986.

Michael V. Fox, ed. *Temple in Society*. Winona Lake, Indiana: Eisenbrauns, 1988.

Michel, Otto. *Prophet und Märtyrer*. Beiträge zur Förderung christlicher Theologie 37.2. Gütersloh: C. Bertelsmann, 1932.

Minear, Paul S. *Images of the Church in the New Testament*. Philadelphia: The Westminster Press, 1960.

Moore, George Foot. *Judaism*. 3 Vols. Cambridge: Harvard University Press, 1927.

Moreau, Jacques. *Die Christenverfolgung im römischen Reich*. Aus der Welt der Religion N. F. 2. Berlin: Alfred Töpelmann, 1961.

Motto, Anna Lydia. *Seneca: Moral Epistles*. American Philological Association: Textbook Series 8. Chico, California: Scholars Press, 1985.

Mowinckel, Sigmund. *He That Cometh*. Translated by G. W. Anderson. Nashville: Abingdon Press, 1954.

Mußner, Franz. *Theologie der Freiheit nach Paulus*. Quaestiones Disputatae 75. Freiburg: Herder, 1976.

Munro, W. *Authority in Paul and Peter: The Identification of a Pastoral Stratum in the Pauline Corpus and 1 Peter*. New Testament Studies Monograph Series 45. Cambridge: Cambridge University Press.

Neill, Stephen. *The Interpretation of the New Testament 1861-1961*. London: Oxford University Press, 1964.

Nestle, Dieter. *Eleutheria*. Vol. 1: *Die Griechen*. Hermeneutische Untersuchungen zur Theologie. Tübingen: J. C. B. Mohr (Paul Siebeck), 1967.

Nieder, Lorenz. *Die Motive der religiös-sittlichen Paränese in den paulinischen Gemeindebriefen*. Münchener theologische Studien 12. München: Karl Zink, 1956.

Niederwimmer, Kurt. *Askese und Mysterium: Über Ehe, Ehescheidung und Eheverzicht in den Aufängen des christlichen Glaubens*. Forschungen zur Religion und Literatur des Alten und Neuen Testaments 113. Göttingen: Vandenhoeck & Ruprecht, 1975.

_____. *Der Begriff der Freiheit im Neuen Testament*. Theologische Bibliothek Töpelmann 11. Berlin: Töpelmann, 1966.

North, Christopher R. *The Suffering Servant in Deutero-Isaiah*. London: Oxford University Press, 1948.

Perdelwitz, Richard. *Die Mysterienreligion und das Problem des 1 Petrusbriefes*. Gießen: Alfred Töpelmann, 1911.

Perrot, Charles, ed. *Études sur la Première Lettre de Pierre*. Lectio Divina 102. Paris: Cerf, 1980.

Peter Hermann. *Der Brief in der römischen Litteratur*. Leipzig: B. G. Teubner, 1901.

Peterson, Erik. *Zeuge der Wahrheit*. Leipzig: Jakob Hegner, 1937.

Pfammatter, Josef. *Die Kirche als Bau*. Analecta Gregoriana 110. Rome: Gregorian Pontifical University, 1960.

Preisker, Herbert. *Das Ethos des Urchristentums*. Gütersloh: C. Bertelsmann, 1949.

Radin, Max. *The Jews among the Greeks and Romans*. Philadelphia: The Jewish Publication Society of America, 1915.

Reicke, Bo. *The Disobedient Spirits and Christian Baptism*. Acta Seminarii Neotestamentici Upsaliensis 13. Kopenhagen: Einar Munksgaard, 1946.

Rendtorff, Heinrich. *Getrostes Wandern: Eine Einführung in den ersten Brief des Petrus*. 7th ed. Die urchristliche Botschaft 20. Hamburg: Furche-Verlag, 1951.

Rengstorf, Karl H. *Mann und Frau im Urchristentum*. Köln: Westdeutscher Verlag, 1954.

Rigaux, Beda. *The Letters of St. Paul*. Translated by Stephen Yonick. Chicago: Franciscan Herald Press, 1968.

Roth, Cecil. *The Historical Background of the Dead Sea Scrolls*. Oxford: Basil Blackwell, 1958.

Safrai, S. and M. Stern, ed. *The Jewish People in the First Century*. 2 Vols. Compendia rerum Iudaicarum ad Novum Testamentum. Philadelphia: Fortress Press, 1976.

Sander, Emilie T. "ΠΥΡΩΣΙΣ and the First Epistle of Peter 4:12." Th.D. dissertation, Harvard University, 1966.

Sanders, E. P. *Jesus and Judaism*. Philadelphia: Fortress Press, 1985.

_____. *Paul and Palestinian Judaism*. Philadelphia: Fortress Press, 1977.

Sanders, Jack T. *The New Testament Christological Hymns: Their Historical Religions Background*. Society for New Testament Studies Monograph Series 15. Cambridge: Cambridge University Press, 1971.

Sanders, Jim Alvin. *Suffering as Divine Discipline in the Old Testament and Post-Biblical Judaism*. Colgate Rochester Divinity Bulletin 28. Rochester, New York: Colgate Rochester Divinity School, 1955.

Scharfe, Ernst. *Die petrinische Strömung der neutestamentlichen Literatur*. Berlin: Reuther & Reichard, 1893.

Schille, Gottfried. *Frühchristliche Hymnen*. Berlin: Evangelische Verlagsanstalt, 1965.

Schlatter, Adolf. *Petrus und Paulus nach dem ersten Petrusbrief.* Stuttgart: Calwer Vereinsbuchhandlung, 1937.

Schmidt, David Henry. "The Peter Writings: Their Redactors and Their Relationships." Ph.D. dissertation, Northwestern University; Evanston, Illinois, 1972.

Schnider, Franz and Werner Stenger. *Studien zum neutestamentlichen Briefformular.* New Testament Tools and Studies 11. Leiden: E. J. Brill, 1987.

Schoeps, Hans Joachim. *Aus Frühchristlicher Zeit: Religionsgeschichtliche Untersuchungen.* Tübingen: J. C. B. Mohr (Paul Siebeck), 1950.

_____. *Paul.* Translated by Harold Knight. Philadelphia: The Westminster Press, 1961.

Schrage, Wolfgang. *Die konkreten Einzelgebote in der paulinischen Paränese.* Gütersloh: Gerd Mohn, 1961.

Schubert, Paul. *The Form and Function of the Pauline Thanksgiving.* Beihefte zur Zeitschrift für die neutestamentliche Wissenschaft 20. Berlin: Alfred Töpelmann, 1939.

Schulze, Johann Daniel. *Der schriftstellerische Charakter und Werth des Petrus, Judas, und Jakobus zum Behuf der Specialhermeneutik ihrer Schriften.* Weißenfels: Böseschen Buchhandlung, 1802.

Schutter, William L. *Hermeneutic and Composition in 1 Peter.* Wissenschaftliche Untersuchungen zum Neuen Testament 2.30. Tübingen: J. C. B. Mohr (Paul Siebeck), 1989.

Schürer, Emil. *The History of the Jewish People in the Age of Jesus Christ (175 B.C.-A.D. 135).* Edited and translated by Geza Vermes, Fergus Millar, and Martin Goodman. 3 Vols. Edinburgh: T. & T. Clark, 1986.

Seeberg, Alfred. *Der Katechismus der Urchristenheit.* Leipzig: A. Deichert, 1903.

Shimada, Kazuhito. "The Formulary Material in First Peter: A Study According to the Method of *Traditionsgeschichte.*" Ph.D. dissertation, Union Theological Seminary, 1966.

Smallwood, E. Mary. *The Jews under Roman Rule from Pompey to Diocletian.* Studies in Judaism in Late Antiquity 20. Leiden: E. J. Brill, 1981.

Spitta, Friedrich. *Christi Predigt an die Geister.* Göttingen: Vandenhoeck & Ruprecht, 1890.

Spörri, Theophil. *Der Gemeindegedanke im ersten Petrusbrief.* Neutestamentliche Forschungen 2. Gütersloh: C. Bertelsmann, 1925.

Stamm, Johann Jakob. *Das Leiden des Unschuldigen in Babylon und Israel.* Abhandlungen zur Theologie des Alten und Neuen Testaments 10. Zürich: Zwingli, 1946.

Stanford, W. Bedell. *Greek Metaphor: Studies in Theory and Practice.* Oxford: Basil Blackwell, 1936.

Stauffer, Ethelbert. *New Testament Theology.* Translated by John Marsh. London: SCM Press, 1955.

Stowers, Stanley K. *Letter Writing in Greco-Roman Antiquity.* Library of Early Christianity. Philadelphia: The Westminster Press, 1986.

Streeter, Burnett Hillman. *The Primitive Church.* New York: The Macmillan Co., 1929.

Surkau, Hans Werner. *Martyrien in jüdischer und frühchristlicher Zeit.* Göttingen: Vandenhoeck & Ruprecht, 1938.

Sutcliffe, Edmund. *Providence and Suffering in the Old and New Testaments.* London: Thomas Nelson, 1953.

Tcherikover, Victor. *Hellenistic Civilization and the Jews.* Translated by Simon Applebaum. New York: Atheneum, 1985.

Thiele, Walter. *Die lateinischen Texte des 1. Petrusbriefes.* Vetus Latina: Aus der Geschichte der lateinischen Bibel 5. Freiburg: Herder, 1965.

Thraede, Klaus. *Grundzüge griechisch-römischer Brieftopik.* Zetemata 48. München: C. H. Beck, 1970.

Vanhoye, Albert. *La structure littéraire de l'Épitre aux Hébreux.* Studia Neotestamentica 1. Paris: Desclée de Brouwer, 1962.

Verner, David C. *The Household of God.* Society of Biblical Literature Dissertation Series 71. Chico, California: Scholars Press, 1983.

Vielhauer, Philipp. *Oikodome.* Theologische Bücherei 65. München: Kaiser, 1979.

Vollenweider, Samuel. *Freiheit als neue Schöpfung: eine Untersuchung zur Eleutheria bei Paulus und in seiner Umwelt.* Forschungen zur Religion und Literatur des Alten und Neuen Testaments 147. Göttingen: Vandenhoeck & Ruprecht, 1989.

Vögtle, Anton. *Die Tugend- und Lasterkataloge im Neuen Testament.* Neutestamentliche Abhandlungen 16. Münster: Aschendorff, 1936.

Völter, Daniel. *Der erste Petrusbrief: seine Entstehung und Stellung in der Geschichte des Urchristentumes.* Strassburg: Heitz & Mündel, 1906.

Weidinger, Karl. *Die Haustafeln: Ein Stück urchristlicher Paraenese.* Untersuchungen zum Neuen Testament 14. Leipzig: J. C. Heinrich, 1928.

Weinrich, Harald. *Sprache in Texten.* Stuttgart: Klett, 1976.

Weiss, Bernhard. *Der erste Petrusbrief und die neuere Kritik.* Biblische Zeit- und Streitfragen 2.9. Berlin: Edwin Runge, 1906.

_____. *Der petrinische Lehrbegriff.* Berlin: Wilhelm Schultze, 1885.

White, John L. *Light from Ancient Letters.* Foundations and Facets: New Testament. Philadelphia: Fortress Press, 1986.

_____. *The Form and Function of the Body of the Greek Letter.* Society of Biblical Literature Dissertation Series 2. Missoula, Montana: Scholars Press, 1972.

Wibbing, Siegfried. *Die Tugend- und Lasterkataloge im Neuen Testament.* Beihefte zur Zeitschrift für die neutestamentliche Wissenschaft 25. Berlin: Alfred Töpelmann, 1959.

Wiles, Gordon P. *Paul's Intercessory Prayers.* Cambridge: Cambridge University Press, 1974.

Yadin, Yigael. *Bar-Kokhba.* New York: Random House, 1971.

_____. *The Message of the Scrolls.* New York: Simon and Schuster, 1957.

Yadin, Yigael. *The Temple Scroll.* New York: Random House, 1985.

Zeitlin, Solomon. *Studies in the Early History of Judaism.* 3 Vols. New York: KTAV
Publishing House, 1973.

Articles

Aalen, Sverre. "Honor." *The New International Dictionary of New Testament Theology.*
Edited by Colin Brown. Vol. 2: *G-Pre*, 44-52. Grand Rapids: Zondervan
Publishing House, 1975.

Achtemeier, E. R. "Righteousness in the OT." *The Interpreter's Dictionary of the Bible.*
Edited by George Arthur Buttrick. Vol. 4: *R-Z*, 80-85. Nashville: Abingdon,
1962.

Achtemeier, P. J. "Righteousness in the NT." *The Interpreter's Dictionary of the Bible.*
Edited by George Arthur Buttrick. Vol. 4: *R-Z*, 91-99. Nashville: Abingdon,
1962.

Applebaum, Shimon. "The Zealots: The Case for Revaluation." *Journal of Roman
Studies* 61 (1971): 155-170.

Bahr, Gordon J. "Paul and Letter Writing in the First Century." *Catholic Biblical
Quarterly* 28 (1966): 465-477.

Balch, David L. "Hellenization/Acculturation in 1 Peter." In *Perspectives on First Peter.*
Edited by Charles H. Talbert, 79-102. National Association of Baptist Professors
of Religion: Special Studies Series 9. Macon, Georgia: Mercer University Press,
1986.

_____. "Household Codes." In *Greco-Roman Literature and the New Testament:
Selected Forms and Genres.* Edited by David E. Aune, 25-50. ·Society of Biblical
Literature Sources for Biblical Study 21. Atlanta, Georgia: Scholars Press, 1988.

Balla, E. "Das Problem des Leides in der Geschichte der israelitisch-jüdischen Religion."
*In EYXAPIΣTHPION: Studien zur Religion und Literatur des Alten und Neuen
Testaments.* Edited by Hans Schmidt, 214-260. Vol. 1: *Zur Religion und Literatur
des Alten Testaments.* Forschungen zur Religion und Literatur des Alten und
Neuen Testaments 36. Göttingen: Vandenhoeck & Ruprecht, 1923.

Bammel, Ernst. "The Commands in 1 Peter 2:17." *New Testament Studies* 11 (1964): 279-281.

Bauer, F. C. "Der erste petrinische Brief." *Theologische Jahrbücher* (1856): 193-240.

Bauernfeind, Otto. "Πόλεμος." *Theological Dictionary of the New Testament*. Edited by Gerhard Friedrich. Vol. 6: Πε–Ρ, 502-515. Grand Rapids: Wm. B. Eerdmans Publishing Co., 1968.

Beare, Francis W. "The Teaching of First Peter." *Anglican Theological Review* 27 (1945): 284-296.

Beck, Brian E. "Imitatio Christi and the Lucan Passion Narrative." In *Suffering and Martyrdom in the New Testament* (Studies Presented to G. M. Styler). Edited by William Horbury and Brian McNeil, 28-47. Cambridge: Cambridge University Press, 1981.

Berger, Klaus, "Hellenistische Gattungen im Neuen Testament." *Aufstieg und Niedergang der römischen Welt* 25.2 (1984): 1033-1431.

_____. "Apostelbrief und apostolische Rede: Zum Formular frühchristlicher Briefe." *Zeitschrift für die neutestamentliche Wissenschaft* 65 (1974): 190-231.

Bertram, Georg. "Στρέφω." *Theological Dictionary of the New Testament*. Edited by Gerhard Friedrich. Vol. 7: Σ, 714-729. Grand Rapids: Wm. B. Eerdmans Publishing Co., 1971.

Best, Ernest. "1 Peter and the Gospel Tradition." *New Testament Studies* 16 (1970): 95-113.

_____. "1 Peter II.4-10: A Reconsideration." *Novum Testamentum* 11 (1969): 270-293.

_____. "Spiritual Sacrifice. General Priesthood in the New Testament." *Interpretation* 14 (1960): 273-299.

Betz, Hans Dieter. "2 Cor 6:14-7:1: An Anti-Pauline Fragment?" *Journal of Biblical Literature* 92 (1973): 88-108.

_____. "Das Problem der Grundlagen der paulinischen Ethik." *Zeitschrift für Theologie und Kirche* 85 (1988): 199-218.

Betz, Hans Dieter. "De fraterno amore (Moralia 478a-492d)." In idem, ed., *Plutarch's Ethical Writings and Early Christian Literature*, 106-134. Studia ad corpus hellenisticum Novi Testamenti 4. Leiden: E. J. Brill, 1978.

————. "Introduction." In idem, ed., *Plutarch's Ethical Writings and Early Christian Literature*, 1-10. Studia ad corpus hellenisticum Novi Testamenti 4. Leiden: E. J. Brill, 1978.

————. "The Problem of Apocalyptic Genre in Greek and Hellenistic Literature: The Case of the Oracle of Trophonius." In *Apocalypticism in the Mediterranean World and the Near East*. Edited by David Hellholm, 577-598. Proceedings of the International Colloquium on Apocalypticism. Tübingen: J. C. B. Mohr (Paul Siebeck), 1983.

Betz, Otto. "Felsenmann und Felsengemeinde." *Zeitschrift für die neutestamentliche Wissenschaft* 48 (1957): 49-77.

Bieder, Werner. "Grund und Kraft der Mission nach dem I. Petrusbrief." *Theologische Studien* 29 (1950): 1-30.

Bishop, Eric F. F. "*Oligoi* in 1 Pet. 3:20." *The Catholic Biblical Quarterly* 13 (1951): 44-45.

Blunck, J. "Freedom." *New International Dictionary of New Testament Theology*. Edited by Colin Brown. Vol. 1: *A-F*, 715-720. Grand Rapids: Zondervan Publishing House, 1975.

Boers, Hendrikus. "The Form Critical Study of Paul's Letters: 1 Thessalonians as a Case Study." *New Testament Studies* 22 (1976): 140-158.

Boismard, M. E. "La typologie baptismale dans la Première Épître de Saint Pierre." *La Vie Spirituelle* 94 (1956): 339-352.

————. "Pierre (Première Épître de)." *Dictionnaire de la Bible*. Edited by Louis Pirot. Supplément 7: *Pastorales-Pirot*, 1415-1455. Paris: Letouzey & Ané, 1966.

————. "Une liturgie baptismale dans la Prima Petri." *Revue Biblique* 63 (1956): 182-208; 64 (1957): 161-183.

Boobyer, G. H. "The Indebtedness of 2 Peter to 1 Peter." In *New Testament Essays* (Studies in Memory of Thomas Walter Manson). Edited by Angus J. B. Higgins, 34-53. Manchester: Manchester University Press, 1959.

Bornemann, W. "Der erste Petrusbrief: Eine Taufrede des Silvanus?" *Zeitschrift für die neutestamentliche Wissenschaft* 19 (1920): 143-165.

Bradley, David G. "The Origins of the Hortatory Material in the Letters of Paul." Ph.D. dissertation, Yale University, 1947.

_____. "The Topos as a Form in the Pauline Paraenesis." *Journal of Biblical Literature* 72 (1953): 238-246.

Brandon, Samuel G. F. "Zealots." *Encyclopaedia Judaica*. Vol. 16: *Ur-Z*, 947-950. New York: The Macmillan Co., 1972.

Brandt, Wilhelm. "Wandel als Zeugnis nach dem 1. Petrusbrief." In *Verbum Dei manet in aeternum* (Festschrift für Otto Schmitz). Edited by Werner Foerster, 10-25. Witten: Luther-Verlag, 1953.

Brinkmann, A. "Der älteste Briefsteller." *Rheinisches Museum für Philologie* 64 (1909): 310-317.

Brooks, Oscar S. "1 Peter 3:21--The Clue to the Literary Structure of the Epistle." *Novum Testamentum* 16 (1974): 290-305.

Brown, John Pairman. "Synoptic Parallels in the Epistles and Form-History." *New Testament Studies* 10 (1963-1964): 27-48.

Brox, Norbert. "Zur pseudepigraphischen Rahmung des ersten Petrusbriefes." *Biblische Zeitschrift* N. F. 19 (1975): 78-96.

Brunt, John C. "More on the *Topos* as a New Testament Form." *Journal of Biblical Literature* 104 (1985): 495-500.

Bultmann, Rudolf. "Bekenntnis- und Liedfragmente im ersten Petrusbrief." *Coniectanea Neotestamentica* 11 (1947): 1-14; reprint, *Exegetica*. Edited by Erich Dinkler, 285-297. Tübingen: J. C. B. Mohr (Paul Siebeck), 1967.

Bultmann, Rudolf. "Das Problem der Ethik bei Paulus." *Zeitschrift für die neutestamentliche Wissenschaft* 23 (1924): 123-140; reprint, *Exegetica*. Edited by Erich Dinkler, 36-54. Tübingen: J. C. B. Mohr (Paul Siebeck), 1967.

Buss, Martin J. "Principles for Morphological Criticism: With Special Reference to Letter Form." In *Orientation by Disorientation* (Studies Presented in Honor of William A. Beardslee). Edited by Richard A. Spencer, 71-86. Pittsburgh Theological Monograph Series 35. Pittsburgh: The Pickwick Press, 1980.

Carrington, Philip. "Saint Peter's Epistle." In *The Joy of Study* (Papers Presented to Honor F. C. Grant). Edited by Sherman E. Johnson, 57-63. New York: The Macmillan Co., 1951.

Cerfaux, Lucien. "Regale sacerdotum." In *Recueil Lucien Cerfaux* 2, 283-315. Bibliotheca Ephemeridum Theologicarum Lovaniensium 7. Gembloux: J. Duculot, 1954.

Chevallier, Max-Alain. "1 Pierre 1/1 à 2/10: Structure littéraire et conséquences exégétiques." *Revue d'histoire et de philosophie religieuses* 51 (1971): 129-142.

Combrink, H. J. B. "The Structure of 1 Peter." *Neotestamentica* 9 (1975): 34-63.

Conley, T. "Philo's Use of Topoi." In *Two Treatises of Philo of Alexandria.* Edited by David Winston and John Dillon, 171-178. Brown Judaic Studies 25. Chico, California: Scholars Press, 1983.

Cothenet, Édouard. "Les orientations actuelles de l'exégèse de la Première Lettre de Pierre." In *Études sur la Première Lettre de Pierre.* Edited by Charles Perrot, 13-42. Lectio Divina 102. Paris: Cerf, 1980.

Coutts, J. "Ephesians I. 13-14 and I Peter I. 3-12. *New Testament Studies* 8 (1956-57): 115-127.

Cranfield, C. E. B. "The Interpretation of I Peter iii. 19 and iv. 6." *The Expository Times* 69 (1958): 369-372.

Cronbach, Abraham. "Righteousness in the OT." *The Interpreter's Dictionary of the Bible.* Edited by George Arthur Buttrick. Vol. 4: *R-Z*, 85-91. Nashville: Abingdon Press, 1962.

Dahl, Nils A. "Adresse und Proömium des Epheserbriefes." *Theologische Zeitschrift* 7 (1951): 241-264.

_____. "Das Volk Gottes." *Skrifter utgitt av det norske Videnskaps-Akademi* 1.2 (1941): 1-351; reprint, Darmstadt: Wissenschaftliche Buchgesellschaft, 1963.

Dalton, W. J. "Interpretation and Tradition: An Example from 1 Peter." *Gregorianum* 49 (1968): 11-37.

Danker, F. W. "1 Peter 1,24-2,17: A Consolatory Pericope." *Zeitschrift für die neutestamentliche Wissenschaft* 58 (1967): 93-102.

Daube, David. "Κερδαίνω as a Missionary Term." *Harvard Theological Review* 40 (1947): 109-120.

_____. "Participle and Imperative in 1 Peter." In E. G. Selwyn, *The First Epistle of Saint Peter*, 467-471. Thornapple Commentaries. Grand Rapids: Baker Book House, 1981.

Dautzenberg, Gerhard. "Σωτηρία ψυχῶν (1 Petr 1,9)." *Biblische Zeitschrift* 8 (1964): 262-276.

Davies, Paul E. "Primitive Christianity in 1 Peter." In *Festschrift to Honor F. Wilbur Gingrich*. Edited by Eugene H. Barth and Ronald E. Cocroft, 115-122. Leiden: E. J. Brill, 1972.

Delling, Gerhard. "Der Bezug der christlichen Existenz auf das Heilshandeln Gottes nach dem ersten Petrusbrief." In *Neues Testament und christliche Existenz* (Festschrift für Herbert Braun). Edited by Hans Dieter Betz and Luise Schottroff, 95-113. Tübingen: J. C. B. Mohr, 1973.

Dijkman, J. H. L. "1 Peter: A Later Pastoral Stratum?" *New Testament Studies* 33 (1987): 265-271.

Dinkler, Erich. "Die Petrus-Rom-Frage." *Theologische Rundschau* N. F. 25 (1959): 189-230; 27 (1961): 33-64.

_____. "Die Taufaussagen des Neuen Testaments." In *Zu Karl Barths Lehre von der Taufe*. Edited by Fritz Viering. Gütersloh: Gerd Mohn, 1971.

Donfried, Karl P. "False Presuppositions in the Study of Romans," *Catholic Biblical Quarterly* 36 (1974): 332-355; reprint, *The Romans Debate*. Edited by idem, 120-148. Minneapolis, Minnesota: Augsburg Publishing House, 1977.

Doty, William G. "The Classification of Epistolary Literature." *Catholic Biblical Quarterly* 31 (1969): 183-199.

_____. "The Concept of Genre in Literary Analysis." In *Society of Biblical Literature Seminar Papers* 2. Edited by Lane C. McGaughy, 413-448. Atlanta, Georgia: Scholars Press, 1972.

Elliott, J. K. "The Language and Style of the Concluding Doxology to the Epistle to the Romans." *Zeitschrift für die neutestamentliche Wissenschaft* 72 (1981): 124-130.

Elliott, John H. "1 Peter, Its Situation and Strategy: A Discussion with David Balch." In *Perspectives on First Peter*. Edited by Charles H. Talbert, 61-78. National Association of Baptist Professors of Religion: Special Studies Series 9. Macon, Georgia: Mercer University Press, 1986.

_____. "Ministry and Church Order in the N.T.: A Traditio-Historical Analysis." *The Catholic Biblical Quarterly* 32 (1970): 367-391.

_____. "The Rehabilitation of an Exegetical Step-Child: 1 Peter in Recent Research." *Journal of Biblical Literature* 95 (1976): 243-254.

Ellis, Earl. E. "II Corinthians V.1-10 in Pauline Eschatology." *New Testament Studies*. 6 (1960): 211-224.

Erbes, K. "Was bedeutet ἀλλοτριοεπίσκοπος 1 Pt 4,15?" *Zeitschrift für die neutestamentliche Wissenschaft* 19 (1920): 39-44.

Fascher, E. "Fremder." *Reallexikon für Antike und Christentum*. Edited by Theodor Klauser. Vol. 8: *Fluchtafel-Gebet I*, 306-347. Stuttgart: Anton Hiersemann, 1972.

Ferguson, Everett. "Spiritual Sacrifice in Early Christianity and Its Environment." *Aufstieg und Niedergang der römischen Welt* 23.2 (1980): 1151-1189.

Feuillet, André. "Les *sacrifices spirituels* du sacerdoce royal des baptisés (1 P 2,5)." *Nouvelle Revue Théologique* 96 (1974): 704-728.

Filson, Floyd, V. "Partakers With Christ: Suffering in I Peter." *Interpretation* 9 (1955): 400-412.

Fiorenza, Elisabeth Schüssler. "Cultic Language in Qumran and in the N.T." *Catholic Biblical Quarterly* 38 (1976): 159-177.

_____. "The Phenomenon of Early Christian Apocalyptic: Some Reflections on Method." In *Apocalypticism in the Mediterranean World and the Near East*. Edited by David Hellholm, 295-316. Proceedings of the International Colloquium on Apocalypticism. Tübingen: J. C. B. Mohr (Paul Siebeck), 1983.

Fitzmyer, Joseph A. "Some Notes on Aramaic Epistolography." *Journal of Biblical Literature* 93 (1974): 201-225.

Francis, Fred O. "The Form and Function of the Opening and Closing Paragraphs of James and 1 John." *Zeitschrift für die neutestamentliche Wissenschaft* 61 (1970): 110-126.

Friedrich, Gerhard. "Lohmeyers These über das paulinische Briefpräskript kritisch beleuchtet." *Theologische Literaturzeitung* 81 (1956): 343-346.

Funk, Robert W. "The Apostolic *Parousia*: Form and Significance." In *Christian History and Interpretation* (Studies Presented to John Knox). Edited by W. R. Farmer, 249-268. Cambridge: Cambridge University Press, 1967.

Gärtner, Burkhard. "Suffer." *The New International Dictionary of New Testament Theology*. Edited by Colin Brown. Vol. 3: *Pri-Z*, 719-726. Grand Rapids: Zondervan, 1979.

Gaudemet, J. "Familie I (Familienrecht)." *Reallexikon für Antike und Christentum*. Edited by Theodor Klauser. Vol, 7, 286-358. Stuttgart: Anton Hiersemann, 1969.

Gerhard, Gustav Adolf. "Untersuchungen zur Geschichte des griechischen Briefes 1." *Philologus* 64 (1905): 27-65.

Goetzmann, J. "House." *The New International Dictionary of New Testament Theology*. Edited by Colin Brown. Vol. 2: *G-Pre*, 247-256. Grand Rapids: Zondervan Publishing House, 1971.

Goldstein, Horst. "Die politischen Paränesen in 1 Petr 2 und Röm 13." *Bibel und Leben* 14 (1973): 88-104.

Goppelt, Leonhard. "Jesus und die, 'Haustafel'-Tradition." In *Orientierung an Jesus,* (Festschrift für Josef Schmid). Edited by Paul Hoffmann, 93-106. Freiburg: Herder, 1973.

Grundmann, Walter. "Δῆμος." *Theological Dictionary of the New Testament.* Edited by Gerhard Kittel. Vol. 2: Δ-H, 63-65. Grand Rapids: Wm. B. Eerdmans Publishing Co., 1964.

_____. "Ταπεινός." *Theological Dictionary of the New Testament.* Edited by Gerhard Friedrich. Vol. 8: T-Υ, 1-26. Grand Rapids: Wm. B. Eerdmans Publishing Co., 1972.

Gundry, Robert H. "'*Verba Christi*' in I Peter: Their Implications Concerning the Authorship of I Peter and the Authenticity of the Gospel Tradition." *New Testament Studies* 13 (1967): 336-350.

_____. "Further *Verba* on *Verba Christi* in First Peter." *Biblica* 55 (1974): 211-232.

Günther, Ernst. "Zeuge und Märtyrer." *Zeitschrift für die neutestamentliche Wissenschaft* 47 (1956): 145-161.

Hahn, Ferdinand. "Die christologische Begründung urchristlicher Paränese." *Zeitschrift für die neutestamentliche Wissenschaft* 72 (1981): 88-99.

Haran, Menahem. "Temple and Community in Ancient Israel." In *Temple in Society.* Edited by Michael Fox, 17-26. Winona Lake, Indiana: Eisenbrauns, 1988.

Harris, J. Rendel. "The Influence of Philo upon the New Testament." *Expository Times* 37 (1926): 565-566.

Hauck, Friedrich. "Κοινός." *Theological Dictionary of the New Testament.* Edited by Gerhard Kittel. Vol. 3: Θ-K, 789-809 Grand Rapids: Wm. B. Eerdmans Publishing Co., 1965.

Hill, David. "On Suffering and Baptism in I Peter." *Novum Testamentum* 18 (1976): 181-189.

Hill, David. "To Offer Spiritual Sacrifices (1 Peter 2:5): Liturgical Formulations and Christian Paraenesis in 1 Peter." *Journal for the Study of the New Testament* 16 (1982): 45-63.

Hiltbrunner, Otto, D. Gorce, and H. Wehr. "Gastfreundschaft." *Reallexikon für Antike und Christentum.* Edited by Theodor Klauser. Vol. 8: *Fluchtafel-Gebet I,* 1061-1123. Stuttgart: Anton Hiersemann, 1972.

Humphreys, W. Lee. "A Life-Style for Diaspora: A Study of the Tales of Esther and Daniel." *Journal of Biblical Literature* 92 (1973): 211-223.

Hunzinger, Claus-Hunno. "Babylon als Deckname für Rom und die Datierung des 1. Petrusbriefes." In *Gottes Wort und Gottes Land* (Festschrift für Hans-Wilhelm Hertzberg). Edited by Henning Graf Reventlow, 67-77. Göttingen: Vandenhoeck & Ruprecht, 1965.

_____. "Zur Struktur der Christus-Hymnen in Phil 2 und 1. Petr 3." In *Der Ruf Jesu und die Antwort der Gemeinde* (Festschrift für Joachim Jeremias). Edited by Eduard Lohse, 142-156. Göttingen: Vandenhoeck & Ruprecht, 1970.

Jeremias, Joachim. "Ποιμήν." *Theological Dictionary of the New Testament.* Edited by Gerhard Friedrich. Vol. 6: *Πε–Ρ,* 485-501. Grand Rapids: Wm. B. Eerdmans Publishing Co., 1968.

_____. "Zwischen Karfreitag und Ostern: Descensus und Ascensus in der Karfreitagstheologie des Neuen Testaments." *Zeitschrift für die neutestamentliche Wissenschaft* 42 (1949): 194-201.

Johnson, Sherman E. "The Preaching to the Dead." *Journal of Biblical Literature* 79 (1960): 48-51.

Jonsen, Albert R. "The Moral Theology of the First Epistle of St. Peter." *Sciences Ecclésiastiques* 16 (1964): 93-105.

Jowett, Robert. "The Form and Function of the Homiletic Benediction." *Anglican Theological Review* 51 (1969): 18-34.

Kamlah, Ehrhard. " ϓΠΟΤΑΣΣΕΣΘΑΙ in den neutestamentlichen Haustafeln." In
Verborum Veritas (Festschrift für Gustav Stählin). Edited by Otto Böcher und
Klaus Haacker, 237-243. Wuppertal: Theologischer Verlag Rolf Brockhaus,
1970.

Katz, Albert. "Norms for 204 Literary and 260 Nonliterary Metaphors on 10
Psychological Dimensions." Metaphor and Symbolic Activity 3 (1988): 191-214.

Kendall, David W. "The Literary and Theological Function of 1 Peter 1:3-12." In
Perspectives on First Peter. Edited by Charles H. Talbert, 103-120. National
Association of Baptist Professors of Religion: Special Studies Series 9.
Macon, Georgia: Mercer University Press, 1986.

Ketter, Peter. "Das allgemeine Priestertum der Gläubigen nach dem ersten Petrusbrief."
Trierer Theologische Zeitschrift 56 (1947): 43-51.

Keyes, Clinton W. "The Greek Letter of Introduction." American Journal of Philology 56
(1935): 28-44.

Kittel, Gerhard. "Δοκέω." Theological Dictionary of the New Testament. Edited by idem.
Vol. 2: Δ-Η, 232-254 Grand Rapids: Wm. B. Eerdmans Publishing Co., 1964.

Knox, John. "Pliny and I Peter: A Note on I Pet 4:14-16 and 3:15." Journal of Biblical
Literature 72 (1953): 187-189.

Koester, Helmut. "1 Thessalonians: Experiment in Christian Writing." In Continuity and
Discontinuity in Church History (Essays Presented to George Hunston Williams).
Edited by F Forrester Church and Timothy George, 33-44. Studies in the History
of Christian Thought 19. Leiden: E. J. Brill, 1979.

Kohler, Kaufmann. "Zealots." The Jewish Encyclopedia. Vol. 12: Talmud-Zweifel, 639-
644. New York: KTAV Publishing House, Inc., 1906.

Koskenniemi, Heikki. "Cicero über die Briefarten." Arctos N. S. 1 (1954): 97-102.

Kraft, Eva. "Christologie und Anthropologie im 1. Petrusbrief." Evangelische Theologie
10 (1950/51): 120-126.

Kübler, B. "Peregrinus." *Paulys Real-Encyclopädie der classischen Altertumswissenschaft.* Edited by Wilhelm Kroll. Vol. 19: *Pech-Petronius,* 639-655. Stuttgart: J. B. Metzler, 1937.

Kuss, Otto. "Zur paulinischen und nachpaulinischen Tauflehre im Neuen Testament." In *Auslegung und Verkündigung I.* Edited by Otto Kuss, 121-150. Regensburg: Friedrich Pustet, 1963.

Lampe, G. W. H. "Martyrdom and Inspiration." In *Suffering and Martyrdom in the New Testament* (Studies Presented to G. M. Styler). Edited by William Horbury and Brian McNeil, 118-135. Cambridge: Cambridge University Press, 1981.

Lau, F. "Diaspora." *Die Religion in Geschichte und Gegenwart.* Vol. 2: *D-G,* 174-180. Tübingen: J. C. B. Mohr (Paul Siebeck), 1958.

LaVerdiere, Eugene A. "A Grammatical Ambiguity in 1 Pet 1:23." *Catholic Biblical Quarterly* 36 (1974): 89-94.

Légasse, S. "La soumission aux autorités d'après 1 Pierre 2. 13-17: Version spécifique d'une parénèse traditionelle." *New Testament Studies* 34 (1988): 378-396.

Lohmeyer, Ernst. "Probleme paulinischer Theologie I: Briefliche Grußüberschriften." *Zeitschrift für die neutestamentliche Wissenschaft* 26 (1927): 158-173.

Lohse, Eduard. "Paränese und Kerygma im 1. Petrusbrief." *Zeitschrift für die neutestamentliche Wissenschaft* 45 (1954): 68-89.

_____. "Parenesis and Kerygma in 1 Peter." Translated by John Steely. In *Perspectives on First Peter.* Edited by Charles H. Talbert, 37-59. National Association of Baptist Professors of Religion: Special Studies Series 9. Macon, Georgia: Mercer University Press, 1986.

Love, Julian Prince. "The First Epistle of Peter." *Interpretation* 8 (1954): 63-87.

Lumpe, A. and H. Karpp. "Eltern." *Reallexikon für Antike und Christentum.* Edited by Theodor Klauser. Vol. 4, 1190-1219. Stuttgart: Anton Hiersemann, 1969.

Lyall, Francis. "Roman Law in the Writings of Paul: Adoption." *Journal of Biblical Literature* 88 (1969): 458-466.

Lyonnet, Stanislas. "Note sur le plan de l'epître aux Romains." *Recherches de science religieuse* 39-40 (1951-1952): 301-316.

Malherbe, Abraham J. "Exhortation in First Thessalonians." *Novum Testamentum* 25 (1983): 238-256.

Manson, T. W. "Review of E. G. Selwyn, The First Epistle of St. Peter." *The Journal of Theological Studies* 47 (1946): 218-227.

Martin, Ralph P. "The Composition of 1 Peter in Recent Study." In idem, ed., *Vox Evangelica: Biblical and Historical Essays*, 29-42. London: Epworth Press, 1962.

McCaughey, J. D. "Three 'Persecution Documents' of the New Testament." *Australian Biblical Review* 17 (1969): 27-40.

McEleney, Neil J. "The Vice Lists of the Pastoral Epistles." *Catholic Biblical Quarterly* 36 (1974): 203-219.

McGuire, Martin R. P. "Letters and Letter Carriers in Christian Antiquity." *The Classical World* 53 (1960): 148-200.

McKay, K. L. "Aspect in Imperatival Constructions in New Testament Greek." *Novum Testamentum* 27 (1985): 201-226.

McKelvey, R. J. "Christ the Cornerstone." *New Testament Studies* 8 (1961): 352-359.

McNicol, Allan J. "The Eschatological Temple in the Qumran Pesher 4QFlorilegium 1:1-7." *Ohio Journal of Religious Studies* 5.2 (1977): 133-141.

Meinhold, Arndt. "Die Gattung der Josephgeschichte und des Estherbuches: Diasporanovelle I." *Zeitschrift für die alttestamentliche Wissenschaft* 87 (1975): 306-324; 88 (1976): 72-93.

Michaelis, Wilhelm. "Πάσχω." *Theological Dictionary of the New Testament*. Edited by Gerhard Kittel. Vol. 5: Ξ-Πα, 904-938. Grand Rapids: Wm. B. Eerdmans Publishing Co., 1968.

Michaels, J. Ramsey. "Eschatology in I Peter III.17." *New Testament Studies* 13 (1966/67): 394-401.

Michaels, J. Ramsey. "Jewish and Christian Apocalyptic Letters: 1 Peter, Revelation, and 2 Baruch 78-87." In *Society of Biblical Literature Seminar Papers* 26. Edited by Kent Harold Richards, 268-275. Atlanta, Georgia: Scholars Press, 1987.

Michel, Otto. "Οἰκοδομέω." *Theological Dictionary of the New Testament*. Edited by Gerhard Friedrich. Vol. 5: Ξ-Πα, 136-144. Grand Rapids: Wm. B. Eerdmans Publishing Co., 1970.

_____. "Leiden im NT." *Die Religion in Geschichte und Gegenwart*. Vol. 4: *Kop-O*, 294-305. Tübingen: J. C. B. Mohr (Paul Siebeck), 1960.

Miller, Donald G. "Deliverance and Destiny. Salvation in I Peter." *Interpretation* 9 (1955): 413-425.

Mitton, C. L. "The Relationship Between 1 Peter and Ephesians." *The Journal of Theological Studies* N.S. 1 (1950): 67-73.

Moule, C. F. D. "Some Reflections on the *Stone* Testimonia in Relation to the Name Peter." *New Testament Studies* 2 (1955): 56-58.

_____. "The Nature and Purpose of 1 Peter." *New Testament Studies* 3 (1956): 1-11.

Mullins, Terence Y. "Disclosure: A Literary Form in the New Testament." *Novum Testamentum* 7 (1964): 44-50.

_____. "Topos as a New Testament Form." *Journal of Biblical Literature* 99 (1980): 541-547.

Nauck, Wolfgang. "Freude im Leiden. Zum Problem einer urchristlichen Verfolgungstradition." *Zeitschrift für die neutestamentliche Wissenschaft* 46 (1955): 68-80.

_____. "Probleme des frühchristlichen Amtsverständnisses (1 Ptr 5:2f.)." *Zeitschrift für die neutestamentliche Wissenschaft* 48 (1957): 200-220.

Nestle, Dieter. "Freiheit." *Reallexikon für Antike und Christentum*. Edited by Theodor Klauser. Vol. 8: *Fluchtafel-Gebet I*, 269-306. Stuttgart: Anton Hiersemann, 1972.

Niederwimmer, Kurt. "Ἐλεύθερος." *Exegetisches Wörterbuch zum Neuen Testament.*
    Edited by Horst Balz and Gerhard Schneider. Vol. 9: Ἀαρων–Ἐνώχ, 1052-1058.
    Stuttgart: Kohlhammer, 1980.

Nixon, R. E. "The Meaning of 'Baptism' in 1 Peter 3, 21." *Texte und Untersuchungen
    zur altchristlichen Literatur* 102 (1968): 437-441.

Oepke, Albrecht. "Παῖς." *Theological Dictionary of the New Testament.* Edited by
    Gerhard Friedrich. Vol. 5: Ξ–Πα, 636-654. Grand Rapids: Wm. B. Eerdmans
    Publishing Co., 1970.

Ohly, Friedrich. "Haus III (Metapher)." *Reallexikon für Antike und Christentum.* Edited
    by Theodor Klauser. Vol. 13, 905-1063. Stuttgart: Anton Hiersemann, 1986.

Olson, David R. "Or What's a Metaphor For?" *Metaphor and Symbolic Acivity* 3 (1988):
    215-222.

Olsson, Tord. "The Apocalyptic Activity: The Case of Jamasp Namag." In
    Apocalypticism in the Mediterranean World and the Near East. Edited by
    David Hellholm, 21-50. Proceedings of the International Colloquium on
    Apocalypticism. Tübingen: J. C. B. Mohr (Paul Siebeck), 1983.

Pardee, Dennis. "An Overview of Ancient Hebrew Epistolography." *Journal of Biblical
    Literature* 97 (1978): 321-346.

Parente, Fausto. "Flavius Josephus' Account of the Anti-Roman Riots Preceding the 66-
    70 War, and its Relevance for the Reconstruction of Jewish Eschatology during the
    First Century A.D." *Journal of the Ancient Near Eastern Society* 16-17 (1984-85):
    183-205.

Patsch, Hermann. "Zum alttestamentlichen Hintergrund von Römer 4:25 und 1. Petrus
    2:24." *Zeitschrift für die neutestamentliche Wissenschaft* 60 (1969): 273-279.

Perdue, Leo G. "Paraenesis and the Epistle of James." *Zeitschrift für die
    neutestamentliche Wissenschaft* 72 (1981): 241-256.

Pesch, Wilhelm. "Zu Texten des Neuen Testamentes über das Priestertum der Getauften."
    In *Verborum Veritas* (Festschrift für Gustav Stählin). Edited by Otto Böcher und
    Klaus Haacker, 303-315. Wuppertal: Rolf Brockhaus, 1970.

Philonenko, Marc. "L'apocalyptique quomrânienne." In *Apocalypticism in the Mediterranean World and the Near East*. Edited by David Hellholm, 211-218. Proceedings of the International Colloquium on Apocalypticism. Tübingen: J. C. B. Mohr (Paul Siebeck), 1983.

Plumpe, J. D. "*Vivum saxum, vivi lapides*: The Concept of 'Living Stone' in Classical Antiquity." *Traditio* 1 (1943): 1-14.

Preisker, Herbert. "Anhang zum ersten Petrusbrief." In Hans Windisch, *Die katholischen Briefe*, 3d ed, 152-162. Handbuch zum Neuen Testament 4.2. Tübingen: J. C. B. Mohr, 1951.

Radermacher, L. "Der erste Petrusbrief und Silvanus." *Zeitschrift für die neutestamentliche Wissenschaft* 25 (1926): 287-299.

Reicke, Bo. "Die Gnosis der Männer nach 1 Ptr 3:7." In *neutestamentliche Studien für Rudolf Bultmann*. Edited by Walther Eltester, 296-304. Beihefte zur Zeitschrift für die neutestamentliche Wissenschaft 21. Berlin: Alfred Töpelmann, 1954.

Reinach, Theodore. "Diaspora." *The Jewish Encyclopaedia*. Vol. 4: *Chazars-Dreyfus*, 559-573. New York: KTAV Publishing House, 1906.

Rengstorf, Karl H. "Die neutestamentlichen Mahnungen an die Frau, sich dem Manne unterzuordnen." In *Verbum Dei manet in aeternum* (Festschrift für O. Schmitz). Edited by Werner Foerster, 131-145. Witten: Luther-Verlag, 1953.

Richard, Earl. "The Functional Christology of First Peter." In *Perspectives on First Peter*. Edited by Charles H. Talbert, 121-140. National Association of Baptist Professors of Religion: Special Studies Series 9. Macon, Georgia: Mercer University Press, 1986.

Robinson, James M. "Die Hodajot-Formel in Gebet und Hymnus des Frühchristentums." In *Apophoreta* (Festschrift für Ernst Haenchen). Edited by Walther Eltester, 194-235. Beihefte zur Zeitschrift für die neutestamentliche Wissenschaft 30. Berlin: Alfred Töpelmann, 1964.

Rossell, William H. "New Testament Adoption: Graeco-Roman or Semitic?" *Journal of Biblical Literature* 71 (1952): 233-234.

Rödding, Gerhard. "Descendit ad inferna." In *Kerygma und Melos* (Festschrift für Christhard Mahrenholz). Edited by Walter Blankenburg, Herwarth von Schade and Kurt Schmidt-Claussen, 95-102. Kassel: Bärenreiter Verlag, 1970.

Sanders, Jack T. "The Transition from Opening Epistolary Thanksgiving to Body in the Letters of the Pauline Corpus." *Journal of Biblical Literature* 81 (1962): 348-362.

Sasson, Haim Hillel Ben. "Galut." *Encyclopaedia Judaica.* Vol.7: *Fr-Ha*, 275-294. New York: Macmillan Co., 1971.

Schelkle, Karl Hermann. "Das Leiden des Gottesknechtes als Form christlichen Lebens." In idem, ed., *Wort und Schrift*, 162-165. Düsseldorf: Patmos Verlag, 1966.

Schlier, Heinrich. "Θλίβω." *Theological Dictionary of the New Testament.* Edited by Gerhard Kittel. Vol. 3: *Θ-K*, 139-147. Grand Rapids: Wm. B. Eerdmans Publishing Co., 1970.

_____. "Vom Wesen der apostolischen Ermahnung nach Röm. 12:1-2." In idem, *Die Zeit der Kirche*. 3d ed. Freiburg: Herder, 1962.

Schmid, Josef. "Petrus *der Fels* und die Petrusgestalt der Urgemeinde." In *Begegnung der Christen* (Festschrift für Otto Karrer). Edited by Maximilian Roesle und Oscar Cullmann, 347-359. Frankfurt: Josef Knecht, 1960.

Schmidt, K. L. "Πάροικος." *Theological Dictionary of the New Testament.* Edited by Gerhard Friedrich. Vol. 5: *Ξ-Πa*, 841-853. Grand Rapids: Wm. B. Eerdmans Publishing Co., 1970.

Schnackenburg, Rudolf. "Episkopos und Hirtenamt." In idem, ed., *Schriften zum Neuen Testament*, 247-267. München: Kösel-Verlag, 1971.

Schoeps, Hans Joachim. "Die Tempelzerstörung des Jahres 70 in der Jüdischen Religionsgeschichte." In idem, *Aus frühchristlicher Zeit*. Tübingen: J. C. B. Mohr (Paul Siebeck), 1950.

Schottroff, Luise. "Die Gegenwart in der Apokalyptik der synoptischen Evangelien." In *Apocalypticism in the Mediterranean World and the Near East*. Edited by David Hellholm, 707-728. Proceedings of the International Colloquium on Apocalypticism. Tübingen: J. C. B. Mohr (Paul Siebeck), 1983.

Schrage, Wolfgang. "Zur Ethik der neutestamentlichen Haustafeln." *New Testament Studies* 21 (1975): 1-22.

Schrenk, Gottlob. "Δίκαιος." *Theological Dictionary of the New Testament.* Edited by Gerhard Kittel. Vol. 2: *Δ-H*, 182-191. Grand Rapids: Wm. B. Eerdmans Publishing Co., 1968.

_____. "Πατήρ." *Theological Dictionary of the New Testament.* Edited by Gerhard Friedrich. Vol. 5: *Ξ-Πα*, 945-959. Grand Rapids: Wm. B. Eerdmans Publishing Co., 1970.

Schroeder, David. "Die Haustafeln des Neuen Testaments." Ph.D. dissertation, Hamburg University, 1959.

_____. "Lists, Ethical." *Interpreter's Dictionary of the Bible. Supplement,* 546-547 Nashville: Abingdon, 1976.

_____. "Parenesis." *Interpreter's Dictionary of the Bible. Supplement,* 643. Nashville: Abingdon, 1976.

Schutter, William L. "1 Peter 4:17, Exekiel 9:6 and Apocalyptic Hermeneutics." In *Society of Biblical Literature Seminar Papers* 26. Edited by Kent Harold Richards, 276-284. Atlanta, Georgia: Scholars Press, 1987.

Schweizer, Eduard. "1. Petrus 4, 6." *Theologische Zeitschrift* 8 (1952): 152-154.

Selwyn, E. G. "Eschatology in I Peter." In *The Background of the New Testament and Its Eschatology.* Edited by W. D. Davies and D. Daube, 394-401. Cambridge: University Press, 1956.

Seyler, Georg. "Über die Gedankenordnung in den Reden und Briefen des Apostels Petrus." *Theologische Studien und Kritiken* 5 (1832): 44-70.

Sieffert, E. A. "Die Heilsbedeutung des Leidens und Sterbens Christi nach dem ersten Briefe des Petrus." *Jahrbücher für deutsche Theologie* 20 (1875): 371-440.

Sleeper, C. Freeman. "Political Responsibility According to 1 Peter." *Novum Testamentum* 10 (1968): 270-286.

Smith, Morton. "On the History of ΑΠΟΚΑΛΥΠΤΩ and ΑΠΟΚΑΛΥΨΙΣ." In *Apocalypticism in the Mediterranean World and the Near East.* Edited by David Hellholm, 9-20. Proceedings of the International Colloquium on Apocalypticism. Tübingen: J. C. B. Mohr (Paul Siebeck), 1983.

_____. "Zealots and Sicarii, Their Origins and Relation." *Harvard Theological Review* 64 (1971): 1-19.

Soucek, Josef B. "Das Gegenüber von Gemeinde und Welt nach dem ersten Petrusbrief." In *Stimmen aus der Kirche der CSSR.* Edited by Bé Ruys und Josef Smolík, 56-69. München: Kaiser Verlag, 1968.

Spicq, Ceslas. "La Ia Petri et la témoignage évangélique de Saint Pierre." *Studia Theologica* 20 (1966): 37-61.

_____. "La place ou de rôle des jeunes dans certaines communautés néotestamentaires." *Revue Biblique* 76 (1969): 508-527.

Stauffer, Ethelbert. "Märtyrertheologie und Täuferbewegung." *Zeitschrift für Kirchengeschichte* 52 (1933): 545-598.

Stählin, Gustav. "Ξένος." *Theological Dictionary of the New Testament.* Edited by Gerhard Friedrich. Vol. 5: Ξ-Πα, 1-36. Grand Rapids: Wm. B. Eerdmans Publishing Co., 1970.

Steen, Henry A. "Les clichés épistolaires dans les lettres sur papyrus greques." *Classica et Mediaevalia* 1 (1938): 119-176.

Stern, Menahem. "Diaspora." *Encyclopaedia Judaica.* Vol. 6: Di-Fo, 8-19 New York: Macmillan Co., 1971.

Strathmann, Hermann. "Μάρτυς." *Theological Dictionary of the New Testament.* Edited by Gerhard Kittel. Vol. 4: Λ-Ν, 474-513. Grand Rapids: Wm. B. Eerdmans Publishing Co., 1967.

_____. "Die Stellung des Petrus in der Urkirche." *Zeitschrift für systematische Theologie* 20 (1943): 223-282.

Strobel, August. "Macht Leiden von Sünde frei? Zur Problematik von 1. Petr. 4, 1f." *Theologische Zeitschrift* 19 (1963): 412-425.

Stuiber, A. "Diaspora." *Reallexikon für Antike und Christentum*. Edited by
   Theodor Klauser. Vol, 3: *Christusbilt-Dogma*,972-982.   Stuttgart:
   Anton Hiersemann, 1957.

Stumpff, Albrecht. "Ζῆλος." *Theological Dictionary of the New Testament*. Edited by
   Gerhard Kittel. Vol. 2: *Δ-H*, 877-888. Grand Rapids: Wm. B. Eerdmans
   Publishing Co., 1964.

Sykutris, J. "Epistolographie." *Paulys Real-Encyclopädie der classischen
   Altertumswissenschaft*. Edited by Wilhelm Kroll. *Supplement*, vol. 4, 185-220.
   Stuttgart: J. B. Metzler, 1924.

Sylva, Dennis. "The Critical Exploration of 1 Peter." In *Perspectives on First Peter*.
   Edited by Charles H. Talbert, 17-36. National Association of Baptist Professors of
   Religion: Special Studies Series 9. Macon, Georgia: Mercer University Press,
   1986.

Talbert, Charles H. "Once Again: The Plan of 1 Peter." In idem, ed., *Perspectives on
   First Peter*, 141-151. National Association of Baptist Professors of Religion:
   Special Studies Series 9. Macon, Georgia: Mercer University Press, 1986.

Theron, D. J. "Adoption in the Pauline Corpus." *Evangelical Quarterly* 28 (1956): 6-14.

Thornton, T. C. G. "1 Peter: A Paschal Liturgy?" *Journal of Theological Studies* N. S.
   12 (1961): 14-26.

Thraede, Klaus. "Ärger mit der Freiheit: Die Bedeutung von Frauen in Theorie und Praxis
   der alten Kirche." In *Die Beziehung von Mann und Frau als Frage an Theologie
   und Kirche*. Edited by Gerta Scharffenorth, 131-181. Berlin: Burckhardthaus,
   1977.

_____. "Zum historischen Hintergrund der Haustafeln des NT." In *Pietas*. Edited by
   Ernst Dassmann and K. Suso Frank, 359-368.   Jahrbuch für Antike und
   Christentum 8. Münster: Aschendorff, 1980.

Toit, A. B. du. "The Significance of Discourse Analysis for New Testament Interpretation
   and Translation: Introductory Remarks with Special Reference to 1 Peter 1:3-13."
   Neotestamentica 8 (1974): 54-79.

Unnik, W. C. van. "A Classical Parallel to 1 Peter ii.14 and 20." *New Testament Studies* 2 (1955): 198-202; reprint, *Sparsa Collecta: The Collected Works of W. C. van Unnik.* Edited by J. Reiling, G. Mussies, and P. W. van der Horst. Vol. 2, 106-110. Supplements to Novum Testamentum 30. Leiden: E. J. Brill, 1973.

_____. "Christianity According to I Peter." *Expository Times* 68 (1956/57): 79-83; reprint, *Sparsa Collecta: The Collected Works of W. C. van Unnik.* Edited by J. Reiling, G. Mussies, and P. W. van der Horst. Vol. 2, 111-122. Supplements to Novum Testamentum 30. Leiden: E. J. Brill, 1973.

_____. "Die Rücksicht auf die Reaktion der Nicht-Christen als Motiv in der altchristlichen Paränese." In *Judentum Urchristentum Kirche* (Festschrift für Joachim Jeremias). Edited by Walther Eltester, 221-234. Beihefte zur Zeitschrift für die neutestamentliche Wissenschaft 26. Berlin: Alfred Töpelmann, 1960; reprint, *Sparsa Collecta: The Collected Works of W. C. van Unnik.* Edited by J. Reiling, G. Mussies, and P. W. van der Horst. Vol. 2, 307-322. Supplements to Novum Testamentum 30. Leiden: E. J. Brill, 1973.

_____. "Peter, First Letter of." *The Interpreter's Dictionary of the Bible.* Edited by George Arthur Buttrick. Vol. 3: *K-Q*, 758-766. Nashville: Abingdon Press, 1962.

_____. "The Critique of Paganism in 1 Peter 1:18." In *Neotestamentica et Semitica* (Studies in Honour of Matthew Black). Edited by E. Earle Ellis and Max Wilcox, 129-142. Edinburgh: T. & T. Clark, 1969.

_____. "The Redemption in 1 Peter 1:18-19 and the Problem of the First Epistle of Peter." In *Sparsa Collecta: The Collected Essays of W. C. van Unnik.* Edited by J. Reiling, G. Mussies, and P. W. van der Horst. Vol. 2, 3-82. Supplements to Novum Testamentum 30. Leiden: E. J. Brill, 1980.

_____. "The Teaching of Good Works in 1 Peter." *New Testament Studies* 1 (1954): 92-110; reprint, *Sparsa Collecta: The Collected Works of W. C. van Unnik.* Edited by J. Reiling, G. Mussies, and P. W. van der Horst. Vol. 2, 83-105. Supplements to Novum Testamentum 30. Leiden: E. J. Brill, 1973.

Villiers, J. L. de. "Joy in Suffering in 1 Peter." *Neotestamentica* 9 (1975): 64-86.

Wand, J. W. C. "The Lessons of 1 Peter: A Survey of Recent Interpretation." *Interpretation* 9 (1955): 387-399.

Weiss, E. "Fremdenrecht." *Paulys Real-Encyclopädie der classischen Altertumswissenschaft.* Edited by Wilhelm Kroll. Supplement 4: *Abacus-Ledon*, 511-516. Stuttgart: J. B. Metzler, 1924.

Wendland, Heinz-Dietrich. "Zur sozialethischen Bedutung der Neutestamentlichen Haustafeln." In *Die Botschaft an die soziale Welt: Beiträge zur Christlichen Sozialethik der Gegenwart.* Edited by Heinz-Dietrich Wendland, 104-114. Hamburg: Furche-Verlag, 1959.

Wenham, David. "Being *Found* on the Last Day: New Light on 2 Peter 3:10 and 2 Corinthians 5:3." *New Testament Studies* 33 (1987): 477-479.

Wenschkewitz, H. "Die Spiritualisierung der Kultusbegriffe Tempel, Priester und Opfer im N. T." *Angelos* 4 (1932): 71-230.

White, John L. "Introductory Formulae in the Body of the Pauline Letter." *Journal of Biblical Literature* 90 (1971): 91-97.

_____. "New Testament Epistolary Literature in the Framework of Ancient Epistolography." *Aufstieg und Niedergang der römischen Welt* 25.2 (1984): 1730-1756.

_____ and Keith A. Kensinger. "Categories of Greek Papyrus Letters." In *Society of Biblical Literature Seminar Papers* 10. Edited by George MacRae, 79-91. Atlanta, Georgia: Scholars Press, 1976.

Wicker, Kathleen O'Brien. "Mulierum virtutes (Moralia 242e-263c)." In *Plutarch's Ethical Writings and Early Christian Literature.* Edited by Hans Dieter Betz, 106-134. Studia ad corpus hellenisticum Novi Testamenti 4. Leiden: E. J. Brill, 1978.

Wifstrand, Alfred. "Stylistic Problems in the Epistles of James and Peter." *Studia Theologica* 1 (1948): 170-182.

Wrede, W. "Miscellen, 3: Bemerkungen zu Harnacks Hypothese über die Adresse des I. Petrusbriefs." *Zeitschrift für die neutestamentliche Wissenschaft* 1 (1900): 75-85.

INDEX OF NON-BIBLICAL PASSAGES

(Bold page numbers indicate the index entry occurs in the notes.)

INDEX OF HEBREW BIBLE PASSAGES

(Bold page numbers indicate the index entry occurs in the notes.)

343

INDEX OF DEUTEROCANONICAL PASSAGES

(Bold page numbers indicate the index entry occurs in the notes.)

INDEX OF NEW TESTAMENT PASSAGES

(Bold page numbers indicate the index entry occurs in the notes.)

INDEX OF ANCIENT PERSONS

(Bold page numbers indicate the index entry occurs in the notes.)

INDEX OF MODERN PERSONS

(Bold page numbers indicate the index entry occurs in the notes.)

INDEX OF GREEK TERMS

(Bold page numbers indicate the index entry occurs in the notes.)

369

INDEX OF SUBJECTS

(Bold page numbers indicate the index entry occurs in the notes.)

Lightning Source UK Ltd.
Milton Keynes UK
UKHW041521080719
345787UK00001B/174/P